ANTHROPOLOGY
AND THE GLOBAL FACTORY

ANTHROPOLOGY
AND THE
GLOBAL FACTORY

Studies of the New Industrialization
in the Late Twentieth Century

EDITED BY FRANCES ABRAHAMER ROTHSTEIN
AND MICHAEL L. BLIM

BERGIN & GARVEY

New York • Westport, Connecticut • London

Library of Congress Cataloging-in-Publication Data

Anthropology and the global factory : studies of the new
   industrialization in the late twentieth century / edited by Frances
   Abrahamer Rothstein and Michael L. Blim.
         p.   cm.
   Includes bibliographical references and index.
   ISBN 0–89789–232–1 (alk. paper). — ISBN 0–89789–233–X (pbk. :
alk. paper)
   1. Industrialization. 2. Capitalism. 3. Economic development.
I. Rothstein, Frances Abrahamer. II. Blim, Michael L.
HD2329.A58   1992
338—dc20   91–18922

British Library Cataloguing in Publication Data is available.

Library of Congress Catalog Card Number: 91–18922
ISBN: 0–89789–232–1 (HB)
       0–89789–233–X (PB)

First published in 1992

Bergin & Garvey, One Madison Avenue, New York, NY 10010
An imprint of Greenwood Publishing Group, Inc.

Printed in the United States of America

The paper used in this book complies with the
Permanent Paper Standard issued by the National
Information Standards Organization (Z39.48–1984).

10 9 8 7 6 5 4 3 2 1

To Our Parents,
the First Workers in Our Worlds

Contents

Tables and Figures   xi

1. Introduction: The Emerging Global Factory and
   Anthropology
   Michael L. Blim   1

**Part I: Global Production and the Mobility of
Capital and Labor**

2. What Happens to the Past? Return Industrial
   Migrants in Latin America
   Frances Abrahamer Rothstein   33

3. Capitalist Production in a Socialist Society: The
   Transfer of Manufacturing from Hong Kong to
   China
   Alan Smart and Josephine Smart   47

4. Nonresident-Indian Investment and India's Drive
   for Industrial Modernization
   Johanna Lessinger   62

Part II: The New Industrial Diversity

5. Small-Scale Industrialization in a Rapidly
   Changing World Market
   Michael L. Blim   85

6. Spanish Galician Industrialization and the Europe
    of 1992: A Contextual Analysis
    Hans C. Buechler and Judith-Maria Buechler   102

7. The Unexpected Entrepreneurs: Small High-
    Technology Firms, Technology Transfer, and
    Regional Development in Wales and Northeast
    England
    Douglas Caulkins   119

8. Rural Industrial Enterprise and "Socialism with
    Chinese Characteristics"
    Eugene Cooper and Xiong Pan   136

9. Informal Sectorization of Egyptian Petty
    Commodity Production
    Kristin Koptiuch   149

10. Industrial Decentralization and Women's
    Employment in South Africa: A Case Study
    Georgina Jaffee   161

**Part III: Worker Struggles and Survival in the
            New Industrial World**

11. Labor-Managed Systems and Industrial
    Redevelopment: Lessons from the Fagor
    Cooperative Group of Mondragón
    Davydd J. Greenwood   177

12. Tobacco, Textiles, and Toyota: Working for
    Multinational Corporations in Rural Kentucky
    Ann E. Kingsolver   191

13. Women as Political Actors in Rural Puerto Rico:
    Continuity and Change
    Ida Susser   206

14. Women Workers and the Labor Movement in
    South Korea
    Seung-kyung Kim   220

15. Conclusion: New Waves and Old—
     Industrialization, Labor, and the Struggle for a
     New World Order
     Frances Abrahamer Rothstein   238

     Bibliography   247

     Index   279

     About the Contributors   283

Tables and Figures

TABLES

1.1	World Economic Growth, 1972–1991	9
1.2	World Trade and Export Volumes, 1972–1991	11
7.1	High-Technology Entrepreneurial Career Types in Samples from Mid Wales and Northeast England	125
8.1	Expansion of Rural Enterprise in Dongguan County, 1978–1984	139
8.2	Expansion of Rural Enterprise in Shunde County, 1978–1984	140
10.1	Worker Composition by Sex for Selected Factories, 1990	167

FIGURES

1.1	World Economic Growth, 1972–1991	10
1.2	Economic Growth by Regions, 1972–1991	11
1.3	World Trade and Export Volumes, 1972–1991	12
5.1	Industrial Production, Marche Region, Italy, 1986–1989	91
5.2	Industrial Employment, Marche Region, Italy, 1986–1989	92
5.3	Capital Investment per Worker, Marche Region, Italy, 1986–1989	95

ANTHROPOLOGY
AND THE GLOBAL FACTORY

1

Introduction: The Emerging Global Factory and Anthropology

Michael L. Blim

The world is becoming a global factory—that is, industrial production for the capitalist world market is now found on every continent and in most regions of the world, a situation that stands in conspicuous contrast to world historical experience before World War II. The rise of this new global factory is marked not simply by the spread of industrialization throughout the world but also by the incorporation of vast new populations of workers in novel production and labor processes manufacturing goods for the world capitalist market. From rural farmsteads and urban garages to small workshops and transnational factories, the work of peasants, artisans, and industrial workers alike is moving through dense and interwoven production and distribution networks to find its place in a world marketplace that is increasingly, if imperfectly, united by new forms of transportation and communication.

In this introductory chapter, I hope to provide a more theoretically and empirically informed judgment about what the new global factory is and about anthropology's role in its understanding. To accomplish this task, I will: (1) critically review competing conceptions of the contemporary capitalist world economy; (2) suggest an alternative theoretical description based on a conceptual formulation of the global factory; (3) assess the empirical character of the global factory; and (4) show how anthropology has contributed and can contribute to its analysis.

ON COMPETING DESCRIPTIONS OF THE WORLD
CAPITALIST ECONOMY

In some real sense, the contemporary capitalist world economy and its development have proven hard to describe. Every attempt to capture the phenomenon has displayed crucial weaknesses. Here, I will examine briefly four of the most prominent neo-Marxist descriptions of contemporary capitalist development: world-systems theory; the articulation approach to the analysis of noncapitalist, precapitalist, and capitalist modes of production; the dependency and underdevelopment thesis; and the new international division of labor hypothesis.[1]

Wallerstein's (1974, 1979) formulation of the world capitalist economy as a social system in which relationships of exploitation between core capitalist societies and late-developing countries are created through unequal exchange in an expanding world market has served as a highly useful heuristic for social research. It highlighted the crucial roles of primitive accumulation, colonial plunder, and unfree labor in the rise of European capitalist economies, and argued convincingly that the developmental fates of all the regions and countries were joined historically in the commercial calculus of mercantile capitalism.

However, the world-systems approach has been criticized—rightly in my view—for its overt determinism, as well as for its theoretical flatness and inability to continence the capacities of local peoples to amend, blunt, or even change its allegedly lawlike operations. Commentators have noted how the theory privileges exchange relations in the marketplace over productive relations in the workplace (Brewer 1980: 165–167; Brenner 1977); reduces class relations to the maximizing strategies of the dominators rather than analyzing the struggles between the capitalists and other classes (Skocpol 1977); and neglects the interplay between class conflicts and the internal dynamics of state formation and policy-making (Skocpol 1977). It has also been suggested that the Wallersteinian perspective radically simplifies the labor forms one finds in the capitalist periphery and seriously underestimates the importance of local production conditions and worker resistance in the determination of local economies and their role in the world capitalist economy (Stern 1988). Others have claimed that Wallerstein is unable to accommodate changes and more subtle stages in the development of world capitalism (Ross and Trachte 1990: 56–61); overlooks cultural diversity and the potential for resistance in and from the periphery (Nash 1981); and ignores the fact that non-European peoples with noncapitalist modes of production, no less than an aggrandizing Europe, have coconstituted the contemporary world (Wolf 1982: 296–298).

However, the very *actuality* of the rough and discontinuous nature of the world economic terrain that subsequently fueled doubts about the value of Wallerstein's schema also prompted the independent invention of a body of theory and research on noncapitalist and precapitalist modes of production. The object was to furnish researchers with ways of talking about and explaining social life in societies where capitalism permeated or abutted but had not yet overwhelmed local social formations. Some researchers tried to restrict the scope of capitalism's spread in the contemporary world by highlighting the persistence of noncapitalist modes (Godelier 1977; Meillassoux 1981), or to invent new precapitalist modes of production (Rey 1975; Hindess and Hirst 1975; Terray 1972).[2] Others sought to show the extensive copresence of noncapitalist with capitalist modes of production, either in history (Amin 1976; Wolf 1982) or in social formations throughout the developing world (Bradby 1980; Morris 1980; Wolpe 1980b; Seddon 1978).

Their solutions, though helpful in highlighting the complex linkages between capitalist and developing societies as well as between capitalist and noncapitalist modes of production within particular social formations, have also created problems that limit the effectiveness of the modes of production approach in capturing the fluid and complex realities posed by the introduction of industrialization worldwide.[3] The proliferation of previously unspecified modes of production, to several sympathetic critics, less resembled discovery than an exercise in nominalism (Brewer 1980: 198–202; Godelier 1979: 17; Clammer 1985: 100–151). Others complained of the deep-seated functionalism and timelessness of some of its various formulations (Roseberry 1988: 170; Rothstein 1986; Raatgever 1985: 298–300; Wolf 1982; 401–402), and noted a tendency toward analytical abstraction at the expense of coherent theoretical accounts that also explain empirical circumstances and acknowledge actors as more than the litter bearers of social and economic structures (Roseberry 1988: 170–171; Raatgever 1985: 300–325).

The proposal of the dependency thesis—that the northern metropolitan capitalist core actively underdeveloped the Third World—anticipated by several years Wallerstein's world-systems theory (Frank 1967, 1970: 4–17; Cardoso and Faletto 1979 [1971]). In fundamental respects, it fell prey to the same criticisms addressed to Wallerstein's work: an overemphasis on world market exchange rather than on the productive and labor processes in developing countries (Laclau 1971: 19–38; Brewer 1980: 158–181); a prejudgment of passivity in the periphery (Roseberry 1988: 165–167; Nash 1981: 402–408); and an inability to countenance significant variation at the local, regional, and national levels of analysis (Nash 1981: 404–417). The last point, the problem of variation, was remedied partly by the stress some researchers placed on the balance of political and economic forces within the

dependent countries themselves and by their arguments for distorted
or dependent development, rather than a unidimensional, universal
process of underdevelopment (Cardoso and Faletto 1979 [1971]; Arrighi
1970; Evans 1979).[4]

This amendment of the "development of underdevelopment" hypothesis of Frank was necessary because empirical events throughout the
Third World simply overtook it. The significant, albeit flawed, economic
development of Mexico and Brazil, as well as the pell-mell industrialization of East Asia, served as strong counterfactuals to the theory
(Berry 1989: 188; Deyo 1987: 13–14; Lipietz 1986: 35). Indeed, the
notion that East Asian development may be qualitatively different
from the path observed in Latin America (Amsden 1990; Ferleger and
Mandle 1989: 139–144) raises the question of whether the dependency
thesis is best understood as a regional, rather than a global, theory
of imperialism.

More recently, scholarly attention has converged on the concept of
the new international division of labor (NIDL), first formally proposed
by Frobel, Heinrichs, and Kreye (1981). The central notion—that core
transnational corporations were redeploying their capital for goods
production to low-cost labor sites in the periphery—shifted the focus
from the Wallersteinian and dependency theory–minded concerns for
the world marketplace and the terms of trade to the locus of production,
where big capital extracts excess surplus value from Third World workers.[5] Production, in their view, was being decomposed, Taylorized, and
subsequently decentralized to locations where optimal profits were
most likely. The rise of export processing zones (EPZs) throughout the
Third World and the recruitment and exploitation of women as the
preferred labor force (Ong 1987; Leacock and Safa 1986; Fernandez-
Kelly 1983; Fuentes and Ehrenreich 1983) were considered as evidence
of this powerful new tendency at work. Sassen-Koob (1988: 9–17)
amended the original proposal by arguing that the globalization of
production is creating a kind of transnational corridor wherein flows
of immigrant labor to capitalist centers like the United States are
stimulated by transnationalist capitalist penetration of client regions
such as the Caribbean and East Asia.

As salutary as the shift back to production from exchange has proved
for explaining the burst of new industrialization around the world, the
new international division of labor thesis unfortunately shared with
the Wallersteinian perspective a highly mechanistic dimension, as if
the calculus of cheap labor were all there was to the capitalist mode
of production. Critics argued, among other things, that the NIDL thesis
treated labor as an exchange good, and thus, like the world-systems
and dependency approaches, neglected the creation of value in production and the emergence of worker struggle through participation
in capitalist social relations of production.[6] Thus, the NIDL thesis

seemed, once more, to attribute a deadly passivity to Third World peoples and failed to examine the key gate-keeping role that states and the class coalitions that support them play in establishing legal-juridical entities like export processing zones. Furthermore, in contrast to what the theory predicted, transnational capital played a relatively unimportant part in the industrial development of East Asia, surely the most spectacular arena of world capitalist expansion over the past 20 years (Berry 1989: 192–193; Haggard and Cheng 1987: 87–93; Barrett and Chin 1987: 39; Evans 1987: 206–208).

Thus, though each theoretical description of the capitalist world economy presents only a partial account of the phenomenon, each provides vital points of interest necessary for its understanding. The conception of the capitalist world economy as a system points to something intuitively right about increasing world economic integration, however fuzzy and ill-defined the parameters and structure of that system is, and about capitalism's highly coercive capacity to ensnare enormous numbers of peoples within its grasp. The careful attention paid to noncapitalist modes of production now enables us to ask about the *extent* of capitalist penetration in social formations throughout the world and to perhaps gauge more accurately the ways in which the current capitalist world economy feeds parasitically on the "off-book" noncapitalist laboring of diverse groups of peoples. Though the dependency thesis initially seems to offer less promise for further application, it provides three crucial caveats for our work here: (1) the gap between north and south has widened, rather than narrowed, even as production was being globalized (Langley 1990: 50–57);[7] (2) unfavorable terms of trade continue to adversely affect economies still tied primarily to raw materials exports instead of manufacturing; and (3) the distorted and exploitative nature of capitalist development has lost none of its edge.

Finally, the concept of the international division of labor, with its emphasis on production and a kind of capitalist logic of serial involvement of late-developing nations and regions in production for the world market, also has a sense of rightness about it. Recent evidence has begun to document the industrial development of the East Asian periphery, from Thailand to mainland China, by East Asian capital searching for cheap-labor populations (Lim 1989: 29).[8] This suggests that the labor-capital calculation has important explanatory power in our evolving conception of the changing world economy.

THEORETICALLY SITUATING THE GLOBAL FACTORY

What, then, are the elements we need to carry forward from the foregoing critique? First is the conception of a structured whole—that is, a description of the contemporary capitalist world economy. In place of the world-systems and NIDL perspectives, proposed here is a description of a totality whose structure is determined no less by the capitalist rules of the game, but whose organization reflects the productive efforts of a variety of agents from individuals and social groups to firms and transnational corporations, and whose activities are mediated in important ways by class struggle and nation-state policies. Hence, the operation of this capitalist system is best understood as more disorderly, decentralized, variable, and open to innovation by its actors than in the usual notion of system.

Second is a conception of process. All four of the major approaches discussed above have attempted to describe the process of capitalist development, and each is situated in some way with respect to several basic theoretical problems entailed by the Marxist research program (Burawoy 1990). The creation of value in capitalism must be located, and this is done typically by placing it amid the relations of production *and/or* of exchange. The placement of the value question also affects the horizon and prospects for successful worker struggle with their capitalist overlords.

What accounts for this capitalist system's dynamics? It is argued here that one needs a fairly robust notion of combined and uneven capitalist development. As Roseberry (1989: 129), in discussing Wolf's creative use of the concept (1982: 296–309, 418–420), noted, references to combined and uneven development tend to be ritualistic and underdeveloped. Hence, some synthetic work needs to be done.[9]

For Marx, unevenness in capitalist development is first largely an *internal* matter that is *externalized* as contradictions arise in the process of value creation itself. It begins as capitalists seek to incorporate into the production process former agricultural and household workers, attempting to transform their variegated needs and relative autonomy into denatured, disciplined interchangeable parts of the machine (Marx 1977: 341–424, 762–870). Not only do capitalists reduce human effort to a commodity like any other, but they produce commodities that are now compared with all others. To compete with all others, they intensify their exploitation of workers, replace living labor with machines, and cheapen their commodities through overproduction. Capitalists then find themselves ensnared in an asymmetrical development process of their own making: "What is now to be expropriated," Marx wrote (1977: 928–929), "is not the self-employed worker, but the capitalist who exploits a large number of workers. . . . One capitalist always strikes down many others." Finally, Marx turned to the development of capital itself, noting how the emerging "departments" of capitalism, the first devoted to the production of capital goods and the second concerned with the production of consumer goods and services necessary for the reproduction of society, find themselves increasingly at odds (Marx 1967: 395–469). Each movement of capitalism, by Marx's logic, creates contradictions internal to the phenomenon, and each forces capitalism to externalize its problems by penetrating new domains and lashing new populations to its mast.

Implicit, then, in Marx's conception of capital was the incommensurability of the objects it tried to combine, the necessary asymmetry of its project, and the inevitability that capitalism as a system would seek its spread as a solution to the contradictions created. Capitalism and the world market become combined:

And whereas in the sixteenth century, and partly still in the seventeenth, the sudden expansion of trade and the creation of a new world market had an overwhelming influence on the defeat of the old mode of production and the rise of the capitalist mode, this happened in reverse on the basis of the capitalist mode of production, once it had been created. The world market itself forms the basis for this mode of production. On the other hand, the immanent need that this has to produce on an ever greater scale drives it to the constant expansion of the world market, so that now it is not trade that revolutionizes industry, but rather industry that constantly revolutionizes trade. (1981: 451)

The capitalist mode of production which once drew its nurturance from colonial plunder and the growth of the world market finally transforms the world economy in service of its own ends.

Both Lenin and Trotsky also placed uneven development at the heart of the Marxist problematic. "Uneven and spasmodic development of individual enterprises, of individual branches of industry and individual countries," Lenin wrote in *Imperialism*, "is inevitable under the capitalist system" (1970: 72). Capitalism would not be capitalism without uneven development, he noted: "Uneven development and a semi-starvation level of existence of the masses are fundamental and inevitable conditions and premises of this mode of production" (1970: 73). Trotsky elevated combined and uneven development to the status of a law of motion in the capitalist system, but stressed that such a law "has nothing in common with a pedantic schematism." On the contrary, he contended, the paradoxical effect of combined and uneven development is to create in late-developing nations "a peculiar combination of different stages in the historic process" and a form of development as a whole that "acquires a planless, complex, combined character" (1964: 85).

The most effective statement of the centrality of combined and uneven development in the evolution of contemporary world capitalist economy is found in the work of Ernest Mandel (1975).[10] His premise, like Marx's, is simple: "Capital by its very nature tolerates no geographical limits to its expansion," and the law of uneven and combined development "is inherent in the capitalist mode of production" (1975: 310–311). Consequently, Mandel asserted that uneven development, though beginning in the locus of capitalist production itself, was embedded in a combined international economic structure from the start (1975: 41–42, 311). The world economy that capitalism transformed has always consisted of differing social relations of production, ranging from precapitalist and semicapitalist, to full-blown capitalist relations of production "linked together by capitalist relations of exchange" (1975: 70). For Mandel, the processes of primitive and capitalist accumulation are not "merely *successive* phases of economic history but also *concurrent* economic processes" (1975: 45–46). In addition, the accelerated pace of technological change through automation, Mandel argued, exacerbates the internal contradictions of the capitalist mode of production, propelling it outward for new sources of value, labor, and exchange (1975: 184–222).

Mandel's treatment of the contemporary capitalist world economy seems particularly congenial for the notion of the global factory. *Global factory*, as used here, is a term meant not to connote a real thing but to stand conceptually for the complex of empirical activities and their intersection in the globalization of industrial production. It is a contemporary manifestation of the continuing combined and uneven development of the world capitalist system in which the production of commodities and the creation of value have dispersed capitalist productive activity throughout the world. It occurs in an environment in which the capitalist relations of production and exchange generate new, if uneven, possibilities for economic growth and for increased exploitation of labor by capital.[11]

EMPIRICALLY CHARACTERIZING THE GLOBAL FACTORY

Grasping the empirical dimensions of this new global factory is difficult, precisely because it is driven by combined and uneven development and thus liable to exhibit to the observer what Trotsky called "a planless, complex, combined character" (1964: 85). To overcome this potential problem in description, I present in propositional form some of the more important tendencies at work in the construction and operation of the global factory.

PROPOSITION 1: The global factory is emerging within the context of expanding, but increasingly combined and uneven, world capitalist economic growth.

The capitalist world economy is expanding, both qualitatively and quantitatively, and these trends have enormous importance for un-

Table 1.1
World Economic Growth, 1972–1991 (annual changes, in percent)

	Average 1972-81	1982	1983	1984	1985	1986	1987	1988	1989	1990	1991
All	3.5	0.5	2.7	4.4	3.3	3	3.4	4.1	3	2.3	3.1
Industrial	3	-0.3	2.7	4.9	3.4	2.7	3.5	4.4	3.5	2.7	2.9
Developing	5	2.1	2.2	4	3.9	4	3.8	4.1	3	3.2	4.5
By region											
Africa	3.2	2	-1.1	0.8	4.1	2.3	1.1	2.3	2.9	2.7	3
Asia	5.6	5.6	8	8.3	6.8	6.8	8	9	5.1	5.4	5.7
Middle East	6	1.3	1.7	-0.9	-0.2	-0.6	-0.8	3.8	3.9	3.2	3.4
Western Hemisphere	5.1	-1.1	-2.8	3.4	3.5	4	2.9	0.3	0.9	1.4	4.2

Source: International Monetary Fund, *World Economic Outlook* (Washington, D.C.; IMF, 1990), pp. 123, 142–43.

derstanding the rise of the new global factory. Qualitatively, the capitalist world economy's developmental fate is now combined through the extension of capitalist relations of production and exchange with the economies of the former socialist societies of Eastern Europe, the Soviet Union, and China, as well with peoples and regions whose ways of life were subsumed historically under noncapitalist and semicapitalist relations of production. Quantitatively, world economic output and world trade have grown over the past 20 years, though differences in economic growth rates among developing regions have been accelerating.[12]

As the data shown in Table 1.1 and Figures 1.1 and 1.2 indicate, total world economic output increased an average per year of 3.5 percent between 1972 and 1981, and an estimated 3 percent per year from 1982 through 1991 (International Monetary Fund 1990: 123). World trade over the past 20 years, as Table 1.2 and Figure 1.3 demonstrate, increased by volume an average of 5.2 percent per year from 1972 through 1981; and from 1982 through 1991, world trade volume increased an estimated average of 5.4 percent per year (International Monetary Fund 1990: 143).

However, an examination of regional growth rates for developing countries discloses that beneath the upward trend lines for the world economy as a whole, discrepancies are growing. An inspection of data displayed in Figure 1.2 shows that since 1981, all the regions of the developing world except Asia have grown more slowly economically than the world economy as a whole. In contrast, between 1972 and 1981, only Africa lagged—and then only slightly—behind world economic growth norms.

Instead, the economic growth record for this past decade has been almost uniformly dismal for every developing region of the world save Asia. Economic growth in the Middle East has slumped from an annual growth rate of 6 percent between 1972 and 1981 to a 1.6 percent growth

Michael L. Blim

Figure 1.1
World Economic Growth, 1972–1991

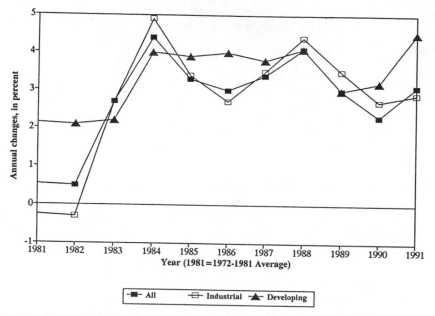

Source: International Monetary Fund, World Economic Outlook (Washington, D.C.: IMF, 1990), pp. 123, 142–43.

rate between 1982 and 1991. For the developing economies of Africa, the growth rate has fallen from an annual average of 3.2 percent between 1972 and 1981 to a 2 percent rate between 1982 and 1991. For the Western Hemisphere, the results have been equally disconcerting—from an annual rate between 1972 and 1981 of 5.1 percent to a 1.7 percent rate over the past decade (International Monetary Fund 1990: 123).[13]

These trends suggest that the new world economic order is becoming increasingly differentiated. Discrepancies between advanced capitalist and developing nations, already yawning, will probably grow over the next decade. At the beginning of the 1980s, almost 80 percent of the world's output was produced by industrial countries (Conference Board 1989: 6–7). Even a doubling of the developing country growth rate will not appreciably alter the balance.[14] The differences in productive capacity are just too great: Consider that in 1987, per capita gross national product in 45 nations with a combined population of 2.7 billion people was still less than U.S. $500 (Conference Board 1989: 7).[15]

Instead, as Gordon (1988) and Petras and Engbarth (1988) have argued, new and important variation is emerging among developing countries. On the one hand, there are the newly industrializing coun-

Figure 1.2
Economic Growth by Regions, 1972–1991

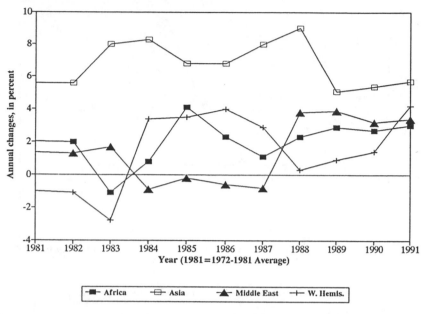

Source: International Monetary Fund, *World Economic Outlook* (Washington, D.C.:
IMF, 1990), pp. 123, 142–43.

Table 1.2
**World Trade and Export Volumes, 1972–1991 (annual changes,
in percent)**

	Average 1972-81	1982	1983	1984	1985	1986	1987	1988	1989	1990	1991
Total Volume	5.2	-1.6	2.9	8.8	3.3	4.9	6.5	9.1	7.2	6.6	5.8
Industrial Exports	6.1	-1.9	3	9.8	4.7	2.3	5	9	7	7.2	6.3
Developing Exports	2.1	-6.2	1.4	6.8	0.8	8.3	11.4	11	7.3	6.6	6.4
Developing Manufacturing Exports	9.7	2.4	9.7	15	4.2	6.9	18.9	11.9	7.7	7	7.2

Source: International Monetary Fund, *World Economic Outlook* (Washington, D.C.:
IMF, 1990), pp. 123, 142–43.

tries (NICs) of East Asia whose growth through exports to advanced
capitalist societies distinguishes them from industrializing Latin
American nations which are now shifting from manufacturing for their
home economies to export production. On the other hand, there are
the oil producers whose further development depends on the erratic

Figure 1.3
World Trade and Export Volumes, 1972–1991

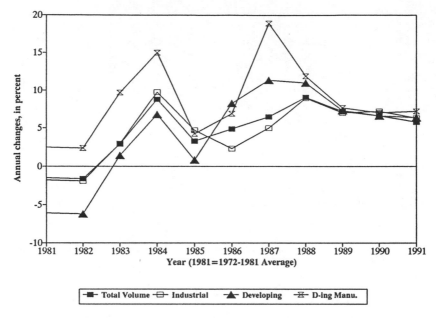

Source: International Monetary Fund, *World Economic Outlook* (Washington, D.C.: 1990), pp. 123, 142–43.

returns from the sale of their primary commodity. Finally, there are 75 to 80 Third World nations that find themselves virtually cut out of the development loop (Gordon 1988: 56–57).[16]

PROPOSITION 2: Manufacturing is the growth engine for the contemporary capitalist world economy.

Manufacturing is driving the capitalist world economy, as advanced capitalist and developing countries alike seek to increased their shares of the wealth of nations. Among advanced capitalist economies, the production of goods and services that support production still account for two-thirds of their total gross product and 60 percent of their jobs (Conference Board 1989: 9). For developing countries, 20 percent of their total gross domestic product was derived in 1980 from manufacturing—up from 13 percent in 1960 (Singh 1989: 105).

For the capitalist world economy as a whole, exports of manufacturing between 1980 and 1986 grew 30 percent in volume, while the overall volume of international trade increased 18 percent for the same period (Lim 1989: 23). For developing countries, the dollar value of their manufacturing exports increased 168 percent between 1982 and 1991, and they have maintained a positive balance of manufacturing exports over imports in 6 of the last 10 years (International Monetary Fund 1990: 162). In 1985, developing countries accounted for 17 percent of all world manufacturing exports—up dramatically from their 7 percent share in 1965 (Singh 1989: 106). Manufacturing exports now account for over half the foreign exchange earnings of the East Asian NICs, Mexico, the Philippines, and Thailand, and are only second to oil for Malaysia and Indonesia (Lim 1989: 23–24; *New York Times*, 25 September, 1990: D7).

In contrast, developing countries reliant on mineral and agricultural exports have suffered significantly from real declines in the value of their products. From 1980 to 1986, world prices for food and industrial raw materials declined 30 percent; between 1954 and 1986, the real loss in value amounted to 50 percent (Lim 1989: 32). In other words, developing countries *not* participating in manufacturing for export have lost ground steadily over the past quarter century. These outcomes surely confirm the prediction of dependency and world systems theorists that unfavorable terms of trade impoverish the already impoverished. However, the same results support our thesis here: namely, that industrialization has transformed the nature and direction of the capitalist world economy—a trend, now florescent, that Marx pointed to more than a century ago.

Some forms of industrial manufacturing are now widely diffused throughout the world economy. There is considerable evidence that manufacturing in textiles, apparel, and electronics assembly is widely dispersed throughout the capitalist world economy. Textiles and apparel production, given easy access to local markets and their relative labor intensity, are often historic start-up industries for late-developing countries moving into manufacturing, in our time no less than in Marx's.[17] In 1984, one-quarter of all manufacturing exports from developing countries consisted of textiles and apparel (Singh 1989: 107). In contrast, though some components of electronics assembly are scattered among a large number of nations and regions, the advanced capitalist countries, along with the East Asian NICS, Malaysia, the Philippines, and Mexico account for the lion's share of electronic product exports of all sorts (Castells and Tyson 1989: 44).[18]

Is industrialization in the developing world acquiring depth? That is, are their economies producing the consumer durable and capital goods that will stimulate more industrial growth? The answer, as of this writing, is mixed. First, the developing world's share of all manufacturing productive capacity, despite its expanded scope and a notable increase in its share of world exports, has grown slowly. In 1985, for instance, developing countries accounted for 18 percent of world manufacturing output, up only slightly from their 15 percent share in 1965 (Singh 1989: 104–105). Thus, there is not that much more productive capacity relative to overall levels in the world manufacturing economy to support a more profound process of capital deepening. Furthermore, the more dramatic advances in manufacturing output appear to be concentrated, depending on the observer, in the European periphery and among the East Asian NICS, according to Gordon (1988: 31), or, according to Singh (1989: 106–107), in the East Asian NICS, India, and China. For sub-Saharan Africa and much of Latin America, industrial manufacturing from the late 1970s through the mid-1980s has lagged behind other regions (Singh 1989: 106–107; Jaycox 1988; 35–38).

Second, increasing capital intensity in the industrial production process of the developing world also appears to be confined to some, but not all, developing economies. For instance, a World Bank study estimated that in 1981 only 12 of 55 low- and middle-income developing countries had 25 percent of their manufacturing value added through production of capital goods, transportation equipment (which includes automobiles), and chemicals. The list includes several of the East Asian NICS and India, but also contains former import-substitution industrializing countries such as Brazil, Chile, Mexico, and Argentina (Petras and Engbarth 1988: 87–90).

This last point concerning the manufacturing activity of former import-substitution industrial countries suggests another potential source for the expansion of worldwide manufacturing. Protracted economic crisis and international debt problems among Latin America's industrial leaders has prompted a redirection of manufacturing capacity from domestic markets to production for export. Though the overall prospects for success are uncertain, a significant proportion of new manufacturing and manufacturing export growth among developing countries, particularly in capital and consumer durable goods production, will probably originate in the factories of former import-substitution industrializers (Balassa 1989: 3–27, 186–226; Reynolds and McCleery 1989; Frischtak 1989; Gordon 1988: 58).

PROPOSITION 3: Production for the new global factory increasingly involves the activities of local and regional networks of petty commodity producers.

The new global factory is progressively harnessing the labors of petty commodity producers throughout the capitalist world economy. Turkish rug makers (Berik 1987), Mexican and Bolivian weavers (Stephen 1991; Buechler 1986), Indian lace makers (Mies 1986: 27–50), Italian shoemakers (Blim 1990b), Hong Kong wood-carvers (Cooper 1980),

Taiwanese garment makers (Gallin 1990: 179–192), Haitian textile producers (Grunwald and Flamm 1985: 180–205), and countless others now find their destinies combined in the development of capitalist production for the world market. Important technological advances in telecommunications, aided by air transportation, have facilitated the creation of new networks of production and labor (Fainstein and Fainstein 1989: 22).

Appraisal of the size and scope of this petty commodity component of the new global factory is difficult. The International Labor Organization estimated in 1984 that very small industrial enterprises generate at least half of Third World countries' manufacturing employment and between 20 and 45 percent of their manufacturing output (Munck 1988b: 36). In advanced capitalist economies, small firms continue to account for a significant portion of manufacturing employment (Granovetter 1984: 323–334; Boissevain 1984). In a late-developing capitalist country such as Italy, for instance, 85 percent of the manufacturing workplaces in 1981 operated with fewer than 10 workers; together, these small firms employ 26 percent of Italy's industrial labor force (Censis 1984: 60–61, 71). In addition, petty commodity production plays an important part in informal economies around the world (see Portes, Castells, and Benton 1989).

The new linkages between petty commodity producers and the world market are diverse as well as complex. Transnational outsourcing, though significant, is not necessarily the primary means by which small producers are engaged in production for the world market. Regional and national merchant capital combines also provide channels for consumer goods made cheaply in the capitalist periphery (Cook 1986; Alonso 1983; Hu 1983; Long and Richardson 1978). State development agencies in search of export earnings may organize, as in the case of Turkey, rural workshops and cooperatives for the production of luxury goods (Berik 1987: 13–22).

Petty commodity production itself constitutes a complex economic environment, and thus, its relationship to the capitalist world economy is complicated. Firms may find themselves occupying a relatively protected production niche within a more elaborate manufacturing network through subcontracting, or in direct competition with large-scale producers (Basok 1989; Capecchi 1989; Dore 1983). On the other hand, firms may alternate between intermediate or finished goods production for local and national markets and transnational customers (Blim 1990b; Benton 1990; Benería and Roldán 1987).

However, it is important to recognize that it is not simply goods that are being produced: Also being produced are new capitalist relations of production. Throughout the countryside hamlets and burgeoning urban squatter settlements of the capitalist peripheries, First World and Third, new forms of social life enmeshed in the capitalist mode of production, consumption, and exchange are emerging. As Hobsbawm argued (1966: 5–62), the expansion of capitalist production both requires and creates new markets for consumption and exchange that transform the fundamental nature of social life. It may well be, as Waterman (1981: 91) hypothesized, that "rather than destroying petty production—the process of peripheral capitalization simply increases the levels and the incorporation of petty- and small-capitalist enterprise." We now will turn to the specific ways in which the global factory is transforming local life.

PROPOSITION 4: The production process of the new global factory is highly networked and flexible, even as its labor process is based increasingly on the incorporation and exploitation of domestic workers.

The global factory is distinguished by a highly fluid interaction between international markets for goods *and* systems of production and labor, and by complex systems of horizontal and vertical economic linkages that incorporate a wide variety of capitalist agents and workers. Several brief case descriptions may help illustrate these new tendencies at work. An itinerant garbage picker in Cali, Colombia, feeds paper scraps into a production cycle headed by an exporting, transnational paper company (Waterman 1981: 89–90). A central Italian women stitching shoe tops contributes her skilled, if undocumented and underpaid, labors to the manufacture of shoes purchased by a Swiss merchant capitalist and resold to the U.S. Bloomingdale's chain (Blim 1990b). In the neighborhoods of Mexico City, homeworkers, small firms, and large factories are linked in labors sometimes as independents and other times as vassals of transnational corporations, and produce goods sometimes for home and other times for export markets (Benería 1989; Benería and Roldán 1987). In Haiti, local entrepreneurs using machinery furnished by their U.S. contractors employ women at a piece rate to produce textiles and assemble garments, which are typically reimported to the United States under highly favorable tariff provisions (Grunwald and Flamm 1985: 180–205).

Combined capitalist development creates these seemingly peculiar, contradictory mixes of exploitation and opportunity, of abject dependence and chimerical autonomy, of production for national markets and export needs. Networks of homeworkers and family-based firms are utilized extensively. The linkage of households to firms and of firms to markets or larger corporations often rests on the self-exploitation of the household and/or the exploitation of some of its members through the manipulation of patriarchal gender and age hierarchies for petty profit (Ward 1990: 1–22; Hadjicostandi 1990: 64–81; Nash 1988; Ong 1987; Benería and Sen 1986).

Transnational corporations, while decisive in the composition and expansion of capitalist global production in some spheres, remain relatively unimportant in others. Surely, their power in the face of capitalist world economic expansion has not diminished: It is estimated that the world output share of the top 200 transnational corporations reached 29 percent by 1980, up from 18 percent in 1970, though as Gordon noted, increasing profit competition among them may be propelling their movement outward into the capitalist periphery (1988: 41–48). Membership in the transnational corporate community is becoming increasingly multinational itself, as South Korea with 6 transnational corporations (TNCs), Brazil with 2 and Mexico with 2 have joined with the advanced capitalist countries in the ranks of the 100 largest transnational corporations (Conference Board 1989: 22–23).

As capital becomes increasingly multinational, the sources of world investment are becoming increasingly diverse and less predictably core-directed. Consider that Brazil and Taiwan are among the world's top 15 direct investors abroad, and that Taiwan has overtaken the United States as the second leading capital exporter after Japan in East Asia. In 1986, five newly industrializing countries—Brazil, Mexico, Singapore, South Africa, and Malaysia—accounted for almost half the foreign investment flowing to developing countries (Lim 1989: 29–31).

And, as astonishing as the TNCs' hold over the world's productive resources is, the distribution of their enterprises and their impact are highly uneven. They remain dominant in the primary materials, agricultural commodities, mining, and materials-processing sectors, and in consumer durable goods production (Gill and Law 1988: 191–223; Raskin and Muller 1974). Though they continue to prosper through their historic involvement in the industrialization of the Latin American import-substituters, they arrived late on the scene in the case of Pacific Rim development. Foreign ownership and investment were not significant in Taiwanese development, and only became a major factor in South Korean capital formation 10 years ago (Barrett and Chin 1987: 39; Haggard and Cheng 1988: 92–93). As a result, only 6 percent of South Korean transnational subsidiaries are wholly owned by their foreign parents; in contrast, fully 50 percent of transnational subsidiaries in Brazil and Mexico are wholly foreign-held (Evans 1987: 208).

The export processing zones (EPZs) are important spheres for productive activities of transnational corporations, and they are widely diffused in one functional equivalent form or another throughout the developing world (Kamel 1990; Frobel et al. 1981). The motivation for their spread, Gordon (1988: 57–58) noted, is not simply a search for cheap labor, but for state-suppressed, politically docile labor, as well as for easy access to nearby local and regional markets. Production in export processing zones is typically narrow in scope and concentrated largely in just three industries: garments, textiles, and electronics (Sassen-Koob 1988: 112–113; Grunwald and Flamm 1985: 217). The Mexican *maquiladoras* program is an important exception to this rule. Given their easy commercial and geographical access to U.S. markets, the Mexican export processing zones are now major assembly points for consumer durables ranging from automobiles to major consumer appliances and kitchen accessories (*New York Times*, 25 September 1990: D7).

Also important to consider is the fact that not all transnational investment in foreign manufacturing follows a specific pattern or accomplishes a similar end for the investors. First, one finds that different national capitalists use foreign export production differently. While Japanese companies often use offshore production from Asian and Mexican EPZs as export platforms for further penetration of local and other foreign markets; U.S., and apparently South Korean and Taiwanese, capitalists tie in local firms and factories for labor-intensive phases of production that they then reimport for final assembly or finishing in their home countries (Sayer 1986: 115–119; Grunwald and Flamm 1985: 3). Second, national capitalists vary in the location of their foreign investments. For instance, the lion's share of direct foreign investment from advanced capitalist countries like the United States, Western Europe, and Japan is to *other* advanced capitalist countries rather than to the Third World (Yin 1991; Berry 1989: 209). In contrast, regional NICs show an increasing tendency to invest in downstream, late-developing countries (Lim 1989: 29–31; Petras and Engbarth 1988: 98–99). Third, the purposes and organization of direct foreign investment also depend importantly on the type of industry in which groups of capitalists find themselves (Grunwald 1985: 217; Sayer 1986: 107–124).

Nonetheless, capitalist penetration of peripheral zones throughout the developing world via transnationally dominated export processing zones have profound and unsettling impacts on their home regions. The EPZs are costly to construct and maintain for the nation-states that sponsor them (Warr 1987), contribute little but their low wages to the local economy, and create health and environmental problems for workers and nearby residents (Kamel 1990; Fuentes and Ehrenreich 1983). Capitalists also exploit ethnic differences and gender inequalities to control the labor process and extract additional surplus value through long and physically punishing work routines (Ward 1990: 12–14; Ong 1987; Fernandez-Kelly 1983).

Though they serve as highly visible reminders of how interconnected global production has become, there are reasons to suspect that the overall importance of EPZs in relation to the growing global factory is limited. Consider that in Mexico, where, through the *maquiladoras* program, the notion of development zones has been taken perhaps to its extreme, the 393,000 workers employed in *maquiladoras* factories in 1989, according to Rothstein (1989), represented only about 10 percent of the Mexican industrial labor force. As a representative example, the world semiconductor industry, one of the key EPZ products, is estimated by Sayer (1986: 109) to employ only some 300,000 workers worldwide, a number smaller than all those employed in the Mexican *maquiladoras* program.

Consequently, a more robust, as well as realistic, conception of the global factory needs to focus on the progressive *generalization* of capitalist relations of production and on the variety of agents that are active in capitalist development. It also needs to consider how these highly variegated productive activities are mediated in important ways by a shifting array of social forces organized as workers, capitalists, classes, communities, and nation-states.

PROPOSITION 5: The global factory is shaped in important ways by the actions of and conflicts between a variety of agents—from nation-states and capitalist classes to workers and communities.

People make their own history, but not any way they please, to paraphrase the inestimable Marx: "They do not make it under circumstances chosen by themselves, but under circumstances directly encountered, given and transmitted from the past" (1963: 15). The contradictions of capitalism arising from the problem of capitalism's tendency to externalize its problems through combined and uneven development both create limits as well as possibilities for an array of actors who constitute themselves in a variety of ways. Within the context of this proposition, I would like to illustrate, rather than definitively explain, a bit of what is known and what may be knowable about the emerging global factory within the local and world social fabric.

State policies and state power are utterly crucial to the construction of the global factory, as are the constellation of internal and external class forces that impinge on state action. As Skocpol pointed out, states are fundamentally "Janus-faced," anchored simultaneously in the international system of states and in a domestic environment inevitably marked by class-divided social structures (1979: 32). On the one hand, they move within the thick political and economic webbings of interstate relations, particularly ones in which certain states acquire hegemonic positions within a changing world order (Chase-Dunn 1989: 131–198). Furthermore, nation-states that achieve some degree of hegemonic advantage also seek to extend their control over the capitalist world economy, as analyses of U.S. attempts to influence international financial and economic development organizations suggest (Gill and Law 1988; Block 1977). The shift of developing countries toward export-oriented industrial development strategies, for example, has been aided in no small part by the actions of international organizations such as the International Monetary Fund and the various regional development banks (Balassa 1989: 65–83, 207–223; Christiansen et al. 1988: 101–103).

Nation-states also exert enormous influence over their national development processes. Such a judgment has been implicit in the earlier discussion showing that nation-states in the post–World War II period have undertaken development approaches ranging from import substitution to export-oriented industrialization, and that states throughout the world capitalist economy have been engaged in inducing capitalist development through the formation of export processing zones and development zones of various sorts. As the record of the newly industrializing countries has come under increasing scholarly scrutiny, the high degree of state involvement in the shape and flow of industrial development has been underscored. Developing states have implemented fiscal and monetary policies favorable to certain forms of industrial growth and have deployed other strategies designed to create labor markets that are more malleable for capitalist exploitation. They have also sought to accelerate the process of capital accumulation, sponsored infrastructure improvements, financed research and development subsidies for new industries, and provided leadership in industrial specialization targeting (Amsden 1985; 1990; Balassa 1990; Kwon 1990; Berry 1989: 197–205; Deyo 1987; Islam and Kirkpatrick 1986; Rueschemeyer and Evans 1985).

Though states are more than mere crystallizations of ruling-class interest or simply the concrete manifestations of class conflicts (Skocpol 1979: 24–29; Evans, Rueschemeyer, and Skocpol 1985: 3–37), they are nonetheless often linked through economic development with organized capitalist interests of various sorts and sizes. As Evans (1979) explained for Brazil, states can be active partners in a triple alliance with international and local capital through the creation of specific forms of dependent economic development. State power is often used to suppress labor movements and unions (Kamel 1990; Munck 1988b: 121–143; Van Hear 1988; Wangel 1988; Fernando 1988; Wolpe 1980b), or to shape them in noncombative, corporatist ways.

Just as states vary in internal composition, power, and policy, so do the national capitalist classes with whom they are in contact. To understand the enormous potential for variation, it is useful to analyze the capitalist class constellations typical in part of Latin America, East Asia, and peripheral Europe. Though these types by no means exhaust the empirical configurations of the regions themselves, they do illustrate the degree to which capitalist class trajectories may mediate the trend toward global production discussed here. In Latin America, dependency theory studies describe a discredited national bourgeoisie— a suspect category of *compradors* who betray the national economic development process in the interests of collaboration with international capital and who ultimately bear the responsibility for the "misdevelopment" of their countries (Cockcroft, Gunder Frank, and Johnson 1972: xviii, 103–106, 429–430). The interests and activities of this *gran bourgeoisie* were often contrasted with quiescent industrialist fractions and a volatile, vulnerable petty bourgeoisie composed of small-business-people, low-level bureaucratic functionaries, professionals, and technicians who alternatively suffered or prospered from the advance of multinational capitalism (Cockcroft, Gunder Frank, and Johnson 1972: xix-xxi, 162–217, 430).

Studies of the capitalist classes in the newly industrializing countries of East Asia suggest a different pattern for national class configurations. At the risk of some oversimplification, it seems that in the cases of South Korea and Taiwan, postwar authoritarian states, having emerged from Japanese colonialism with a greatly weakened agrarian bourgeoisie, organized a new bourgeoisie based in industrial development. These states directly controlled certain basic industrial sectors and retained certain Japanese innovations, notably the encouragement of the growth of large financial–industrial combines. At the same time, they supported the formation of a competitive, petty entrepreneurial sector and class to support the emergent monopoly sectors and to more efficiently utilize low-cost rural labor in the production of cheap consumer goods for domestic consumption (Amsden 1985; 1990; Koo 1987; Evans 1987; Greenhalgh 1988).

The late-developing nations of the European periphery present still another historic class constellation. The national capitalist classes of peripheral Europe got off to a late start relative to their northern European counterparts and were none too successful in establishing political hegemony in the face of resistance from the agrarian bourgeoisie, peasants, and workers. After the authoritarian interlude, which for the Iberian peninsula lingered until only recently and for Greece reappeared for an extended period during the 1970s, capitalist states emerged that have attempted to support the growth of a national bourgeoisie. At the same time, there is evidence that the peripheral states have countenanced or actively supported the expansion of a petty bourgeoisie, in part entrepreneurial, that might serve both as a bul-

wark against working-class militance and as an element in a procap-
italist democratic consensus (Giner 1985; Pizzorno 1974; Berger 1980:
86–124; Tarrow 1985; Lange 1985; Arrighi 1985a; Wallerstein 1985).

What kind of capitalist class might be expected to materialize
through the further globalization of production? One might hazard two
predictions: first, that national class structures will become increasingly differentiated; and second, that one will observe the rise of an
entrepreneurial petty bourgeoisie, both of the micro-industrial and of
the merchant capitalist sorts, in areas most affected by capitalist expansion. As we have observed, there are a variety of productive sources
for the global factory, ranging from transnational corporations and
state and national capitalist enterprises to the coupling of petty commodity production to world markets through merchant, national, and
transnational capital. In addition, we have noted the more multinational nature of finance capital and its more variable investment behavior. These phenomena would seem to support both possibilities,
though the future of this new petty bourgeoisie is probably exceedingly
fragile and vulnerable to steadily increasing perils of proletarianization (see Roldan in Munck 1988b: 211).

It should also be anticipated that diverse national capitalist class
fractions will begin to cluster in self-conscious ways and form associations directed at affecting the political process. Through interest-
based organizations and political parties, they will likely engage in
increased competition for state sponsorship of initiatives supportive of
their respective growth trajectories.

What of labor? The strategies that capitalists use to appropriate
value and maximize the level of the exploitation of labor have been
identified exhaustively through more than a century of research into
the political economy of capitalism.[19] However, the emergence of the
global factory, precisely because it derives from the spread of combined
and uneven capitalist development, promises to upset easy character-
izations of developmental stages and phases and to capsize quick judg-
ments about potential evolutionary patterns and processes in the
worldwide capitalist labor process. Instead, following from this description of the global factory, perhaps the most sanguine prediction
possible is to expect an even more eclectic mix of value-maximizing
strategies deployed by capital against labor. As networks of production
stretch from one continent to another, from the backrooms and small
shops to markets, or to factories and corporate boardrooms, the forms
of labor and the forms of exploitation may themselves become as combined as the development that prompts them. The key, given this context, is to eschew universalizing current conceptualizations of labor
process regimes and social structures of accumulation and to utilize
them as heuristics in a structural analysis of the variety of contem-

porary world capitalist terrains.[20] The watchword may well be to treat our conceptual schemas as local theories if and until they show themselves handy in explaining the new contours of capitalist expansion and change.

Capitalism's search for labor that is cheap, potentially docile, and politically suppressed, disorganized, and divided against itself will probably not diminish much. To paraphrase Lenin, capitalism would not be capitalism without it. Agents, ranging from merchant capitalists and petty entrepreneurs to corporations and nation-states, will likely continue to exploit divergent levels of social development and differences among workers in gender, ethnicity, and race and to deploy wage forms that disguise appropriation, foster coercion, and encourage cooperation. The novel element reflected in our analysis of the global factory is that capitalism now seeks to achieve its goals simultaneously in a moment of worldwide production. This shift poses an extraordinary challenge for analysis and description.

This prospect is no less daunting for workers and their communities. Working-class formation typically begins as a local phenomenon: For the working class, this fact is a source of strength, as well as weakness. Locality presents the disadvantage of relative immobility in the face of an increasingly mobile, flexible, expansive capitalist foe. The nub of it is that workers, save those who migrate, cannot be in two places at the same time, but capital, by virtue of its networking of production, can. However, this same limitation yields an important potential strength, namely, the capacity of workers and their communities to mobilize a variety of social and cultural ties that already bind them in creating a politically viable social movement. Following Thompson's lead (1986 [1963]), historical and anthropological case studies have indicated how working-class movements have mobilized ties of residence, kinship, gender, race and ethnicity, craft and work culture, and religion, as well as more generalized cultural identities and dispositions in developing effective bases for anticapitalist struggles.[21]

As Sacks (1989) has argued, the meanings and experiences of working-class membership have been typically coextensive historically with the meanings and experiences of community membership. An abbreviated account of labor agitation among shoe workers in a central Italian region linked since the late 1950s with the world market may illustrate how the coincidence of industry, class, and community can unleash an increased potential for working-class militancy in the global factory. At first glance, one might have given labor a scant chance in a monocultural industrial region where workplaces consist of thousands of small factories and shops and where illegal labor by homeworkers and others is central to the labor process. Small-plot sharecropping, for 500 years the major economic activity before the

postwar rise of shoe production, had created a set of cultural dispositions favorable to petty entrepreneurialism located in household reproduction among landlords and sharecroppers alike. The social
relations of production internal to the household were ordered by
patriarchal norms; a mix of clientelism and paternalism cloaked the
typically exploitative external relations between sharecropping hous-
esholds and landlords. In all, a tremendous export boom in the shoe
industry during the 1960s that provided first-time wage labor for many
individuals and profitable small businesses for a quarter of the local
households would seem to have created an inauspicious base for a
progressive labor movement (Blim 1990b: 105–175).

Nonetheless, shoe workers in the region nurtured a union movement
from the early 1960s onward, culminating in three industrywide and
communitywide strikes in 1967, 1971, and 1974. The 1971 strike was
the most spectacular and resulted in local entrepreneurial acceptance
of the national shoe industrial contract. Barricades obstructing traffic
in and out of the bevy of central Italian hilltowns were erected and
controlled by workers and their families. Autonomous groups of women
factory workers constructed and superintended their own blockades.
The strikers, as in many other labor struggles, won by successfully
shutting down the entire shoe industry which, in practice, amounted
to the entire economy of the area (Blim 1990b: 224–228).

There were, perhaps, four discernible reasons for their success. First,
external circumstances were favorable for local action. Successful national labor militancy, as exemplified by Italy's 1969 "Hot Autumn"
period of labor agitation, in which workers and unions won major
concessions for labor on the factory floor and in national wage and
working conditions legislation; increased organizational support of local workers by the national labor confederations; and the growing
national and regional strength of the Communist party all contributed
to nurturing local awareness and will. Second, the success of the shoe
industry fueled an expansion of production that fast outstripped both
the available local productive capacity and the labor force. The remedy,
a dramatic shift from workshop to factory production, necessitated a
shift in the rhythm and routines of work and increased the use of the
drive system (Gordon, Reich and Edwards 1982: 14–15) rather than
paternalism as the exclusive form of labor control. These factors increased the vulnerability of entrepreneurs to labor's claims.

Third, industry and community had become coextensive forms of
social life: What the industry did, and what workers got, determined
the life chances of the community itself. Both workers and entrepreneurs could claim virtually identical historical biographies; large portions of both groups had emerged from the same penurious system of
petty exploitation as sharecroppers or had come from a town center

household that scratched out a living in handicraft production. As worker discontent grew, the common cultural heritage that at times had bound workers and entrepreneurs in a common cause cut several different ways. On the one hand, the combination of newfound entrepreneurial wealth accompanied by widespread diffusion of the drive system of labor control fostered a sense among workers that entrepreneurs were exceeding the rather wide, socially tolerable band of rewards and social conduct that both workers and entrepreneurs, collectively former veterans of the captive labor market of sharecropping, had customarily expected. In a word, some exploitation was endured by workers in the interests of the greater community good, progress, development, and so on. After all, many workers reasoned, either they or their children might become entrepreneurs some day. However, the entrepreneurs had overstepped the boundaries of the customary contract between unequals that had prevailed from the old form of labor in the fields to the new forms of labor in the factory.

On the other hand, workers were well "accustomed" to the modus operandi of the entrepreneurs, precisely because, through participation in sharecropping, they had seen it all before. There was no surprise in the "zero-sum" nature of the game, no "shock of the new" that mobilized them. Rather, it was a canny collective perception of the old in the new, the rediscovery of the landlord in the factory boss, that lent coherence to their analysis and cohesiveness to their organization.

Finally, the strike was supported by households and their kin networks, and outward through these dense, interconnected social ties, which were sustained by the community itself. The women who took leading roles in the strike were factory workers, a status in the community that seemed to have enabled them to overcome the pervasive gender inequalities embodied in the household relations and the use of women's labor in underpaid, illegal shoe homework. It should also be noted, however, that the strike only improved wages and working conditions for men and women factory workers, and not for children or homeworkers of both sexes (Blim 1990b: 130–175).

To be sure, this case is only one among many potential accounts of worker resistance in the emerging global factory. It may provide some insight into the special problems and possibilities one might find in petty commodity production zones presently surfacing in the world capitalist economy. Other productive environments will require other explanations. Koo (1990), for instance, argued that proletarianization of a more recognizable sort is occurring as a consequence of South Korean development, albeit more abruptly and intensely than—with the case of Europe in mind—one might have been imagined. State repression as well as deep state involvement in development, in tandem with an artisanal production tradition, have slowed and weakened the workers' collective response. Trade union militancy has shaped in important ways further capitalist development in countries such as Argentina and Nigeria (Munck 1988a; Van Hear 1988). A number of studies of worker resistance in export processing zones show that even the states' artificial design of isolated, instant company towns creates potential for labor militancy (Kamel 1990; Ong 1987; Fuentes and Ehrenreich 1983).

It would be mistaken, following Sacks's premise (1989), I think, to confine analysis of sites of resistance to shop floors and factory gates. The global factory, as discussed here, simply represents more concretely the progressive incorporation of peoples throughout the world in capitalist production for the world market. Popular resistance to this process of subsumption of work and everyday life to the norms of capitalist relations of production, consumption, and exchange is widespread. As Walton and Ragin (1990) demonstrated, so-called International Monetary Fund (IMF) riots and other popular struggles against economic austerity policies imposed on developing countries by international agencies are extraordinarily widespread, extending to 26 of the 80 world debtor countries. Other studies of popular movements in Latin America (Stephen and Logan 1990; Gledhill 1988) also highlight how local protests, in times of economic crisis, often acquire an anticapitalist character.

Consequently, one of the principal products of the global factory is struggle in a variety of forms and with a plenitude of potentials. The highly variable interaction between and among these pervasive classes of agents furnishes anthropology with a formidable research agenda.

ANTHROPOLOGY AND THE GLOBAL FACTORY

Anthropology has a vital part to play in understanding the new global factory. Like its forerunner, the anthropology of industrialization and development, an anthropology of the global factory can disclose the variety of ways in which local peoples incorporate themselves and are incorporated into global production for the world market.[22] As an empirical matter, the evolving structure of the global factory *demands* the kind of field research that anthropologists do because the phenomenon entails activities at the level of the household, the kin group, and the community before moving up to and including regions, states, and world markets. An anthropology focusing on the global factory can investigate the ways in which local peoples mobilize culturally distinctive capacities to shape their unfolding economic destinies as well as documenting their struggles to resist the world capitalist logic in whole or in part. In the final paragraphs of this chapter, I try to reconstruct, through the discussion of some illustrative texts, some prefigurative and prospective tendencies that an anthropology of the global factory might skillfully use.

If one looks carefully at the field studies of industrialization produced before the Vietnam War, one finds that they serve as a somewhat refreshing corrective to the oft-heard complaint that anthropologists present disconnected and inward-turning accounts of small societies. Warner et al.'s *Yankee City* study (1947), as well as the Lynds' influential *Middletown* community study (1929, 1937), exhibit an outward-looking perspective as well as a keen interest in how industrialization links study towns to the larger society and recasts daily life, the class structures, and the power struggles of their respective local communities. After World War II, active anthropological participation in world economic development studies produced work that, though filtered through the lenses of modernization theory, was no less concerned with how local societies could provide culturally diverse responses to an expanding capitalist world order. Both Nash (1958) and Geertz (1963) demonstrated the importance of local cultural variation in the industrial development process while calling for anthropological studies that reached beyond their villages to incorporate an understanding of the world economy as a profound motor for social change. At the same time, careful studies of the dimensions and effects of the plantation economy on Puerto Rican society by Steward, Wolf, and Mintz (Steward 1956; Wolf 1959; Mintz 1959) prefigured later Latin American research on dependency, development, and the proletarianization process.[23]

Research on postwar African industrialization during the 1950s also tied local studies to macro-social economic processes. The impacts of labor migration and the formation of urban networks in the industrial towns in Zimbabwe and Zambia on tribal associations and identities were carefully analyzed. Moreover, particular attention was paid to the interaction between achieved statuses in workplaces and union organizations on tribal identities and the prospects for intertribal worker solidarity (Epstein 1978; Mitchell 1973; Powdermaker 1962; Gluckman 1961).

By the mid-1970s, anthropological work on industrialization more explicitly embraced both a world market orientation and an identification with peoples in regions caught up in a maelstrom of economic and social change not of their own making. Wolfe (1977) argued for the analysis of the impact of transnational corporations on the internationalization of production, while Safa (1974) analyzed the influence of Puerto Rican industrial development on the creation of a culture of poverty. Nash (1979) and Taussig (1980), both of whom studied tin mining and economic dependency in Bolivia, pointed to rituals and indigenous cultures of resistance to capitalist encirclement and degradation of the local ways of life.

By the 1980s, the study of anthropology and industry was located decisively within the framework of the world capitalist economy and within the context of an international division of labor. Positions within the world economic order were pinpointed (Benton 1990; Cooper 1980), and novel forms of production such as export processing zones were explored in detail (Nash and Fernandez-Kelly 1983; Fernandez-Kelly 1983; Ong 1987). Appreciative attention was given to working-class formation and struggle (Blim 1990b; Nash 1989; Lamphere 1987; Rothstein 1982). The different and unequal consequences of industrial development for women as well as the impact of the expansion of capitalist relations of production on household reproduction enriched the broader anthropological investigation of gender (Ong 1987; Lamphere 1987; Benería and Roldán 1987; Rothstein 1982). Finally, the deeply historical characters of some industrial transformations were analyzed in detail to reveal how capitalism achieves a hegemonic role in local economies and the tensions its successes as well as crises create (Blim 1990b; Nash 1989; Lamphere 1987).

In fashioning an anthropology of the global factory for the 1990s, therefore, certain important analytical strengths from anthropology's historical record can be carried forward and used creatively. First, the outward-looking perspective, with an emphasis on linkages and structures that impinge on and partly shape the everyday realities of local life, is essential. Second, the demonstrated anthropological openness to a wide range of analytical units from households, kin networks, and communities to corporations, classes, nation-states, and the world economy can enable us to capture the *actuality* of the global factory and its flexible, highly changeable shapes in ways that are unique and valuable. Third, anthropology's inclination to pay attention to, and thereby legitimize, local voices and expressions, individual and collective, of resistance to involvement in and dependency on the evolving capitalist economy provides the moral edge necessary for more profound knowledge of the world in which we live today.

In this spirit, this book has been assembled as a tool for deeper understanding. It is hoped that our collective efforts may spark further awareness and study of this profound process of social transformation which is only imperfectly captured through the gloss of the global factory.

NOTES

My thanks to Frances Rothstein, Daniel Faber, and Alan Klein for comments on earlier drafts of this chapter. My thanks also to Ying Yin and Luis Falcon for assistance in assembling the tables and figures used in this chapter.

1. For classic statements of modernization theory, see Eisenstadt (1966), Levy (1960), Parsons (1977), and Rostow (1971).

2. For an extensive review and critique of the mode of production alternative as a theoretical solution, see Brewer (1980: 183–274), Wolpe (1980a: 1–44), Clammer (1978: 1–30), and Foster-Carter (1978a: 1978b).

3. To reform the Wallersteinian thesis, Chase-Dunn (1989: 26–28) has proposed a revitalized world-systems theory in which he envisions appropriating the concept of modes of production, their articulation and contradiction, in understanding the flow and direction of change within a global social formation.

4. Roseberry (1988: 166) made this point nicely.

5. Walton (1985) has argued that the "new" international division of labor in which transnational corporations organize worldwide production is the third in so many international divisions of labor, the first consisting of the organization of the periphery for raw materials exports, and the second comprising the import substitution industrialization common in leading Third World countries in the 1950s and 1960s.

6. The NIDL thesis has been criticized strongly on a variety of grounds. For more extensive critiques, consult Berry (1989); Munck (1988b: 32–33); McMichael (1982: 115–146); Southall (1988: 1–34); Petras and Engbarth (1988); Sayer (1986).

7. Langley (1990: 50) noted that between 1980 and 1988, Third World international indebtedness increased dramatically such that the percentage of export earnings needed to repay the debt increased from 81.6 percent of exports to 160.7 percent.

8. A recent report on foreign investment in Thailand (*New York Times*, 10 May 1990, pp. D1, D9) suggests how well advanced is this new investment cycle *within* the Asian economy. As might be expected, Japan leads the list of national investors with over US $3.5 billion in 1989. The next principal investor is Taiwan ($871 million); and among the top 10 investing countries, one finds Hong Kong ($563 million), Singapore ($408 million), and South Korea ($171 million). Number 13 on the list is Malaysia ($71 million). For the record, the United States finds itself 5 on the list with a 1989 investment total in Thailand of $551 million.

9. Walton (1987) has argued that non-Marxist accounts of capitalism, including work by Max Weber, Karl Polanyi, and Joseph Schumpeter, also feature uneven development prominently in their explanation of growth and change within capitalist economies.

10. Trimberger (1979) presented an early and highly cogent comparison of dependency theory with notions of combined and uneven development.

11. A number of observers have pointed to recent tendencies on the part of world capitalist development toward flexible, post-Fordist production (Piore and Sabel 1984), increasing disorganization (Lash and Urry 1987), and more flexible accumulation strategies (Harvey 1989). Each of these sets of observations, in theory, can be used as evidence for the thesis set forth here that capitalism is embarked on a new phase in its trajectory of crisis and growth.

12. It should be emphasized that the subsequent discussion in the text concerning uneven economic growth and increasing growth inequalities among

developing countries does not bear directly on Marxist predictions that profit rates equalize and decline among capitalist firms and, finally, economies over time, the phenomena that for Mandel (1975) provide the motive force for combined and uneven development. The data ostensibly provide a structural account of the symptoms and consequences of combined and uneven development rather than an account of its causes.

13. A recent Inter-American Development Bank report (*New York Times*, 30 October 1990: D6) suggests an upturn in Latin American development fortunes, with an average annual economic growth rate of 5.5 percent for the years 1992–1995.

14. Berry (1989: 207) has argued that to match the success of the East Asian NICS, late-developing countries would need to increase their manufacturing exports by more than 700 percent, a trend, he judged, that would be resisted by advanced capitalist and newly industrializing countries alike.

15. Per capita gross national product in Latin America dropped dramatically in most countries between 1981 and 1989. That of Mexico declined 9.2 percent; Venezuela, 24.9 percent; Brazil, 0.4 percent; Ecuador, 11.9 percent; Peru, 24.7 percent; and Argentina, 23.5 percent. The only major gainers were Colombia with a 13.9 percent increase and Chile with a 9.6 percent increase (*New York Times*, 11 February 1990: E3).

16. McMichael (1982: 127–130) distinguished between semi-industrial, sub-imperial states such as Argentina, Brazil, Mexico, and India, where export-oriented manufacturing proceeds from a mature industrial base, and the East Asia NICs, which have been incorporated into the production networks of the core capitalist societies. Krugman et al. (1989) used indebtedness and export capacity to divide the developing world into four categories of countries.

17. The list of nations exporting textiles, footwear, and apparel is too long to name. For some more indications, consult Balassa (1989); Purcell (1989); Grunwald and Flamm (1985); and Frobel, Heinrichs, and Kreye (1981).

18. Sayer (1986) argued, for instance, that factors such as the structure of the semiconductor industrial sector, particularly its production process, capital intensity, and technological deployment, along with competitive pressures for improved quality control within the industry, often influence decisions concerning industrial location more than does the availability of cheap labor.

19. For useful research on the labor process of contemporary capitalism, see Burawoy (1979, 1983); Braverman (1974); Edwards (1979); Gordon, Reich, and Edwards (1982); Bendix (1956).

20. Burawoy's highly useful conceptualization of labor regimes (1983), as well as work of the regulationist school (Aglietta 1979; Lipietz 1986: 16–40) and their U.S. counterparts (Gordon, Reich, and Edwards 1982), offer important possibilities for application. Given the increased complexity of the world capitalist economy, care in their use seems important.

21. For a summary and review of recent historical literature on class formation, see Katznelson (1986). I will discuss some exemplary anthropological analyses of class formation and culture in the final section of the chapter.

22. For excellent reviews of the literature on industrialization and development, see Walton (1987); Holzberg and Giovannini (1981); and Nash (1981).

23. Mintz (1985) has provided a compelling account of how the industrialization of sugar as a commodity for the world market profoundly altered the social lives of peoples in both producing and consuming societies.

Part I

Global Production and the Mobility of Capital and Labor

2

What Happens to the Past? Return Industrial Migrants in Latin America

Frances Abrahamer Rothstein

In this chapter Frances Rothstein shows not only that labor moves toward cities and centers of capital investment but that Latin American workers who leave their rural villages eventually return home in large numbers. Even before they physically return they often send economic and political support. One frequently overlooked consequence of so much return migration is that "development" has occurred in rural Latin America and therefore the rural divide is disappearing. A second important consequence of this pattern of return migration is that, in contemporary industrialization, labor is not cut off from family and community ties as it was in the first industrial experience.

Many anthropologists argue that contemporary Third World development and industrialization cannot be understood in terms of Euro-American models (Collins 1986; Rothstein 1986; Keren 1988). One of the problems of these models is that development is presented as representing a sharp break with the past. This chapter will examine wage-labor migration in Latin America and show how the past and present are combined in the widespread practice of return migration.

Migration studies is one of the areas in which a break with the past is usually stressed. Models of migration in the First World have emphasized one-way movement *away* from the past. Not surprisingly, the same models have prevailed in studies of migration in the Third World. This is evident in the fact that, despite a huge literature on migration in Latin America and repeated assertions that migration involves a

two-way flow, return migration has received little systematic attention
from Latin Americanists.[1] The purpose of this chapter is twofold. First,
I suggest that although return migration may not be the only pattern
in Latin America, it has nonetheless been an important pattern involving thousands of rural–urban workers, their households, and their
home and host communities. Second, I will show that the effects of
return migration are more significant than is usually acknowledged.

The chapter is based in part on my longitudinal anthropological
research in San Cosme Mazatecochco, a rural community of approximately 6,000 people in central Mexico, and on a review of case studies
of migration elsewhere in Latin America. For the purposes of this
analysis, I define *return-migration* broadly (following Connell et al.
1976) to include seasonal return, repeated return, and permanent
return.[2]

It is often suggested that the neglect of return migration is due to
methodological difficulties. Butterworth and Chance (1981), for example, suggested that return migration is the aspect of migration that
is the "least amenable to quantification" (73). Analysis of return migration does require some sort of diachronic study, either by using case
histories, such as the migration life histories used by Feindt and
Browning (1972) or longitudinal research in which the investigator
compares residence at different time periods. I suggest, however, it is
not so much our methods as our theories that have led to neglecting
return migration.

Although careful longitudinal study is ultimately necessary to describe and analyze return migration, we do not ask even the simple
questions that we might pose. Nelson (1976) noted, for example, that
it is so widely assumed that migration to Latin American cities is
permanent that few studies ask migrants if they plan on staying. One
method that is often used as a proxy indicator of return migration,
particularly in comparing different countries, is the ratio of males to
females. It is assumed that where the number of men in cities is substantially greater than the number of women, much of the explanation
lies in the return of men to their home communities (Nelson 1976:
724). This is one of the reasons why Latin America is thought to have
less return migration than countries in Africa or Asia. Using the male/
female ratio as a proxy indicator, however, assumes that women do
not migrate autonomously. Not only will the ratio of males to females
in cities (and thus, the estimates of return migration) be affected by
the autonomous migration of women, but in some areas and in some
stages of capitalist development, women represent a significant part
of a return migration flow that has only rarely been examined (Rudolf
1983).

More broadly, the assumptions that return migration and the au-

3RD Floor JZ1318.G582

Cross - national drug policy / special editors Robert Maccom

3rd floor. HV5801.C76

Positive development :
3rd BF721.P67

then the .06 + x becomes just .06. We are
to the .06 it is being added to and so it can be

Health and the environment

(special ed. of this vol)

4th floor. RA566.3.H43

#2002

Globalization and democracy /
special editors

nimportant in Latin America are
oretical perspectives on migration
ntations that have dominated our
theory and the dependency per-
variations on dependency such as
e change as a unilineal and uni-
tional" or "precapitalist" to "mod-
lustrializing." In the view of such
(1963), for example, traditional
to how far they have moved along
. In the dependency perspective,
not moving along a developmental
ependencistas also assume a single
aches differ in their explanations
move along their expected devel-
eorists, internal obstacles are usu-
for dependency theorists, external
country from developing. The two
crucial characteristics of "devel-
ient path is, but they share a com-
th on which all societies move (or
ates.

n the dependency perspective, lack
the urban, modern, industrial, de-
ough such a view would seem to
gration (after all, return migrants
l urbanity back), both dependency
ture, either the traditional village
re, as too powerful a constraining
spective, when migrants do return
assumed that traditional customs,
ep them from making significant
spective, because capitalism draws
off so much of the rural area's resources and orients migrants to urban
capitalism, return migrants are prevented from having any lasting
effect on the home area.

Behind their unidirectional and overly structural approaches, the
common problem with both the modernization and dependency perspectives to migration is that they ignore and/or underestimate changing class relations and human agency. Modernization theorists, who
often ignore class altogether, see only the continuities and similarities
between return migrants and nonmigrants in their home areas and
the differences between return migrants and some idealized version of
middle-class urbanites. Dependency theorists, despite their stress on

20. What works in preventing crime?
HV 7431 . W42 .3rd

capitalism, often also ignore class. Even the more recent approaches of world-systems theorists or articulationists, which do focus on class, often attribute almost complete power to capitalists and ignore or underestimate working-class efforts.

As I have argued elsewhere (1986), a narrow and historically specific view of class is often imposed by social scientists on workers at all times and places. Just because contemporary Third World workers do not think and act in the same ways as workers in Europe or North America at some particular point in time does not mean that they are not "true" workers or that they are "semiproletarians." The return migrants whom most anthropologists and other social scientists discuss *are* workers. Moving is one of the ways in which they deal with the fact that they have to sell their labor. Moving, per se, contrary to the assumptions of both modernization and dependency theorists, cannot change the structure of capitalism. It may, however, affect relations within and between classes. In what follows, I suggest that return migration is quantitatively more significant than social scientists have assumed and that it may have important functions in bridging relations between rural and urban workers and between workers in different sectors of the economy.

Despite the neglect of return migration and the theoretical formulations that ignore class and assume that return migration is insignificant, there are numerous hints in the literature on rural communities, wage labor, rural–urban migration, on remittances and on migrant associations, that by the 1970s and 1980s, if not before, return migration had become quantitatively and qualitatively significant throughout Latin America. Many studies contain vague or general assertions of such significance. Altamirano (1984: 59) claimed that there is "considerable return migration" in the Peruvian highlands. Portes and Walton (1981: 59) suggested "substantial proportions of return migration." Some studies give numerical estimates or actual counts of returns. These seem to indicate that as many as 30 to 40 percent of the adults in some rural communities are return migrants. In San Cosme, 27 percent of the economically active men live or lived in Mexico City or elsewhere and return regularly to the community, usually weekly.[3] More than two-thirds of San Cosme's households had one or more members who had lived elsewhere and who repeatedly or permanently returned.[4] In Cedral, another rural community in Mexico, 30 percent of the men had been elsewhere (Feindt and Browning 1972). In Copa Bitoo, Oaxaca, over 40 percent of the adults had been outside the community (Young 1982). In the Morelos Highlands, de la Pena (1981) found that more than half the household heads were migrants.

Similar rates have been reported for other areas in Latin America. Brush (1980) found that 31 percent of the households in a rural com-

munity in Peru had returnees. A study of rural Colombia found that between one-fifth and one-third of the men had lived in a large city
(Simmons and Cardona 1972). Rudolf (personal communication, 1988)
found that by the mid-1980s most of the adult men and women in a rural Panamanian community had lived elsewhere. Although most rural
dwellers in Latin America may not be return migrants, there do seem
to be a significant number who have lived and worked elsewhere.

ECONOMIC EFFECTS OF RETURN MIGRATION

In addition to largely ignoring the topic, much of the literature
underestimates the effect of return migrants and return migration on
the home communities. Some studies of particular communities suggest that return migrants and return migration have contributed to
local development, but most of the research stresses the failures of
migrants and/or migration with regards to development. Interestingly,
such pessimism is shared by modernization and dependency theorists,
although dependency theorists blame capitalism and uneven development and modernization theorists blame rural populations and their
resistance to change. In both formulations, it should be noted, rural
dwellers are viewed as the passive pawns of either capitalism or
tradition.

The most common arguments that the impact of return migration
is negative or negligible include the following points: (1) The productive
capacity of the rural community is not increased and in some cases is
decreased; (2) new employment opportunities are not generated locally;
and (3) migrants return without having learned new or appropriate
skills. In addition, the "pessimists" argue that migrants spend their
earnings on purchases that benefit individuals rather than the entire
community and on consumption goods rather than productive investment. A related argument suggests that a "tradition of migration"
encourages people to look toward migration rather than economic or
political organization (Grindle 1988: 116–117).

I do not disagree with the overall conclusion of the pessimists that the
gap between rich and poor nations or regions is not lessened by migration or return migration. That, however, has more to do with the structure of capitalism, uneven development, and class conflict than it does
with migration. The migrants that we are talking about are migrant
workers; that is, they are working-class and/or peasant migrants. Ask-
ing if return migrants or return migration significantly alter the local
productive structure or generate new employment opportunities are
the wrong questions. Migrants are cheap labor, not Horatio Algers. We
must rid ourselves of the myth that migration is the answer to uneven
development. Then, we can rid ourselves also of the unreasonable ex-

pectation that return migrants are, by virtue of their return, going to radically alter the structure of capitalism. Although dependency theorists do not adhere to the myth that migration is the answer to Third World poverty and inequality, since so much of their work is geared to refuting that myth, it dominates their results and, more important, distorts their findings so that they too underestimate the impact of return migration on rural communities.[5] In what follows, I suggest that although I do not doubt that capital gains more from migration and return migration than does labor, return migrants and return migration are changing rural economies and political relations.

One of the most important ways in which return migration affects and changes rural areas is through its effect on small-scale subsistence production. Return migration is closely associated with access to some land. Whether it is through inheritance of family land or use rights to communal land, or because it is possible to buy or seize small parcels of land, most return migrants have or acquire land.[6]

Many writers have focused on the negative consequences of the tie between migrants and land. They point out that in some areas, agricultural productivity and/or production have declined because wage labor is more profitable than subsistence cultivation and migrants sometimes hold on to land but do not cultivate it or do not cultivate it intensively. It has also been argued that by holding on to land, migrants contribute to inflationary land prices which limit peasants' access to land and perpetuate exploitative tenant–landlord relations (e.g., Dinerman 1978).

My research in San Cosme and studies such as those of Bartra (1974) and Edelman (1980) suggest that in Mexico, and I suspect elsewhere also, it is not migration but the relative productivity of capitalist production compared to small-scale subsistence cultivation that accounts for the decision to not cultivate or to cultivate less intensively. By favoring capitalist industry and large-scale agriculture, development policy in Mexico has led to significant increases in productivity in the capitalist sector. Small-scale peasant production has generally not received credit or new technological inputs and peasant productivity has not increased. Consequently, the peasant economy cannot compete with the more dynamic capitalist economy (Rothstein 1982: 65).

Although they cannot compete with large-scale capitalist agriculture or industry, because they retained or bought land with their wages, migrants in San Cosme usually do cultivate a few hectares of land and supplement their wage incomes with subsistence production. Even in 1980, when wages in Mexico were relatively high, I estimated that one family, which included both return migrants and nonmigrant wage workers and which did not cultivate their slightly larger than average holdings very intensively, relied on their own subsistence cultivation for about 20 percent of their consumption. By the mid-1980s, when wages had fallen and prices risen, this family, like others in San Cosme, had intensified their subsistence production. They went more frequently to their fields to weed in order to improve yields, to provide weeds for fodder and fuel, or to gather small amounts of ripe corn or sugarcane, even if the whole field was not ready for harvesting. Heavier reliance on subsistence production during the economic crisis of the 1980s suggests that whether they use their land, use it not very intensively, or do not use it every year, even a small parcel of land gives San Cosme's wage workers some degree of autonomy and makes them slightly less vulnerable to the fluctuations and crises of the capitalist labor and commodity markets.

Reliance on subsistence production, such as I am describing, is sometimes viewed, for example, by Meillassoux (1972), as a way for capitalists to pay urban workers less. Others have suggested, however, that not only does subsistence production subsidize capitalism, but capitalism also subsidizes the peasant economy. Many contemporary "peasant" farms, as noted by Figueroa (1984) and Arizpe (1982) among others, could not survive without the income derived from capitalist wage labor. Even if they invest in only a few hectares of not very productive subsistence land, return migrants help to maintain the peasant economy or, more accurately, a modified version of it.[7] This peasant economy, in turn, supports segments of the population that are disadvantaged in, discarded by, or perhaps resistant to, the capitalist labor market, including the unemployed, the underemployed, the old, and women, particularly those with children. The continued existence of even a modified form of peasant production also provides wage workers with an alternative model of society to that provided by capitalism.

A second direct economic effect of return migration is that migrants bring with them money and goods. Even when migrants do not actually return, if they expect to do so they are more likely to send remittances and the remittances will be larger (Rempel and Lobdell 1978). The supposedly negative side of this is that the money is spent on such consumer items as housing, sewing machines, televisions, radios, stereos, and bicycles. Pessimists point out only that these expenditures fail to generate wealth or jobs. What they fail to consider, however, is that although the purchases do not generate large numbers of full-time formal sector jobs, they often generate some local wage labor and self-employment possibilities. Combined with small-scale subsistence production, these activities enable some rural dwellers to avoid migration and complete reliance on wage labor.

In San Cosme, peasants have supplemented subsistence production with wage labor or commerce for as long as they can remember. Until

recently, the main supplementary activity was agricultural labor, usually in the fields of factory workers in neighboring villages (Nutini and
Isaac 1974; Rothstein 1982) and later in San Cosme. In the 1940s, as
industrialization began to develop, first because of World War II and
then increasingly because of Mexico's import-substitution industrialization policies, some men from San Cosme were able to obtain jobs in
textile factories in Mexico City, which is about three hours by bus from
the community. As the value of their agricultural production declined
and as the prices of the items that they bought went up, San Cosmeros
sold their labor more. Most peasants families in San Cosme now send
their sons, and, to a lesser extent, their daughters, out of the community
to work, but many rely also on locally available wage labor or commercial activities.

One peasant family, for example, supports itself through small-scale
cultivation, sheepherding, raising a few pigs, and the sale of labor by
the father locally as a mason. Another peasant family relies on the
increased opportunities, provided in part by return migrants, for the
husband to work as a musician. Because return migrants and other
full-time wage workers spend more cash on weddings, birthday parties,
and such community celebrations as Carnival and the Saint's Day,
musicians and artisans (e.g., women who embroider capes for Carnival)
can earn cash locally. The availability of more cash in the community
has also led to more grocery stores, more butchers, a stationery store,
a *tortilleria* (a tortilla store), a store that sells fabric, another that sells
shoes, an ice cream stand, and several establishments. Some people
have invested their wages or cash from other sources in trucks, tractors,
and taxis, for which there is now an increased demand. These are all
small and limited enterprises, but they do provide some opportunities
in the rural area, and they bring it a greater variety of goods and
services. As Alderson-Smith (1984: 224) noted for rural Peru, "Migration has, in recent years, become a means of broadening the economic
base of the village enterprise." In the past, Peruvian peasants wove
together a series of economic activities in different climatic zones. Now,
in Alderson-Smith's words, "A modern version of vertical ecology takes
place in which interdependence between climatic zones is replaced by
ties between a range of economic 'zones' " (1984: 225). Peasants in San
Cosme similarly weave together a variety of agricultural and nonagricultural activities. Although these activities are pursued more by
families without full-time wage laborers, they are dependent on full-
time wage laborers for their market.

Many of the new enterprises correspond to the kinds of activities
that are described for the informal sector. They are small-scale, they
employ few people and rely heavily on unpaid family labor, and they
are not regulated by the state. Most of the literature on the informal

sector has focused on urban areas (e.g., Portes, Castells, and Benton 1989). Perhaps one of the important consequences of return migration is the growth of the informal sector in rural areas. Whether one sees this as a process of diffusion in which return migrants bring the urban informal sector to the countryside and/or as a consequence of dependent capitalism and the inability of the formal sector to absorb labor, the countryside *is* changing and is increasingly characterized by the same class relations as the city. Return migration is an important factor in the changes and may be the means through which workers with common class interests transcend the rural–urban divide.

RETURN MIGRANTS AND NEW SKILLS

Another point raised by those who stress the failures of return migrants and return migration is that return migrants rarely come back with new skills. Ironically, however, the most common effect noted for return migration and/or remittances is increased education. Almost every study of how migrants' wages are used in rural communities mentions schooling, usually for siblings or offspring but occasionally also for migrants themselves. Migrants have affected rural educational levels also not only by channeling their cash to education; their experiences outside the rural community often provide the motivation for more education. In San Cosme, it was not only through wages and motivation but also through ties outside the community that educational improvements were made. Men, and occasionally women, who worked in Puebla or Mexico City used their contacts with union officials and other political leaders to get state and federal support to build schools and provide teachers and supplies. Through their cash and contracts, educational facilities in San Cosme have increased from one fourth grade school in the early 1960s to two six-year primary schools, a kindergarten which has recently been enlarged, and a tele-secondary school (a secondary school in which some subjects are taught by television) that has twice been expanded. In addition, migrants' contacts also provide the children of San Cosme with housing and/or jobs so that they can study elsewhere.

Social scientists often point out that increased education has not had significant implications for rural development because there are not enough good jobs for the newly educated sector. Although more education does not guarantee getting ahead, and few individuals do experience mobility, education has become necessary in most Third World countries to keep from falling back. Even the unskilled and semiskilled jobs in textile factories on temporary contracts which men from San Cosme have been filling for 40 years with only a few years of education now require completion of primary school. Higher paying, but also assembly-line, jobs in transnational firms require a secondary school diploma.

Increased education has also meant some limited occupational mobility. Most sons and daughters of San Cosme are *obreros* (workers) and homemakers like their fathers and mothers (Rothstein 1982). However, a few have become teachers, lawyers, nurses, doctors, technicians, and accountants. Another, more general effect of increased education is a very sharp decline in illiteracy. From about one-half of the adult population being illiterate in 1960, the proportion had dropped to less than one-third (29 percent) in 1980. Among those between the ages of fifteen and nineteen, illiteracy has almost disappeared (the literacy rate is 95 percent).

In addition to schools, return migrants in San Cosme and elsewhere have used their cash and political contacts to improve other aspects of the local infrastructure. Migrants' wages and contacts are used to improve roads and to get potable water, electricity, and health centers. In San Cosme the efforts to become a free municipality and to get bus service and a paved road, as well as other community services, were all spearheaded by return migrants.

POLITICS AND RETURN MIGRATION

It is probably with regard to their impact on politics that return migration and return migrants are said to have their least impact. Two reasons are usually suggested for this limited impact; one has to do with migration, and the other with return.

The first argument is that because migration offers an economic alternative to politics, it encourages political acquiescence. For example, after recognizing the significant impact of remittance income and development brought by migration to Union, a rural community in Mexico, Grindle suggested that "the possibility of migration helps explain why the residents of Union do not organize economically or politically to find solutions to their economic problems" (1988: 116–117). Unfortunately, Grindle seems to have assumed that the factionalism and *caciquismo* (form of politics in which a regional leader or leaders dominate), which, she noted, existed in Union, had no short- or long-term effect on their economic problems, despite the fact that Craig and Cornelius (1984) suggested that particularistic politics do sometimes result in material rewards for rural Mexicans. Elsewhere, Grindle (1989: 209) also suggested that an effective state apparatus controls political organization and limits the participation of the rural poor, but that various forms of rural protest were evident in the 1980s. Grindle rightly suggested that we should not look only at the dramatic ways, such as collective protest, in which people deal with their economic problems, to the neglect of such household-based strategies as migration. However, her assertion that "economic responses to crisis occur within the peasant household, *not in the public arena*" (1989: 191, emphasis added) is refuted by her own evidence of rural political activity.

The other argument about lack of migrants' political activity focuses not on migration as an alternative but on return as an alternative. In this argument it is suggested that return migrants (in this context, frequently called semiproletarians or peasant-workers), because they expect to return to their rural homes and maintain rural ties and concerns, do not develop "true" workers' consciousness and do not protest against capitalism. As I have argued elsewhere (1986), despite the numerous assertions about the lack of true workers' consciousness, few studies have actually examined the consciousness of Third World workers in general or of return migrants in particular. Furthermore, critics of these workers, such as Laite (1981), have ignored the numerous instances in which workers who actively oppose the status quo are co-opted, arrested, killed, or "disappeared."

Regardless of what their consciousness may or may not be, the political behavior of return migrants suggests that they are often politically active. Urban migrants who plan on returning home are often heavily involved in rural politics, and many of those who are most active in rural areas are return migrants. Migrants from San Cosme often returned home to hold office; to vote, especially in controversial elections; or to engage in other political activity. Numerous studies, especially of regional associations, show that rural–urban migrants frequently work politically in the city on behalf of their home communities. Altamirano (1984) found that regional associations of highlighted migrants in Peru organized opposition to *hacendados* and agitated for land reform. Mangin (1965) cited an example, from Lima, of a meeting of a regional association during which most of the items on the agenda concerned hometown affairs. In Mexico, Orellana (1973) found that in addition to lobbying for such community projects as schools, migrants from Oaxaca worked to get a settlement from a foreign mining company. Isbell (1978) gave numerous examples of migrants in Lima and villagers in Chuschi cooperating politically to expel the priest, get independent *communidad* status, and to invade some neighboring *hacienda* land. In these and other similar cases, in addition to working in the city lobbying government officials and politicians, migrants return home to hold local political office and/or to participate in confrontational political activities, such as land invasions.

Another important characteristic of the politics of return migrants is that they are both reformist and radical. At times return migrants in San Cosme and elsewhere work through the existing system, and at times they oppose it. Many of the community improvements described above for San Cosme and elsewhere were achieved through patron–client relations (which are often dismissed by observers as sim-

ply maintaining the status quo). However, patron–client relations depend on "payoffs." The people of San Cosme and many other rural
communities have not only received numerous payoffs, they have come
to expect them. Furthermore, there are indications that when patron–
client relations and the existing political structure do not "pay off,"
return migrants look for alternatives. In San Cosme, when their efforts,
through patron–client relations and the Institutional Revolutionary
Party (PRI) to get a higher price for some land they were selling to
several new factories failed, San Cosmeros turned to the P.S.U.M. (the
socialist party). Recently, they elected a municipal president from the
Cardenista Front. In other cases also—for example, the Nahuatl villages studied by Schryer (1987) in Puebla—return migrants participated in more radical political activity. Isbell also cited a situation in
which residents of Chuschi, including migrants and nonmigrants, decided to invade a *hacienda*'s land to resolve a dispute that had been
going on for 20 years.

CONCLUSION

In conclusion, I suggest that return migration is quantitatively and
qualitatively more significant than most Latin Americanists have assumed. I suggest also that migration is not only an individual or even
household-based strategy. There are important community-level associations and involvements. These are apparent in the community-
based organizations that migrants form in the host cities, in the community development efforts of migrants and return migrants on behalf
of their home communities, and in the community control that is often
exerted in particular factories and other employment sites. Return
migration also encourages or allows certain kinds of communities and
certain ties from the past, such as those of family and community. The
consequences of return migration described here—the maintenance of
subsistence cultivation, increased nonagricultural informal-sector activity, improved education and other public services, and greater political activity on behalf of rural communities and interests—are more
than individual and household solutions, and may have important implications beyond simple survival.

In order to appreciate the significance of return migration, however,
it is necessary to revise our views of both "the rural world" and "the
Third World." Whether they rely on modernization theory or the dependency perspective, most social scientists have tended to treat rural
communities as isolated, bounded, and inherently static units. Change
is seen as coming from, or as prevented from coming from, the modern,
urban, capitalist world. Furthermore, change, if it occurs at all, is seen
as following a single path from traditional to modern or from precap-

italist to capitalist. Even the dependency approach, which acknowl-
edges two recent paths, precapitalist to developed capitalist and
precapitalist to underdeveloped capitalist, usually sees the second path
as a deformed route in which "normal" capitalist development has been
stymied. What both these approaches fail to value sufficiently is the
fact that return migrants, other rural dwellers, and urban dwellers
are all part of a capitalist system in which the parts are integrated,
in terms of cooperation and conflict, by class. As Leeds (1979) argued,
the view, common in much of the social science literature on migration,
of contemporary society which opposes the urban and the rural, is
ethno- and tempocentric because it is based on the particular urban
experience of medieval Europe and capitalist urbanism. Leeds went
on to suggest that capitalist urban structure and process (which are
only one form of urban structure or society), unlike medieval feudal
society, which was characterized by fixity and immutability, requires
labor mobility.

As the properties of the [capitalist] system become increasingly defined and
increasingly dominant, a labor supply is needed which is increasingly detachable from geographical contexts. It must be removable from localities of origin
to points of concentration of capital. It must also be detachable from social
contexts of origin, specifically from community and family, and, later, also
from associations (e.g. unions). (Leeds 1979: 236)

This detachment from family, community, and associations functions
to separate workers from "any sort of social group that might act in a
corporate way against the interests of capitalist encroachment" (Leeds
1979: 235).

Viewed in terms of Leeds's model, return migration has the important function of maintaining ties with social groups, such as the community and family, which might act corporately against capitalism
(1979: 236). His model, as well as the evidence of return migrants'
political activity, suggests that we need to consider the implications
of return migration and return migrants' politics more carefully than
we have done thus far. We need to look, for example, at the effects of
stronger family and community ties on resistance and at the variety
of ways that local action can affect the larger structure. As I suggested
above, both dependency and modernization theories tend to view return
migrants as passive victims of either capitalism or tradition. I do not
deny the influence of capitalism or that capitalists constantly struggle
to increase their profits. However, consciously or not, workers (full-
time, part-time, migrant, and nonmigrant) also struggle. Often, their
struggles, like those of many of us, are channeled into ways that do
not alter the basic structure. Most writers suggest that migration and

return migration are examples of such strategies which simply help
individuals and/or families survive but do not affect the larger structure (except perhaps to benefit it) or offer any real solution. I suggest,
however, that because we have assumed that return migration in Latin
America is inconsequential, both qualitatively and quantitatively, we
have not really examined its extent or impact. Contemporary industrialization is characterized by an unprecedented movement of capital
and labor. Most studies have stressed the extent of mobility and the
ways in which the mobility both of labor and of capital contribute to
capital accumulation at the core. Return migration suggests that in
the contemporary world, movement of labor not only is more frequent
than before but is also taking new forms which combine the present
and the past. Perhaps this combination of the present and the past will
lead also to new relations among and between classes.

NOTES

A total of two years was spent in San Cosme between 1971 and 1989. I am
grateful to Towson State University and the Wenner-Gren Foundation for
Anthropological Research for supporting various phases of the research.

1. The literature on Africa indicates a great deal of return migration. Much
of it, however, sees return migration as preventing change. For useful reviews
of the literature on return migration, see Nelson (1976), Wiest (1979), and
Gmelch (1980).

2. Ultimately, return migration (like migration, as Leeds [1987] noted in
his concept of "degree of migrancy") should be seen on a continuum. At one
end would be long-term migrants who move from an area and hope to return.
At the other end would be migrants who leave for brief periods, usually to do
seasonal agricultural labor. Here, because of the nature of the available literature, I have focused on males who have returned to their home communities.
It is not always clear where migrants are returning from or what kind of wage
work they were engaged in, but to the extent possible, especially in the discussion of effects, my concern is with return migrants who have participated
in industrial wage labor or other urban activities rather than agricultural
labor. In addition, although the literature on international migration has relevance for the subject of this chapter, because that literature raises additional
issues of state policy, this analysis focuses on internal migration.

3. Author's census, 1984.

4. Author's censuses, 1971, 1980, and 1984.

5. See, for example, Dinerman (1978) and Rubinstein (1983).

6. Nelson (1976: 736) suggested that one of the reasons why return migration
is less common in Latin America than Africa or Asia is that access to land is
rarer in Latin America. However, access to land should not be treated as static.

7. For a discussion of some of the ways in which small-scale cultivation
today differs from "traditional" peasant production, see Rothstein (1986).

3

Capitalist Production in a Socialist Society: The Transfer of Manufacturing from Hong Kong to China

Alan Smart and Josephine Smart

Like Rothstein, Alan and Josephine Smart show the importance of social ties. Here, however, the ties are between Chinese emigrants who migrated to Hong Kong and nonmigrants, and they are used not by workers but by entrepreneurs who invest in China. (For an analysis of the effect of such investment on the receiving area, see Chapter 8 in this volume.)

In this chapter we will examine a distinctive form of the international division of labor: the transfer of the majority of its manufacturing production from a capitalist society, Hong Kong, into offshore production in a socialist society, the People's Republic of China. Although Hong Kong is not the only capitalist society transferring production into China, it accounts for 65 percent or more of the total foreign direct investment. Furthermore, while the proportion of the total industrial production of Japan or the United States that is carried out in China is minuscule, Hong Kong employs more manufacturing workers in China than within Hong Kong.

We will first discuss some of the literature on capitalist investment in socialist societies and distinguish the Hong Kong situation from these other cases. Second, we will outline the character and reasons for the development of Hong Kong's investment in China. Third, we will examine the social processes involved in facilitating this type of investment by examining in detail one particular case of investment.

Although use is made in this chapter of statistical information collected by the two governments, press reports, and the secondary literature, most of the analysis is based on ethnographic information. Our research on Hong Kong investment in China has its roots in previous, apparently unrelated, fieldwork in Hong Kong on squatter areas (A. Smart 1986, 1989) and street hawkers (J. Smart 1989). Our research serendipitously uncovered cases of small-scale entrepreneurs establishing factories in China, generally in their native place (i.e., the place in China where their patrilineal ancestors lived, whether or not they or their father actually lived there). This phenomenon interested and surprised us, because the literature on foreign investment in China tended to concentrate on the experiences of large multinationals. This literature also tended to claim that investing in China involved years of difficult negotiations and that the investor had to be in for the long term and even be willing to lose money at first in order to establish good working relations. The ability of very small-scale entrepreneurs (sometimes with investments of less than US$1,500)[1] to establish themselves in China conflicted with these views and raised the question of how they accomplished this. Our initial research suggested that there was a second pattern of investment in China, one that was approved at the local level rather than by central authorities, socially mediated rather than bureaucratic, and rapid and flexible rather than slow and long-term.

CAPITALIST INVESTMENT IN SOCIALIST ECONOMIES

In the last decade, China has attracted US$30 billion in foreign investment, including both direct investment and loans (South China Morning Post 6 July 1989: B3; henceforth *SCMP*). China had 2,187 joint ventures and 46 wholly owned foreign enterprises in 1987 (People's Republic of China, State Statistical Bureau 1988: 733) and at least 19,000 "foreign-backed firms," mostly export processing arrangements in 1989 (*SCMP* 8 November 89: B3). By contrast, attempts to encourage joint ventures in Eastern Europe have reaped 300 in Hungary, less than 400 in Yugoslavia, and approximately 100 in Poland (Beedham 1989: 57).

Capitalist investment also took place in Eastern Europe in the 1970s on a wide scale, but it occurred primarily in the form of foreign loans, and that is a very different type of economic interrelationship. International lending is less likely to produce the kind of transformations produced by direct investment, since the central authorities retain control over the incoming funds. It has been suggested that this kind of lending has actually delayed economic reforms by supporting inefficient industrial and economic structures (Brada, Hewett, and Wolf 1988).

In China, state monopoly over capitalist investment has not been retained, and the multiple channels for trade and investment approved by local rather than central authorities have produced a situation in which the breadth and strength of the integration between Hong Kong and parts of China are dramatically greater than any other comparable arrangement. This kind of impact does not occur without resistance. While these restructuring tendencies are evident, China claims to be undertaking "socialist modernization" in order to strengthen the nation and ultimately bolster its effort to forge a true socialism (Dirlik 1989: 36).

Petras (1988), on the other hand, has explained the resistance as deriving from a tradition of "workerist solidarity" shared by state enterprises and urban workers which the Chinese state is attempting to undermine. The strength of this resistance has frustrated attempts to reform the state sector and led the reformers to adopt a strategy based on the countryside and the new special economic zones in order to shrink the size of the state sector (Petras 1988: 9).

Whether this is "postsocialism" (Dirlik 1989), "capitalist restoration" (Chossudovsky 1986), or simply "socialist modernization," it is clear that the interaction between China and capitalist forces, spearheaded by the "expatriate bourgeoisie" of Hong Kong, is resulting in a dramatic transformation of the relations of production in China (Scobell 1988), and that it is urgent that this interaction be more clearly understood than it is at present.

HONG KONG AND CAPITALIST DEVELOPMENT IN CHINA

We argue that direct foreign investment in China, primarily from Hong Kong, has brought China into the international division of labor in a way unprecedented for the socialist nations, as it serves as an offshore production base for consumer manufactures in a way more commonly found among capitalist less-developed countries such as the Philippines or Mexico. The role of Hong Kong in integrating China within the new international division of labor is central. Since the People's Republic of China's adoption of the Open Door Policy in 1978, and the signing in 1984 of the Sino-British Joint Declaration on Hong Kong's future, the intergration of the economies of Hong Kong and China has occurred at a remarkable rate (Scobell 1988: 599). Although the political crisis of 1989 has temporarily slowed this integration, already it is estimated that some Hong Kong industries carry out 80 to 90 percent of their production in China (*SCMP* 8 June 1989: 3).

Estimates of the number of workers employed in Hong Kong–invested firms in China range from 1.5 million to 4 million, with around

2 million being the most common estimate (Hong Kong: Trade Development Council 1988; *SCMP* 18 June 1989: M13), which is substantially more than the 900,000 employed in Hong Kong manufacturing. China is Hong Kong's largest supplier of imports, accounting for 31 percent of the total compared to 19 percent and 8 percent for Japan and the United States (Hong Kong, Census and Statistics Department 1989: 9). It is also the largest market for Hong Kong's reexports (34 percent of the total), which is important since 55.8 percent of Hong Kong's total exports are reexports. China is also the main country of origin for Hong Kong's reexports—48 percent of the total (Hong Kong, Census and Statistics Department 1989: 11).

The volume of reexports represents the emergence of widespread industrial cooperation across the border, where raw materials are imported to Hong Kong, reexported to joint ventures and export-processing firms in China, and then brought back to Hong Kong for finishing or packaging before finally being exported. This is illustrated by the fact that 39 percent of Hong Kong's reexports were raw materials and semimanufactures (Hong Kong, Census and Statistics Department 1989: 10). According to a survey of 2,000 Hong Kong companies, at least 55 percent of Hong Kong reexports of Chinese products were actually goods produced by Hong Kong companies in China (specifically Guangdong) under processing/assembly arrangement (Hong Kong, Trade Development Council 1988: 11). It is also worth noting that Hong Kong's customs statistics do not include an enterprise's products that were shipped directly from supply sources to overseas customers, estimated to total US$17.95 billion in 1988 (Hong Kong, Trade Development Council 1988: 11).

Despite difficulties in the quantification of total foreign investment in China, one undisputed observation that arises is the dominance of Hong Kong and Macao investment in China. Observers suggest that 60 percent (US$4.5 billion) of the total US$7.45 billion direct foreign investment in China by the end of 1983 came from Hong Kong and Macao sources (Hua 1986: 67; Tong 1984: 17). Between 1980 and 1984, of US$1.4 billion invested in 931 equity joint ventures, Hong Kong alone contributed US$800 million in 700 such ventures (Jacobs 1986: 116). Hong Kong's Trade Development Council estimated that Hong Kong investment accounted for about 79 percent of the foreign projects in China, although only 65 percent by value (*SCMP* 10 March 1988: B4).

The dominance of Hong Kong foreign investment in southern China is particularly impressive. In 1985, investment from Hong Kong and Macao in Guangzhou (capital of the Province of Guangdong) totaled US$409.4 million or nearly 88 percent of the total foreign investment in that city (Almanac Editorial Board 1986: 236). In mid-1988, Hong Kong had an estimated total direct investment of between US$4.7 and

US$5.1 billion in Guangdong Province, involving 13,000 to 15,000 enterprises (Hong Kong, Trade Development Council 1988: 5). In the Shenzhen Special Economic Zone, it is usually estimated that 80 to 90 percent of foreign investment originates from Hong Kong (Jacobs 1986: 116). Hong Kong provides about two-thirds of the direct foreign investment in Fujian Province, one-quarter of it in manufacturing (Wong 1987: 81).

In particular, Hong Kong and Macao investment more or less monopolizes the small-scale export processing agreements in southern China. During the initial period after the Open Door Policy almost all the foreign investment in Guangdong was in the form of processing agreements. The portfolio of foreign investment has diversified since then, but export processing is still a significant source of foreign investment in southern China. One source estimates that in Guangdong Province there were over 60,000 export processing and assembly agreements and only 2,000 manufacturing joint ventures or wholly owned ventures in 1986. The export processing agreements accounted for 42 percent of total direct foreign investment (Economic Research Department 1987: 3; Sit 1985: 237). The Hong Kong Trade Development Council's estimates are more modest, suggesting that 11,000 to 12,000 enterprises are involved in export processing (note that "enterprises involved" and "contracts" may differ, since one enterprise might be involved in more than one contract), with a total investment of US$1.8 to 1.9 billion, employing 850,000 to 1.2 million Chinese workers and having paid US$2 billion in processing fees from 1979 to 1987 (Hong Kong, Trade Development Council 1988: 5). In some regions of the province, export processing remains the fastest growing form of foreign investment. For instance, export processing investment in Dongguan County in the Pearl River Delta of Guangdong Province grew from US$2.35 million in 1979 to US$62.69 million in 1986 (Kung and Chan 1987: 17–19).

To understand the Hong Kong style of investment, some background information on how it is conducted is necessary. In the early years of the Open Door Policy, all decisions concerning foreign investment were made by central authorities or by state-owned organizations. Eventually, some decision making was decentralized to give local authorities and enterprises the power to conduct business directly with foreign corporations (Hua 1986: 61). However, this local autonomy applies only to small or medium enterprises which do not involve key sectors of the economy, such as transportation, energy, steel, and so forth. In Guangshou, for example, foreign investments that involve more than US$10 million must still be approved by central authorities (Wang 1988: 173). The decentralization of authority to negotiate agreements with foreign investors to individual firms or local authorities, together with the availability of the export processing form of foreign investment, provides the structural basis that makes possible the rapid expansion of small-scale investments that attract many Hong Kong investors. In 1980, the average investment per processing agreement was only US$11,538, increasing to US$25,641 in 1981 (Sit 1985: 237). These Hong Kong investments, though small-scale in each instance, are quite significant in the aggregate.

Why do Hong Kong investors dominate small-scale investment in China? Although there are many small investors involved in investment in China, there are also many economically powerful investors who are very capable of engaging in large-scale ventures but prefer not to do so. The rationale has little to do with financial power but everything to do with strategic thinking. At the heart of the concerns about investing in China are worries about dealing with the Chinese bureaucracy.

Given the problems arising from the incompatibilities of the two diverse and different economic systems of socialism and capitalism, there is a risk that a single large joint venture may get bogged down in negotiations with central authorities or aborted. The Hong Kong investors circumvent such risks by setting up a number of independent units, each responsible for their own activities, so that any delays in one will not affect the whole investment. Small-scale investment is a strategy to reduce or minimize the economic risk associated with the problems of doing capitalist production within a socialist economy. The decentralization of decision making fits very will with this strategy, and, indeed, largely makes it possible. Under a centralized system, a dozen small investments would have to go through the same procedure and be scrutinized by the same officials. With decentralization, however, a different authority (or enterprise or collective) is involved in each agreement, so a bureaucratic hitch is unlikely to affect all other negotiations or agreements.

However, the heavy participation of Hong Kong investors in this form of investment venture must be placed in the context of the macroeconomic situations of Hong Kong and the global market economy. Hong Kong's export manufacturing industries rely on an abundant supply of legal and illegal Chinese immigrants who are willing to work hard and long for a fraction of the wage that unionized Western workers would get for the same work (see Chen 1982; England and Rear 1975; Hopkins 1971; Sit, Wong, and Kiang 1979). As the supply of immigrant workers stabilized and the economy of Hong Kong diversified to offer many other economic opportunities, the manufacturing sector has found itself increasingly squeezed between the twin pressures of labor shortages and demands for higher wages. These problems are aggravated by the growing competition from other newly developed countries in the Pacific Rim such as South Korea, Thailand, Taiwan, and the Philippines which seek a share of the world market for their products.

One way in which Hong Kong responds is by capitalizing on the relatively cheap cost of labor offered by China in an attempt to retain its export competitiveness (Baran 1985: 12, Chai 1983; Gressel 1987: 2; Wong 1987: 80; Economist Intelligence Unit 1987).

Taking into consideration wages and other overhead costs, the production cost in Shenzhen can be 50 percent lower than in Hong Kong, and even lower in other parts of the Pearl River Delta. Often, only part of the production, the most labor-intensive processes, are shifted to China, while the processes requiring more skilled labor or sophisticated technology will be carried out in Hong Kong. The attraction of the small-scale export processing ventures in China is thus closely related to the forces of capitalist competition in the world market and Hong Kong's dependence on its export manufacturing economy (Hong Kong 1987: 45).

The economic reforms and the geographical concentration of foreign investment have caused a great deal of social change and disruption. Limitations of space preclude an adequate discussion here, and we will restrict ourselves to one important issue: labor migration and the emergence of labor markets in China (Kim 1988). In addition to officially sanctioned migration to areas of labor shortage (Andors 1988: 26), there has also developed in China a "floating population," which is estimated to be as large as 50 million people. These job searchers are usually peasants with insufficient land to work or construction workers rendered unemployed by the austerity measures. This development has been encouraged by the 1984 policy allowing villagers to move to urban areas if they provide their own grain provisions (Xu and Zhang 1989: 36). These migrants have caused problems in all major cities, but Guangdong seems to be receiving a large share of it, fueled by rumors of high-paying jobs with foreign firms. Guangdong is estimated to have a floating population of at least 3 million, despite efforts to send back an influx of 2 million in the spring of 1989 alone (SCMP, 26 June 1989: B11). These temporary residents, even if they locate work, have no rights to rationed goods or to medical or educational services. They are often housed in makeshift shanties or even sleep in railway stations or on the street. Almost all the workers in the factory discussed in the case study below belong in this category of temporary migrant labor.

GIFT EXCHANGE AND FOREIGN INVESTMENT: A CASE STUDY

The following analysis and case study is intended as a contribution to an understanding of the actual relations of production and social conditions engendered by the extension of capitalist forms of production into Guangdong Province.

Hong Kong entrepreneurs commonly invest in parts of China where they have preexisting social connections and pay a great deal of attention to cultivating good *guanxi* (a Chinese concept of central importance meaning "relationships" or "social connections"). The importance of this strategy can be better appreciated by realizing that although economies are dominated by a particular mode of production, they are never homogenous entities but rather contain distinct forms of production or exchange with different characteristics. Our research on Hong Kong investment strategies indicated that a conscious utilization of the gift economy (Yang 1989: 37) supports the economic and social interests of overseas Chinese investors and their local counterparts by modifying the operation of state power in China (Smart and Smart 1989). In so doing, the gift economy bridges some of the extreme incompatibilities between these diverse economic systems, thereby making possible a more effective integration between the capitalist interests involved in foreign investment and the socialist redistributive principles. The gift mode of exchange, which is neither socialist nor capitalist, is part of social and economic interaction in both Hong Kong and China and acts as a buffer to overcome the difficulties resulting from the differences and incompatibilities between the socialist and capitalist modes of production.

In 1986, three Hong Kong entrepreneurs came together and worked out an investment plan in China. With capital of just under US$40,000 and based on equal shares among the investors, they planned to set up a small-scale shoe manufacturing plant in Henggang, which is 17 kilometers north of Hong Kong and just outside the Shenzhen Special Economic Zone. There is a single road connecting Henggang with Shenzhen. It is the only road to all destinations in the north, east, or west of Guangdong Province from Hong Kong or Shenzhen. With the onset of rapid industrialization and urbanization in recent years, this road is grossly overused and major traffic congestions have become a regular and frequent occurrence. Without traffic problems, it takes about 2 hours to travel to Henggang from Hong Kong. It takes about 45 minutes to reach the border by train, which starts in Hunghom in Kowloon; then 30 minutes or less to go through customs; and then 30 to 45 minutes by bus or taxi to Henggang. On a bad day, however, it can take 6 to 8 hours to travel the 17 kilometers between the border and Henggang. Work has been underway for over two years now to construct and widen the road to accommodate the growing demand of vehicular traffic, but as yet, the construction has had the opposite effect of aggravating the traffic problem. Henggang itself is now at the mercy of heavy dust during dry days and muddy road conditions during rainy days.

For a variety of reasons, then, Henggang seemed a poor choice for Hong Kong investors. It was a small agricultural township of under 10,000 people of Hakka ethnic background. It offered little of the facilities or infrastructure necessary to accommodate the demand of industrial production and the housing needs of workers. The handful of Hong Kong invested industries in the area at that time were frequently affected by power failures. Goods and material had to be transported by vehicles, and possible delays due to traffic congestion were a concern. Henggang is not near a rail line or any waterway, so there still is no other means of transport for goods and materials between Hong Kong and Henggang.

In this particular case, the three entrepreneurs were attracted to Henggang for one specific reason. One of the entrepreneurs was the nephew of a local official who headed an institution that occupied a large piece of underused land. Negotiation between uncle and nephew resulted in an attractive package for the entrepreneurs: The institution would rent them the factory space in one of its existing buildings at a rate that was at least 50 percent lower than that charged in Shenzhen; the institution would pay for all the utilities, which was a significant saving for the entrepreneurs; and a new factory with dormitory, kitchen, and washroom facilities would be built at the institution's expense. Thus, the feasibility of the initial investment plan was based to a large extent on the kinship relationship between one of the investors and his or her counterpart in Henggang.

In the early period of the economic reform in China under the Open Door Policy, many Hong Kong investments followed this kinship factor, so it was common for investors to set up their factories in their home village or in places where they had strong kinship links with local officials or power brokers. As more Hong Kong enterprises are set up in various locations, it is now becoming more common for people to direct their investment according to the advice or observation of friends who have already invested in the same locale. Despite the changing focus from kinship- to non–kinship-based social relations, it remains true that preexisting social relations in the locale where an investment is intended remain a significant factor in the Hong Kong investors' decision about investment in China.

The establishment of the shoe factory was preceded by rounds of dinner parties during the many discussion sessions on terms and conditions between the institution officials and Hong Kong investors. The Hong Kong investors in this case were more fortunate than most others because they had relatively few local counterparts with whom to deal in China. Once their rental contract with the institution/local landlord had been signed, the institution officials carried on from there to deal with the local government officials and provincial officials in Shenzhen to complete the investment registration and approval. Bureaucratic red tape was thereby kept to a minimum.

As was true for the three Hong Kong investors, there are many obvious advantages to having preexisting social relations in the place where investment is intended. The social links can provide an investor with entree to the right power brokers who may expedite the negotiation and secure better terms and conditions, and they allow an investor to enter into a gift exchange with his counterparts in China. The cultivation and maintenance of strategic social relations can be instrumental in smoothing out all kinds of problems, particularly in terms of personnel management and bureaucratic red tape (see Smart and Smart 1989).

The participation in the local gift economy in China by Hong Kong investors is sometimes misunderstood by others as a form of corruption or bribery. From our perspective, the gift economy facilitates

the personal exchange and articulation of gifts, favors, [and] banquets. . . . The art in *guanxi* exchange lies in the skillful mobilization of moral and cultural imperatives such as obligation and reciprocity in pursuit of both diffuse social ends and calculated instrumental ends. (Yang 1989: 35)

Furthermore, the gift economy or the art of *guanxi* is based on the "ethics of obligation, reciprocity, and mutual aid, and the responsibilities of friendship and kinship" (Yang 1989: 36). The term *guanxi* means relationships or social connections built on "preexisting relationships of classmates, people from the same native-place, relatives, superior and subordinate in the same workplace, and so forth" (Yang 1989: 41).

Most Hong Kong investors have *guanxi* in locations in China where they intend to invest, and this gives them an advantage over those who do not. In interviews with Japanese managers in Shenzhen, Andors (1988: 35) found that they "resented the Hong Kong Chinese because their *guanxi* with local officials accorded them special privileges." However, it must be emphasized that *guanxi* is not a social given; its strength and depth are determined largely by the intensity of exchange relations between the parties involved, even for individuals who are bound by kinship.

The initial round of dinner exchanges (mostly paid for by the Hong Kong investors) during negotiation for the establishment of the shoe factory was later replaced with other forms of exchange relationships. The institution officials responsible for putting together the contract receive gifts of dried seafood, liquor, imported cigarettes, and other seasonal items from the investors at all major festivities such as Chinese New Year and Mid-Autumn Festival. When the head of the institution was on a work-related trip to Hong Kong last year, one of the investors was called on to accompany him to shop for a large-screen color television, a stereo system, and other major appliances. The investors graciously presented these as gifts. It was the first time any official from the institution had made a trip overseas, and the investors no doubt hope it will be a long time before another trip is made.

It is common for the institution officials to take their important visitors on an inspection tour of the shoe factory. Almost all visitors want one or two pairs of the nice leather shoes manufactured at the site which are well above the average quality and style of the shoes made for domestic consumption. Many pairs of shoes were taken away as "gifts" over the years, and the few that were paid for were charged at a greatly reduced price close to cost. The local security bureau personnel are also known to pay regular visits to the shoe factory because of the attraction of the shoes. At first, the investors gave away the shoes, but as the visits from the security bureau personnel increased, they decided to charge them. The investors know that they do not have to go out of their way to get on the good side of the security bureau because they are housed within the premises of the institution and the head of the institution will make sure that good security is maintained. To the Hong Kong investors, having good local *guanxi* in China means getting things done more quickly and effectively: It is good business strategy.

When the niece of a key official in the institution was appointed the manager of the factory, the investors agreed to pay her in Hong Kong dollars instead of Chinese renminbi, as she requested. As payment for her appointment, she pays the institution one-third of her wages. The manager is responsible for most of the paperwork and dealings with the local officials. She makes sure that the appropriate duties are paid and that all migrant workers have their temporary residence permits in order. Most important, she assists the investors in their constant struggle to avoid the official exchange rate which is nearly half the black market rate. In theory, the wages of all workers must be remitted in Hong Kong dollars through the Bank of China. The official exchange rate is HK$100 = Y47, but the black market rate before June 1988 was a staggering HK$100 = Y90. Even the lower rate of HK$100 = Y82 after June 1988 is still a lot more attractive than the official rate.

One of the ways in which investors can cut down on the loss through official exchange is to underreport the number of workers so that the total wage remitted through the bank can be reduced, and there are many other ways to go around the official exchange trap. In order to

do it effectively, however, a foreign investor must get the full cooperation of the local manager assigned to his or her factory because it
is the manager who keeps records of the number of workers in an
enterprise, the total amount imported and exported, and the total value
added to the production. It is, thus, of little surprise that local managers
are usually involved in gift exchange relationships with their employers from Hong Kong. Cash bonuses at major festivals are a common
gift. A less common but highly valued and desired gift is an all-expense-
paid trip to Hong Kong. Similarly, the manager in the shoe factory
received a much valued 20-inch Japanese color television last year. It
is extremely difficult and expensive to buy an imported Japanese television in China. The manager asked her employers to get her one from
Hong Kong and said she would pay for it (the cost is equivalent to 16
months of her current net income), but so far she has not made any
obvious attempt to do so and the Hong Kong investors are not pressing
the matter.

Any material gifts and favors bestowed on the appointed managers,
and, to a lesser extent, on the factory workers, are intended to bind
their loyalty to the Hong Kong employers and the foreign enterprise.
Many strategies are employed to keep good *guanxi* with workers. One
Hong Kong manager mentioned that he always tells the kitchen staff
to cook a snack for the workers whenever they work overtime. Another
investor spends as much time as possible talking to his workers and
listening to their problems. In the shoe factory, the "good and reliable"
workers can get an advance on their wages for their occasional visits
home. There is a color television in the office and all workers are
welcome to watch Hong Kong programs after dinner or during lunch
breaks. The investors are talking about getting a television installed
in each of the dormitories so that the workers can watch even on
Sundays when the office is closed. One female worker, a distant relative
of one of the investors who has been with the factory from the beginning, received a gold ring for her wedding two years ago. She was given
a month of maternity leave and was provided with separate accom-
modations when she returned with her child and husband. (All the
other workers stay in a dormitory with bunk beds.) When this worker's
teenage sister-in-law came to look after the child so that the mother
could work more efficiently, the sister-in-law was allowed to stay in
the workers' dormitory. The husband is now also working in the same
factory. The two investors who are most involved with the production
in China both have relatives from their home village working in their
factory. Many of them came when the factory started in 1987. This
stable body of permanent skilled workers is extremely valuable because
they can be depended on to work overtime whenever it is needed, to
work efficiently, and to help train new workers.

Participation in the gift economy is not without its problems. First, there is the question of who should be included in the exchange network. This is particularly problematic for investors who have to deal with many government officials from different departments and of different ranks outside the kin- and social-based network. Some believe it is important to establish good *guanxi* only with senior officials who have decision-making power, while others suggest that it is equally important to include low-ranking officials since they are part of the general Chinese bureaucracy.

Second, there is the widespread problem of incomplete or ineffective exchange. Exchange relationships are based on the principle of reciprocity (Polanyi 1944; Mauss 1954). When one receives, one is obliged to return. When two individuals involved in an exchange relation are bound by multiple social and economic ties, neither party is likely to interrupt the rhythm of giving and receiving because too much is at stake. However, the same cannot be said when the exchange relationship is not bound by trust and obligation mediated through kinship and other social forces. For many investors, their exchange partners in China will include a large number of officials and individuals who fall outside their preexisting social network in the country. Almost all Hong Kong investors have a story or two to tell about an incomplete exchange relationship. It is clear that investors with preexisting connections in the location of investment, particularly with key officials and personnel who are in a position to determine or influence the terms and management of the investment, are more likely to succeed than those who lack similar local connections.

Third, what begins as a personalized, reciprocal relation of gift exchange can become institutionalized and unilateral: a "squeeze" rather than a gift exchange. Although both are perceived from the outside as corruption, they are seen rather differently from the perspective of the investors who are being squeezed. This raises the whole issue of the morality of engagement in the gift economy and the question of where one draws the line between bribery or corruption and gift exchange. The boundary is historically variable and generally disputed. Much of what was traditionally considered acceptable, and even expected, gift exchange between officials and citizens became illegal after 1949. The problem is that liberalization and commercialization have once again shifted the boundaries between legal and illegal and gift and bribe but without making the position of the new boundary clear. In fact, the boundary shifts with the political breeze, and what is acceptable may depend on one's position and the perspective of the observer (Myers 1989: 206). As a result, participation in the gift economy in China can sometimes involve the exchange partners in illegal activities. The gift economy, argued Yang (1989: 37), "alters and weakens in a piecemeal fashion the structural principles and smooth operation of state power" in China. When a Hong Kong investor gives his or her local counterpart a Japanese television as a gift, he or she is intervening in the socialist egalitarian redistributive economy. When the counterpart returns with a favor of underreporting the number of workers in the factory in order to help reduce the monetary loss through wage remittance at the official exchange rate, this action can be interpreted as doing the country a disservice in undermining the country's interest in favor of the investor's interest and for personal gain. The gift economy clearly helps to support the economic and social interests of overseas Chinese investors and their local counterparts by modifying the operation of state power in China. As such, there is a danger that some of the gift exchange activities are illegal and that the parties involved may eventually face legal repercussions.

CONCLUSION

Although Hong Kong investments in China operate on a basically capitalist organization of production, they are influenced by their location within a society dominated by socialism. This situation produces a constant stream of challenges and problems, mitigated by the low cost of labor (itself in part a result of socialism) and the concern of the Chinese government to prevent worker unrest and independent unionism (Leung 1988). Many Hong Kong investors respond to this situation in a manner distinct from that of investors from other capitalist countries. Most Hong Kong investments are relatively small-scale enterprises set up in locations where the investors have preexisting social connections or *guanxi*. These enterprises are managed primarily by the Hong Kong investors and their Hong Kong–based management staff and skilled technicians. Unlike large-scale multinational investments which involve negotiations with central authorities and may take several years to finalize their terms and conditions, Hong Kong investors generally negotiate directly with local officials, and the negotiations are usually socially mediated through their local *guanxi*. It rarely takes more than a year to sign an investment contract. The apparent greater efficiency and success of Hong Kong entrepreneurs in investment ventures is due largely to their distinct approach to investment, although other overseas Chinese investors share this to a lesser extent. International investors can utilize the advantages possessed by the Hong Kong investors by using them as subcontractors, and this is, indeed, very common.

The social linkages and cultural commonalities of Hong Kong investors and their Chinese counterparts, combined with the decentralization of investment approval and economic liberalization, result in a pattern of capitalist investment that is based in the grass roots of society, and is difficult for the central government to control. It also has a great potential for inducing social changes in Guangdong, precisely because it is widespread and diffuse rather than concentrated, and because it is closely integrated into other types of social relations.

NOTES

Fieldwork was conducted in Hong Kong from May to August 1987 and June to August 1989, and in China during July 1987 and June and July 1989. Research for this chapter was supported by a University of Calgary Research Grant. We are grateful for the support of the Centre of Asian Studies, Hong Kong, and Zhongshan University, Guangzhou, and for the advice of many other scholars. We are particularly indebted to the generous assistance of Hong Kong investors and of government officials in both China and Hong Kong.

1. Currency has been converted to U.S. dollars at the rate of US$1 = HK$7.8.

4

Nonresident-Indian Investment and India's Drive for Industrial Modernization

Johanna Lessinger

*Capital following social networks that span the globe is also the
focus of this chapter. The movement of capital is often discussed as
if there were no people involved. Here Johanna Lessinger describes
how Indian state policy, immigration of more affluent sectors of the
population (highly educated middle class), and social and cultural
ties combine to encourage a new form of capitalist industrialization
based on investment by Indians living in the United States and
Western Europe.*

India, a country with a longer history of industrialization than most
Third World countries, is currently in the midst of a concerted drive
to strengthen its economy by reshaping it along advanced capitalist
lines. Part of that campaign involves state-directed efforts to modernize
the country's industrial sector. For the first time the Indian government is actively seeking foreign investment in a wide range of its
industries. This contrasts with earlier investment policies which effectively discouraged many foreign firms.

One segment of the new economic policy has sought to involve Indian
immigrants now living overseas. Since the early 1980s the Indian government has solicited this group to establish savings accounts in Indian
banks and to invest directly in Indian industry. It is this policy, and
the immigrant investors themselves, that form the subject of this chapter. Since the policy is still new and the Indian government is remarkably reticent about its success, many questions remain
unanswered. Some trends are already clear, however.

What makes India's strategy possible is a recent historical shift within global alignments of capital and labor, so that for the first time some immigrants are strategically located within the technical and financial elites of their more developed adopted countries. As some of these immigrants return "home" in the role of international investor, they further transform their class status. Ironically, this industrialization strategy is one that places unusual emphasis on nationalist sentiment and the rhetoric of a common culture at the very moment at which capitalist pressures toward internationalization are at a new high in India. This suggests that we need to broaden our understanding of the relationship between industrial development and contemporary migration.

From the standpoint of the Indian government, the decision to involve immigrants in the modernization process represents a compromise in an ongoing struggle among planners and politicians about development strategies and philosophies. Between those who want to keep Indian development independent of foreign influences and those who want to immerse India more thoroughly in global economic dependencies, the government seems to view Indian immigrants as a kind of "third force," appealing because they are neither wholly Indian nor wholly foreign. The immigrants presently appear more malleable, more committed to Indian national interests, less threatening to Indian self-sufficiency, and more adaptable to the Indian business milieu than foreigners, while simultaneously offering more technical sophistication and more "rationality" and "efficiency" than local capitalists. However, the immigrants' semi-insider, semi-outsider status also renders them potentially troublesome as forces of social and political disruption.

The government campaign urges Indians living overseas, known as nonresident Indians (NRIs), to use their foreign skills and capital in India to become shareholders, to found new industries, or to resuscitate old ones. In 1989 an Indian government official announced that there were some 957 NRI ventures operating in India, with more in the planning stages ("NRI Investment on the Rise" 1989: 9). These businesses are as yet just a small fraction of the estimated 10,000 foreign companies that have invested in India since 1957 (Indian Investment Centre n.d.: 1), but they represent a significant trend.

A concurrent campaign aimed at those NRIs with less direct entrepreneurial interests offers highly favorable terms to those putting their savings (in the form of precious "hard" currencies) into Indian banks; this money is used to finance the government's role in the NRI investment process as well as to finance other imports needed to modernize and upgrade indigenous Indian industry.

This two-pronged promotional effort recognizes that overseas Indians, part of the wave of outmigration that has siphoned off so many

members of India's highly educated urban middle class over the past
25 years, have utilized their education, skill, and access to capital to
become very prosperous in their new homes. Embedded in the technically oriented business and financial bourgeoisies in their adopted
countries, and prosperous and full of entrepreneurial drive, NRIs are
eagerly receptive to the state offers. For most, however, their entry
into international investment might not have occurred without the
stimulus of the new Indian state policies. These policies now designate
those who retain Indian citizenship, those whose parents or grandpar-
ents were Indian citizens, and their spouses as a special category of
investor, eligible for facilities denied to local entrepreneurs and also
to other foreign investors.

Those immigrants most drawn to the offers of the Indian state are
the large colonies of recent Indian immigrants in North America, Europe, the Middle East, Southeast Asia, and Africa, rather than the
older Indian immigrant populations in the Caribbean and the Pacific.
The latter lack the skills, the wealth, and the recent networks within
India which make NRI investment viable.

At present, therefore, Indian state policy is one of the forces shaping
a new class, a group of transnational entrepreneurs whose activities
occur in several different social arenas as they shuttle between India
and their adopted countries (see Glick-Schiller and Fouron [1990], and
Basch, Glick-Schiller, and Szanton [in press] for discussions of trans-
nationalism as a global phenomenon). As NRI investors become more
numerous and more adept at manipulating their transnational social
networks, their primary interest in this form of investment becomes,
first, the profits to be made from the skilled and extremely low-wage
work force in India, and, second, the country's huge internal consumer
market. As a result, non-immigrant Indian workers face exploitation
by their former compatriots within an international division of labor.

Earlier phases of capitalist development produced outmigration from
India; the global capitalist process helped to "underdevelop" India to
the point where some of its population could only find a livelihood in
areas under the control of more advanced capitalist states. At present
India is scrambling to redefine its place in a competitive global system
that places great emphasis on high-technology manufacturing, both
for export and for internal consumption by a growing middle class.
Presently India's most immediate competitors are other Asian countries. In such a situation India's relationship with its own migrants
has changed. They and their capital need to be lured back.

Still relatively few in number, NRI investors and the businesses
they found promise to have a distinct impact on Indian society. NRI
control of relatively large amounts of capital and receipt of government
assistance makes this group economically privileged. Moreover, NRIs

are the transmitters of sophisticated technology and Western management techniques, and they move easily between the two cultures. Although NRIs are emerging as potential agents of social change, their impact, heightened as it is by its close association with the new consumer culture sweeping India, is not always of the positive kind that Indian planners had envisioned. Within India's emergent national culture, a debate about the role of NRIs has become intertwined with the ongoing debate about modernization and Westernization in which every former colonial state engages.

The Indian experience raises the question of whether development strategies based on the return of immigrant capital may not backfire in social and political terms. NRIs themselves have begun to demand a political role in India, their special privileges have antagonized an indigenous capitalist class, and their development projects, business methods, and consumption standards have accentuated class tensions within the country. At present, Indian planners remain highly satisfied with the path they have chosen. However, the Indian business class, Indian progressives and sectors of the general public are less sure.

INDIAN ECONOMIC DEVELOPMENT AND THE DEBATE ABOUT SELF-SUFFICIENCY

India, unlike some other Third World countries, did not start its present industrialization drive "from scratch." India's present industrial base is an outgrowth of British colonial domination, and many of India's current major manufacturers—machinery, cement, steel, jute, processed food, textiles, and clothing—are a legacy of British capital, gradually transferred after India achieved independence in 1947. Critics like Bagchi (1973) have charged that Indian industry might have both grown and diversified further in the colonial period if the British had not undercut indigenous capitalists in order to preserve their economic domination. Nevertheless, an Indian business class did grow significantly during this period and moved into whatever areas were not closed to it.

After independence, foreign investment (much of it British) shifted from the plantation and extractive industries of the colonial era to more technologically intensive manufacturing fields (Balasubramanyam 1984: 149). This was not enough, however, to give India the kind of industrial growth rate needed for rapid development in a country whose large population was extremely poor and still 80 percent rural. Succeeding governments have wrestled with the problem of how to speed Indian industrialization; employ an impoverished, ever-growing population; and redistribute wealth without recreating neocolonial dependence on foreign capital.

From 1947 until the late 1970s, industry and the industrialization process were highly regulated by the government in programs that some called socialist but that might have been better labeled populist. Succeeding Five-Year Plans set forth the goals of national self-reliance and legal production of both the public sector of strategic goods and services and the small-business sector. "Self-reliance" discouraged both foreign investment and foreign imports and insulated Indian industry somewhat from foreign competition. Stringent controls on currency exchange furthered this by protecting the value of the Indian rupee inside India. Large-scale private-sector industries were hedged in by restrictions and licensing requirements. To a certain extent, these tactics succeeded. India's small-business sector flourishes, and foreign capital has, until recently, been kept at arm's length.

In particular, the Indian government has been hostile to multinational corporations, despite injured cries from international capital, political pressure from the United States, and internal argument from conservative Indian economists. Multinationals were commonly viewed as conglomerates able to act as extraterritorial powers, interfere in local politics, juggle exchange rates, and make enormous hidden profits (Patwardhan 1986: 73). In fact, in several cases, multinationals—the British oil company Burma Shell and the North American firms Coca Cola and IBM—withdrew from India rather than comply with the 1973 Foreign Exchange Regulations Act (FERA) which mandated majority Indian shareholding in all foreign firms in the country and put a cap on the repatriation of profits (Patwardhan 1986; Ninan 1989: 52).

However, by the mid-1970s the Indian economy had also become a morass of government policies and controls that, many critics felt, combined the worst features of both capitalism and socialism. Amid the red tape and welter of regulations, industrial growth was slow (an average of around 3.5 percent annual growth before 1974), particularly in the public and large industry private sectors. An Indian economist summing up the relative achievements of the period 1950–1976 also noted a long list of failures: poor industrial productivity, slow growth of employment, slow growth of exports, little attention to production costs or quality of finished goods, little emphasis on upgrading industry, and overwhelming emphasis on regulation (Ahluwalia 1988: 151–152).

In the mid- and late 1970s, a period of economic reform—basically, partial deregulation—began. Industrial policy moved toward more active promotion of industrial growth, although policies protecting small-scale industry remained in place. The first round of reforms had modest success. In the period 1974–1985 the average annual growth rate rose to 4.5 percent annually (Ninan 1989: 36)—painfully low in comparison with most industrial countries. Industrial employment still lagged. In 1981 only about 6 million Indians were employed in the industrial sector out of a population of 665 million (Lucas 1988: 185–186). Agriculture and the enormous informal sector still employed the bulk of workers.

The move to reform the Indian economy and Indian economic planning coincided with the spectacular industrial growth of other parts of Asia. South Korea, Taiwan, Hong Kong, Malaysia, and Thailand were in the midst of a boom in export-oriented production, spurred by foreign investment. In a world clearly in the process of economic restructuring, Indian economists, politicians, and planners, who had for years been pressing to simultaneously modernize the country's industry, reduce its emphasis on import-substitution, and seek foreign investment began to get a more respectful hearing. Their position suddenly began to seem nationalist, designed to protect India from being left behind in a changing world order. India's seventh Five-Year Plan for 1985–1990 expanded the kinds of businesses and investments open to large industries, removed licensing requirements from many kinds of industries, liberalized imports of capital goods, and placed great emphasis on technology transfer as an essential component of foreign investment.

This modernizing trend, combined with an active search for foreign investment, was vastly accelerated when the late Rajiv Gandhi came to power in late 1984. Gandhi was a personal enthusiast for modern technology, Western management techniques, and modernity in many forms. He brought into the government a group of Western-oriented technocrats charged with carrying out his campaign slogan, "Into the twenty-first century." Gandhi's 1991 assassination did not reverse these trends.

The results evoked cautious satisfaction in Indian planners up to 1990, although several rapid changes of government and the oil price increases brought about by the Gulf War and a severe recession threaten to slow growth. An overall growth rate of 8.5 percent (an industrial growth rate of 8.8 percent), an expansion in the Indian stock market, and a growth in exports were offset by a sharp decline in foreign currency reserves plus a growth in external debt and in India's still-low debt service ratio (Reserve Bank of India 1989). Multinationals began to return cautiously—among them Pepsi Cola and Coca Cola. Foreign investment has increased, although collaboration with Indian firms and provision of technology transfer are still required. The numbers of approvals for foreign collaboration issued by the government each year has risen steadily, from 271 in 1975 (Reserve Bank of India 1985: 1) to 957 in 1986 and 853 in 1987 (Indian Investment Centre n.d.: 1). The largest numbers of these collaborations still come from

Britain; followed by the United States; various Western European countries such as West Germany, Switzerland, the Netherlands, and France; and Japan.

THE IMMIGRATION THAT MAKES NRI INVESTMENT POSSIBLE

Outmigration is not a new phenomenon in Indian society, and an estimated 10 million people of Indian origin live outside the country now, their migration shaped by almost 200 years of capitalist penetration. The most immediate cause of migration has been lack of land or employment. Agricultural stagnation dating back at least a hundred years and an industrial sector lagging since the 1950s have left much of India's population un- or underemployed. Some migration was actively promoted by the colonial state. From the mid-nineteenth century until the 1920s, Britain sponsored the migration of thousands of poor Indians as indentured laborers to the Caribbean, Pacific islands such as Fiji and Mauritius, Southeast Asia, Africa, and western Canada. Most worked initially on plantations, in the lumber industry, or as laborers. The majority of these early immigrants lost touch with India and never returned but rather stayed to become farmers, entrepreneurs, or, in succeeding generations, professionals. Today, Indians in Fiji, the Caribbean, and South Africa may still identify themselves as Indian, but they rarely know India or its culture at first hand.

A new flow of migration out of India began in the 1950s when thousands of South Asians, most of them rural people, flocked to Britain on Commonwealth passports in response to that country's postwar labor shortage. Smaller numbers of Indians from similar social backgrounds migrated to Canada. People from this wave of migration are now parts of the working classes or pretty bourgeoisies of their adopted countries. Britain's Indian community has also produced some major industrialists. (One such tycoon was recently involved in a series of takeover bids in India that rocked industrialists there).

The most recent migration, in which skilled urban professionals are very prominent, began in the mid-1960s and accelerated in the two subsequent decades as Western countries began to seek highly skilled, technically trained labor power. A perceived shortage of professionals, scientists, and medical personnel lay behind the 1965 revision of U.S. immigration laws. An estimated 650,000 to 800,000 Indians to date have entered the United States. Despite poverty and downward mobility for some Indian immigrants (Lessinger 1989), for most, prosperity plus modern technology have allowed maintenance of close contact with India. This generation of migrants is truly transnational in orientation; among other things, a constant stream of information about immigration strategies and job opportunities flows from successful migrants back to friends and relatives in India. As a result, the current stream of outmigration is constantly reproduced.

In a startling change from the situation 20 years ago, virtually every urban middle-class Indian family (and a significant part of the rural bourgeoisie as well) has at least one member of the extended kin network living abroad. Whether these are small manufacturers in Britain, Silicon Valley engineers, or oil-field workers in the Middle East, their earnings are still fabulous by Indian standards. The younger generation in India, faced with a shortage of good jobs, is yearning to follow and is willing to pursue any path to go abroad.

Much of this migration is spurred not only by lack of employment in India but also by the process of capital penetration itself. Western-oriented and highly technical systems of higher education as well as the growing number of foreign firms in India that hire graduates of the best educational institutions, and often send them abroad for further training, all play a role. Meanwhile, a Western-style consumer culture flourishing in Indian cities both intensifies the desire to migrate and ensures familiarity with Western cultural patterns. (Illsoo Kim, in his 1981 study of Korean immigration to the United States, noted a similar process at work in Korea.)

The "brain drain" created by the emigration of its most highly trained citizens has worried the Indian government, which recognizes the country's shortage of doctors, scientists, and trained managers. Critics note that many of these professional immigrants have received publicly funded educations in India's premier science, technology, and medical schools. The Indian sociologist Haribabu Ejnavarzala pinpointed the extraordinary number of science graduates from the Indian Institute of Technology at Kanpur who eventually migrate to the United States after receiving U.S.-style training on state scholarship at an institution founded with U.S. aid (1986).

However, the Indian government has done little to address this loss of talented young people. It is generally agreed that in India, jobs for educated people are scarce and usually obtainable only through patronage. Working conditions are poor. The infrastructure needed to sustain Western-style research, medical practice, or management systems is largely absent. Many universities, scientific laboratories, and medical establishments lack essential equipment. Transactions in large banks are still recorded by hand in ledgers. Patronage, petty corruption, and social discrimination are rife in work situations. Indian businesspeople and professionals in the United States speak feelingly in interviews about the sense of freedom, autonomy, and accomplishment they found in moving to the United States (Lessinger 1986). In addition, immigrants can attain levels of material comfort abroad that are increasingly elusive for many of India's urban middle class.

A profile of Indian immigrants in the United States suggests the suitability of these NRIs for the Indian government's industrial development drive. Unlike many other U.S. immigrant groups, the Indians who arrived here after 1965 have largely been able to maintain or enhance the middle-class professional status that they arrived with. With money to spare, years of Western technical and management experience, important networks within Western scientific, industrial, and financial institutions, and a burning desire to make good, NRIs are, in fact, the answer to a planner's prayer. For instance, in 1988, almost 43 percent of the Indian immigrants in the United States held managerial or professional positions, and another 36 percent held technical, sales, and administrative support jobs (Ray 1989: 15, reporting figures compiled by U.S. Census Bureau statistician Amara Bachu). Some 45 percent of the adult, foreign-born Indians in the United States earned $25,000 or more a year, with 30 percent of them earning $35,000 or more annually (Dutt 1989: 12, citing figures compiled by Bachu.) These relatively high individual incomes are augmented because families of Indian immigrant professionals typically contain two or more earners. Many such households also practice a kind of frugality unknown to most native-born Americans.

An important group of Indian entrepreneurs has also settled in the U.S. This group already had extensive business ties with India, even before NRI investment became possible. Indeed their pattern of interweaving their Indian and overseas business and social ties foreshadowed the way that NRI investors have come to operate. Importers of diamonds and gemstones, textiles, clothing, leather goods, and food items use family-owned firms and business ties in their natal areas of India to supply their businesses in the United States. For such entrepreneurs, Indian government NRI incentives are simply an inducement to do more of what they have been doing all along.

At the top of the immigrant status hierarchy is an extremely successful group of people who are probably wealthier and more influential than they were in India: doctors, engineers, scientific researchers, stockbrokers or financial consultants, real estate magnates, and owners of large-scale firms. Work and schooling in the United States have situated these people in industries, research organizations, and banks and financial organizations in which they have access to technology, management skills, financial know-how, and credit. Furthermore, this group retains strong social links with India—links that are intensified precisely because these people are wealthy and successful enough to travel frequently, sponsor the immigration of relatives, buy property in India, and even dabble in Indian local politics.

The entrepreneurial drive of this group is evident in a variety of situations. For instance, it is very typical for professionals such as engineers or financial analysts to start working in U.S. firms and eventually to found their own companies, perhaps with U.S. as well as Indian partners. Equally, many salaried professionals are also involved as investors in the business ventures of fellow Indians. This means that the Indian immigrant community is criss-crossed by a web of economic transactions reinforcing the links between the professionals and the business people (Lessinger 1986). In this milieu, Indian government concessions to NRI investors, plus the surplus value to be extracted from India's abundant supply of cheap, skilled labor, prove potent lures. Many NRIs understand that their knowledge of Indian languages and Indian culture plus the active social ties they retain in India offer them a competitive edge over other foreign investors in that country.

Moral and emotional considerations also play a role, albeit a secondary one, in attracting NRI investors to India. Most first-generation Indian immigrants retain a deep emotional involvement in the country of their birth, along with a deep ambivalence about where their cultural allegiances lie. Most go on thinking of themselves as Indian, most feel some guilt in having left India, and most toy, at some period in their lives, with the idea of returning there to live permanently. Thus, NRIs are not wholly hypocritical when they talk about investment in terms of a moral obligation to provide jobs and technical know-how to a country they left because it was too poor and backward to accommodate their ambitions.

In a more specific way, NRIs see investment in India in the context of their own ongoing social involvement with that country and their own potential return. Friendships, patronage relationships, and obligations to kin can be maintained now that telephones, jet travel, and the video camera make regular contact possible. Most people try to provide regular remittances to parents or siblings and to shoulder financial responsibility for schooling, weddings, and other life-cycle events within the family circle.

NRI savings accounts and annuities, placed with the State Bank of India at interest rates higher than those available to Indians (and, at one period, also higher than those available to bank customers in the United States), thus have enormous emotional appeal to NRIs, speaking as they do to the possibility of helping relatives or retiring in India oneself. The highly favorable currency exchange regulations for those with NRI savings accounts are a way of channeling money legally to relatives who remain in India.

Both the savings and involvement in an Indian business can also pave the way for an immigrant's return into a society where outmigration is resented as well as envied. People might not be willing, or able, to return to a job in an Indian firm, yet with a comfortable savings account and a business of their own, they can come back to an affluent life-style and congenial working conditions. Advertisements in the U.S. immigrant press remind the potential NRI investor that it is possible to have the "best of both worlds."

The Indian government plays, quite openly, on all these sentiments. Government spokespeople use immigrant cultural events celebrating Indian-ness as forums in which to solicit NRI investment. Their sales pitches play heavily on the moral aspect—on NRIs' obligations to the country that bred and trained them. At the same time, the wide-open nature of the investment field and the profits to be made are emphasized. Since there is regional competition within India for NRI money, state governments send officials to address immigrant gatherings whenever possible, urging people to invest not just in India but in their home state. A Bengali literary society meeting, a Kannada cultural conference, or the appearance of a Tamil film star in the United States all become occasions for investment appeals tinged with interregional chauvinism.

At the present period, investment in India may also seem more attractive as Indian immigrants confront social tensions, economic uncertainty, and an "outsider" role in their adopted countries. India's relative political stability and its devotion to capitalist economic forms ("Now that Rajiv has given up all that socialism rubbish," as one businessman sniffed shortly before Gandhi was voted out of office) seem increasingly comforting. The immigrant sense of precariousness, unease, and fear of racism is expressed most clearly by Indian entrepreneurs now living in the Middle East, Southeast Asia, and Africa. The kind of dispossession and expulsion they fear already became visible during the coup d'état in Fiji and amid the more recent upheavals in Kuwait and Iraq. Indians in Singapore and even in the old immigrant communities in British Guyana and Trinidad feel threatened by religious and ethnic chauvinism as well. Even in the more politically stable Western countries, racism and nativism bubbling beneath the surface have made many Indians nervous. The soundness of U.S. banks and the stability of the U.S. stock market are further sources of unease for immigrants in this country.

Interviews suggest that the inability of many Indian businesspeople in the United States to handle this country's tense race and labor relations may weight their preference toward investing in Indian factories. A New York City clothing importer was asked whether it would not be cheaper and easier to manufacture the rapidly changing lines of clothing in the United States rather than in family-owned firms in India. At the time he was explaining how he sent a U.S. fashion designer to India four times a year to introduce up-to-the-minute designs and colors; he also sent a host of inspectors back and forth to ensure that design and quality standards were maintained. In addition he, like other clothing importers, struggled with the yearly shifts in U.S. textile import quotas.

The man said bluntly that neither he nor his sons felt they could manage the kind of black and Hispanic work force they would have to recruit if they opened a factory in New Jersey. In contrast, he said he "knew" his Indian workers; he and his relatives could manage them well. This suggests, therefore, that the whole Indian cultural ambience of highly personalized workplace and business relationships, which characterizes Indian small industry and which dismays Western investors, may actually prove appealing to the immigrant investor.

WHAT NRI INVESTORS GET AND HOW THEY GET IT

In broad terms, many of the government incentives offered to NRI investors are similar to those offered to other foreign investors. The guidelines themselves are constantly undergoing adjustment and liberalization, but the general parameters have remained similar for several years. Foreign ownership or partnership, the removal of capital and profits from India, the licensing of new firms, the import of components, and the export of goods are all carefully regulated. The amount of foreign equity allowed and the percentage of profits that can be repatriated overseas are directly related to the type of industry involved and its location. Priority industries (which include most high-technology firms), industries geared to import-substitution, export-oriented industries, and those located in some of the more backward and underindustrialized areas are permitted more foreign equity and a higher level of profit repatriation.

Thus, according to 1987 government guidelines, NRIs, like other foreign investors, can contribute up to 40 percent of the capital in an ordinary venture; the rest must be contributed by Indian investors. In such a case the foreign investor can take 40 percent of the profits or dividends out of the country. Those percentages can rise to 74 percent in the case of priority industries, those in poorly developed areas, or those that undertake to export 60 to 75 percent of their output. It can rise to 100 percent for industries exporting their total output (Jain 1987).

In addition, NRIs and other foreign industrialists are permitted to import certain capital goods, components, and raw materials, and to buy other raw materials at controlled prices. A variety of taxes are waived or postponed. All these provisions are denied to Indian industrialists, and obtaining them is an incentive for Indian companies to take on foreign or NRI collaborators or shareholders.

Some privileges pertain only to NRI investors. For instance, NRI firms are not required to provide technology transfer, as foreign firms must. Moreover, NRIs who do not wish to repatriate their profits or their capital can invest in virtually anything in India aside from speculative real estate or agriculture. They can even invest in the Indian stock market if profits are kept in India.

The Indian government favors NRI investors most openly in the area of special services. To guide investment into priority areas and to streamline a byzantine bureaucratic process, the newly created Trade Development Authority in India works with Indian consular offices abroad; the Indian Investment Centre also has offices around the world. Some Indian state governments are also setting up their own organizations, such as the State Industrial and Investment Corporation of Maharashtra, which promotes investment in the highly industrialized corridor between Bombay and Pune. All these organizations officially give potential NRI investors advice about where and how to invest and act as advocates in steering licensing applications through committees. Informally, they throw governmental weight behind applications, discouraging obstructions from local interests.

An important function of these groups is to help the NRI investor assemble the groups of Indian coinvestors needed in virtually any NRI venture. With fair regularity, Indian state governments themselves become partners and/or lenders in NRI projects as well as offering improvements in infrastructure as part of interregional competition for new industry. At least one regional politician has promised to curb trade unions within the export zone of his region.

The level of lending may allow NRIs with comparatively little capital of their own to embark on large projects. The State Bank of India began its present loan policy in 1987, when it began to use reserves, created by the growing number of NRI deposits, to provide project loans for NRI industries. These same foreign currency reserves may be released to allow NRI investors to import needed components or equipment. The state bank also helps NRI industrialists to raise further capital on the Indian stock market ("SBI Helps NRIs" 1989). The governments of various Indian states often provide additional loans and investment packages, as well as tax holidays, cheap land and access to electricity and water.

One of the rationales behind the extensive assistance that the Indian government offers NRI investment is that projects are likely to be proposed by people new to the stringencies of international investment, whether single entrepreneurs or consortia of individual investors. Although NRI investments seem to run the gamut from very small to very large, officials suggest that many are smaller than the ordinary foreign collaboration which is usually carried out by a large multinational. One of the added roles of government assistance, therefore, is to even out some of the inequities that small individual investors initially face. Some Indian officials have complained of NRI investor inexperience, blaming it for a relatively high failure rate among NRI businesses ("NRI Entrepreneurs" 1989). However, it is probable that this novice quality, making many NRI ventures initially dependent on the government, is part of their political, if not their economic, charm in government eyes. These are not large, established multinationals whose corporate bases elsewhere give them political leverage in India. The combination of NRI inexperience and the elaborate approval process gives the government considerable power to shape where such firms locate, what they will produce, and who their Indian collaborators will be.

At the same time one should not overemphasize the dependency of NRI investors, who often have a social base of their own in India. It is this social base that gives them a competitive edge over foreign competitors and makes them desirable partners in joint ventures. Independently of the government agencies set up to assist them, NRIs usually know the right people and the right approaches to maneuver through the Indian bureaucratic maze. It is clear that many, if not most, NRIs choose to locate their businesses in their native regions where they know the language, the local tastes, and the political climate. Relatives or friends are hired as local managers to handle day-to-day affairs if the NRI investor cannot relocate to India.

Presently there is no breakdown available to indicate where in India the 900-plus NRI ventures are currently in operation. The very partial information available from interviews and media accounts suggests that a great many NRI firms are located either in Maharashtra State, outside Bombay; in Andhra Pradesh state, particularly around Hyderabad; and around Bangalore in Karnataka State. All are areas that have experienced considerable industrial growth in the last 20 years. This pattern makes sound economic sense from the point of view of the investor, since preexisting urban industrial areas tend to have more reliable sources of electricity, water, and transport, as well as pools of skilled workers. However, it suggests that NRI investment is being primarily directed toward the industrialized urban areas, which have already produced large numbers of immigrants, rather than toward India's more backward and underindustrialized areas, as the government might hope. The upshot may well be a further spurring of out-migration from these urban industrial areas.

Nor is it clear just what industries attract the most NRI investment.

Again, very fragmentary data suggests a range from small, relatively low-technology plants assembling portable radios to at least one British NRI steel plant (made possible by the government decision to open the formerly reserved state sector to private investment.) Many NRI plants seem to concentrate on the production of machine tools or electronic components. Electronic components (along with computer software) and medical supplies represent both priority industries and the kind of export commodity India is anxious to promote. Steel, portable radios, machine tools, and coated papers fall into the realm of import substitution which becomes increasingly important with the growth of India's avidly consuming middle class. NRIs have recently announced the opening of several medical products plants making eyeglass lenses, eye care products, or surgical latex gloves; all are destined for export to the West. A new NRI plant producing coumarin, a perfume fixative, and another plant producing coated papers used in packaging, are making goods intended to replace Indian imports of these products, (see "SICOM" 1990). Another major area of non-factory investment is in the construction of hospitals and luxury hotels. Luxury hotels—built from imported designs and run with Western management techniques—are central to the kind of high-profit tourist industry India is anxious to promote. (NRIs, as well as Westerners, are increasingly the target of Indian tourism advertising.) Hospitals, on the other hand, represent a government attempt to build up the country's dilapidated infrastructure and to provide a vital service for which there is tremendous demand among India's middle classes.

NRI ventures are clearly intended to generate employment for Indian citizens, including the skilled working class, those privileged enough to have a high school or college degree, and a professional/managerial class that is extremely vocal about its own problems with un- and underemployment. At the same time, these industrial ventures are expected to help reverse the "brain drain" by drawing immigrant members of the educated elite back to the land of their birth.

Clearly, many of these industries fulfill expectations on all fronts. They do create local employment (although there are no figures on the numbers of people they hire), and at least some NRIs do move back to India permanently in order to run their businesses. Several of the author's friends and acquaintances who are contemplating this kind of NRI investment clearly see the move as part of a set of complicated life decisions they are making about whether, when, and how to return to India. On the other hand, a number of cases collected in the United States suggest that a whole group of NRI investors are currently retaining their positions in U.S. society while shuttling back and forth between a firm in India run by relatives and a firm or professional position in the United States. Some of this is sheer prudence—why abandon your U.S. livelihood while the firm in India is new and un-tried? Some of this is also indicative of the transnational perspective of many immigrants, who find they can live quite successfully in two social spheres. Indeed, their ultimate success as overseas investors may depend on their ability to keep roots in their adopted countries.

The following brief cases, drawn from my own research and from detailed cases recounted in the Indian and Indian immigrant presses, suggest some of the range among NRI investors. The first case is of a small business, indicating the continuity between NRI strategies and those of a traditional business class that used its Indian social networks to develop an import-based business abroad. For this group the avail-ability of the government of India help has eased matters, but it has not yet significantly changed their orientation.

Mr. B., based in New York, imports Indian foodstuffs. He sells these retail and acts as a distributor to other Indian grocery shops all over the United States. He uses family ties in Africa (a source of lentils) and in Indian rice-growing areas. Some years ago Mr. B. decided that there was a good market in the United States for a regional variety of home-style hot pickle.

Mr. B. provided the capital that allowed a former pickle supplier to expand his tiny factory outside Bombay. In return for the capital and a share of the profits, Mr. B. is allotted all the factory's output. The factory involves little fancy technology. Mr. B. takes advantage of the regulations which permit him to repatriate 100 percent of his profits since this is a 100 percent export busi-ness. Mr. B.'s cousin handles the shipping of the pickles and keeps a general eye on the concern.

The next case involves an NRI investor whose scientific and indus-trial experience makes him more typical. In fact, he is almost ideal from the Indian government's point of view: scientifically trained and versed in Western production and management techniques, with an established company track record and a good credit rating, he has transferred his technological skills to plants in India making electronic components. This is precisely the kind of NRI investor the Indian gov-ernment has envisioned, since India is anxious to develop its own sup-plies of such goods rather than rely on imports from South Korea, Taiwan, and Japan, now the major producers of capacitors. Typically, these firms give employment to the major investor's relatives. They also, as the owner told me with pride, help some employees to come to the United States, nominally for advanced training. The owner and I both understood that those who come to the United States for training will do their best to convert student visas into permanent resident visas.

K.L. came to the United States originally for graduate study in engineering. Today he owns and operates a medium-sized factory in New Jersey which makes electrolytic capacitors, components used in making electronic goods.

In his underindustrialized home state of Bihar, K.L. and his family run two factories making ceramic capacitors. All output is sold in India. One factory is owned by K.L., his family, and other stockholders, among whom are both U.S.-based NRIs, U.S. engineer friends of K.L., and family friends in India. The other factory is a joint venture with the Bihar state government, which provided 70 percent of the financing and helped organize a group of Indian investors.

That factory, which is semiautomated, uses imported Japanese machinery and hires 65 people. Most of the employees are local high-school graduates who are given on-the-job training. Several of these young employees moved on to jobs with other multinationals, and two eventually came to the United States for further training.

K.L. is trying to develop Indian sources for the raw materials in the capacitors, since the present imported raw materials are a major expense.

Daily operations of both factories are supervised by K.L.'s older brother, a doctor, and by his father, a retired civil servant. K.L. travels to Bihar himself several times a year to supervise operations, but he has no intention of giving up his New Jersey plant.

Another case relating to the vast scheme to open a hospital/medical research/medical training center in Hyderabad, in Andhra Pradesh state, can be followed through hugh double-paged ads in the immigrant newspaper *India Abroad*. The scheme, put together by a large group of South Indian doctors in the United States, is described as a charity but is actually a form of investment, since donor/investors are offered a chance to buy building plots and to practice medicine in the new facility, which is equipped with all the latest medical devices. Furthermore, the hospital, if it succeeds, will inevitably make money for its sponsors.

One of the implications of this scheme, if it comes to fruition, is that it will potentially offer Western-style medical care to NRIs who return, or to their aging relatives. It may also offer medical school training to NRIs' children at a fraction of the cost of such training in the West.

The political criticism directed in India against other such clinics and hospitals which are tailored to the elite probably accounts for this scheme's promise to train local medical personnel and to offer free treatment to poor patients. Much in the prospectus needs to be taken with a grain of salt.

The International Medical Science City will, when completed, offer: the most advanced medical research facilities; training for Indian and foreign doctors; free medical care for 40 percent of its patients; subsidized by charges to the other 60 percent; a gleaming, well-equipped new hospital; 200 house plots available for sale to those who donate $10,000; a "core group of 100 physicians" drawn from among the institution's trainees; a visiting facility drawn from among those who contribute $10,000 a year; free medical care for the families of those who contribute $10,000. All donations are tax deductible since this is a charity.

The institution is shown in accompanying photos as still in the early phases of construction. However the prospectus lists 90 "patrons and benefactors" from 22 American states who are said to have donated more than $500,000 and to have pledged three quarters of a million dollars. (*International Medical Science City* 1990)

THE BACKLASH AGAINST NRI INVESTING

If Indian government officials are generally pleased with the drive for NRI investment, there is nevertheless a backlash against the phenomenon within India. It comes from a variety of quarters: from the Indian business class, from progressives, from politicians, and from within a general cultural debate about what it means to be Indian at a time of rapid economic and social change.

Some of the reaction against NRIs is part of a general backlash against current development and industrialization policies (see, for instance, Mehta 1988: 203). NRI investors are vulnerable to political attack as a highly visible and much-discussed sector of the new industrial bourgeoisie. They have come to symbolize the damaging inroads that foreign influence is perceived to be making on Indian culture. Touted by the Indian government as the bearers of Western-style technology, expertise, and outlook, NRIs bear the brunt of a good deal of resentment and cultural chauvinism. They are considered "not Indian," weaklings who deserted their motherland in favor of easy living (and emotional and moral sterility) abroad. At a time of great social tensions exacerbated by economic change, divisions between peasant and urbanite, underdeveloped and developed regions, and worker and capitalist are often symbolized in terms of Indian versus Western. Even the current wave of Hindu fundamentalism sometimes confounds its "secularist" enemies with Westernized ones. In these conflicts, NRIs are a highly visible target. They, as a group, have not eased matters when they demand still greater economic privileges, the right to vote in Indian elections, and special cabinet-level representation.

The progressive attack on the current "economic liberalization" policies also emphasizes the degree to which these policies largely benefit foreign corporations and India's growing industrial elite. In this regard the lavish loans and technical assistance that NRI industries enjoy stand out strikingly. Although the Indian government can and does argue that it is spending money to generate jobs, bolster infrastructure, and produce more consumer goods for the Indian public, many critics have asked whether that money could not be better spent on Indian endeavors. Of course, the Indian business class, already pressed by competitors in India and abroad, is bitterly resentful. Other social critics are more concerned about growing disparities of income and access to basic amenities—inequalities that current development policies accentuate.

A particular focus of angry debate is the large, lush, NRI-funded medical institutes and hospitals that are springing up, particularly in South India. As discussed, these have multiple functions for their NRI investors, providing money-making investments, sites for returned NRIs' medical practices, and up-to-date medical care for NRIs' aging parents. Nonetheless, they are striking within India's stratified health system, which itself provides a vivid, concrete vision of class privilege. Many rural people get no almost no modern medical care at all. The urban poor do have access to large public hospitals, where basic medical equipment and supplies are frequently lacking. The well-to-do fear the crowds and dirt of public hospitals, and use private clinics and nursing homes instead. The very rich go to the few premier medical institutions in major cities which offer the most sophisticated diagnostic facilities.

In this situation, NRI-funded medical centers, which are geared to the rich but heavily subsidized by state governments, are a political affront, highlighting the class conflicts inherent in the situation. The state and municipal governments that offer the medical centers cheap building sites, water connections, power lines, telephone service, access roads, and bus service are the same institutions that cannot provide clean drinking water to their citizens, let alone maintain adequate public hospitals and clinics. Tax holidays mean revenue foregone, while state loans tie up capital that might otherwise finance public services. This kind of development, and the outcry surrounding it, is precisely what Indian politicians want to avoid in a country already dangerously polarized by class, ethnic, and regional inequalities.

CONCLUSIONS

Any conclusions about the NRI investment phenomenon in India must be prefaced by a string of unanswered questions. It is possible that this form of investment is a short-lived phenomenon, workable only while India is in a state of reentry into a new world economy. NRI investors may eventually be pushed aside by larger, more powerful multinationals, once they have tested the waters. If NRI investment is associated with a certain amount of return migration, will these investors retain their transnational perspective or will they soon be reabsorbed into a purely Indian social setting?

On the other hand, the Indian example, however ephemeral, raises theoretical questions about the relationships between late capitalist industrialization and migration. Global economic changes of the last 25 years have created, for a number of countries as well as India, educated, technically skilled, and wealthy expatriate populations. Strategically placed in class terms, expatriates may serve as a source of development capital and entrepreneurial skills for less-developed countries if they can be wooed back to their countries of origin. They offer former colonies some "third force" alternative to dependence on multinational corporations or international lending agencies, although nobody would suggest that immigrant capital alone can modernize an economy.

The Indian example also highlights the role of the state, not just in setting industrial development policy but in actively soliciting and supporting a chosen group of capitalists as a counterweight to too-powerful foreign capital and impotent local capital. NRI investors are, with the backing of the Indian government, transforming themselves from expatriate professionals and entrepreneurs into members of an international business class controlling investments that are, by Indian standards, vast. If this new class of investors is, at present, malleable and dependent on the state, it may nevertheless eventually begin to assert its own independent class interests—interests not always consonant with those of the Indian state. Already NRI demands for a major political role in India have shaken the political establishment.

Central to the whole NRI phenomenon, and to other development strategies like it, is the importance of cultural and national identity. These are the ideological lures with which NRI investors are persuaded to part with their money and to return to a country they thought they had left for good. Dual cultural identity is central to planners' vision of NRI investment success, since it depends on these investors' ability to bridge two very different cultural settings. The question of cultural identity (as well as that of class interests) is also at the heart of local opposition to NRI investment. However, this formulation of a special investor class defined by culture—even transnational culture—flies in the face of scholars' general assumption that both capital and labor are anonymous and interchangeable. Clearly this kind of particularism, which links nations with their expatriate populations, is still part of the general configuration of development in many former Third World countries.

Finally, the political risk of this kind of industrialization strategy, which is dependent on the capital of returned immigrants, has already been alluded to. The kind of unequal distribution of scarce resources, highly visible in the case of NRI investors, can only heighten class tensions and class divisions in a country like India. Meanwhile, the creation of an international entrepreneurial class with one foot in India, thanks to shared language and culture, but with the other in a richer, more powerful society, can only hasten the kinds of rapid, tumultuous, social and economic changes that Indian planners have hoped to guard against.

Part II

The New Industrial Diversity

5

Small-Scale Industrialization in a Rapidly Changing World Market

Michael L. Blim

In this chapter Michael Blim gives a diachronic analysis of the shoe industry in the Marche region of Italy and shows how kin networks, which are important in generating labor and capital in the initial development of small-scale industry, are ultimately too limited to allow such firms to compete successfully in an international market.

This chapter analyzes some of the potentials and limits to a strategy of flexibly specialized industrialization for late-developing regions in the emerging global factory. Based on a study of the rise and decline of small-scale industries in postwar central and northeastern Italy, I argue that regions embarking on programs of petty entrepreneurial production of consumer and capital goods for the contemporary world market may find their success short-lived. Obstacles to adequate capital accumulation arising from the small-scale industrial project itself sometimes inhibit the capacities of entrepreneurs to adapt to the rapidly changing world market demand on which their initial prosperity was founded. My observations reflect an analysis of data collected over the course of two years of fieldwork conducted between 1981 and 1990 in the Adriatic coastal region of the Marche among shoe producers.

I would like to explore briefly several major topics that arise from the central-northeastern Italian case and its theoretical implications. First, I will summarize its main points of interest. Second, I will examine its relative importance in current economic development thinking and discuss some possible reasons why it has taken on an exaggerated significance within key economic policy circles. Third, I will analyze the causes of the rise and decline of one central-northeastern Italian industry and suggest possible implications for other regions engaging in small-scale industrial production for the world market.

THE CENTRAL-NORTHEASTERN ITALIAN CASE

Central-northeastern Italy is the land of Benetton clothes and Vespa motorbikes, and of the now-famous "Made in Italy" designer label. Goods ranging from machine tools, small appliances, and auto parts to textiles, ceramics, and shoes are produced in formal industrial districts throughout the seven central-northeastern regions that comprise what Arnaldo Bagnasco has defined as the "Third Italy" (1977). In the study site region of the Marche, monocultural industrial districts have formed around the manufacture of shoes, furniture, apparel, and musical instruments.

In economic terms, central-northeastern Italian development has been extraordinarily successful. Because of the boom, family income for the people in all but two of central-northeastern Italy's seven regions now equals or exceeds the national average—an extraordinary gain made at a time when Italy's national income grew at a greater rate than any other modern capitalist economy except Japan ("Survey of the Italian Economy" 1988). Key to this success is petty entrepreneurship. Industrial development has produced a vast entrepreneurial–small-business class. For the study site region of the Marche, 36 percent of those who were economically active in 1985 were self-employed—a proportion exceeding the Italian mean by 7 percent (Istituto Centrale di Statistica 1986: 89–91). In San Lorenzo Marche, a pseudonym for the field study site and one of a half dozen Marche region towns that dominate the area's shoe industry, 27 percent of the household heads own and operate shoe production firms, and another 12 percent of the family heads are small-business people. For the town, then, a total of 39 percent of the household heads are petty entrepreneurs (Blim 1990b: 2).

Also crucial to Third Italian industrial growth is the formation of a flexible labor force (Brusco 1986). Many factors create a labor market conducive in many ways to accumulation, as my research in the Marche shoe zone suggests. First, most Marche industrial firms arise from a base in a particular household and its kin networks, and many, especially the small artisan workshops with fewer than 10 employees that comprise 83 percent of the region's manufacturing firms (Merli 1984: 140–141), recruit kin and friends of kin to fill laboring needs above and beyond what the household itself provides.[1] Through kin ties, women, children, and pensioners are often engaged in a labor process that cloaks poor pay and bad, often dangerous, working conditions in the disguise of family loyalty and household reproduction imperatives (Blim 1990b: 153–156).

Second, the Italian state plays no small part in composing a flexible labor force. On the one hand, it provides no unemployment compensation for workplaces with fewer than 20 employees, the laboring nexus of the Third Italy (Garonna and Pisani 1986: 114–172; Lazerson 1988: 330–342). Hence, labor discipline is direct: When workshops fail, workers are fired; when entrepreneurs have no orders, workers are furloughed without pay. On the other hand, the Italian state, by reason of inefficiency or convenient inaction, countenances widespread use by employers of illegal labor practices that place the worker in the unenviable position of having to bid individually for a workplace post wherein everything—from workday length to hourly wages as well as pension and medical care benefits—is put in play. *Lavoro nero* or "black labor," the term by which these practices are known, renders the Third Italian labor market more flexible for employers and makes business more profitable. For instance, I found in my study of the Marche shoe industry that *lavoro nero* and the tax evasion that accompanies the unreported earnings deriving from under-the-table labor account for 26 percent of the profits of the typical shoe firm (Blim 1990b: 162–171).

The economic transformation of the Marche region (1981 population: 1.4 million) was perhaps the most dramatic take-off among the seven regions. Though emerging from World War II most committed among the regions to agriculture, usually in the form of the *mezzadria* (sharecropping) the Marche region made an enormous about-face in less than 30 years: In 1951, 60 percent of the region's active population was still engaged in agriculture; by 1981, the proportion had shrunk to 15 percent, while industry employment for the same year accounted for 44 percent of the active work force. Moreover, the accelerating rate of industrialization has been equally impressive: The number of industrial workers, having increased by 41 percent between 1951 and 1971, jumped another 50 percent between 1971 and 1981—a rate of increase for those years exceeded by only 2 of Italy's 17 other regions (Anselmi 1983: 14; Balloni and Vicarelli 1979: 43–47; Mazzoni 1983: 49, 58; Ascoli n.d.).

Though informal industrial districts capitalizing on other preindustrial specialties such as apparel, furniture making, and musical instruments have sprung up, the shoe industry has proved the most important of the local motors of development. In 1987, it accounted for 46 percent of the manufacturing employment and one-quarter of its regional domestic product. Throughout its honeycomb of hill towns, 25 percent of Italy's shoes and 17 percent of its shoe exports are produced (Unione Regionale delle Camere di Commercio delle Marche, 1988b).

In San Lorenzo Marche, the locus of the two-year field study, shoe making is the preponderant economic activity of the town's 7,500 inhabitants. In 1981, 25 shoe factories and 225 small artisan firms officially employed approximately 2,500 workers and also as many as 1,000 additional workers illegally. In 1982, I created a sample of 15 factories and 25 artisan firms, and I have followed their progress through successive re-studies in 1984 and 1987.

THE THIRD ITALY AND DEVELOPMENT THEORY

This extraordinary economic success has attracted a great deal of attention among scholars and planners interested in development and redevelopment. Postwar industrialization of the Third Italy, in fact, has become well known in neoliberal development theory because it is, at once, spontaneous, small-scale, export-led, and flexible in production method; niche-finding in marketing; familial in organization; and petty entrepreneurial in character. This simultaneity of circumstances fit well with an emergent neoliberal critique of advanced capitalist industrial decline and with economic redevelopment remedies for U.S. society. The central-northeastern Italian example received, if anything, more attention relative to its success claims probably because nation-state and monopoly-capitalist involvements were virtually absent—a situation in stark contrast to development by military dictatorship in Latin America or the state-sponsored triumphs of Japan, South Korea, Taiwan, and the city-states of the Pacific Rim (Amsden, 1985; Clammer 1987; Deyo 1987; Islam and Kirkpatrick 1986; Mason et al. 1980).

First highlighted in the United States in early work by Suzanne Berger and Michael Piore (1980), as well as by Charles Sabel (1982), the central-northeastern Italian case featured prominently in Piore and Sabel's influential book, *The Second Industrial Divide* (1984). The Proudhonian vision of successful craft production by egalitarian artisan groups, Piore and Sabel believed, was realized in the postwar industrialization of the Third Italy. These low-tech, mid-tech, and occasionally high-tech Italian versions of California's Silicon Valley and Boston's Route 128 represented important instances of how some advanced capitalist cultures created economic variations more fitting for an increasingly erratic, crisis-prone, and saturated world market.

Their thesis, that the capitalist world economy had reached a "second industrial divide" in which mass production would give way to craft production for more specialized market niches, has achieved a certain widespread currency, in part because it converged in a timely fashion with other neoliberal industrial reform proposals circulating in the early and mid–1980s.[2] U.S. big-city economic development planners, regional research institutes, and progressive trade unions have shown interest in transplanting the Italian notion of the small-scale industrial district populated by petty entrepreneurs and unskilled labor as a possible solution to chronic inner-city unemployment and poverty.[3] Though Piore and Sabel's proposals have been criticized on several grounds (Williams et al. 1987; Stinchcombe 1987), the central-north-eastern Italian example that undergirds the thesis has remained relatively untouched and unexamined. A closer look thus far has been lost among the well-deserved accolades for an Italian economy that is now the sixth most powerful economy in the capitalist world.

RISE AND DECLINE

Some Causes for the Rise

In trying to account for the Third Italy's success, Italian scholars have offered several possibilities.[4] Some have emphasized its neoclassical roots (Fua and Zacchia 1983; Goodman et al. 1989). Others have offered explanations from a political-economic perspective. The contribution of Italy's position as a semiperipheral economy within the international division of labor to the Third Italy's development was analyzed (Paci 1973, 1980, 1982). The relatively unique indigenous linkages between the regions' social formation and small, familial enterprises were examined with great historical care (Bagnasco 1988; Bagnasco, Pini, and Trigilia 1981; Capecchi 1989).

My own research, undertaken since 1981, supports several arguments as to "the reason(s) why." Key neoclassical factors such as expanding markets, underutilized rural labor, and product specialization leading to a comparative advantage offered a partial explanation for the phenomenon. The neo-Marxist emphasis on cheap, easily exploitable peripheral laboring populations fit too. More important was the heritage of area involvement in petty capitalist entrepreneurialism, either through commercialized agriculture in the form of small-plot sharecropping or in proto-industrial handicraft production. Four hundred years of capitalist penetration during the Papal State regime, which ended only with the unification of Italy in 1870, provided perhaps a dubious but nonetheless useful social historical backdrop for post-World War II economic development (Blim 1987, 1990b).

Decline and Its Causes

Even by the time I had begun the first fieldwork in 1981, certain disquieting signs of industrial difficulty in the shoe sector were already apparent. The factory movement—that is, the development of larger, more mechanized, functionally integrated workplaces of 50 workers or more—had crested. Though employment in the Marche region shoe sector between 1971 and 1981 had increased by 80 percent, the proportion of those workers found in factories had declined from 42 percent of the shoe work force in 1971 to 33 percent of the work force in 1981. Further productive decentralization rather than concentration had characterized the shoe boom of the 1970s, as by 1981, artisans with fewer than 20 workers still accounted for over 90 percent of the region's shoe firms (Regione Marche 1982: 48–49; Merli 1984: 144–147).

Even as the Marche shoe industry grew throughout the 1970s horizontally across the coastal plain, past the foothills, and toward the Apennine hinterlands, San Lorenzo Marche, as one of the early microindustrial magnets in the region's development, felt the first shocks of decline. From 1971 to 1981, the number of shoe factories in San Lorenzo Marche tumbled from 51 to 25. At the same time, both the number of artisan shops and the number of workers employed in the shoe sector increased. Consequently, firm size in both industrial and artisan workplaces also dropped noticeably between 1971 and 1981 (Blim 1990b: 117–123, 153–158).

After the 1984 re-study, I concluded that the shoe sector was caught in a devolutive phase of capitalist development. Rising market competition and low rates of investment and technology transfer were stifling innovation and further industrial growth. Continued reliance on undocumented labor and fiscal evasion were blocking industrial rationalization and a more efficient deployment of resources in larger, more capital-intensive firms (Blim, 1990b: 162–171).

By the summer of 1987, the town shoe industry was in total disarray. Regardless of strategy, market, model, or price, full retreat was the order of the day for all save a handful of producers whose success, given the environment, seemed almost anomalous. More factories were closing (by the fall of 1988, 7 of the 15 factories in my industrial sample had closed); owners were buying and marketing shoes and leather made abroad, and were seeking to produce shoes in Brazil, Hong Kong, Mauritius, and southern Italy. Artisan production overall had declined sharply, and small-firm owners were making deals with middling-quality shoe chains in England and the United States to produce shoes designed by the foreign clients at little more than cost. Other artisans under contract to prominent shoe boutique designer labels were being forewarned by their clients to prepare themselves for the time, two

Figure 5.1
Industrial Production, Marche Region, Italy, 1986–1989

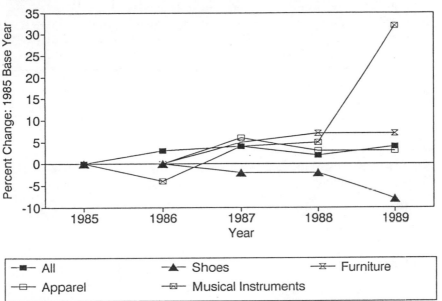

years hence, when all contracts would be shifted to Brazilian producers. To add injury to injury, town producers watched helplessly as the Italian national market was flooded with Asian imports which now claim a 40 percent market share.

The regional shoe industry's decline has been slower, and though more gradual, no less apparent. As the data represented in Figures 5.1 and 5.2 suggest, both shoe production and employment dropped significantly from 1986 through 1989. During the same period, production and employment in the Marche region's other major industries—furniture, apparel, and musical instruments—either stabilized or improved slightly. I will comment on the meaning of the apparent uneven progress of the region's industries later in this chapter.

For the Marche shoe industry, the problem is markets: that is, firms are not finding new markets or holding on to old ones, and this, above all else, is the presenting symptom of their distress. Their price is no longer competitive for the low- and medium-cost markets. Their quality is not on par with established high-end producers in England, the United States, and northern Italy. Some producers have tried to run away to countries with low labor costs, but without success. They lack the capital and the mass-production know-how to manufacture simple, yet technologically sophisticated, shoes with inexperienced, unskilled foreign labor.

Figure 5.2
Industrial Employment, Marche Region, Italy, 1986–1989

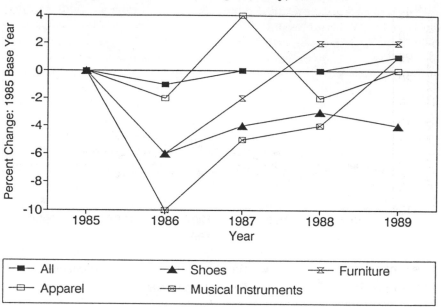

Unemployment, not the chronic underemployment characteristic of a previously subsistence-based sharecropping peasant population, is now common. For the years 1987 through 1989, between 7 and 8 percent of the region's shoe factory work force was drawing unemployment compensation under Italy's *Cassa Integrazione di Guadagni*. Other workers not eligible for unemployment compensation and not counted by any reputable employment index have been idled or have slipped into retirement or into illegal, casual labor for the remaining shoe entrepreneurs. The proportion of those still employed by the shoe industry who are working out of their homes has been increasing steadily, rising from 8 percent of the shoe work force in 1987 to 11 percent in 1988 and 12 percent in 1989 (Unione Regionale Camere di Commercio delle Marche 1988a; 1989, 1990).

In the town of San Lorenzo Marche, skilled male workers whom I had watched for half a dozen years bargain with new employers for under-the-table bounties and monthly bonuses as conditions of employment now searched for work at the plant and workshop gates of the surviving firms or sat drinking in the neighborhood bars. If they were offered work, it was at less than the minimum wage and under the table. Some were encouraged to set up their own shops. By receiving work in this way, their contractors (no longer, technically, their employers) could shift the burden of health, unemployment compensation, and pension costs onto their newfound subcontractors, and perhaps illegally avoid taxation on the products or services as well. Skilled women let go from failing firms either returned to illegal labor or piecework at home, or went into business as artisans, absorbing, like men, the risks of intermittent employment and the costs of their benefits. Unskilled workers of both sexes sought jobs in the town and surrounding villages; given the monocultural economy of the area, jobs outside the shoe business are few and far between.

The working class, only less than a generation ago released from the near servitude of petty sharecropping, has not yet formed a coherent, politically conscious whole and cannot easily avail itself of established organizational support in seeking to reverse economic decline.[5] Workplace organization is difficult: Most factories and workshops are small and composed of kin, friends, and friends of kin. Union militancy, after a 1976 burst of spontaneous energy which resulted in local factory recognition of the national union contract, has faltered badly. Industrial crisis and the diversion of union organizing energies into Italian Communist party regional political activities over the past decade have undermined, if not effectively eliminated, union leadership potential. The regional Italian Communist party (now renamed Democratic Party of the Left), in a search for political dominance, has forsaken labor struggles for fair wages and working conditions and for an end to illegal labor exploitation. Instead, the party has pursued a pro–growth and civic development line, hoping to enlist a multiclass coalition in their causes.

These are the facts of the decline of an industrial monoculture and a particular mode of economic organization by which it flourished. Shoes will continue to be made in volume for some period of time, though the future modus operandi seems to be taking at least two directions simultaneously. First, productive decentralization is accelerating, pulverizing the industry into even more tiny units. This option temporarily lowers labor costs and increases the opportunities for undocumented labor and fiscal evasion. Second, a few producers are radically improving the quality of their work, finding high-end fashion markets, often through a brand name, and employing several hundred workers apiece in world-class production lines. However, the industry, spread in the hands of hundreds of fiscally healthy small firms and employing at progressively higher wages every able-bodied person, directly and indirectly, in the district, probably is finished. Industrial reconversion, probably of a very diffused and heterogeneous sort; growth in the tertiary sector; and emigration of the young educated and professional labor incapable of finding sufficient work in the service sector are among the likely future trends.

UNDERSTANDING DECLINE

The decline of the Marche shoe industry, albeit of crucial importance for the well-being of one of the Third Italy's seven regions, does not undo by itself the central-northeastern Italian economic miracle, though an understanding of its decline might suggest some of the structural frailties to which the flexible specialization model is heir. For the near term, success or failure of each of the Third Italy's informal industrial districts probably depends as much on the secular trends of its particular product sector, the international competition, and the vagaries of the world market itself as it does on the internal structure and operation of the local industry. In this section, I will try to make some more general sense of this sort of household-rooted flexible industrial production system by comparing the decline of the shoe industry with the results obtained by other manufacturing sectors that compose, with shoes, the regional industrial base.

As the data highlighted in Figures 5.1 and 5.2 suggest, the economic outcomes achieved by the region's principal industries have varied considerably over the past several years and are some indication, I believe, of the typical unevenness of microindustrial economic terrains.[6] Let me emphasize at the outset of this analysis that there are no significant differences in the economic or social organization of the various regional manufacturing industries: All are overwhelmingly small-scale and rooted in household production of consumer goods, half of which find themselves for sale on the world market.[7] Hence, the potential discrepancies disclosed, it is argued, are related to the ways in which each industry adapts to the general conditions of the world market and to the specific requirements of its particular world market sector.

First, all Marche region manufacturing production has grown slowly since 1985, as Figure 5.1 indicates. From 1986 to 1989, all manufacturing production increased by only 2 to 4 percent per year. However, the amplitude of the spread among the performances of the various industries has grown significantly over the four-year period. Shoe production has declined steadily—in marked contrast to the other industries, which posted slow but steady gains (furniture); showed dramatic increases (musical instruments); or simply muddled along, albeit on the plus side of the ledger (apparel).

Regional manufacturing employment as a whole, as Figure 5.2 suggests, is stagnating, but the outlook is less stark for some industrial workers as opposed to others. Shoe employment dropped no less than 4 percent a year from 1986 through 1989, while employment in furniture and musical instrument production, after two years of decline,

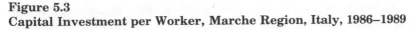

Figure 5.3
Capital Investment per Worker, Marche Region, Italy, 1986–1989

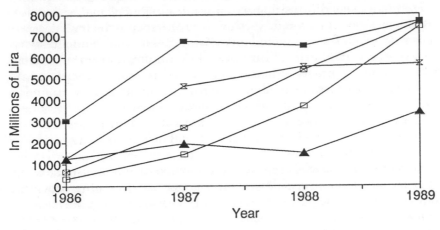

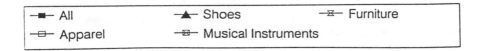

has begun to grow again. Apparel employment, much like its record in output, meanders along, not having declined or grown much over the past four years.

Examination of other data collected on the Marche region manufacturing sector suggests that the paramount problem for the shoe industry is its low level of capital investment. In 1982 (the last year for which these data are available), fixed capital in the regional shoe industry amounted to only 8 percent of total shoe output, some 6 percent below the Marche region manufacturing mean of 14 percent of total output (Italy, Regione Marche 1982: 56, 82). From 1986 through 1989, capital investment per shoe worker did not keep pace with the Marche region industrial investment average: In 1986, it approximated only 41 percent of typical regional industrial capital outlays; in 1987, it constituted only 30 percent of the regional industrial average. After sinking to a four-year low of 23 percent of the investment outlays of all regional industrial manufacturers in 1988, shoe capital investment bounced back to 44 percent of the typical outlay for 1989 (Unione Regionale Camere di Commercio delle Marche 1987, 1988a, 1989, 1990).

Investment patterns for the principal Marche region manufacturing industries, as Figure 5.3 shows, have varied widely from 1986 onward. However, growing investment—except in the shoe industry—seems to be the overall trend. Between 1986 through 1989, investment in the musical instruments and apparel industry climbed steadily, so that by 1989, these expenditures approximated the regional mean. The furniture industry—in 1986, investing, like the shoe industry, at a rate of less than half the regional industrial mean—had climbed incrementally to a 1989 expenditure per worker equivalent to 72 percent of the regional average. In marked contrast, investment per worker in the shoe industry has lagged well behind the industrial mean and in 1989 showed only marginal signs of improvement.

The downward trajectory of the region's shoe industry, when compared with its slow-growing microindustrial neighbors, may have several broader implications. First, small-scale industrial specialization in goods for the world market and the mobilization of households and their kin networks in speeding capital accumulation and in providing a flexible labor supply do not seem to relieve industries of the classical capitalist imperative to increase the capital intensity of their enterprises. Following Marxist or neoclassical economic reasoning, the way out of a declining competitive spiral is to increase productivity through capital investment and to lower unit costs through economies of scale. In particular, assembly lines worldwide in all goods are being transformed and made more flexible and efficient through the use of computer-aided numerically controlled machines (CNC) and computer-assisted design and manufacturing processes (CAD-CAM) that are high-tech spin-offs from advances in the fields of robotics and computers (Noble 1984; United States Congress, Office of Technology Assessment 1984; Colombo 1987). All industries, whether heretofore considered "traditional," such as shoes, or "advanced," such as machine tools, can be expected to undergo high-tech renovations of this sort (Cohen and Zysman 1987; 206; Piore and Sabel 1984: 213–234).

These new technologies, however, have made little impact on the region's shoe industry. Though the regional manufacturing association has undertaken several initiatives to encourage technological innovation, only a few of the several hundred industrial and artisan firms with which I am familiar in San Lorenzo Marche have experimented with state-of-the-art technologies embodied in CNC machines. In the three cases where I have firsthand knowledge, producers use an outside subcontractor for more intricate top-stitching designs on upscale market goods such as boots, which constitute only a fraction of their total output. The technology, as of this writing, is applied as a useful adjunct but not as an integral element in local manufacture. Consequently, the region's workshops and factories have improved their very low rates of productivity only slightly, if at all, during the nine years I have studied them.

If it is reasonable to argue for greater capital investment on the part of the Marche region shoe sector and to note critically the absence of new, computer-driven technologies, it is also important to ask: Why aren't they being used? The short-term answer is that the producers have lost confidence in the near-term survival of their firms. As one informant (an artisan shoe producer with a workshop employing eight persons along with his partner in the manufacture of children's shoes) whom I have known since 1981 told me in the summer of 1990: "I go to all of the shoe machinery trade fairs, and having the machines would be wonderful. Given a market as shaky as this one, how can I take out a large loan? All I would need is for a major customer to withdraw or go bankrupt, and I would lose the machines—and probably the firm." Other informants shared his reservations.

The long-term problem is chronic capital shortage. Small producers, in the main, produce small profits. Only a handful of firms, already prosperous and armed with cash reserves, can afford to take the plunge. For the vast majority, on whom the remarkable burst of regional prosperity depended and who were innovatively inactive during better times, catch-up in a time of crisis appears beyond their ken.

Moreover, at base, the very attributes of the small producers' flexible production system, such as the dispersion of capital risk through sub-contracting and widespread, relatively egalitarian patterns of accumulation, prevent the easy recycling of local capital assets. As firms have failed, their factories—instead of being used by other local producers to increase output—have become abandoned or have been recovered by creditors and leased to wholesalers as warehouses or to retailers for such things as new car agencies.

There is also an inevitable complication arising from the fact that firm profits are also family profits. Typically, the social reproductive needs of the household and kin networks compete with the purely "business needs" such as capital investment in the firm. In the cases of several informants, there have been times when firm needs, reasonably enough, have lost out.

There are distinct disadvantages to small firm size that may increasingly counter the advantage of flexibility. World markets in consumer goods such as shoes are notoriously open, so much so that most late-developing nations usually rely on shoes, apparel, and textiles in the first industrial phases. In the past 15 years, for instance, Taiwan, South Korea, and Brazil have become important world shoe exporters and have provided highly damaging competition for low-cost shoe producers in Spain as well as in central-northeastern Italy. Given a relatively open world market environment for shoes, transnational corporations do not achieve strict monopoly or oligopoly status, but they do make markets for products, influence the development of innovative technologies, absorb the lion's share of capital goods, and exert enormous downward pressure on prices. They also have access to capital markets at lower interest rates, and organize production and distribution networks incorporating small firms such as those found in central-northeastern Italy as dependent producers. Many a San Lorenzo Marche small producer has been picked up by a transnational combine, a sort of mega-putting-out firm, only to be squeezed or dropped in successive years in ways that either bankrupt or endanger the survival of the firm.

To gain leverage in the world market, the region's shoe firms could try to standardize production and coordinate marketing. After all, Marche regional shoe production is substantial: Recall that it accounts for one-quarter of Italy's shoe production and 17 percent of Italy's shoe exports. It would appear, however, that the further pulverization and dispersion of production into the hands of smaller and smaller firms—a trend now at least 10 years old—mitigates against the concentration that is probably necessary to establish the "industrial firm leaders" that are able to innovate in hard times. Furthermore, to counter shifting, unstable market demand and lower margins, the region's producers have already forsaken a series of market niches such as children's shoes that could have served as foci for specialized production and marketing efforts. Finally, I have not yet found any movement on the part of entrepreneurs to forsake the ideology of "making it on your own," which is so essential to petty entrepreneurial development and so evidently successful in the building phase, and which seems now to inhibit cooperative efforts of all sorts among firm owners. Their solution to troubled times thus far has been to pull harder on their bootstraps.

Can labor salvage the situation and launch an industrial reprise? First, it would be necessary for the organizations currently most able to advance worker-based initiatives, the national trade unions and the Communist Party, to articulate a renewal strategy and to mobilize their national political muscle behind a program. State intervention, particularly to make substantial amounts of credit available for capital improvements as well as for buy-outs and the formation of worker-owned cooperatives, would seem critical to success.

Second, an avenue for change must be created. Perhaps the most viable option would be the encouragement of worker-owned cooperatives. The initial advantage of this approach is that current Italian law provides preferential tax treatment for cooperatives, thus enabling worker-owners to retain more earnings while also preserving their jobs. However, absent state support for a renewal of the industry as a whole, the more equitable and innovative solution of worker-owned cooperatives is unlikely to succeed. Unless cooperative workers engage in massive self-exploitation (and given the exploitative edge to laboring in the shoe industry now, it is hard to imagine that much more can be squeezed out of the workers even by the workers themselves), there is no reason to think they will succeed where the petty entrepreneurs did not.[8] Also, because the regional cooperative movement is young and relatively weak, support for a cooperative strategy must come from the shoemaking community and from regional and local governments, no less than from the state and the political forces that influence its industrial policy.

Looking back at the broader issue of the value of flexible specialization for success in a rapidly changing world market, what can be learned from this case? The overarching lesson seems to be that several capitalist rules of the game, however fuzzy, apply to firms large and small, "Fordist" and craft alike. Flexible specialization and the use of adaptable labor pools drawn from households and kin do not override the needs for increasing investment and the capital intensification of production. Also, it would appear that small-scale industries must redress the power imbalances between them and their large-scale, often oligopolistic, competitors by innovative, specialized products that match their resourceful production process. Marketing cooperatives and investment, once again, seem to be important concomitants to a strategy of developing specialized product niches.

It may well be that the global factory now emerging is not what Henry Ford, or Karl Marx for that matter, might have imagined. An analysis of the Marche regional industrial mosaic suggests that small-scale producers for the world market can bend the rules of capitalism to suit their needs—particularly in the beginning. Once in the race for world markets, however, they may ignore the deeper logic of capitalism only at their own peril.

NOTES

The research on which this chapter is based was supported by a Fulbright fellowship and grants from the Wenner-Gren Foundation for Anthropological Research, the Italian Studies Center of the University of Pennsylvania, the Commission of the European Communities, and the Brodolini Foundation. Portions of this chapter appeared in an earlier version published as "Economic Development and Decline in the Emerging Global Factory: Some Italian Lessons," *Politics and Society*, 18, no. 1 (1990), 143–163.

1. The connections between kinship ties and firm operations are strong, as several findings from my study of 40 shoe firms in San Lorenzo Marche reveal. Twelve of the 15 industrial firms were owned and operated by proprietors who were kin to each other. The kin configurations varied from firms controlled by nuclear households and extended households to firms constituted by first cousins. Kin coowners in factory settings usually composed the management and supervisory staff. Among the 25 artisan firms surveyed, 21 were owned and operated among kin, typically by one household, either nuclear or extended.

Taken in sum, 42 percent of the 25 artisan-firm labor force was composed of proprietors and their kin (Blim 1990b: 119–130).

2. Throughout the first five years of the 1980s, there was a plethora of industrial policy schemes presented, of which Piore and Sabel's was one of the more theoretically ambitious. Rohatyn (1981) advocated a new reconstruction finance corporation. Reich and Magaziner (1982) argued for state intervention in the development of a national industrial policy, while Reich (1983) introduced the flexible specialization argument. From the left side of the redevelopment spectrum, Bluestone and Harrison (1982) attempted to bell the capitalist cat with the responsibility for U.S. economic decline. Dahl (1985) attacked the antidemocratic nature of corporate capitalism and endorsed the development of worker-owned and cooperative economic schemes as a more democratic solution for economic policy.

Each of these formulas has influenced policy debates over the course of the 1980s. Piore and Sabel's concept of the "second industrial divide," and particularly their conclusion that the age of mass production is over and that future economic growth will henceforth obey a post-Fordist logic of small-batch production and market segmentation, has been widely cited and often partly accepted, though their view that more cooperative and humane small-scale economic organizations are likely has been treated more skeptically. See Cohen and Zysman (1987: 83, 168, 274nn. 10, 12), Lash and Urry (1987: 196–200, 357 n. 17), and Sirianni (1987: 6–9, 28nn. 16, 20). Piore and Sabel's analysis of the transformed world economy has been incorporated significantly into the recent influential Massachusetts Institute of Technology Commission on Industrial Productivity report on the restructuring of the U.S. economy (Dertouzos et al. 1989: 46–52). Benton (1990) provides a highly useful application of the flexible specialization argument with respect to understanding recent Spanish industrial development.

3. Research conducted under the theoretical rubric of flexible specialization, as interpreted by Piore and Sabel, has proceeded apace. See, for instance, a collection of papers edited by Jonathan Zeitlin, an early collaborator of Sabel, in *Economy and Society* 18, no. 4 (1989). Another collection (Goodman and Bamford with Saynor 1989), analyzes the structure of Italian industrial districts with an eye toward identifying the characteristics that make flexible specialization possible.

4. See Blim (1990a) for a summary.

5. For a useful discussion of the elements entailed by the concept of class formation, see Katznelson (1986: 3–44).

6. The data represented in Figures 5.1 and 5.2 are reported in Unione Regionale delle Camere di Commercio delle Marche (1987, 1988a, 1989, 1990). My thanks to Luis Falcon and Ying Yin for assistance in developing the graphics.

7. The Third Italy's reliance on industrial firms with fewer than 10 employees is matched as well by Italy as a whole. The 1981 Industrial Census shows that 84.7 percent of all industrial firms were composed of fewer than 10 employees (Censis 1984: 56–58).

8. Russell (1984: 253–294) has provided a chastening account of some of the important drawbacks to employee ownership in the U.S. context which suggest

caution in expressing excessive enthusiasm for the cooperative option. There is some danger in the Marche region, too, of the development of "lemon" capitalism resulting from buy-outs of uncompetitive firms made by workers who are unsupported by a general initiative for regional industrial renewal.

6

Spanish Galician Industrialization and the Europe of 1992: A Contextual Analysis

Hans C. Buechler and Judith-Maria Buechler

By taking a regional focus, Hans Buechler and Judith-Maria Buechler show how government policy at different levels, a declining agriculture, and new forms of industrialization interact in rural Spain. Like many of the other contributions, their analysis suggests that industrialization in previously rural areas is not an automatic panacea for problems generated by unequal distribution of wealth.

Industrial development is often regarded as a *Ding an Sich*, a phenomenon that can be treated without considering the sociopolitical and economic framework. In this chapter we shall take a more holistic approach and examine a series of industrial developments that we observed during our fieldwork in Spanish Galicia in the wider contexts of changing political differentiation and integration of the region in the nation state and the European Community, and the changing patterns in agriculture, which, together with fishing, is still the region's major economic sector.

Galicia, a historically marginalized area, is one of the poorest regions of Spain. In 1972–1973, when we first undertook research in the region, Galicia had just recently begun a push toward industrialization. In 1973 only 41 percent of the economically active population worked in salaried employment as opposed to 72 percent in the country as a whole and 85 percent in developed countries (Vence Deza 1986: 160). Nevertheless, this represented an increase of one-third over 1960 and was due largely to a boom in industry and construction. However, the industrial boom was short-lived. Between 1976 and 1983, the years of economic crisis in Spain, industrial employment in Galicia decreased by 33,800, far more than the net employment increase of 21,248 between 1960 and 1973. Even during the boom period, development often meant the establishment of highly polluting industries and the construction of hydroelectric projects that benefited other regions while destroying prime agricultural land. In agriculture only the most onerous tasks were beginning to be mechanized. Moreover, the region's major source of revenue continued to be the remittances from the massive flow of migrants working in Switzerland, West Germany, and other more industrialized European countries. Moreover, like Galician electrical power, a large share of these remittances was also funneled into the more developed areas of Spain.

Two symbolic dates dominate discussions of the future of Galicia and the other Spanish regions: 1992, marking the prospective full economic integration of the Common Market, and 1979, marking the establishment of the first *autonomías*, or autonomous regional governments. In this chapter we shall explore the implications for agriculture and industrialization of the reemergence of Galicia as an autonomous region and its insertion in the larger context of the Common Market.

The Common Market has outlined a bold plan in which the 12 nations involved will form a single economic entity. Should this vision materialize, the economies of Spain and the two other relatively poor newcomers to the Common Market—Greece and Portugal—will, by 1992, be transformed from relative national insularity to multinational integration. The member countries are still jockeying for position in the European Economic Community (EEC). Indeed, many of the premises of the 1992 concept are far from universally accepted. Given these uncertainties, what are the prospects of specific *regions* within these countries? On the one hand, regions will, theoretically, have direct access to the center of economic decision making in Brussels. For Galicia, early indications point to both considerable opportunities and potential further marginalization. The EEC (under pressure from Spain) has already promised to double assistance to disadvantaged regions by 1992, a category under which all regions of Spain are presently included. On the other hand, this increase is unlikely to be enough to change the well-established trend toward increasingly greater disparity between rich and poor regions in the Common Market (cf. Meixide Vecino 1985: 305; Pérez Touriño 1985: 23). In addition, the nations remain the principal economic actors in the EEC. Thus, production quotas for agricultural products subsidized by the EEC are negotiated by each member nation. A country may well sacrifice the well-being of a particular region in return for rulings favorable to the central economic interests of the nation.

At the same time that Spain has entered the European arena, it is in the process of reorganizing its internal political structure as a second step in the transition to democracy. At present, the relationships between nation and region, nation and the traditional subdivisions of the country (i.e., the provinces), region and province, region and municipality, and province and municipality are all in a state of flux. Any economic decision must take into account the intersection of these different levels of economic and political integration.

Spanish social scientists and politicians alike have generally interpreted the formation of *autonomías* entirely as an internal matter. While they disagree about the degree of autonomy that regions should be allowed to have, most agree that decentralization is at the same time a safeguard against fascism and an essential step toward democratization (cf., e.g., Solé Tura 1985: 62–67).

The strengthening of regional identification can, however, also be interpreted as dependent on events in arenas larger than the nation state. Thus, participants in a recent symposium on the role of regions within the Common Market American Anthropological Association (1988) came to the conclusion that membership in the European Economic Community may often promote the opportunities of individual regions, which, thanks to the structure and policies of the EEC, can bypass the nation-states of which they form a part. They may, for example, deal directly with the Common Market government in Brussels (and, one could add, with multinational corporations). Some of the participants argued that this trend has had the additional effects of encouraging individual regions in member countries to stress their unique features and even of furthering the search for regional identity in those areas with historically weak separate identities. At the same time, however, at least one of the members of the same panel stressed the dangers of further marginalization of the poorer segments of Common Market countries (Shutes 1988).

In this chapter we will first explore the direct involvement of the local, provincial, regional, and national levels of government in development. Then we shall investigate the changes in the regional economy as exemplified in agriculture and industry, and in turn relate these changes to one another and to changes in government, this time including the EEC.

DEVELOPMENT AND THE INTERACTION OF DIFFERENT LEVELS OF GOVERNMENT

Returning to Galicia in 1987 after an absence of nine years we were struck by the marked improvement in the road network. The new widened and improved road to Madrid is impressive by any standards. The major cities of El Ferrol, La Coruña, and Santiago are linked by

a divided limited-access throughway that will soon extend to Pontevedra and Vigo. Castiñeiro (a pseudonym), the capital of the district
where we did most of our research, is now also connected to La Coruña
by a wide modern highway, for the planners are aiming to attract
industry into the area. Finally, even the most isolated hamlets, some
of which could only be reached after long hikes in the early 1970s, are
now linked to the major highways by a maze of mostly asphalted or
at least hard-surfaced roads. Improvements in the electricity net and
the (still incipient) extension of the telephone services have followed
suit.

Further inquiry revealed that these and other changes had been
initiated on various governmental levels. An understanding of the
political dynamics involved in instituting these changes requires a
brief exegesis into the complex changes set in motion after the death
of General Francisco Franco.[1]

The process of democratization entailed a redefinition of the relationships between different levels of government. Foremost in this
process of restructuring was the question of regional autonomy. The
new process of according regional autonomy is based, in part, on the
concept of "historic regions" which, in turn, is rooted in the fact that
many regions of Spain were once independent kingdoms or city-states
and were accorded more rights in earlier experiments at decentralization. As a corollary, the regions are not necessarily accorded identical
rights, nor, indeed, do they follow identical procedures to acquire autonomous status. There has been and continues to be considerable
disagreement and shifting of positions among the various political parties about the degree of independence that should be accorded to the
regions. The final statutes governing *autonomías* have left many areas
open to interpretation and ample room for political maneuvering both
on the part of individual regions and on the part of the central government. Hence, it may take a long time for the *autonomías* to take
their final form.

Also far from finalized is the position accorded to the provinces (especially where these do not coincide with the *autonomía*). Some of our
informants felt that the central government has taken advantage of
these uncertainties to bolster support for the ruling party. In 1987,
some Galician provinces were governed by the Socialists, the party in
power in Madrid, while until August of that year the conservative
Alianza Popular (AP) party held power in Santiago, the capital of
Galicia. Our informants attributed the dynamic role of the provincial
government of La Coruña in road construction to the central government support they were able to muster because of their party
affiliation.[2]

Whatever the merit of these criticisms may be, the massive increase in public works also shows that now regional as well as provincial governments are clearly being held more accountable for their actions or lack thereof than they were during the dictatorship. The province of La Coruña was regarded by some informants as particularly responsive to the needs of the rural population. Unlike the provincial government of Pontevedra which was deemed to be more interested in urban than rural development, the governor of La Coruña has apparently earmarked three-quarters of the budget for the *aldeas* (rural hamlets).

Local governments have also become more responsive to requests for infrastructural development, requests that are becoming increasingly frequent as funds have become more available. While some Galicians continue to complain that such amenities as roads and telephone lines still depend heavily on patronage ties, most agree that local politicians are far more active than in the past.

The final shape of Galician politics on all levels of government must await the completion of the structure of the Xunta (regional government). In 1988 this process was far from complete. Slowed down by partisan politics, Xunta politicians seem more intent in shaping the *autonomía* government to their own advantage than addressing current issues and defending the interests of Galicia in the national and EEC arenas, a luxury that the region may not be able to afford, given the rapid pace of events.

GALICIAN AGRICULTURE AND THE COMMON MARKET

The reorganization of the power structure in these areas and the success of integration into the EEC must ultimately be judged by their ability to alleviate economic hardship, particularly the high rate of unemployment. It has been estimated that 13.5 percent of the economically active persons in Galicia were out of work in 1986, and unemployment in the region has risen more rapidly than in the country as a whole. The changes that are being brought about in agriculture through Spanish integration into the Common Market have so far aggravated, rather than alleviated, unemployment in the area.

The transformation of Galician agriculture provides examples of the subordination of regional concerns to national and Common Market interests with only token attempts at providing longer-term solutions to regional problems. In order to enter the Common Market, Spain was forced to make some major concessions. One was the reduction of dairy farming, the predominant agricultural activity in Galicia, which was in direct competition with well-established Common Market partners and was not deemed of vital concern to the country's economy. From the 1960s on, dairy farming had enjoyed the stimulus of generous federal subsidies. Not only were these eliminated from one day to the next, but small dairy farmers are now actively discouraged from raising or even maintaining production. Retired farmers are not allowed to sell milk in their own name while collecting pensions. Younger farmers are given monetary incentives if they agree to sell their dairy cows and keep the land out of dairy production for 10 years. Those who promise to do so for three generations are paid a sum equivalent to 10 years of continued production. Marginal milk producers, (i.e., those without refrigerated tanks or whose milk has a low fat content or a high bacterial count) face price penalties. In one of the hamlets of Santa María, a parish we studied intensively in 1971 and revisited in 1974, 1978, and 1987, only seven households, most of whom had already built modern cement barns, had retained herds of the same size as before. The remainder had substantially reduced their herds or given them up entirely.

However, there are some countervailing tendencies. A large milk-processing plant owned by a farmer cooperative has continued to expand and diversity its production, in part with financial support from the autonomous government of Galicia (cf. Buechler 1989). Moreover, the autonomous government and farmer groups are still trying to prevail on the government and the Common Market to increase the milk quota.

Possible answers to Galicia's dilemma are being sought on many different levels. The individual farmer has faced the decreasing support of dairy farming and the spiraling cost of such inputs as fertilizer by boosting production through increased mechanization, including group purchases of farming equipment that can be shared with neighbors. Nevertheless, production costs are high because plots are small and dispersed, so even those machines that are shared with others stand idle most of the time. The second land concentration program, which was initiated in 1987, may alleviate land dispersal to some extent, but it is unlikely to be enough.

A new, more technologically sophisticated, level of subsistence farming has come into existence. In the past, when Antonio and Celia García came back from Switzerland and wanted to buy a freezer, the people in the store in the municipal capital said that in Spain one ate fresh meat. Disgusted, the couple turned around and left, saying that if the store did not want to sell freezers, that was their problem. Now, even the poorer households have freezers to store pork, which was traditionally salted, and other fresh produce that used to be available only in season. Moreover, farmers are increasingly slaughtering and freezing their own calves rather than selling them on the market. As one small-scale farmer put it: "If you go to the butcher, he will charge you

500 pesetas per kilo of veal, while you will only get 200 pesetas. You pay [more than] double and a kilo of meat is barely enough for three persons." This family relies on the husband's pension money and income from the wife and daughter's sewing in addition to farming. They even purchase some of their meat in the market. Under such circumstances, gearing their farm production primarily toward subsistence makes a lot of sense.

Conversely, many farmers are also experimenting with new forms of market-oriented production from tomatoes and kiwi fruit to quail and bison. They are also obviating the climatic limitations on agriculture by constructing plastic greenhouses in which lettuce, tomatoes and other vegetables can be grown throughout the year. Finally, there are simpler ways of adapting to the changing situation, most of which are geared toward labor inputs. Wheat is once again cultivated more extensively, not so much because it is lucrative but because it requires no hand labor and at least keeps the fields from becoming overgrown with weeds. Moreover, the tractor has replaced the cow-drawn plow even for such tasks as planting potatoes.

The *autonomía* intervenes in these activities in a number of ways. It subsidizes tractor fuel and fosters the construction of plastic greenhouses by contributing a considerable share of the cost (20 percent of the cost of a greenhouse, for example). The main problem seems to be commercializing the new crops. Reliable marketing channels have yet to be secured. One farmer who experimented with soy beans was rewarded with a bumper crop but was unable to sell them. The soybean distributors were tied in to North American suppliers and had no interest in the local crop. Attempts to shift dairy farming to veal production has faced similar barriers. Middlemen shun locally fattened calves, preferring to purchase very young animals and prepare them for market in the east of Spain. Some farmers hope that such monopolies will be reduced with the greater liberalization of markets in the Common Market of 1992.

The specter of 1992 has also generated a new involvement of U.S. firms. Fearful of being excluded from the Common Market, one U.S. firm has rented a large tract of common land to experiment with different varieties of soybeans for eventual export within the market. The project has received substantial assistance from the *autonomía*.

An overly narrow focus on agriculture would make one lose sight of the fact that rural Galician households commonly supplement and combine agriculture with other activities and sources of income: small service enterprises, temporary and permanent wage labor at home and abroad, unemployment benefits, and pensions. These multiple sources have permitted Galicians to manage to get along.

THE PROCESS OF INDUSTRIALIZATION

In view of declining agriculture and the reduction of opportunities of migrating abroad—the traditional safety valve for economic pressures in the region—it is not surprising that rural Galicians are becoming increasingly involved in the process of industrialization. The last few years have seen the collapse of the shipbuilding industry. At the same time, however, a number of other industries have emerged.

Some of these processes of industrialization are based on distinctive features of the local economy. We have already mentioned the expansion of milk processing. A second example is the renaissance of the garment industry. While at least one antiquated clothing factory has been forced into bankruptcy, several new or restructured ones based on the Italian/Mexican model of combining factory-based mass manufacture with (often clandestine) home industry have emerged. This system of production gives a firm considerable flexibility to both adapt to seasonal demand and increase the variety of garments that can be produced simultaneously. Spearheaded by a family firm of designer/producers in the city of Santiago, whose clothing is already well known nationally, the garment industry has grown very rapidly in recent years. By 1987 the industry was even publishing its own fashion magazine, *Galicia Moda*.

One of the largest firms of this kind, which is based in Arteijo, employs some 750 assembly-line workers and an estimated additional 5,000 people working either in smaller semi-independent factories or full- or part-time at home. In 1986, total sales amounted to more than 15 million pesetas.[3]

The core of the firm is constituted by eight factories, each with its own name and management and founded at a different time since 1964, and a chain of stores specializing in the production and sale of low-cost but fashionable garments, partly of its own design. The factories that form the core of the firm produce those items, such as men's shirts, that can be made in large volume and are not sensitive to changing demand. They also make the designs and do the cutting for all garments.

The dependent factories range from declining older plants whose services are enlisted whenever the need arises to dynamic newcomers who also work directly for individual stores and chains and may simultaneously be involved in the retail trade. One such operation, located in the small town of Castiñeiro, even exports clothing to Germany. It was founded by Mr. Alvarez, who had worked in France for four years. After his apprenticeship in Spain he was introduced to the manufacture of ready-made clothing by a Basque refugee near

Paris, where he later worked in a small factory. He also had a three-year stint in a factory in Berne, Switzerland, manufacturing military uniforms. When Mr. Alvarez returned to Castiñeiras around 1972, he set up one of the first clothing workshops in the town. Today he has a small factory where he works with eight young women, three apprentices and five who have been trained in specialized institutes subsidized by the government of Galicia. The apprentices are also subsidized by the *autonomía* which pays 75 percent of their wages. To be eligible for this benefit, an employer must agree to hire an apprentice for the full two-year duration of the apprenticeship. An individual may even take a course administered by an academy in her own home. Mr. Alvarez gives classes to such persons in his factory. Since work is seasonal, only two of the workers work for him on a year-round basis; all the others have seasonal contracts.

Mr. Alvarez sells clothing in his own retail store, to other small retailers, to large chain stores, and to other factories. Often he works with designers from the factories and wholesalers from whom he obtains subcontracts. From the firm in Arteijo he receives precut garments. Aware of the scarcity of Galician designers, he has sent his son to a newly established school for design and pattern production, for he expects Galician clothing design to become as well known in the EEC as it already is in Spain.

Entry into the Common Market is only slowly leading to changes in the Arteijo factory's involvement in the international market. Thus, the firm would like to import German fabrics whose coloration is more even than Spanish ones, but until now only token amounts were imported because some de facto barriers remain in place.

Unlike Mr. Alvarez, most other clothing producers in Castiëiras appear to be clandestine operations that send their in-house workers out the back door every time a municipal official knocks at the front door. These firms cut garments in a central location and then distribute them to homeworkers or merely act as middlemen and assembly points for large factories.

The Arteijo firm also hires such homeworkers either directly or through middlemen. Most of the homeworkers come from rural communities or small towns, where there are few employment opportunities that pay more than the minimum wage. A large part form part of producer cooperatives, most of which were originally established by priests in the province of Orense. In addition to protection from exploitation by intermediaries, cooperatives have the advantage of lower contributions for social security than individuals. The rest work for entrepreneurs or for seamstresses who also sew. The large number of skilled seamstresses in the Galician countryside provides a valuable base for the industry.

One such seamstress, Remedios Fraga, told us that she would still have plenty of work if she took on individual clients but that she could earn more working for the factory because her productivity was higher. Working as a homeworker for a factory has meant considerable changes in Mrs. Fraga's mode of operation. She is often forced to work very long hours to meet deadlines: Not uncommonly, she toils 15 hours a day and, if she has other things to do, often overnight. She works much harder than she used to. Before, she had no fixed schedule. Many years ago (probably in the 1950s), when she began working as a seamstress, she used to go to work in other people's homes, where she might work for about 8 hours. Later, when she worked at home, she might work 12 hours on some days and not at all on days when she took care of household chores. At the time, she did not feel compelled to work every day. Even if someone wanted a garment finished urgently, it could still wait an extra day. She also had much less work. "But I also did not earn what I am earning today. Life followed a different rhythm. Being a seamstress was different." Mrs. Fraga expresses a lot of loyalty to the company. She says proudly that for the first time, if necessary, her family could live from her work alone. The improvement in her standard of living was apparent from the fact that she has built a beautiful new kitchen since we last visited her in 1978.

In addition to changes in the work schedule, Mrs. Fraga has also experienced other changes. She not only sews herself, she also earns from supervising less experienced workers in the hamlet. She prefers to work with young girls because she finds it difficult to tell older women, especially those who have sewn a lot, that they are making mistakes. However, older women apparently also work for her.

From Remedios Fraga's perspective, her transition from independent artisan to homeworker/manager has been a positive experience. This point of view is not shared by all such workers. For one thing, Mrs. Fraga has no children and can thus allocate longer hours to her work. In addition, she benefits from the fact that her husband pays less for electricity because he works for an electric company. She is also covered by his health insurance. Many of her coworkers are not so covered and, at the same time, they can ill afford the available individual coverage which, according to Mrs. Fraga, would entail the payment of a premium of some 16,000 pesetas per month.

For example, when Mrs. Vazquez, an elderly resident of Santa María whose career is very similar to that of Mrs. Fraga, became ill, her family had difficulties making ends meet. Although her medical expenses were covered by her husband's farm insurance, they sorely missed her income, all the more so because Mr. Vazquez has not been able to work for wages for the past five years because of chronic illness and is barely able to help on the family farm. In spite of the fact that he had worked for a long time in construction and had also paid into the farmer's insurance benefits fund, he had only recently been able to obtain invalid insurance benefits. Sewing skirts brings in some 30,000 pesetas a month before subtracting some 5,000 to 6,000 pesetas for electricity and without counting amortization for two industrial sewing machines, the more powerful of which is presently worth 200,000 pesetas. This is far less than the 50,000 pesetas per month that she estimates she would earn if she worked in a clothing factory, where she would also have unemployment insurance and one month's vacation, but it is three or four times what she earned just two years earlier when she was engaging in homework for a firm in Castiñeiras, a job she had held for the six previous years. Also, as Mrs. Vazquez puts it: "One has to include into one's calculations the fact that one is at home, that one does not have to go anywhere and even if it is not much, it still is welcome." Fortunately, their twenty-one-year-old daughter, who also sews, lives with them; she contributes to the household and helps with the farm work. In addition, the Vazquezes can rely on their neighbors for help. In return, Mrs. Vazquez sews whatever they need without charge. The factory closes for a month in the summer, which gives her plenty of time for this neighborly duty. As a result the family produces much of what they eat.

Given the unfavorable conditions, it is not surprising that many women engage in homework only when they have no other alternative. The case of one farmer from the area around Castiñeiras may serve as an example of sporadic involvement in homework. She decided to take in work from a factory in Arteijo when her husband came back from his last stint in Switzerland and was out of work, for the family could not subsist on agriculture alone. Unlike Mrs. Fraga and Mrs. Vazquez, who have the cut pieces delivered to their homes, she would have to pick up the work personally in Arteijo unless the factory had a lot of work, and, like the other women, she had to provide her own sewing machine as well as the thread. It meant working many hours and with no insurance. Having worked for a long time in Switzerland under better conditions, she felt badly exploited. Therefore, as soon as her husband found regular work, she stopped sewing and concentrated all her efforts on farming again. For women, then, past work experiences and family configurations influence present work strategies and consciousness.

Our research suggests that subcontracting certainly must be seen as a way in which capital controls and cheapens female labor, but the female labor force maintains some control by assuming a managerial role, combining the work with reproductive tasks and subsistence farming, or moving in and out of the labor pool according to household needs or at different stages of the domestic cycle.

Our third example illustrates the place and prospects of a smaller, town-based plastics factory. It was set up by three siblings, one hamlet neighbor, and an acquaintance from elsewhere in the province who pooled their labor and financial resources and obtained substantial bank credit and support from the autonomous government for a total investment of between 50 and 60 million pesetas. The loan/subsidy from the *autonomía* was predicated on the creation of new workplaces. The factory also benefited from the tolerance of the municipal government with respect to the plant's environmental impact.

The firm's founders have transferred many of the values that traditionally governed rural family enterprises to the firm. Sofía, one of the three Garcia siblings who used to farm and still helps run a family store cum bar in a hamlet nearby experiences the conflict between working for profit as the sales manager and secretary of the firm and providing a community service. She regards the bar/store as unprofitable and very difficult to manage simultaneously with the household and the factory job. In addition, she considers the bar a bad influence on her sons, the older of whom takes care of customers when not in school. However, her mother, who is also active in all the family ventures run from their home, worries about the fate of the village drunks if they can no longer find asylum in the bar. One Sunday, when the family went to the beach and closed shop, she became nervous and, indeed, when they came home, two of the regulars were standing forlornly in front of the locked door. In many ways Sofía has transferred these values to her factory job. Neither she nor her brother Gerardo, who is the manager, receive any compensation for their countless hours of overtime. The fact that improving her standard of living is not her only, and perhaps not even the principal, motivation in her involvement in the factory becomes apparent by the fact that she has been offered double or triple her present salary by another factory. She sees her long hours and relatively poor recompense as a service to her kin, just as the bar/store and telephone provide a community service.

The ideology of work as a service to the extended family, which is held primarily, but not only, by women, and the value placed on controlling an enterprise of one's own, which is held more by the men, in turn have measurable benefits for the survival of the firm. The manager is well aware of the fact that one of the reasons why their firm can compete with larger ones is their lower management costs. Individuals without a personal stake in the firm cannot be expected to make the kind of sacrifices necessary to launch this kind of venture. Thus, the only outsider that the firm ever hired, a technician who was familiar with its machinery, left after only a year because of burnout and disagreements with the manager. Newer equipment also decreases labor costs. In addition, Gerardo regards an excess of workers as one of the principal problems of traditional Spanish factories. As a result of their strategies, the factory's labor costs amount to only some 10 percent of total expenditures, while those of other firms reaches 23 percent. The goal in this case is not primarily to cheapen each unit of labor by mechanization but to maintain control over the firm by keeping the work relations constant.

A smaller firm can also respond to demand with more flexibility. This does not mean, however, that the firm is geared toward clients with less demand nor toward a regional market. Rather than viewing the firm's role as a provider to small enterprises in whom the larger firms have little interest, Gerardo sees the role of the factory as a provider of expensive but high-quality goods and better service. He prefers larger firms as clients, and has successfully courted national corporations located all over Spain. At the same time, this fact has not fostered an elitist attitude. Instead, both siblings foster all ties that have the potential of promoting the enterprise. While Gerardo spends a lot of time with powerful business executives, he often obtains addresses of promising potential customers by talking to taxi drivers. His years as a salesman have given him a sixth sense about nonverbal cues in dress and comportment that indicate an individual's occupation which enables him to strike up conversations wherever he happens to be. This personal approach extends to periodic visits to regular clients. Similarly, Sofía spends a lot of time on the telephone enquiring about individuals whom she has never met in person.

The traditional personalistic concerns for coparticipants in the firm extend to working conditions. Both Sofía and Gerardo expect the firm to invest considerable capital in providing a better working environment. While many firms still load and unload trucks by hand, they have already purchased an expensive forklift. The forklift provides a job for a responsible, hardworking older brother who has a bad back. Their plans for the future also involve further modifications to improve working conditions, including heating and ventilation. However, these moves are also made and planned because, in the long run, they are expected to increase productivity. The improvement in controlling the temperature in the factory will also improve the quality of the product and the reliability of the machinery.

Given the fact that the firm was able to amortize its entire bank debt in two years, the factory has done very well. Profits for 1987 were estimated at between 25 and 30 million pesetas. Gerardo figures net profit at 15 percent, which he hopes to further increase by installing another plastic sheet-making machine and another cutter that would require only one additional worker.

The projected more-integrated Common Market of 1992 should enable factories like this to import raw materials more reasonably, secure additional credit earmarked for poorer regions and for small- and medium-sized firms (Castro Cotón 1985: 406), and benefit from programs geared towards retraining special-sector workers, former migrants, and displaced farmers. Indeed, the European Community Commission has specifically decided to foster small and medium enterprises in predominantly rural areas (European Community Commission 1988).[4] Moreover, returned migrants may be able to use their skills, entrepreneurial abilities, and ties established abroad to open new markets.

Regardless of the economic prospects of firms like the ones discussed, the direction they are taking is unlikely to improve income distribution. While sewing cooperatives may have thwarted exploitation by middlemen, cooperativism has not increased wage rates beyond the minimum. Similarly, the active involvement of members of farm families in factory management has not changed the basic fact that most of the fruits of their labor are earmarked for those with the largest investments in the company and it is they who will benefit most from the subsidies conceded by the autonomous government by increasing the assets of each member in proportion to his or her investment in the firm. Women remain in a disadvantaged position vis-à-vis men in such firms because of their familiar obligations. Thus, even if Sofía decided to put pressure on her business partners to increase her salary, the fact that she would probably have to commute a considerable distance to find more lucrative employment would diminish her leverage. As *la de casa* (the child—at present, usually the daughter—who stays at home and takes care of her parents in their old age), her geographical mobility is limited. Finally, some of the industrial changes may not provide stable employment. Thus, programmable machines may eventually lead to the demise of the putting-out system of clothing manufacturing. The Italian experience with the shoe industry suggests that such industries may also practically disappear altogether from an entire region (see Chapter 5 in this volume).

CONCLUSION

The processes of Galician industrialization are best viewed in the context of the manifold changes that this marginal, predominantly agricultural region has experienced during the last decades. A more focused approach would not have shown the intimate linkage between industrial promotion and the blooming of local political action which, in turn, is dependent on the processes of regional autonomy and its countertrends which are manifested in the national government's new interest in the provinces which form a part of state-controlled political hierarchies. At the same time, industrial development is tied more directly to the economic policies of the fledgling *autonomías*. Similarly, the growth of the garment industry based on out-work must be placed into the context of agricultural decline which, in turn, is influenced by rising labor and input costs as well as the agricultural policies of the Common Market. In what follows we shall summarize the major socioeconomic and sociopolitical developments observed and relate them to industrial development in more detail. More specifically, let us examine the role of marginal regions in the Common Market and its repercussions on industrial development.

From the perspective of Galicia, the expansion of interaction spheres in Western Europe may not promote regionalism and regional economic advancement as maintained by the members of the symposium mentioned earlier. Historically, linkages with larger economic theaters have certainly been a factor in promoting regional identity in Spain. Catalonia, like other Mediterranean city-states, gained its strength through pan-Mediterranean commerce. Even Galicia itself based its medieval identity on contacts with distant Flanders. In the case of Catalonia, it is plausible to argue that its present strong regionalism is a renewed attempt at capitalizing on its geographic position and historical links with other European countries to maximize its position within the EEC. However, in marginal regions of Spain, like Galicia, it is difficult to argue that the process of formation of *autonomías* has been strongly influenced by the region's wish to gain a more direct access to European centers of power. It may, in fact, be more plausible to predict that the region will be doubly marginalized: within the nation and within the European Economic Community.[5] At this stage, Galician regional identity is still largely predicated on redefining its position vis-à-vis Madrid.

However, this does not mean that Galicians are not actively attempting to address the problems brought about by Spain's entry into the Common Market. On the contrary, our examples of farmers and industrial producers show that Galicians have taken major steps to find a role in the Europe of 1992, a process that demands that they adapt simultaneously on a variety of levels of sociocultural integration.

In agriculture, government policies aimed at reducing dairy farming have certainly had a major impact. The need of women to supplement agriculture with sewing for the garment industry may be regarded as a direct effect of these policies. On the other hand, farmers have often been able to resist some of these pressures through subterfuge, and, more positively, through the adoption of technologically sophisticated subsistence strategies. They are also experimenting with new forms of market-oriented production, including new crops and food products. Thus, local agricultural initiatives may, albeit at a considerable cost, partially counterbalance detrimental state policies and the autonomous government's lack of concern.

Perhaps the very fact that Galician agriculture has been marginalized in the past may paradoxically give small-scale farmers more leeway in making production decisions. The previous government-promoted move into dairy farming was generally *not* debt-dependent. Even when credit was obtained—usually by farmers with at least 20 to 30 head of cattle—it was short-term credit, often at subsidized rates, and has now been mostly paid off (see also Sullivan 1979: fn. p. 217, Harding 1984: 130). As a result one can, at the very least, expect that the smallholders will not be forced to sell off their land to large farmers at unfavorable prices and thus obviate the process described by Gröger (1979) for rural France. The unpredictable nature of government policies (e.g., their assiduous promotion of dairy farming only to attempt to dismantle it again) is likely to make farmers wary of putting all their eggs into the same basket or to risk becoming too heavily indebted. Their experience has already lead them to resist being forced out of dairy farming.

Some of the same mechanisms are operating in industry as well. The prevalence of short-term over long-term loans may lead to the failure of some new industries during the first years of their existence, but may provide the ones that survive with greater flexibility to weather market fluctuations thereafter. A reliance on homeworkers who can be dismissed without notice rather than on capital-intensive mechanization is an additional mechanism for increasing such flexibility. Similarly, risk may be devolved to smaller or older factories which, in turn, would have to maintain a particularly high degree of flexibility as they would bear the brunt of an economic downturn.

As indicated by the training grants, grants to factories for new jobs created, and even the bending of local zoning regulations that were observed in our case studies, the role of local and regional governments appears to be more favorable to industry than to agriculture. Indeed, industrial development is regarded as a high-priority concern.

In summary, it is plausible to argue that marginality has encouraged both multiple and conservative economic strategies in both agriculture and industry, a fact that may, in turn, facilitate survival in the Europe of 1992. Ultimately, the success of these adaptive strategies will depend heavily on a strong and directed regional government as well as a national and Common Market commitment to a policy of more even regional development. Although some progress has been made, much remains to be done. Our contribution to this problem is to begin to spell out and unravel the multiple levels of renegotiation, from the bindividual to the state, that are involved in understanding European integration and its relation to industrialization from a Galician perspective.

NOTES

Research on which this article is based was carried out between 1972 and 1987. It was supported by grants from the Swiss National Science Foundation, Syracuse University, and Hobart and William Smith colleges.

1. In addition to interviews with local politicians and a careful reading of newspaper reports during our stay in Galicia and Madrid between August and December 1987, this discussion is based on an unpublished paper by Stephanie Buechler, 1987.

2. However, as José Cazorla has pointed out (personal communication, 1989) loyalty to the Socialist party does not necessarily mean privileged status. Thus regions like Andalusia, which are staunch supporters of the PSOE (Socialist party), are often taken for granted by the central government and so receive little government attention.

3. In mid-1987 the exchange rate to the U.S. dollar was 120 pesetas.

4. In addition to their job creation potential, the interest in small- and medium-sized firms may also be related to the slowdown of the economic growth in big firms.

5. Thus, Keating and Jones (1985, p. 6) argued that community competition policy has been in the interest of the economically powerful German *Länder* but has had severe effects on the economy of marginal northern Ireland.

7

The Unexpected Entrepreneurs: Small High-Technology Firms, Technology Transfer, and Regional Development in Wales and Northeast England

Douglas Caulkins

As in the chapters by Lessinger and by Smart and Smart, Douglas Caulkins focuses on capitalists. Unlike their analyses, however, his emphasis is on differentiation among high-technology entrepreneurs in small firms and regional development and policy aimed at peripheral areas of Europe.

During the past decade the officials of many economically stagnating regions in North America and Europe have looked on new high-technology industries as a means of reversing their economic fortunes (Amin and Goddard 1986: 1–22; Breheny and McQuaid 1987; United States Congress: Office of Technology Assessment 1984; Williams 1985: 117–135). "Every city in the advanced industrial world, it now seems, is struggling to open its science park as the answer to decaying steel mills and rusting automobile plants," mused Hall and Markusen (1985: vii). This effort is particularly notable in the United Kingdom (U.K.), where government policies have encouraged the development of high-technology industry as a means of creating employment in the deindustrialized peripheral regions of Wales, Scotland, and the North of England (Hall 1985: 41; Martin 1986: 253; Monck 1985). The initial successes in creating a new electronics industry in these regions came about through inward investment by foreign and multinational corporations, predominantly U.S. and Japanese. These corporations were anxious to establish branch assembly plants within the European Economic Community (EEC) market area in order to avoid import tariffs and take advantage of government grants and other investment incentives (Sayer and Morgan 1987: 22–27). More than most industrial economies, the United Kingdom is dominated by multinationals (Cowling 1986). To mitigate this economic vulnerability and to promote a truly indigenous electronics industry within the deindustrialized regions, British policymakers have increased support for small start-up firms directed by British entrepreneurs. Many authorities are convinced that new, small firms (with 2 to 50 employees) are more likely than large, well-established corporations to provide the kind of industrial innovation and rapid growth in employment needed to launch and sustain an economic regeneration (Breheny and McQuaid 1987; Oakey 1985: 114; Rothwell and Zegveld 1982; Williams 1985: 92–122). This policy emphasis on small business is a response, first, to optimistic but controversial research on the job-generating capacity of small firms (Birch 1987: 96; Keeble and Wever 1986: 24–25; Oakey and Rothwell 1986: 258; Storey 1986) and, second, to the ideological commitment of the Margaret Thatcher government to an "enterprise culture" (Ritchie 1991) that celebrates the individualistic, hard-working entrepreneur as a new cultural hero. Lord Young of Graffham (1985: 15), the secretary of state for employment, has argued that Britain should have a change of culture so that "the importance of enterprise, small firms, and new technology to wealth creation and employment are universally recognized." The high-technology entrepreneur who develops and markets new computer or electronic products is particularly revered in this ideology. Unfortunately for regional development policy, however, new high-technology firms are not attracted to old industrial areas but cluster in different regions entirely, a tendency illustrated by the development of the Silicon Valley semiconductor industry in California (Hall and Markusen 1985: 144–147). The United Kingdom's most extensive concentration of high-technology firms developed along the M11 and M4 motorways between Cambridge, London, and Bristol (Breheny and McQuaid 1987: 316–324). A region of comparative prosperity, this part of Southeast England benefits from a high rate of defense contract spending and a high concentration of skilled technical workers, industrial services, and corporate headquarters (Breheny, Cheshire, and Langridge 1985). Unexpectedly, however, we find a small but growing number of new, high-tech entrepreneurs in the deindustrialized peripheries of the U.K. outside Southeast England.

Who are these British entrepreneurs? In this chapter I examine the career patterns of 31 high-technology entrepreneurs, founders of small electronics and computer firms, in two peripheral regions of the United Kingdom: Mid Wales and the Northeast of England.[1] I pose three questions: Are there discernible career patterns for these indigenous entrepreneurs? Do the contrasting regions of Mid Wales, which is predominantly rural, and Northeast England, which is more urban and industrial, attract different kinds of entrepreneurs? Are some kinds of firms and their owner/managers more successful in promoting technology transfer than others? As will become apparent, these entrepreneurs, mainly engineers and technicians, are "unexpected" in at least two senses. First, most of them anticipated careers working for others rather than founding their own firms. Second, as will be shown in detail, neither of the regions has the cultural and economic conditions considered supportive of new firm formation (Storey 1982: 193–202; Segenberger and Loveman 1987: 101 quoted in Hudson 1989: 23).

DEINDUSTRIALIZATION AND HIGH-TECH REINDUSTRIALIZATION

Northeast England

The Northeast of England "currently is, and for the foreseeable future will remain, an industrial wasteland" according to geographer Ray Hudson (1986: 169). Certainly, the region between the Tyne River on the north and the Tees on the south no longer possesses the industrial base of heavy engineering, shipbuilding, and coal mining for which it was noted during the nineteenth and early twentieth centuries. Between 1979 and 1987, employment in manufacturing declined by 35.9 percent (Smith 1989: 133). Historically a region of large firms, the Northeast is now dependent on multinational corporations, particularly in petrochemicals, for much of the local employment. The present study focuses on areas in the central and southern part of the region, County Durham and the enterprise zone in Middlesbrough in adjacent County Cleveland.

Employment in coal mining in County Durham declined from a high of 170,000 in 1923 (Bulmer 1978: 150) to under 8,000 in 1987. Consett, the center of the steel industry in the county for 140 years, underwent massive unemployment when the British Steel Corporation closed down the mill in 1980 (Smith 1989: 132). Middlesbrough, in the neighboring county of Cleveland, had a thriving steel industry until the 1960s. Following the decline of this technologically obsolete industry, the unemployment rate in Middlesbrough rose to 20 percent, among the highest in the mainland United Kingdom. To counter this problem of industrial obsolescence, central government policies encourage "indigenous development in general and technological innovation in particular" (Amin and Goddard 1986: 8). Indeed, the most tangible evidence of this strategy in the Northeast is the new Computer Aided Design and Manufacture (CADCAM) Centre, which rises like a steel and glass phoenix from the rubble on the former site of the mills along Middlesbrough's industrial waterfront. This location was recently designated an Enterprise Zone, with tax advantages to attract private development to the area. The purpose of the CADCAM Centre, with its associated small factory units each linked to the central computer, is to help transfer or diffuse the latest industrial computer technology to local industry so that it can better compete in the global economy. Consett too has a series of new industrial parks, where advanced technology is strongly encouraged. Other important institutions for the regeneration of the region include the Mountjoy Industrial Research Laboratory at the University of Durham and the two New Towns of Peterlee and Newton Aycliffe, centers of light industry and commerce that have drawn much of their population from the former mining villages. Fourteen of the founders of high-tech firms in the Northeast that I interviewed have premises located in the industrial parks of towns in County Durham; the remaining 7 have premises in the CAD-CAM Centre in Middlesbrough. These firms design and manufacture circuit boards, industrial robots, automation systems, test equipment, electronic tagging systems, scientific instruments, industrial process systems, and computer systems and software.

Wales

Unlike the neighboring regions of North and South Wales, Mid Wales, encompassing the counties of Powys and Gwynedd, had little industry beyond textiles and the now-defunct lead and slate mines. During much of the twentieth century the economy of the region was based on agriculture, principally sheep farming. In common with many other upland regions in Western Europe, Wales experienced accelerating depopulation, a process arrested in the last decade through the efforts of local authorities and the Mid Wales Development Board, the central government's main agency of regional policy. The largest town in the region, and the main focus of industrial development, is Newtown, the center of the Welsh flannel industry in the nineteenth century. The town's population declined with the collapse of that industry and only recently climbed beyond its earlier peak of 7,000 to approximately 11,000 today. Newtown's technology park, built by Mid Wales Development, has attracted a number of growing firms. At Aberystwyth, the second major town, a science park associated with the university provides a model for cooperation between industry and education.

Although Mid Wales has none of the locational criteria usually cited as conducive to the development of high-technology industry (Hall 1985: 43; see also Breheny and McQuaid 1987), the Mid Wales Development Board (MWDB) has been successful in diversifying the economy: More workers are now employed in industry than in farming

(Humphrys 1977: 189). MWDB, the primary industrial landlord in the region, builds advance factories, offering them to prospective tenants at competitive rental rates. Virtually every small town in the region has an industrial park, often bordered by sheep and cattle pastures. The most notable local industrial success is the expansion of facilities of Laura Ashley Limited, the upscale women's clothing and home furnishings company, with retail outlets throughout Europe and the United States.

As Humphrys (1977: 179) noted, Mid Wales must attract industry by "acquired, rather than natural, advantages." Mid Wales, however, is geographically closer to the high technology region of the Southeast than Durham, a factor that is potentially important for attracting new firms. The 1983–1984 annual report of the Development Board for Rural Wales (United Kingdom 1984: 10) noted that in earlier years, "too much emphasis was being placed on the development of indigenous potential" since the modest industrial base in Mid Wales was developed only during the last 20 years and was "not in itself yet strong enough to provide a platform for future growth." As a consequence, the agency continues to place a high priority on attracting companies from elsewhere, primarily from across the border in England. Nine of the 10 entrepreneurs in my sample were English rather than Welsh. The firms of the 10 entrepreneurs interviewed in Mid Wales are engaged in the design and the manufacture of computer software, electronic industrial equipment, scientific instruments, printed circuit boards, and consumer electronics.

AN ANTIENTREPRENEURIAL ENVIRONMENT?

Why should entrepreneurs want to found new, high-technology firms in the Northeast and Mid Wales? According to development specialist David Storey these regions "could at best be described as antipathetic to the individualistic idealism of entrepreneurship" (1982: 3; see also Morgan 1986: 343–344). Indeed, according to Storey's evidence, the Northeast and Mid Wales are the least congenial of the British regions for the development of new firms (Storey 1982: 196). Both regions have low net rates of new firm formation compared with the more prosperous regions of the United Kingdom (Martin 1986: 281). The Northeast has been dominated by large national and multinational corporations and has a low proportion of the small companies that typically nurture the budding entrepreneur. The area is characterized by an "employee" culture, according to Scott (1987: 14), "in which there is a natural tendency to look for large companies to provide employment." The Northeast and Wales have a "stronger tradition of collectivism" than Southeast England, and therefore are less entrepreneurial, according to Storey (1982: 197). One aspect of that collectivist orientation is the northeasterners' strong regional identification, encapsulated in the folk notion that northeasterners who move away will always return to their native region.

CAREERS OF FOUNDERS OF NEW HIGH-TECH FIRMS

In spite of these apparent disadvantages, a modest inventory of small high-technology firms has emerged in the Northeast and Mid Wales during the last 15 years. The careers of the founders of the firms in the sample can be described by four patterns that I call the *local hero*, the *returning native*, the *life-style immigrant*, and the *entrepreneurial immigrant*.[2] This heuristic typology directs attention to important processes in the experience of the new entrepreneurs. Both the local heroes and the returning natives were born and raised in the region where they establish new firms. The local hero never leaves the region; in contrast, the returning native leaves to work for large, perhaps multinational, corporations early in his career. Returning natives tend to be familiar with the global business opportunities in their field while local heroes have a more restricted view as a result of their narrower experience.

Immigrants, those entrepreneurs born and raised outside the Northeast or Mid Wales, are distinguished by two types of motivation.[3] One moves to the region primarily to achieve a way of life that contrasts with that of the congested, expensive, fast-paced Southeast of England. The other moves because of particular business advantages such as lower labor costs and government financial incentives. Obviously, both kinds of motivation can figure in a career decision, but one tends to be more central. As we will see, life-style immigrants are reluctant to allow their businesses to grow rapidly enough to threaten their adopted life-style, whereas entrepreneurial immigrants are interested in business expansion.

Many of the founders of the new firms are highly trained engineers who had established successful careers with major industrial firms in England. All of them experienced barriers to career advancement at some point, and only then did they seriously consider starting their own enterprises. During the industrial restructuring of the past decade, many such engineers found themselves unemployed as large firms cut or scaled down their research and development operations. Rather than find similar work with other large firms, some of these disillusioned engineers decided instead to work with small English companies where they would have greater control over their activities, while others launched directly into their own enterprises. In more than one-third

Table 7.1
High-Technology Entrepreneurial Career Types in Samples from Mid Wales and Northeast England

	Mid Wales	Northeast England	Total
Natives			
Local Heroes	1	8	9
Returning Natives	0	6	6
Immigrants			
Life-style	6	0	6
Entrepreneurial	3	7	10
	10	21	31

of the new firms, the engineer cofounded the business with an experienced manager/accountant, thus increasing the range of skills of the entrepreneurial team.

Regional Variations in Careers

Not all career types are equally prevalent in the two regions. Each has a distinct profile of entrepreneurial careers, showing a different pattern of constraints and opportunities. Native entrepreneurs of either type, for example, are rare in Mid Wales. At this stage in industrial development, virtually all the high-tech entrepreneurs in Mid Wales are English. As will become clear, local heroes can only emerge where there has been both an industrial base and locally available technical training, and Mid Wales has had neither until recently. Both types of immigrant owner/managers come to Wales, but life-style immigrants are in the majority (see Table 7.1).

The Northeast, in contrast, has all the career types *except* the life-style immigrant. Because of the negative (and largely erroneous) stereotypes often associated with the Northeast—relative poverty, industrial blight, environmental degradation, and a narrow working-class culture—high-technology entrepreneurs from the South of England are unlikely to think of that region first when seeking a pleasant refuge from the pressures of congested urban life. While the two regions attract approximately the same proportion of entrepreneurial immigrants (see Table 7.1), the Northeast produces more local heroes than any other career type.

Let us consider these career types in more detail, starting with the local hero, who accounts for 8 of the 21 firms in the Northeast, and 1 from Wales.

THE LOCAL HERO IN THE NORTHEAST

The local hero grew up in the region, received his engineering or technical education there, worked locally, and subsequently started his own firm, perhaps after working for one of the major companies such as ICI, the giant petrochemical conglomerate. As Storey noted (1982: 198), when southern English businesses expanded into the Northeast, attracted by the government subsidies of the 1960s and 1970s, many of the locals employed by them found that they had to transfer to branches in other parts of the country if they were to move up in the management or technical hierarchy. "If he is ambitious he will move and the region will lose an individual who might otherwise have become an entrepreneur, if there had been a greater variety of managerial positions open to him," Storey contended (1982: 198). The less ambitious workers may stay in the region but, lacking in entrepreneurial drive, these men are unlikely to start their own firms, according to Storey (1982: 198). Because their achievement is apparently so unusual, according to Storey's career scenario, I call these stay-at-home entrepreneurs "local heroes."

One local hero, who currently operates a research and development consulting firm, worked for a large company in the Northeast until he and several other individuals encountered career disappointments and decided to start up their own business. When the cofounders wanted to move to an industrial center near London, he withdrew and established his own local firm, employing two technicians as well as his wife. These founders have strong localized social networks, especially as they tend to marry other northeasterners.

Two local heroes established second-generation spin-off firms after working for one of the oldest small, high-tech companies in the area. One, the son of the original founder, completed his training in business and management and then established a new firm in cooperation with his engineer father. A former employee of the original firm also established an independent consulting service to meet the growing demand for printed circuit board design among local manufacturers. The lone Welsh example of this career type was previously employed by Mid Wales' largest company before starting his own computer service business for the local market.

Because local heroes have not worked outside the region, their business connections are predominantly localized patron-client networks, typically with linkages to large national or multinational corporations with branches in the Northeast, where they have personal relationships with engineers and other former colleagues. The *Economist* noted that small businesses in the Northeast that were formally dependent on government contracts now serve such major corporations as Nissan, which has established a large assembly plant near Durham. "They are reluctant to tout for business outside the north-east, let alone the continent" ("Turning on the Northern Lights" 1989: 41). These large firms often subcontract research and development projects to the local heroes, who operate industrial service and small-batch manufacturing businesses. This arrangement is preferred by the large patron corporations because it is more economical than maintaining a research and development capability in-house.

Dependence on the patronage of a few large firms, however, can lead to boom-and-bust cycles for the local heroes' businesses, and some founders, who are wary of this problem, have declined lucrative contracts with large corporations. One small business decided not to accept a computer maintenance contract with a multinational corporation because the managers preferred to grow more slowly and maintain a diverse customer base rather than risk the future of the firm by depending on one major customer.[4]

Most of the firms created by local heroes serve an industrial service niche and are unlikely to employ more than a half dozen workers, and usually have fewer. Often they started the firm with personal savings or a bank loan using their homes as collateral. Any growth in the firm is usually financed through profits rather than outside funding. While virtually all small businesses are eligible for some form of government grant—for training, market analysis, consulting, capital equipment, and so forth—few of the local heroes are major beneficiaries of government assistance. The owner of one electronics firm in Middlesbrough argued that government grants applications are too time-consuming and tend to benefit hired consultants more than they do the target businesses. Local heroes, whose businesses are often chronically undercapitalized, view government grants with suspicion, perceiving them as more trouble than they are worth. Furthermore, they often see banks as fair-weather partners, quick to offer more money when it is needed least and quicker to restrict funds in a crisis.

RETURNING NATIVES

Returning natives also identify with the region in which they were born. Their careers have taken them out of the Northeast and often out of the United Kingdom. Many were upwardly mobile locals whose entrepreneurial potential, according to David Storey's scenario, was lost to the region. Storey has failed to consider that a substantial number of these ambitious individuals may later return to their natal region, having gained technical and managerial experience, ideas, and business contacts in their jobs elsewhere.

While the local heroes are usually confined to a local or regional market for their products or services, the returning natives are likely to have a wider market. Their business networks are dense with contacts developed in the South and abroad. Several of these returnees noted that their previous jobs gave them an overview of the entire industry and an opportunity to make many business contacts, a major advantage for developing their own firms. As part of the global economy, all the returnees either export products and services abroad or, in the case of two computer firms, import hardware for local installation. In addition to their national and international business relations, they rapidly develop contacts in the rather sparse northeastern electronics industry and the regional technical colleges. Often the returnees' local personal networks are quite dense as, in stereotypical northeastern fashion, they have kept up connections with family and friends while living in the South or abroad. Returning immigrants are also proud of hiring a locally born work force and are conscious of their potential importance as creators of jobs in the industrial regeneration of the region. Many of these returnee founders are explicitly egalitarian, often contrasting their own firms with what they regard as the excessively hierarchical organization of business in the South of England. Like an embattled minority, the members of the firm see a need to protect themselves and their coregionalists from a hostile business environment, centered in the South.[5] These firms are larger, on average, than those founded by local heroes, ranging from 2 to 40 employees.

Compared with local heroes, returning natives are more likely to have some form of outside funding, including bank loans and government grants, for starting or expanding the firm. Although some returning natives note that banks are reluctant to extend loans to firms in the high-risk electronics industry, especially when banks have little expertise for evaluating the business plans of these new firms, most of these owners have evolved good relationships with banks. Returning natives also report a more positive experience with government granting agencies, and one entrepreneur in Consett reported that "it would have been difficult for us to expand down South in an unassisted area."

LIFE-STYLE IMMIGRANTS

For the third type of owner/manager, a major attraction is the uncrowded rural character of Mid Wales, with its sheep-grazed hills, tumbling streams, wooded valleys, traditional stone or half-timbered houses, and moderate cost of living. The founders of the six firms in this category chose Wales primarily for the quality of life that they anticipated rather than for the financial incentives offered by the development agency. Four of the firms are computer software or business systems companies. Two of these sell educational and accounting software by mail order throughout the United Kingdom while the other two software firms serve a local clientele.

The manager of one of these custom software/business equipment firms moved to Newtown from South London, a vast leap in social as well as geographical space. A tall, thin young man wearing a pony tail fastened with a rubber band, this escapee from the urban scene is one of what the locals call the "good life" people—people without family roots in the area who nevertheless have become passionately devoted to the slower-paced, more personal environment of rural Wales. Because there have been few barriers to entry into this comparatively new field, computer software development has been a refuge for several of the life-style immigrants who developed computer skills as a hobby or through on-the-job training.

Trained in science teaching and social administration, a husband–wife team decided to transform a hobby into a business by establishing an educational software firm. They found premises in one of the small industrial units built by MWDB in a remote mountain town. Although raised in England, they preferred to settle in Wales upon completing their university degrees at Aberystwyth. After exploring other occupations, they launched the software firm as a means of staying in their chosen location while seeking a nonlocal market. Since they sell their products by mail, they find little commercial disadvantage to this remote location, even though it is far from the population centers and the secondary schools that are their customers.

Another engineer regards Wales as the source of a dedicated and reliable work force that can be a (nonunionized) happy family, interested in crafting a limited quantity of excellent products for people who will appreciate them. His discourse is laced with metaphors about the genuine and authentic society of Wales, and how it differs from the "money-grubbing" environment of the Southeast where he worked previously.

For the life-style immigrants, the good life in Wales and interesting work are high priorities; managing a firm is a means to an end. While most of these people definitely prefer to be self-employed rather than working for others, they are not anxious to become embroiled in the problems of managing a large number of employees. Like many small-business owners in other sectors (Scase and Goffee 1980: 34), the life-style immigrants regard business expansion as a possible trap that would restrict their independence. "I'm not going to try to sell another 500 boxes of computer paper just to have a bit of extra money," one

owner assured me. Their firms employ from two to a dozen persons
and are unlikely to increase beyond the upper end of that range.

Like local heroes, life-style immigrants tend to finance their firms
with personal capital, and expand, if at all, by reinvesting the profits.
They are not enthusiastic applicants for government grants, although
they are happy to bargain for whatever assistance is available from
MWDB, their local development agency.

ENTREPRENEURIAL IMMIGRANT

In contrast to the first three types of founders, the entrepreneurial
immigrant, who typically comes from the South of England, has no
particular loyalty to the region and no preexisting local social network.
His business network, however, is likely to encompass the heartland
of the electronics industry in the Southeast and perhaps abroad. Lower
costs of production, the availability of government grants and tax incentives, and the ease of dealing with local authorities are the prime
reasons for establishing a business in a peripheral region. Immigrants
recognize that they have to make trade-offs to start businesses in these
regions. One owner/manager noted that in the early years of his new
firm he had difficulty convincing top technical people to move to Wales,
a problem that has disappeared now that his firm's reputation in the
industry is secure.

Of the four career models, the entrepreneurial immigrant most
closely resembles the one celebrated by the Thatcher government. Several of these new entrepreneurs had a long-standing interest in starting
their own business and, unlike the others, they did not expect to remain
employees for their entire careers. These owner/managers are interested in expanding their businesses, either by increasing their production facilities or by adding subsidiary or spin-off firms. They may,
in fact, escape the small-business category and grow beyond 50 employees. In the process, several of these firms have sought financing
beyond bank loans and small grants. Some are actively seeking venture
capital, although few firms have had any success in attracting interest
from the venture capital industry concentrated in the South. As one
entrepreneur cynically noted, few of those financiers want to "venture"
into the provincial regions, and when they do they only want to invest
in sure things. Even entrepreneurs who are interested in steady expansion have difficulty securing financing when they outgrow their
loan arrangements with local banks.

TECHNOLOGY TRANSFER

The four entrepreneurial career types are not equally successful in
supporting technology transfer, the diffusion of innovative industrial

products and processes. Companies founded by local heroes are not very active in technology transfer, since their primary mission is to develop engineering solutions to problems that the large firms in the area find inconvenient to tackle. This patron/client relationship can discourage technology transfer because these engineering solutions rarely result in a marketable process or product that could become the basis of substantial growth by the small company. One of the local heroes noted that his firm is "parasitic" on a few larger businesses; it does no original design work but merely assembles systems out of well-known components. He claims that he has insufficient time to develop new products or search for new customers. Furthermore, he noted, he has neither the time nor the incentive to upgrade his skills with computer aided design (CAD) facilities. Another small firm, which is closely linked to a few large corporations, produces innovations that could be marketed more widely, but the flow of contracts for the firm is so steady that the local hero owner/manager has indefinitely postponed his plans for developing and marketing these products. This is one case of a more general tendency in industry known as the "British problem," a failure to convert technological innovation into commercially successful products (Hendry 1990).

The returnees and the immigrants both are active in technology transfer, unlike the local heroes. While the returnees have the broadest range of technology transfer, including product, process, and service innovations, the entrepreneurial immigrants tend to specialize in product innovations: Manufacturing costs may be less in the peripheral regions.

Partly as a consequence of their ramifying national and international business network, the returnees are active in technology transfer, building their business around new products and processes to a greater degree than the local heroes. In some cases the returnees bring product innovations to Wales and the Northeast, such as new computer hardware from the United States, an electronic tracking system for oil-rig workers, improved accounting software, new scientific instruments, or more adaptable industrial robots. Others are engaged in process innovation, such as the use of CAD techniques in industrial process design, or service innovations, such as a small-batch printed circuit board design and manufacture.

It may be true, as Goddard, Thwaites, and Gibbs (1986: 153) have contended that

The peripheral regions are generally dependent on the core area for sources of technological knowledge and do not seem to provide a supporting environment for innovation, especially amongst the smaller and medium-sized enterprises that form the focal point of many contemporary regional industrial development initiatives.

However, this perspective oversimplifies the relationship between core and peripheral regions and fails to provide an analytic approach for discovering which types of entrepreneurial careers are likely to foster innovation and technology transfer. Informed by the analytic perspective advocated here, policy initiatives can be more sensitive to the needs of the different entrepreneurial career types. This study suggests that returning natives and entrepreneurial immigrants are well positioned both to develop innovations and to transfer new technology into the peripheral region. The local heroes, whose potential for innovation seems real but frustrated by the constraints of their customer base, might be targeted for assistance in developing those innovations. Life-style immigrants should not be ignored, although development agencies must recognize that the priorities of these entrepreneurs are not likely to be compatible with rapid business growth.

SUMMARY AND CONCLUSION

Storey (1986: 215) noted that most of the research on firms that is undertaken by economists in the United Kingdom concerns enterprises with more than 200 employees, while public policy "is increasingly directed toward firms with between two and fifty employees." This study focuses on the kind of small high-technology firm targeted by government policy and established by entrepreneurs in the two British regions least likely to support such enterprises, according to the macrostructural indicators of industrial geography. The analysis of the careers of the 31 founders of the small high-technology firms studied in Mid Wales and Northeast England shows that most did not expect to become entrepreneurs. Instead, they changed career paths only when their prospects for advancement as employees were blocked.

The two regions attracted different career types: Mid Wales draws life-style immigrants and a few entrepreneurial immigrants, while the Northeast retains a mix of local heroes, returning natives, and entrepreneurial immigrants, but draws no life-style immigrants. Over time, both regions are likely to attract the entrepreneurial types that they now lack. As the narrow industrial base of Mid Wales broadens, more indigenous entrepreneurs will find local careers appealing. The Northeast is likely to attract life-style immigrants as soon as residents of southern England, where the quality of life is deteriorating, discover that many of the negative stereotypes of the Northeast are not well founded. Favorable stories in the national press (e.g., "The New North:

The Success Story the South of England Has Hardly Noticed," *Sunday Times Magazine*, 6 May 1990) may help change this stereotype.

While the founders of new enterprises have made a modest contribution toward job creation, entrepreneurial role modeling, and technology transfer in their regions, the high-technology reindustrialization of the Northeast and Wales is not imminent. Britain's manufacturing sector has suffered from a widening gap between inward investment from abroad and outward investment in other countries, with the consequence that manufacturing may decline even further (Amin and Smith 1986: 73). Perhaps ironically, the electronics industry, in which rather more hope than capital has been invested, provides less employment now than at the peak year of employment in 1974 when the industry had 435,000 workers (Sayer and Morgan 1986: 160–64). Relative to the United States and Japan, Britain's electronics industry is in decline. For a variety of reasons, high technology cannot provide the sole solution to regional economic problems (Sayer and Morgan 1986), but it can be part of a diversified regional strategy. The dominance of the northeastern regional economy by large firms, including multinationals, may retard the development of small high-technology firms, especially those founded by local heroes locked into restricting patron/client relationships. Preliminary evidence from my study of indigenous entrepreneurs in central Scotland ("Silicon Glen") suggests that as the regional electronics industry becomes more diversified, local heroes are no longer at such a disadvantage because their business networks become less restricted (Caulkins 1988a). Those founders who have global or extraregional business networks are more likely to provide the important growth points for the industry in the future. Similarly, technology transfer is not occurring as rapidly or evenly as the popular "technoevangelists" had hoped.[6] The incremental additions, particularly of the returning natives and the immigrants, may allow the Northeast and Mid Wales to develop a concentration of new technology in some industrial sectors during the next decade. For example, some of my case studies showing increasing synergy between the new electronics and computer software firms as they learn to cooperate in the development of new products.

Less optimistically, however, we must also recognize that the unanticipated consequences of government policies can retard or subvert the transfer of innovations even in high-technology businesses. Occasionally, for instance, employment schemes and technology modernization programs work at cross purposes. Ironically, this conflict in government policies was illustrated in a small robotics factory in the CADCAM Centre that Margaret Thatcher toured, in full view of the television cameras, as part of her 1987 campaign for reelection. The cameras showed Thatcher walking the rubble-strewn graveyard of the earlier industrial era of Teeside (Middlesbrough-Stockton), then tracked her on an optimistic tour of the new firms in the CADCAM Centre. What Thatcher may not have learned in touring the robotics factory is that all the designs and blueprints for these high-tech products were drawn by hand, using old-fashioned, low-tech equipment rather than the sophisticated computer aided design facilities that are available but underutilized in the center. Why resort to this low-tech design process? It is temporarily more cost-effective: The trainee drafter who does the drawings is on a government-subsidized employment scheme, learning skills that other government programs will make obsolete.

NOTES

An earlier version of this chapter was presented at the annual American Anthropological Association meetings in Phoenix, Arizona, on November 1988. I am grateful to the British entrepreneurs who were so generous with their time and information. Thanks to Michael Scott, Chris Turnbull, Alan Bilsborough, Robert Layton, Charles Gullick, James Barber, Deborah Lavin, and the staff of the Anthropology Department of the University of Durham, England, for their kind assistance during my time in 1987 as a visiting fellow in the department. Thanks also to Alf Johnsen for his generous support of Grinnell College's Western European Studies Program.

1. The data come from semistructured interviews, ranging from 45 minutes to 2 hours, with the founding owner/managers of 31 small, indigenous high-technology firms in Mid Wales (10 firms) and Northeast England (22 firms), and carried out between January and November 1987. One northeasterner manages two firms. "Indigenous" small firms are locally owned and managed main-unit establishments with 50 employees or fewer. Foreign-owned firms and branch plants of large corporations are excluded. In this context, the term "high technology" is restricted to the domain of electronics, instruments, and computer hardware and software manufacturing or service. Finally, because the study focuses on potentially innovative firms, only those with at least a minimal research and development program were included in the sample.

2. All the technically trained founders in my sample are male, as might be expected from the predominance of males in British engineering schools. Some of the firms in the sample were founded by husband–wife teams in which the husband concentrates on product design and development while the wife deals with personnel, accounting, management, and marketing tasks. Sometimes the wife is an officially recognized part of the management team with her own separate business card. In any case, as one entrepreneur remarked, "Wives play an important role in any small business." That role, which is insufficiently recognized by the public, would be an appropriate topic for additional study.

3. Litvak and Maule (1976) similarly found both life-style and financial factors to be important in their study of entrepreneurs in Canada, the United States, and the United Kingdom. For a more pessimistic assessment of entrepreneurs' motives, see Scase and Goffee (1980: 29).

4. When translated into Mary Douglas's (1978, 1982) familiar grid/group framework, the companies of local heroes are low group, having a sparse business network, and high grid, or highly constrained by the expectations of the large firms that are their patrons. Among the constant concerns of these small-business founders is to push their organization further down grid, to become less dependent on the large corporations, and to expand their business networks.

5. In this way, the returnees resemble the survival collectivists or sectarians of Mary Douglas's (1978, 1982) grid/group framework, while the immigrant entrepreneurs, who bring their hierarchical models with them, are more clearly in the entreprencurial quadrant. For an expanded discussion, see Caulkins (1988a, 1988b).

6. For example, consider the cautions suggested by United States, Office of Technology Assessment (1984); Goddard, Thwaites, and Gibbs (1986); and Delbecq and Weiss (1988).

8

Rural Industrial Enterprise and "Socialism with Chinese Characteristics"

Eugene Cooper and Xiong Pan

Eugene Cooper and Xiong Pan compare rural industry in two districts in China. One district (Changping) is in a county where export processing (described also by Smart and Smart in Chapter 3) is very pronounced; the other (Guizhou) is in a county in which collective rural enterprise is geared to the domestic market. Despite many differences, both regions show a mix of private and collective enterprises and have experienced important changes in their standards of living.

The promotion of rural industrial enterprise has come to occupy a strategic place in the People's Republic of China's economic development strategy as planners grope to establish a balance between state-planned and private sectors of the economy. Under a bewilderingly diverse set of administrative arrangements, and encompassing a wide variety of domestically and internationally marketed commodities, such enterprises have performed very favorably in the state-sponsored effort to employ individual initiative in advancing the productive forces of society. The enterprises have succeeded in putting underemployed labor power to productive work, providing nonagricultural employment in the countryside, increasing rural income, reducing push factors in urban migration, filling lacunae in the planned state sector, and providing resources for cultural and welfare facilities previously unavailable in rural areas. They have also provided alternative avenues for unofficial upward mobility, and, in many places, shaken up the bipolar (bureaucrat/peasant) class structure of the Chinese rural communities where they operate.

This chapter examines the performance of two districts, Changping in Dongguan County and Guizhou in Shunde County, which are located in the Pearl River Delta of Guangdong Province. The analysis shows how the two districts have created different developmental trajectories and demonstrates the flexibility and adaptability of rural enterprise in China. Each pattern of development, though remarkably different from each other, has provided a measure of economic prosperity for Chinese peasants in the countryside.

The Chinese term for rural enterprise, *xiang zhen qi ye*, is a cover term for a variety of enterprises with disparate characteristics. It refers to two levels of rural administration, *xiang* or subdistrict, and *zhen* or town, and is itself a revision of the term *she dui qi ye*. This latter term translates as "commune and brigade enterprise," and refers to the two analogous levels of rural administration that prevailed when the collective regime in agriculture was still in place. The lowest level of rural administration in that period was the production team (*xiao dui*).

With collective administration in agriculture abandoned in favor of the so-called household responsibility system, *she dui* enterprises have become *xiang zhen* enterprises. However, the change is more than one of name, for while state- and collectively managed enterprises remain in operation, there has been a proliferation of lower-level collective-, individual-, and joint household—managed firms throughout the countryside in recent years.

China's *xiang* (subdistricts) and *zhen* (towns) are bureaucratic levels in an administrative structure that includes *xian* (county), *zhen* (town), *qu* (district), *xiang* (subdistrict), *cun* (village), and *hu* (household), in descending order. All but the latter are represented in a hierarchical structure of administration in the countryside, and rural industrial enterprises are administered at all levels. Generally speaking, state-run and large collective enterprises can be found at the county, town and district levels, whereas enterprises at the subdistrict level and below are dominated by smaller (nonstate) collective, private, and/or joint household ownership and management.

Thus, the cover term *xiang zhen qi ye* refers to a multitude of forms, from large state-run and collective enterprises employing hundreds of workers to small individual enterprises employing no more than a handful of workers, some of whom may be kin. Included also are high-tech export processing factories owned and managed by Hong Kong— and Macau-based Chinese businesses or by multinational corporations, in joint venture or compensation trade agreements with local organs at varying administrative levels in the countryside.

The general strategy of rural enterprise is summed up in the phrases:

"employ local materials, employ local skills, serve local needs, buy and sell in local markets" (*jiu di qu cai, jiu di jia gong, jiu di fu wu, jiu di shao zhi*). In other words, rural industry should develop in accord with local resources and talents to meet local needs. Thus, rural enterprises occupy a niche intermediate between the agricultural and centrally planned state sectors, where they improve the distribution of consumer goods, and often even introduce a competitive challenge to the hegemony of state enterprises in similar product lines.

Central government encouragement of rural enterprise dates from 1978, the year immediately following the Third Plenum of the Chinese Communist Party Central Committee. At that time, rural enterprise was declared a positive force rather than a capitalist deviation. Between 1978 and 1982, total national value of rural enterprise production nearly doubled from Y49,060,000,000 (US $18 billion) to Y84,070,000,000 (US $31 billion).

The Pearl River Delta occupies an area about the size of greater Los Angeles, some 11,300 square miles. It is particularly well situated to take advantage of the participation of Hong Kong and Macau businessmen in rural enterprise development, and as part of the Guangdong Province "special administrative open region," the Pearl River Delta contains a high proportion of enterprises financed by Hong Kong and Macau capital. Well endowed with convenient water and land transport, and with a history of early involvement in China's export trade, the delta has experienced a particularly rich and diversified development of rural enterprise in recent years. In 1983, total income from rural enterprise in Guangdong Province was Y8,160,000,000 (US $3.2 billion); it increased to Y12,130,000,000 (US $4.5 billion) in 1984. However, a still more dramatic increase is indicated in figures for income from individual and joint household enterprises which rose from Y890,000,000 (US $330 million) in 1983, to Y3,300,000,000 (US $1.2 billion) in 1984—an increase of some 270 percent.

The Pearl River Delta extends into 11 counties of Guangdong Province, two of which, Dongguan (1983 population 1.1 million) and Shunde (1983 population 825,000) counties, are the sites for this comparative study. Dongguan County is heavily committed to the processing of imported materials for re-export. Its development has proceeded under a policy of *san lai yi bu*—three imports, one compensation: (1) import the raw material, and the enterprise adds labor; (2) import the pattern, and the enterprise provides the product; (3) import the parts, and the enterprise assembles the product. Compensation refers to trade in which investors are reimbursed and profits are paid in kind, in commodities produced by the enterprise.

The county seat of Dongguan is already a minor city and at present is experiencing an almost breathtaking construction boom. The rhythm

Table 8.1
Expansion of Rural Enterprise in Dongguan County, 1978–1984

	1978	1984	% growth
# rural enterprises	2,618	3,490	33.3%
# employees	72,495	148,056	104.8%
total APV Y 000,000's	130.7	589.2	350%
fixed capit Y 000,000's	90.7	307	238.5%

Source: People's Republic of China, Rural Industrial Bureau, *Xiang Zhen Qi Ye* (Rural Enterprise). Beijing, 1985.

and bustle of the town are reminiscent of the New Territories towns of Hong Kong—Tsuen Wan and Taipo, which in the late 1960s were similarly poised to become minor urban industrial centers. In 1984, 57 percent of the combined value of agricultural and industrial production in Dongguan County came from rural enterprise. Before 1978, the average annual per capita income was about Y150, but by 1983 wages from rural enterprise had expanded that figure nearly four times, to Y589.5. Table 8.1 shows the expansion in scope of rural enterprise in Dongguan County between 1978 and 1984. The chart shows that in 1984 there were more than twice as many workers employed in rural enterprise as in 1978, and the per capita value of production in 1984 was more than twice that of 1978. In 1978, each factory had an average of 27.7 workers, while in 1984 there were 42.5 workers. Factories in Dongguan process imported materials for export such as woolens, clothing, small metal items, toys, electrical goods, plastics, and leather goods. In 1983, income from processing and assembling foreign materials was Y120,000,000 (US $45,880,000), an amount equal to county government income from all other sources.

Dongguan's geographic location is ideally suited to this export processing strategy. The Kowloon–Canton railway runs within its borders for 64 kilometers, one-fourth of its total length, and a road for vehicular traffic also provides a direct link to Hong Kong's New Territories. In addition, labor costs are about one-eighth those of Hong Kong, rents are exceedingly low, and storage of materials and finished products is nearly free. Furthermore, there are nearly 150,000 Dongguan natives overseas and some 650,000 Dongguan natives in Hong Kong and Macau. Dongguan has been able to take advantage of the recent open

Table 8.2
Expansion of Rural Enterprise in Shunde County, 1978–1984

	1978	1984	% growth
# rural enterprs.	ca. 1,900	3,257	71%
# employees	ca. 67,000	107,523	60%
total (Y)	263,394,510	936,340,000	255%
fix capit. mill. Yuan	90.7	307	239%

Source: People's Republic of China, Rural Industrial Bureau. *Xiang Zhen Qi Ye* (Rural Enterprise). Beijing, 1985.

policies to call on its extensive expatriate population to contribute money, resources, and management skills to its rural development.

In the Maoist period, such external kinship relations were regarded as a source of corrupting influences, although remittances from overseas were never interrupted. More recently, the Chinese leadership has recognized the importance of overseas kin investment and have incorporated privately invested capital from expatriates into the development picture as part of what makes Chinese socialism "distinctive."

Shunde County, on the other hand, has virtually no income from such export processing enterprises. Average peasant income of Shunde is not particularly high because the county had a deliberate policy of paying fewer dividends and reinvesting a greater proportion of its earnings in enterprise expansion. Its firms are dominated by larger non–state sector collective firms managed by local government operatives at the district level, and in the past depended more heavily on the marketing of commodities domestically through state-controlled marketing organs.

Rural enterprise began early in Shunde County under the sponsorship of communes and production brigades. In 1978 it already had 1,900 large and small rural factories with 67,000 employees earning about Y50 (US $19) a month. In 1984, rural enterprise contributed 66 percent of the total value of agricultural and industrial production in the county. (See Table 8.2.)

Shunde County's strategy, which was devised in a period prior to Chinese encouragement of private and foreign investment, has been to take advantage of its proximity to Canton (*Guangzhou*) to develop enterprises geared to the domestic market. Large-scale district-run enterprises have been its dominant industrial form.

District (*qu*) enterprises in Shunde are disproportionately large, employ more workers, and produce more goods for broader markets than enterprises at other levels in the county administrative hierarchy. The predominance of district enterprises is a reflection of the importance that earlier commune-run enterprises have had in the industrial development of Shunde, and indicates that collective property still occupies a commanding position in the country. The total value of individually managed enterprises is only 5 percent of total production value.

Of the 380 district-run enterprises, 40 are so-called "core" factories. These 40 factories had a total production value in 1984 of Y414,520,000 (US $154 million), or 66 percent of total district enterprise production. The production value of the other 340 enterprises represented only one-third. The per capita worker productivity figures of district core factories rival those of general factories in the cities.

Of the total of 3,257 enterprises in Shunde County, only 100 are export processing firms, and these have come on-line rather late. However, agents from the county have become more active in their cultivation of ties with Hong Kong in recent years, and this probably reflects a desire on the part of county officials to expand the export processing sector.

The development of Shunde's rural enterprise has thus far been based for the most part around the so-called "Big 6" industries, and so has that of Guizhou district. Most important among these "Big 6" is the household appliance industry, which came into existence in the county when farm tool and farm machinery factories run by the communes and brigades were dismantled and retooled. The household appliance industry accounted for 43.2 percent of the total value of district-run enterprise production in Shunde in 1984. The other five industries of the "Big 6" are plastics, furniture, weaving, clothing, and construction materials. This emphasis on light industrial consumer goods is deemed to "fit local conditions." So successful have these enterprises been that urban state-run enterprises in Canton have been forced to respond by reorganizing production with an eye to matching their greater "efficiency."

While the array of "cradle to grave" benefits provided by state-run enterprises continues to make them attractive careerwise, rural enterprises often pay wages that surpass those of state-run factories on a month to month basis. While they cannot offer guarantees of steady and secure employment or the health or retirement benefits common in the state sector, they provide workers in the nonstate sector with a competitive wage.

THE CHANGPING DISTRICT OF
DONGGUAN COUNTY

Changping District, one of 31 in Dongguan County, lies in the western portion of Dongguan County, at the eastern periphery of the Pearl River Delta. A favorable geographic location and overseas kin ties have been significant in Changping District's reliance on export processing enterprise in its development.

Changping District is composed of 23 subdistricts (*xiang*) and 211 villages with a population in 1983 of about 50,000 people. Its economy is based on a diversified agriculture consisting of irrigated rice fields, orchards, and fish ponds. Prior to 1978, it placed last in Dongguan County in per capita income (Y127 = US $43), due largely to a national policy of "taking grain as the key link," under which local conditions and natural endowments were ignored, and ponds and orchards were converted to rice production.

After six years of development of export processing industries (in 1984), the average annual per capita income in Changping was Y1,024 (US $378), highest in Dongguan County, and its diversified agricultural economy was reestablished on a firm basis. Between 1978 and 1985, the number of enterprises in Changping District expanded from 19 to 92, and construction of new industrial space is continuing. In 1978, the district received approximately $200,000 in export processing fees, whereas in 1984 that figure was nearly $9,000,000. Of the total labor force of 24,000 in the district, some 60 percent or 14,400 are employed in rural industrial or service enterprises.

Income generated from export processing enterprises currently accounts for approximately 80 percent of peasant income. Since 1979, some 6,000 households have built new two-story houses of reinforced concrete construction at a cost of some Y10,000 (US $3,700) each, and the district people's bank absorbed some Y30,000,000 (US $4.6 million) in new deposits. The new enterprises have been an extremely important factor in alleviating rural poverty in Changping.

The district government managed some 10 processing factories in 1984, employing 2,113 workers. These factories earned Y12,400,000 (US $4.6 million) in processing fees in the same year. After taxes, capital depreciation, and profit pay-outs to the district government, Y5,320,000 (US $2 million) was retained for reinvestment in production, construction of social welfare facilities, and improvements in other institutions of collective consumption.

Between 1979 and 1984, about Y9,200,000 (US $3.4 million) was spent on the construction of two new industrial complexes, roads, bridges, a covered market, and a new hotel. A middle school, a central primary school, a kindergarten, a recreation center, a clinic, and a worker's dorm were also built in Changping. These improvements to rural life were the direct result of revenues generated by rural industrial development.

In addition to providing employment for workers of Changping itself, the rural enterprises in the district employ about 6,000 workers from outside the district, giving new meaning to the phrase *li tu bu li xiang*, "leave agriculture without leaving the countryside," meaning to leave one's village but find employment in the countryside rather than the already overcrowded cities. Indeed, the development of rural enterprise and the relatively high wages they pay have stemmed, and even reversed to some extent, the flow of population from countryside to city. Workers from outside Dongguan County are able, in increasing numbers, to find employment in the rural enterprises of Changping District. They retain their official rural household registration (*hu kou*) in the village of their birth (that is, they rely on the output of their native household plot for grain), but they spend the greater part of the year as wage earners in Changping District. It is not uncommon for enterprises in Changping to hire buses at factory expense during the New Year's festival to return these workers to their native counties for the traditional holidays. Rural enterprises in Changping not only put their own citizens to work but are also able to absorb a portion of the underemployed labor power from other districts in the region. Such developments have important implications for alleviating overcrowding in China's cities.

In sum, the social life of Changping District has literally been made over in the past decade, and the promotion of rural industrial enterprise has been central to that process.

GUIZHOU DISTRICT OF SHUNDE COUNTY

The development pattern of rural industrial enterprise in Guizhou District provides an interesting contrast to that of Changping. Guizhou District, 1 of 10 in Shunde County, is located on the western bank of the Pearl River in the central delta region. The district is composed of 19 subdistricts and 232 villages, with a population in 1983 of about 75,000 people.

The highway from Canton to Macau crosses the district and connects it to the principal port of the county, Yangqi. A key center of water transport in the delta, traffic to Canton along the West and North rivers passes Yangqi. In recent years commercial development between Guizhou and Yangqi has stretched out along both sides of the highway, and the boundary between the two towns can no longer be easily demarcated.

Despite its tradition of a mixed agricultural regime of fish pond,

mulberry (silkworm), sugar, and grain production, Guizhou, like
Changping District in Dongguan, was also held back in its development
by the policies of enforced grain production which prevailed under the
collectivist regime. Per capita annual income in 1978 was Y260 (US
$96), nearly twice that of Changping but still quite low. By 1984, per
capita income had jumped to Y981 (US $363) per year. Between those
years, production value in rural enterprises expanded from
Y34,350,000 (US $12.7 million) to Y247,000,000 (US $91.5 million).
Accumulated savings at the end of 1985 amounted to Y79,270,000 (US
$29.4 million). These figures are quite impressive and surpass the
figures for growth in production value of the most industrially developed districts in the state sector of suburban Canton. In 1985, there
were 526 rural enterprises in Guizhou District, turning out electrical
appliances, heaters, cable, light bulbs, woolens, down products, printed
books, clothing, and plastic products.

Guizhou, however, is also noted for its subdistrict (*xiang*)–level development. Shunde county had seven subdistricts among its total of
220, with annual production values exceeding Y10,000,000 (US $3.7
million). Three of those seven were in Guizhou District. Among these
in Hongqi Subdistrict, whose cooperative electric fan factory, alone,
had an annual production value exceeding Y30,000,000 (US $11 mil-
lion). Not surprisingly, the enterprise has attracted provincial and
national attention and has been visited by leading national figures.

Dramatic increases in local government spending for education, rec-
reation, and welfare, however, have not taken place in Guizhou District. Rural industries have remained, for the most part, under the
supervision of those who administered them as commune enterprises.
While at present these bureaucratic entrepreneurs enjoy considerably
greater scope to operate autonomously, the district has generally been
more conservative than Changping in allocating its newly acquired
revenue to social programs.

In Guizhou, the enterprises have remained more of an adjunct of the
collective institutions under which they were organized much earlier
than the enterprises of Changping. In Guizhou, the two-level class
structure of rural society, as it evolved under the Maoist collective
regime, with its bureaucrats and masses, has been disrupted far less
by the development of rural industry than the latecomer Changping.

Like Changping, Guizhou is also possessed of extensive expatriate
networks in Hong Kong and the United States, and remittances from
these individuals have long figured in the household budgets of its
inhabitants. To date, however, these networks have not played a role
in investment in or development of rural enterprise on a scale ap-
proaching that in Changping.

In Guizhou the district has remained in command, and licensing of enterprises at lower administrative levels has been far less extensive than in Changping. However, Guizhou has more recently been affected by a national policy of decentralizing responsibility in enterprise management. Subcontracting, or so-called *cheng bao* arrangements, have become widespread in industrial enterprise management in recent years. Generally, a village, subdistrict, district, or town will farm out the management of a formerly collective enterprise to an individual, family, or management committee for a substantial fee. A formal contract is drawn up, usually in the *gong ban* (industrial office) at the appropriate administrative level, in which the management undertakes to produce a certain quantity of goods and to return a percentage of its proceeds from the contracted production to its administrative unit. Production and profit beyond the contracted obligations to the village, subdistrict, district, or town that grants the enterprise its license to operate, accrues to the management, with smaller bonuses awarded to members of the work force in accord with a variety of incentive schemes. Failure to meet contracted obligations results in rather stiff fines for management.

In recent years, industrial offices in the Chinese countryside have pushed *cheng bao* to its limits, selling off previously subcontracted enterprises to their individual managers outright, and even assisting in the arrangement of financing through state commercial banks and local private mortgage companies. While our data and observations of Guizhou predate these more recent developments, it is reasonable to assume that the privatization of enterprise they brought in their wake did not leave Guizhou unaffected.

GENERAL DISCUSSION

From the data presented above, we easily recognize two rather different developmental trajectories in which rural industrial enterprises have played a role—one based on processing imported materials for export, and one based on the use of largely local materials in larger collective enterprises producing primarily for domestic markets.

Under both circumstances, rural enterprises have made major contributions, setting underemployed labor power to productive work and alleviating rural poverty at little or no cost to the central government. The wages paid have had a positive impact on rural income, while representing for the export processor a small portion of similar costs in Hong Kong or Macau.

Rural enterprises, both individual and collective, rely on local and/ or expatriate resources for capital, organization, labor power, and management skills. When they show losses or go bankrupt, the national government has no direct responsibility. Workers who are laid off return to the family farm. When the enterprises earn money, the state takes a cut in taxes.

The dismantling of the collective agricultural system and the establishment of the household responsibility system in agriculture along with the institutionalization of subcontracting (*cheng bao*) since the late 1970s seems to have liberated an enormous amount of energy. The rural markets of Guangdong Province have been overflowing in recent years with grain produced by individual households above a fairly minimal state production quota. The policy of "leave the land, don't leave the countryside" has created greater opportunities for mobility than Chinese peasants have ever enjoyed since 1949, and the labor force on the land has been dramatically reduced as rural enterprises have attracted large numbers out of agricultural employment. Rural industrialization has replaced agricultural mechanization as the primary means of achieving rural prosperity and may yet encourage wider adoption of mechanized agriculture by reducing the labor force on the land.

There are also a growing number of larger-scale private enterprises in the Chinese countryside, generating for their owners profits that dwarf by many magnitudes the "fortunes" for which "evil landlords" of the old society were submitted to revolutionary justice. Substantial fortunes make it possible, among other things, for some individuals to flaunt population controls by paying the fines for having larger families with impunity; this is among the more serious of the contradictions that rural industry has brought in its wake.

Increased polarization of classes in the rural areas is a serious problem in its own right. Ironically, it was fear of class polarization in the countryside that served as a rationale for suppressing rural enterprise under the radical egalitarian policies of the Maoist period.

Clearly, Changping has experienced a more significant polarization than Guizhou, but it has also produced a substantially larger entrepreneurial class; more people are wealthy. The gulf that divides Changping's entrepreneurs from their workers may be several times greater than in Guizhou, but a greater proportion of previously unprivileged people are in the upper social strata. Guizhou's enterprises have also contributed to the enhancement of rural income, and one might argue that the proceeds have been distributed there in a more egalitarian fashion. However, while the Guizhou pattern might be seen to have advantages along these lines, in general it has represented less of a threat to, and indeed may even be said to have strengthened, local Communist party hegemony in the countryside, giving the party control over new strategic resources and sources of revenue. From our present perspective, the creation of spheres of nonparty economic power in the countryside represents one of the more positive and refreshing contributions of rural industry to contemporary Chinese social life.

The Changping pattern has introduced new opportunities for upward mobility into the rural milieu. Many party members have profited handsomely from rural industry in Changping, to be sure, either in management roles, where they are constrained by objective economic criteria of performance, or through various forms of manipulation of people and resources associated with the rural industrial sector that their political positions make possible. However, the rewards of success in rural enterprise rival in economic terms those associated with official channels of upward mobility through the Communist party and/or recognition as a "model" worker or manager in the state sector. The private rural industrial sector gives ordinary individuals—those without appropriate political credentials or connections, or with "political problems" in their life histories—a rewarding avenue for investment of their time and resources, and a greater degree of autonomy in organizing their lives than they have ever enjoyed before. Such unofficial alternatives for mobility are far fewer under the Guizhou model.

The private sector in China's economy has nevertheless developed a reputation for some unsavory practices such as hoarding and profiteering. The uncertain availability of raw materials and a rather serious inflation of the people's currency encourage a madcap accumulation of back stocks, which not only drives prices up but has also caused disruptions in the supply of state-sector enterprises. More recently, steps have been taken to give state enterprises priority in raw materials markets, fulfilling the prophecies that hoarding is meant to forestall. Good relations with strategically placed party officials can be important in securing supplies and overcoming bottlenecks that can mean the difference between meeting orders or going out of business.

While we possess no direct evidence of corruption in the counties investigated here, official corruption is perceived to be extremely widespread nationally. In particular, as legitimate opportunities for private gain have expanded, many officials have sought to avail themselves of some of the proceeds through bribery and extortion. Indeed, the nationwide student demonstrations of 1989 singled out official corruption as one of their principal objects of protest.

The inflation that plagues the people's currency also punishes those who have not profited so handsomely from entrepreneurial activity or who lack family members employed in the rural industrial sector. While families untouched by rural enterprise are increasingly unusual, the state seems prepared to sacrifice egalitarianism at this stage in favor of the overall positive effect that rural industrial development has exerted on the level of the productive forces of society as a whole.

Inflation also encourages a widespread black market in foreign exchange, which is valued not only as a more secure store of wealth but also for its ability to purchase imported luxury consumer goods which circulate in a sphere that the people's currency is not allowed to penetrate. Nevertheless, the fact that people have accumulated sufficient wealth to aspire to ownership of such goods, and that they have sufficient surplus to seek out foreign exchange on the black market in order to obtain them, is something of an index of the greater prosperity wrought in the rural areas by industrial enterprises.

Unfortunately, rural enterprises have operated without much concern for the environment. Untreated effluents are regularly expelled into local waterways and streams, and consciousness of the long-term destructive effects of such practices has been obscured in the short-term rush to maximize profits. More recently, the state, anxious over its grain quota, has stepped in to more strictly regulate the conversion of agricultural land to industrial uses, but much remains to be done by way of protection against the despoiling of an already fragile physical environment.

Notwithstanding these difficulties, rural industrial enterprise has quite literally transformed the Chinese countryside. It has succeeded in raising the overall rural standard of living, in enhancing the technical level of the rural work force, in loosening the bureaucratic constraints on the ordinary citizen, and in providing an opportunity for those citizens to seize control of their own destinies and make of them what they can.

China's central planners have yet to establish anything like a consensus as to what an appropriate proportion of private and planned enterprise should be in the economy as a whole. Indeed, the state has recently raised the cost of credit in an effort to cool down the private sector of the economy, and no one is sure how the recent political suppression of the Peking student movement will affect foreign investment or central government policies toward the private rural industrial sector.

Nevertheless, the present prosperity of China's rural areas testifies to the greater general weal created by present policies, implemented in accord with differing local conditions and endowments; and China's rural industrial enterprises, private as well as collective, can be expected to remain an important part of what gives Chinese socialism its distinctive characteristics.

NOTE

This chapter is based on fieldwork by its authors in Changping and Guizhou districts of Dongguan and Shunde counties respectively, the former a peripheral county and the latter a central county in the delta. Cooper visited the area in the winter of 1985, and Pan conducted fieldwork over the several years immediately before.

9

Informal Sectorization of Egyptian Petty Commodity Production

Kristin Koptiuch

Like the analyses by Blim, Caulkins, Cooper and Pan, and the Buechlers, Kristin Koptiuch's chapter discusses small-scale production. Rather than focusing on the local context, however, she uses such production as a point of departure to address a series of broader issues. She suggests that the promotion of petty commodity production, that is, the informal sector, by developmentalists (planners, bankers, and transnational finance capitalists) was a response to a "subtle rebellion" by Egyptian workers in which they struggled for higher wages by emigrating.

By the late 1970s, Egyptian petty commodity production had become a concern for both international development agency research and Egypt's national reconstruction in a transnational field. These artisanal, small-scale industries and craftspeople were also made the butt of complaints in the press and among the popular classes in Egypt. Such stubbornly persistent, sweatshop-style craft activities have long provided local markets with quotidian commodities and services and engaged a majority of urban laboring men and women. However, they had not garnered much attention since the early twentieth century. In this essay I examine the reemergence of petty commodity production as both an allegorical figure and an object of institutional policy in the discursive and social fields of often conflicting interests. This renewed concern can best be understood as the result of a disruption of the social reproduction of conditions that had made possible Egypt's modern capitalist productive relations since the turn of the century. The impetus for this crisis, I argue, must be sought in the culture of the subaltern classes and in their changing position in relation to shifts in international capitalism. More specifically, I will suggest that the stress placed by development experts and policymakers on what came to be known as the informal sector represented an effort to keep down the costs of social reproduction at a time when workers' recourse to migration in order to raise their wages was increasing reproductive costs.

PRELUDE

When Ahmad returned to Egypt in 1978 after two years of work as a construction laborer in Saudi Arabia, he used his savings to set up a pottery workshop in the new section of old Cairo's pottery manufacturing zone, 'Ullaliya Gadida. The spacious shop with three potter's wheels and huge kiln outside was a capital investment that, though minimal by modern industrial standards, never could have been accumulated by working as a skilled turner in the one-wheel workshop that his recently deceased father had run in the older section of 'Ullaliya. Understandably, Ahmad had little nostalgia for that workshop, which was destroyed several years back, along with many others, by an aborted government construction project whose gaping foundation hole now covers over with emptiness what was once a plenitude of potteries. This displacement seemed to be more than compensated for by labor displacement abroad and the earnings that permitted Ahmad's own younger generation of potters to rekindle their archaic but still vital craft. Another migrant, the young son of a potter, returned in 1980 from construction work in Kuwait with earnings to finance, with great fanfare, his "traditional" marriage celebration, before leaving again for another tour of labor. As if to offset his local reputation as a bit of a rake, brightly colored graffiti drawn on his father's freshly painted house proudly narrated for the neighborhood the young man's pilgrimage to Mecca, which he made en route home from Kuwait.

Yet another potter returned to put a down payment on a small apartment building near the pottery district. He now occupies the top floor with his wife and five children and rents out the other two floors. He took up his old job as a journeyman potter in a workshop whose potter-owner had trouble finding a replacement while he was away. Like others, this workshop owner complained that he had difficulty finding skilled pottery throwers who were willing to work for the wages he could offer since so many had left the pottery trade either to work abroad or to enter more lucrative trades, such as construction, replacing other skilled workers who had already emigrated. This was despite the fact that already in 1980 the standard potter's wages had nearly doubled since my first visit to 'Ullaliya three years earlier. Not infrequently, serviceable wheels remained idle in the workshops because potters could not hire the minimally paid young apprentices without whose assistance it is difficult to practice efficient piecework.

Embedded in this summary evocation of the plight of Egypt's pottery trade are the threads of a narrative common to many petty commodity trades and small industries that have been affected by the upheavals of a new transnational division of labor and restructuring of global capital. It would be entirely inappropriate to represent those apparently traditional forms of artisanal production persisting today as anachronistic, vestigial remnants of a precapitalist era or as unchanging, nostalgic evidence of "cultural continuity" that must be salvaged before they vanish. Nor does the persistence of petty commodity production (to an extent unanticipated by Marx) validate an image simply of backward, "transnational" modes of manufacture that must be hastened under the wheels of modernization and inevitable supersession by modern industry. The most cogent analyses in the debate on petty commodity production have recognized the necessity to move beyond an empiricist reading of history to show that persistent precapitalist forms are by no means survivals, but in fact were "profoundly transformed by the impact of colonial capital and the development of indigenous capital" (Alavi 1982: 173; see also Smith 1984a, 1984b). The placement of old forms within new frameworks—here charged by a new transnational division of labor and the discontinuous history of capital itself—has radically altered their meaning. Thus, an anthropological interpretation must carefully historicize the persistence of these "traditional" social relations, productive arrangements, and cultural practices.

INFORMAL DEVELOPMENTS

The turn of the twentieth century marked a turning point in economic and class relations within Egypt, in the emergent consciousness of its people caught between class and nation as well as in its advanced integration into the transforming, crisis-ridden, global capitalist system poised at the moment of modernism.[1] Inscribed in the interimperial and national class struggles that took as one of their terrains the most adequate representation of Egypt's artisanry is the historical shift in its relation from dissolution to a rather paradoxical preservation. *Paradoxical preservation* is essentially the subsumption of a new, modern form of petty commodity production (that nonetheless retains the persistent image of tradition) to colonial capital by virtue of this new form's inability to realize its own reproduction except as that reproduction was tied to the expanded reproduction circuits of peripheral capitalism.[2] Perhaps not unexpectedly, the relations of reproduction established at the turn of the century have become problematic today as a result of another shift in global and national struggles between the interests of capital and labor.

In the postcolonial era, the status of petty commodity production has become doubly paradoxical: The life of many premodern forms of production and culture has been rejuvenated by the postmodern pull of the transnational division of labor. These changes are in turn discursively inflected in the recent shift in development research strategies and in Egypt's attempt at national reconstruction in a new transnational frame.

Beginning in the mid-1970s, a global accumulation crisis, prompted by national labor and anti-imperial struggles around the world, brought back into the limelight the mode of reproduction that had served Egypt since the beginning of the century. Crisis was the effect of a challenge to the modern capitalist order, which responded with measures that have brought about a new transnational division of labor whose circuits and flows have colonized spheres social and cultural, as well as economic and territorial. Foreign "aid" channeled from the West to the Third World, particularly to geopolitically strategic countries like Egypt, is one of the technologies that have been quite successfully deployed to influence the recomposition of labor and social reproduction.[3] Among the institutions and fields of knowledge constituted by this terrain of struggle and counterinsurgency is the discourse of "development," the more recent incarnation of its earlier counterparts, the legitimizing code of progress and modernization. In the Egyptian case, as elsewhere, a sense of the current crisis could be glimpsed in the urgency that haunted development discourse during the 1970s, as suddenly petty commodity production, now rechristened the "informal sector," was made the object of enthusiastic information retrieval. By this time the emigration of many Egyptian petty commodity producers had made possible an official awareness of their critical function in providing the possible conditions for an efficient postmodern capitalism in the nation—and their capacity for disrupting those conditions.

The informal sector emerged as a key focus of development research and policy planning throughout the Third World, including Egypt.[4] In conjunction with strategies of family planning designed to curb the Third World's burdensome "population explosion," development planners began to take a keen interest in explaining how minimal employment opportunity in highly capitalized industry coexisted with a relatively low overall unemployment rate. Attention of development planners and others focused on the critical role that the informal sector plays in maintaining the balance. Considerable research on the informal sector has been undertaken by international development agencies, and monographs have described and defined its internal organization and relations of production in many "underdeveloped" countries.[5]

In Egypt, a series of surveys and feasibility studies of Egyptian "small-scale" and "artisanal" industries were funded during the late 1970s by the World Bank, the International Labour Organization, and the U.S. Agency for International Development (AID). A frequently cited survey dating from the mid-1970s profiled Egypt's private-sector industries and brings us about as close as we can get to a statistical sense of an economic sector that historically has eluded statistical census (World Bank 1978; Hansen and Radwan 1982: 64–65). In 1974, some 97 percent of Egypt's 116,926 private-sector establishments were artisanal firms employing less than 10 workers, with half employing less than 5. These workers amounted to 80 percent of the private-sector industrial work force, which in total represented 54 percent of all industrial employment. Their main production was in consumer staples, including clothes, furniture, food processing, metal products, shoes, and leather products. Of the artisanal firms, 74 percent had fixed capital assets of less than LE100 (US $150 in 1980), and 97 percent had less than LE1,000 (US $1,500), underscoring the low capital-intensity of the vast majority of these petty commodity enterprises.

This profile of Egypt's informal sector thus far matches data for small enterprises elsewhere in the Third World. A summation of the characteristics of this sector shows why international agencies have found it very interesting, even as trade unions and labor historians have not. The data strongly suggest that, given its minimal capitalization, the informal sector constitutes a highly effective mode of labor absorption, employing a substantial portion of the "nonfarm" work force in a large number of enterprises with very few workers in each. The availability of cheap commodities and services provided by these labor-intensive enterprises that fall outside the formal industrial sector contributes to the maintenance of a comparatively low cost of living. This cheap cost of living enables highly capitalized enterprises in much of the Third World to extract a high ratio of surplus value by paying workers the low wages that recently in many regions have proved to be a strong magnet of attraction for multinational corporate interests. In the succinct assessment of the World Bank, "as firm size increases: (1) capital investment per worker rises, (2) value added per worker rises, (3) the wage rate rises, and (4) value added per unit of capital *falls*" (1978: 19, emphasis in original).

Finally, the facts that the small workshops of the informal sector favor a "familial" idiom of work relations and that their workers are seldom organized into trades unions makes this form of labor deployment consequential to the maintenance of "political stability" in Third World regions. It is noteworthy that informal sector enterprises are not often touted in development reports for their productive capacity to contribute to the gross national product (GNP), nor for their ability to accumulate capital. The reports envisage the informal sector's potential less in terms of growth than maintenance. The World Bank, for example, favored assistance to those small-scale industries that cater to specialized or low-priced market niches, or that fulfill activities "complementary" to larger firms, including "efficient import substitution." It recommended an approach that would "ensure that small-scale industries fill interstices, command an interlocking position within the industrial structure, and constitute vital parts of a functionally integrated whole" (1977: v). The bank was impressed that "despite the uninviting climate [of Egypt's state-controlled, "socialist" economy], small-scale industry has managed to hold its own and even grow" (1977: i). This growth was clearly less a matter of capital accumulation and expansion of individual firms than it was a rampant, involutionary proliferation.

It is less a matter of concern here that the recommendations of development reports may not have been implemented than that the small-scale industries emerged therein as a figure of increasing importance in the broader discourse on the fate of Egypt's private sector. The extensive discussion of the informal sector in effect amounted to nothing less than the discursive rehabilitation of petty commodity industries, and ipso facto, the "neglected" private sector; "informal sector" became an emblem of legitimacy for the newly assigned place of Egyptian workers in the global economy. Thus, the discursive process of formal/informal *sectorization* may be aptly construed as a strategic deployment in the discourse of reprivatization that has preoccupied state and international interests since Anwar Sadat announced his Open Door economic liberalization policy (*infitah*) in 1973.

Encouragement given the informal sector has been consequential less to the owners of small workshops or their laborers than to those who stand to benefit from the overall reorganization of Egypt's economy towards the private sector. These small-scale entrepreneurial activities may be small and inefficient by "modern" standards. However, since the Nasser-era nationalization of most large-scale industrial enterprises during the 1950s and 1960s, Egypt's public sector effectively included most of what could be considered formal enterprises, tied to the legacy of "socialism" burdened by an overinflated, inefficient government bureaucracy. In effect, the small-scale industries that comprised the informal sector at the beginning of the decade *were* Egypt's private sector. In a discourse of political legitimation, the private and the informal sectors are interchangeable doubles. The latter seems to lack the more obvious political overtones of the former, yet along a symbolic chain of signification, the one slides easily into the other's discursive place. Is the attention given to petty commodity forms of production in the atmosphere of Open Door liberalization genuinely designed to encourage their growth into full-fledged capital-accumulating enterprises? Or has the informal sector sector served as a politically expedient pretext to get the foot of the private sector and its Western corporate allies into that door? Given that Egypt's public sector historically was intimately associated with the state capitalism of Egypt's socialist era, this favoritism toward the private sector takes on political resonance in the new postcolonial context of Egypt's realignment with the West.

EMIGRATION AND CRISIS

Like many of its counterparts in the Third World, during the late 1970s Egypt faced a labor shortage. This shortage, of course, was relative, not absolute: a shortage of workers willing to work for the going wage in certain sectors of the economy, and especially seasonal shortages in rural labor.[6] The post-1973 oil price boom and the ensuing frenzy of construction and development in the oil-rich Arabian Gulf states and Libya sucked in entire segments of skilled and semiskilled workers from the neighboring Arab world and South Asia, leaving gaping holes in the labor structure of these countries (Sivanandan 1979) and in the family structures of those left behind (Hammam 1986). Emigration became the response of many Egyptian farm laborers and skilled craftsworkers (as well as the brain drain of professionals) to the lure of lucrative wages. Contracts and documents required for work abroad were much coveted by Egyptian laborers, and the state loosened restrictions on emigration as one solution to its internal political and economic tensions. The remittances of several million Egyptian workers quickly became a leading source of Egypt's foreign-exchange earnings (bringing in about $4 billion yearly in the mid–1980s), outpacing revenues from tourism, the Suez Canal, oil exports, and foreign aid (Moench 1988).

Egyptians used short-term emigration as an income strategy, as marriage patterns among families of craftsworkers reveal. The appeal once accorded to secure, though low-salaried, public-sector employment gave way to easy money from abroad. Wages earned abroad often covered the culturally requisite costs of marriage and simultaneously redefined those costs upward; they also inflated the costs of "key money" which is required in advance before leasing a flat. Planning for the emigration of one of their members often became a matter of familial strategy—or at least a dream—in which everyone participated. With at least 10 percent of the labor force having emigrated over a 10-year period, a great many Egyptian families could claim some benefits from the remitted wages of a family member who worked abroad for a year or two, or even longer. Unlike other forms of foreign aid, whose trickle-down effects seemed scarcely to matter to the everyday lives of the multitude, workers' remittances amounted to a sort of direct foreign-aid subsidy of the domestic family wage.

By no means were the cost of living and prices of domestic commodities an insignificant issue during this recent period. The state-funded subsidy of food staples, a subvention of foreign aid programs, constitutes implicit recognition of the importance of maintaining the cheap social reproduction of the labor force. The precariously low level of subsistence imposed on most Egyptians was made uncomfortably clear when, in January 1977 under pressure from the International Monetary Fund to reduce state expenditures on food subsidies, Sadat nearly doubled the cost of basic foodstuffs overnight, and all Egypt was rocked by three days of spontaneous "food riots."[7] Though the price increases were rescinded at that time, funding agencies and the United States have continued to push Egypt to reduce subsidies and dismantle the "socialist" public sector as conditions for debt rescheduling (Moench 1988). Inflation became another response of the state to the political turbulence that challenged Sadat's regime during this same year.[8]

To keep wages down in the formal sector, including government employment, the economy needed the informal sector's cheap reproduction. However, emigration meant that craftsproducers could not easily find cheap labor. Many workshop owners or managers whom I interviewed, most of whom presided over and worked in their own shops, claimed that they had difficulty finding trained workers. They nevertheless recognized that this was only to be expected, given that they could not compete with the high wages offered abroad, or even in the local construction industry. Craftsworkers similarly complained that young apprentice-helpers had become flighty, lazy, and not properly deferential; the demand for the young urchins became so great that they simply would move to another employer rather than submit to overbearing authority or undue demands which were formerly accepted as par for the course. Institutional recognition of these problems led to attempts by the state to create new pools of skilled labor by setting up training centers and apprenticeship programs. One scheme, introduced in 1980, offered exemption from social security payments, an issue of complaint by small craftspersons, as an incentive to workshops and production cooperatives to train apprentices for four years (*Al-Ahram*, 3 December 1980). Another scheme got US $40 million credit from the International Development Agency to set up occupational training centers (*Middle East Economic Digest*, 21 November 1980: 24).

While representing the problem as a deficiency in skills and training certainly appealed to assessments made by the public at large, it clearly sidestepped the more relevant issue of the enormous wage differential at home and abroad. Clearly, the question of labor shortages in Egypt must be seen in relation to wage rates, the determination of which was no longer confined to factors within the nation. Contradicting an earlier study that recommended training programs as a remedy (World Bank 1977), a 1978 AID report stated the issue more baldly: The problem was the shortage of skilled workers willing to work at the very low wages offered in Egypt (Berger 1978). In this light, apprenticeship incentive schemes might more aptly be viewed as attempts to recreate a form of minimally remunerated indentured service based on the model of precapitalist trade guilds. "Filling the gaps" in the labor market makes sense as a strategy to ensure cheap social reproduction by creating new ways to more efficiently exploit Egyptian workers and simultaneously to supply the informal sector with *its* conditions of reproduction in a tightened labor market. Widening the analytical frame, such measures are among the disciplinary technologies that, in effect, serve to reconstitute local workers as proper producers for a new international division of labor abroad and an expanding private sector at home.

WORKER SHORTAGE, EMIGRATION, AND STRUGGLE

The disruptions provoked by the emigration of skilled and semi-skilled Egyptian workers lends credence to the importance that development agents ascribed to the informal sector. By 1980 it seemed that this sort of compromise had disrupted the Egyptian economy. From the viewpoint of Egyptian capital, all this pointed to nothing short of a crisis: Its rate of profit was threatened with reduction and the state's advocacy and protection of their interests had been shaken because the mode of capital accumulation that had served it since the early twentieth century was being contested right at its heart: the relations by which its material and social hegemony had been reproduced. This crisis is better construed as one impelled not by an aberrant—or even inherent—"maladjustment" between employment sectors, but by active *class struggle* in the context of global transformations in capital accumulation.[9] It is a struggle motivated less by an organized labor movement than by what Gramsci called the socially constructed "common sense" embedded in working-class culture.[10] This culture is defined both by "productive" and "unproductive" workers, for the income strategy of most extended families typically depends on both.[11]

The emigration of Egyptian laborers, often to tougher work and social conditions abroad (see Ismael 1986), represents, I would argue, an active, critical contestation over the division of the wage itself (Castells 1980: 48). Just as multinational corporate interests were beginning to get a foot *in* Egypt's Open Door, emigrants were taking a step *out*: By "voting with their feet," Egyptian workers extricated themselves from conditions of economic hardship at home and demonstrably articulated a demand for the expansion of their interests and socially recognized needs.

In a sense, the Egyptian workers' will to resist, their articulation of a demand for new accepted standards for their traditional way of life, can best be read in the sense of crisis their practical strategies produced in authoritative discourse: in this case, the discourses of the state and development. This subtle rebellion has been more often than not concealed as such by its assimilation into revised and discordant hegemonic narratives. On the one hand, there are laudatory invocations praising the emigrants for sending home the remittances that have become a mainstay subsidy to the Egyptian economy. On the other hand, there are denunciations of the emigrants' individual avarice and of their imitation of the profit-maximizing pursuits of capital itself (as in the case of state-orchestrated and popular blame leveled at emigrating petty commodity producers for rising prices, unavailability of services, and so on). The impossibility of reconciling these two often conflicting discourses of the state and development belies official attempts to displace class inequalities in the name of collective belt tightening for the sake of the nation or in the name of an imagined authenticity accorded to the industrious but complacent "community" of informal-sector and peasant workers.

CRISIS AND INFORMALIZATION

To see the decline in the rate of profit as impelled by class struggle permits us to reframe with greater understanding the impetus behind the present efforts to recuperate petty commodity production and to simultaneously retain and constrain informal sector enterprises. In effect, the production of the concept of "informal sector" within the discourse of development redefines the functioning of the global capitalist economy; it represents a discursive effort by hegemonic international and class interests to assert their control over the mode of reproduction of capital accumulation. As long as the social reproduction of capitalist relations of production was more or less smoothly assured, the ideology of development was content to project the semblance of a unified capitalist identity across a social and economic field polarized by primeval otherness, a field of eternally distinct alterity: capitalist self and precapitalist other. Framed by the idea of progress and the theory of stages of development, this neat opposition effectively concealed the historical marks of antagonism and inequality that had riddled the development of capitalism with fissures; it imposed, as well, an artificial synchronicity on traditional forms of production and social relations.[12] Once that reproduction had been disrupted in Egypt's case by workers' refusal to labor and live within the constraints imposed by capital and the rate of profit had been threatened by crisis, the developmentalist structuration of the domain of production into preferred and residual categories had to be altered.

Developmentalist discourse could no longer allow formally noncapitalist forms of production and their associated social relations and cultural practices to stand materially—or even conceptually—outside the capitalist mode of production. Having denied in the past the importance and productivity of petty commodity enterprises, destined as they were to fall under the wheels of "progress," development planners, bankers, and transnational financial capitalists had to rehabilitate these forms and make them into "real" industries by naming and defining them as such. Only after suppressing the heterogeneity of these traditional forms and forcing them into the mold of a restructured dual economy could their constituents be subjected to the laws of imperialism charged by a new transnational division of labor.

For Egypt, this significance has become ever more apparent since the mid–1970s as informal-sector workers have been siphoned off by the stronger, transnational pull of oil-fattened wages. Thus renaming Egypt's petty commodity production from outmoded artisanat to the microentrepreneurial informal sector discursively stages one form of the current global reterritorialization of labor, reinventing archaic productive forms while minimizing the emergence of "the clean contours of a 'working class' " (Spivak 1985: 140; also see Mies 1986). However, even while men and women engaged in the informal sector are rehabilitated as "workers" by development planners, opposition and labor organizations continue to ignore this status, thereby losing a critical opportunity to broaden the basis of secular opposition politics and consigning these workers to the organizational machinations of a resurgent fundamentalist Islam and statist campaigns.

If political organization were to be reconstituted on the broadened terrain of struggle established by these "other" workers in an effort to start from and to make ideologically coherent what Gramsci called the "common sense which is the spontaneous philosophy of the multitude" (1971: 421), new forms of class struggle might soon present a more powerful counterhegemonic threat.

NOTES

This chapter is part of a larger work on the poetics of Egyptian petty commodity production. The study is based on a year of ethnographic fieldwork in

Cairo, conducted in 1980, among potters and other petty commodity producers and their families; and on historical research into Egyptian artisanry since the nineteenth century. The research was conducted under a joint fellowship from the Social Science Research Council/American Council of Learned Societies and the American Research Center in Egypt.

1. For general discussions of the development of capitalism in Egypt during this period, see Beinin and Lockman (1987), Davis (1983), Owen (1981), and Richards (1982).

2. On this process of incorporation in general, see Meillassoux (1981 [1975]) and Rey (1973). For the Middle East, with an emphasis on women's domestic labor, see Hammam (1986).

3. See Morsey (1986: 359).

4. Moser (1978) discussed the shift in development strategies and the research on the informal sector that was initiated in 1969 with the establishment of the World Employment Program of the International Labour Organization. For development policy issues from the perspective of international institutions, see, for example, World Bank (1978).

5. See, for example, Barker and Smith (1986); Bromley (1978); Bromley and Gerry (1979); Hugon (1980); Portes (1983); and Smith (1984a).

6. On labor shortages in agriculture, see Richards, Martin, and Nagaar (1983), Taylor-Awny (1987), and Toth (1984).

7. On the 1977 "food riots," see "Egypt in Crisis" 1977; Waterbury 1983: 229.

8. See Lawson (1985: 54) for details on the social struggles of 1977, and other struggles that occurred in 1965, 1974, and 1980.

9. For important discussions of Marxist crisis theory that have informed my views here, see Bell (1977), Bell and Cleaver (1982), Castells (1980), Negri (1984) and O'Connor (1981, 1987).

10. On "common sense," see Gramsci (1971: 326, 328, 419–424). See also Hall (1981: 227) on the importance of common sense and popular traditions.

11. This indeed characterized Western industrial development, at least since the emergence in the late-nineteenth century of the "separate spheres" model in which gender was deployed as a wedge between home and work (Benería and Stimpson 1987). "Housewives" in the domestic sphere were certainly aware of struggles faced by their "breadwinning" spouses on the shop floor and often played crucial roles in supporting strikes and in constructing in common a working-class culture. Here, too, capitalist interests (including those of the state) nonetheless treated women's unwaged work as invisible (Mies 1986).

12. The primeval otherness of non-Western societies is further reinforced in anthropological practice by what Johannes Fabian has called the "denial of coevalness," "a persistent and systematic tendency to place the referent(s) of anthropology in a Time other than the present of the producer of anthropological discourse" (1983: 31).

10

Industrial Decentralization and Women's Employment in South Africa: A Case Study

Georgina Jaffee

In this chapter Georgina Jaffee describes some of the effects of the South African government's industrial decentralization policy on bantustan women. Although government reports that focus on the economic and political effects of decentralization have suggested that the effects are minimal and/or negative, Jaffee argues that the policy has had important consequences for bantustan women. Unlike the situation described, for example, by Fernandez-Kelly (1983), where women's employment in the new international division of labor does not improve their positions in their households, Jaffee suggests that in her South African case, despite the patriarchal context of their employment, women's employment has transformed household relations.

Decentralization of industrial production has been part of the South African government's industrial policy since the 1960s. This regional development policy has attempted to lend political and economic credibility to the *bantustans*, or black homelands, in an attempt to limit the integration of African people into the metropolitan economy. Consequently, the pattern of regional development is predicated on the distinction between "white" South Africa and the bantustans or homelands. Decentralized production has occurred both within bantustans and on their borders.

Up to the mid-1970s the bantustans functioned primarily to reproduce a supply of cheap labor to the metropolitan areas of South Africa. The supply and control of labor was regulated by influx control policies.

Since this period, the bantustans' main function has been to contain
and control the increasing surplus population. Consequently, the formation of regional industrial areas, encouraged by government incentives, developed in an environment in which the work force has
experienced high levels of repression and control from both bantustan
authorities and the South African police. Repressive measures continued to ensure a relatively unorganized and subordinate work force in
decentralized areas.

The development of regional productive activities has had an enormous effect on rural social relations. Industrial growth incorporated
people who were trapped in bantustans as a regional working class.
In particular, women, who had never previously been part of an industrial work force, became incorporated into industrial production in
the regional industrial economy. This participation in industrial production as part of a new regional working class has led to a restructuring of gender and class relations within households and the rural
community.

This chapter is based on a case study of the Brits industrial zone.
Brits is one of the eight decentralized areas in South Africa. It analyzes
the lives of female industrial workers from a rural village who commute
daily to an industrial deconcentration point some 40 kilometers from
where they live. It examines the place women occupy in the industrial
hierarchy, showing how gender inequality has played a role in labor-
force formation. Furthermore, the study focuses on the relationship
between domestic life and wage labor through exploring household
organization.

INDUSTRIAL DECENTRALIZATION

Since 1948 the government of South Africa has focused much of its
policy-making on the political and social segregation of various racially
defined populations. As a result, the government designated 10 predominantly rural areas as homelands. Together, these areas constitute
less than 13 percent of the South African land. In the late 1960s the
government tightened its policy of influx control in order to curb the
flow of black people from rural to urban areas. These policies, combined
with the notorious mass removals of people, displaced urbanization to
the bantustans and laid a basis for the formation of a labor force that
was to be incorporated into industry created in decentralized zones.
The increase in population movement from the rural to urban areas
was caused by the destruction of a rural subsistence base that had
previously enabled migrants to maintain a link to the rural base. The
new influx control measures led to the concentration of large numbers

of potentially economically active people trapped in concentrated settlements in specifically designated areas (Hindson 1987: 74).

Industrial decentralization has gone through two distinct phases.
The first phase (up to 1981) maintained the centrality of the bantustans
as part of the regional development policy. Between 1960 and 1981,
only 7,500 jobs were created per year in areas where over 100,000
people were coming onto the job market annually. In 1981, a new
development plan dividing South Africa into eight development regions
created new growth points for various types of industry. These boundaries cut across bantustan borders and correspond to the new patterns
of capital location and population settlement since the 1960s (Cobbett
et al. 1986). Incentives including subsidies of up to R110 (US$42) per
worker per month, rebates on railage, road transport, shipping, air
freight, interest concessions, rent concessions, interest subsidy on housing, income tax concession, and concessions on sales were introduced.
In 1983 the Development Bank was set up to oversee this process. As
a combined result of these measures, 25,000 jobs per year have been
created in the new development areas since the early 1980s.

WOMEN AND THE NEW DECENTRALIZED
WORK FORCE

A key characteristic of the new labor force that was formed when
industries were set up in these zones is the predominance of women.
Various writers on this topic have shown that the incorporation of
women into the industrial labor force in these areas served as a means
to restructure the reserve army of labor and is a direct social, economic,
and political requirement of the apartheid capitalist state (Mager
1989). Influx control, which prevented women from moving to the cities,
was not designed to establish a basis for cheap labor power but rather
was intended to hold down the numbers of people who would move to
urban areas and thus pose a political threat. In addition, by controlling
these populations in bantustans, the government hoped to keep down
the cost of welfare services.

Decentralized industry led to the formation of a new type of labor
force. Long-distance migration to the cities was replaced by commuter
labor. By the mid-1980s, there were almost a million workers who fit
into this category. Both men and women were drawn into the labor
force from newly developed townships set up adjacent to industry or
from preexisting landless rural villages.

This new labor force is also highly exploited and exploitable. In the
mid-1970s there was no legislation for industrial protection and minimum wage regulation. Currently, less than 10 percent of the work
force in deconcentration points is organized, despite the legislative

changes that are slowly taking place in bantustans. Though unions are gaining official recognition in most bantustans, they were initially outlawed in the decentralized industrial zones. In particular, women are concentrated in the least skilled jobs and are paid lower wages than men. Although some areas differed, a number of studies have confirmed women's lower pay (Mager 1989).

Unions in South African industry have been vociferous since the mid-1970s in their condemnation of the decentralization policy. A great number of urban factories closed and moved to border areas. Not only was union power in urban areas declining due to loss of membership, but low wages in the decentralized areas created competition with urban workers and drove down their wages as well. Despite this tendency, urban unions in the 1980s have gained strength and have managed to influence the political process of industrial policy-making.

Overall, female employment patterns in South Africa are consistent with worldwide trends that indicate an increase in the numbers of women employed in industry. In South Africa, women's employment is subject to two interrelated forms of domination—those of gender and race. African women were the last to enter the industrial sector in the 1960s, following the integration of white, colored, and Indian women into the industrial labor force. Three broad phases in the incorporation of women into industry have been identified. Between 1915 and 1945, white, predominantly Afrikaans women formed almost three-quarters of the female industrial labor. These women were forced to look for employment due to the rural transformation and poverty of the 1920s, and were encouraged by "civilised labor policies" that were set up to protect whites from black competition. The second period, from 1945 to 1960, led to the advancement of colored women into industrial occupations. After 1965, African women moved into industrial employment (Martin and Rogerson 1984).

The occupational hierarchy follows a specific pattern in which white men occupy the most highly specialized positions, followed by white women. At the bottom of the hierarchy are African men, followed by African women, with coloreds and Indians occupying the intermediate positions. Women have also been clustered in certain occupational categories, such as food, clothing, and textiles (Martin and Rogerson 1984: 39). These patterns, which were set up in the mid-1960s, have changed very little.

The regional development policies in the post-1960s period opened the way for a new pattern of women's employment in industry. Over a period of time, women in regional industry have outstripped the number of men. In the Transkei, a large bantustan with numerous decentralized industrial points, women's employment in manufacturing increased from 6 percent in 1980 to 13 percent in 1985, compared to only a 2 percent increase in male employment (Green and Hirsch 1982; Jaffee 1988). Overall, the female percentage of the work force increased from 8.1 percent in 1970 to 16.6 percent in 1980 in the occupational categories of production and transport. Over the same period, women employed in sales increased from 25.4 percent to 50.5 percent (Jaffee 1988).

Women's incorporation into regional industry also created a geographical hierarchy. Women in decentralized industry find themselves in positions of extreme exploitability, as their wages are lower than their male counterparts and lower than women and men employed in industry in metropolitan areas. In well-organized factories in metropolitan areas, women in the same occupational categories as men are paid less due to discriminatory job-grading systems.

BRITS STUDY BACKGROUND

The population of Brits, a small farming town, totals 16,800 people and is composed of 12,000 whites, 200 coloreds, 1,600 Asians, and 3,000 blacks. The black people live in a squalid township 2 kilometers outside the main town. There is no infrastructure in the township, and the government has been attempting to remove the population into a neighboring bantustan for many years. Brits lies 80 kilometers northwest of Johannesburg and 40 kilometers west of Pretoria. There are a further 365,000 people who live in districts surrounding Brits.

Brits was proclaimed a border industrial area in 1968, and rapid industrial expansion has ensued. Surrounded by the "independent" bantustan of Bophuthatswana, the industrial park that developed in the mid-1970s has had easy access to large numbers of unskilled commuter labor. Due to the zone's proximity to the metropolitan area of Johannesburg and the generous incentive scheme, Brits grew rapidly from an initial 22 factories in 1968 to 92 factories in 1990. A significant portion of companies originally relocated from the urban metropolitan area of Johannesburg, and many were multinational subsidiaries.

Fifteen thousand people commuted from neighboring Bophuthatswana to the Brits industrial zone out of a total of 116,000 people who commuted from Bophuthatswana in 1985 on a daily basis to various places in South Africa. One-third of the commuters were women. Workers were recruited for jobs at the various factories both at the gate of the factory and through the labor bureau, where work seekers can apply for jobs. Companies did not use education as a criterion for job placements. Women who were interviewed about their work complained bitterly that they deserved better opportunities because they had obtained relatively high levels of secondary school education.

Most workers, except those who live in a nearby township, travel from at least eight different rural areas from within Bophuthatswana. Some villages are located up to 90 kilometers from Brits. Despite transport subsidization, these journeys constitute an enormous expense for daily commuters. Commuting is also time-consuming: Many workers spend up to three hours a day on buses. Commuters living furthest away from the industrial site leave home at 4:30 A.M. and return at 7:00 P.M. Commuter workers thus have very limited time during the working week for relaxation. The rigid timetable imposed on commuter labor is particularly burdensome for women workers, who are expected to carry out most of the domestic tasks at home.

Close links with parent companies and worker organizations in the metropolitan area led to the rapid organization of workers. As a result, by the mid-1980s, many companies in the zone had been forced to recognize the unions. It took barely five years for a militant working-class culture to emerge in the region. In most cases, union recognition took place after lengthy and violent industrial disputes with the close involvement of the South African police. Many unionists were arrested, and hundreds of workers were maimed in these often bloody confrontations. Multinational firms in the industrial zone—sensitive to divestment pressure—were often the first to recognize the unions. Their organization by unions has provided a bridgehead for union growth in the zone, although other firms have sought to blunt growing labor militancy in the Brits zone by relocating their factories in nearby bantustans.

TYPES OF INDUSTRY

A survey in 1990 of all the 92 companies in Brits revealed an extraordinary industrial variety. Major concentrations included engineering (15 percent), furniture (28 percent), motor components and accessories (10 percent), building supplies (13 percent), and plastics (7 percent). Small firms were also engaged in producing pharmaceuticals, weapons, food products, agricultural equipment, luxury consumer goods, and clothing.

Half the companies surveyed in Brits were part of a larger production process and thus owned by larger groups. Five companies were multinationals. The half that were not linked to other companies were much smaller, with an average work force of 55. The highest number of workers in one plant was 500 and the lowest was 19. The average number of workers was 160. One-third of the work force overall consisted of women.

Women's work in industrial labor has grown worldwide, and patriarchy has been a key element in organizing women's gendered employment in the new international division of labor. Lim (1983: 70–92) has

Table 10.1
Worker Composition by Sex for Selected Factories, 1990

	Total	Male	Female
Electrical	208	101	107
Furniture	235	105	130
Motors	512	302	210
Cable	407	192	215
Motor Components	600	300	300

argued that although firms take advantage of women's inferior position in the labor market, for some women, jobs in export factories do purchase freedom from patriarchal household structures and increase income and consumption levels, as well as expanding women's capacities for individual choices. Fuentes and Ehrenreich (1983) have demonstrated how young women who come to work for multinational companies face poor work conditions and low wages while obtaining a certain amount of independence. In contrast, Fernandez-Kelly (1983) has shown that women enter the labor force as household members; thus, employment does not increase their independence because their wages are delivered to fathers, mothers, or husbands. She also argued that their domestic power is not increased as most of the women still submit to male power.

The results of the Brits study support a gendered description of the new industrial division of labor and the importance of patriarchy in its emergence. The data suggest that women in the Brits zone are more dominant in certain types of manufacturing units and that within those units they were at the lowest end of the industrial hierarchy. For instance, the study showed that 50 percent of the women worked in motor components, 25 percent in electrical goods, and 25 percent in furniture.

A more detailed analysis of five factories with higher proportions of women workers was conducted. Some of the results are reported in Table 10.1.

In the factories surveyed above, women in the same occupational categories as men received a lower average wage than men. The difference was between R10 (US $3) and R40 (US $16), with the greatest difference in more highly skilled jobs. Over two-thirds of the women working in these factories occupied positions at the lowest end of the industrial hierarchy. There was no difference in their industrial experience to justify a lower salary level. Results from a questionnaire distributed in one of the electrical factories showed that 50 percent of the work force reported that there was no difference between men and women's work. An additional 25 percent said that there was no difference in the work even though women worked harder and were paid less than men.

The Brits survey revealed that there was no differential skill that had been acquired before coming into the factory, as the majority of workers acquired their first industrial experience in their present workplace. The mean age for women was 34 and for men, 35. Many employees had entered the work force in the 1980s in their late twenties. Women workers had an average of nine years education, and men, seven.

The occupational structures of decentralized industry is a clear example of how capital inherits and exploits sex segregation. Patriarchal ideology was used to exploit gender differences in order to render greater profits through the payment of lower wages to women. Sexist ideology has affected the way in which women have been positioned in the labor market, a finding corroborated by other studies of women in South Africa's decentralized industries (Mager 1989).

THE WOMEN AT HOME: HOUSEHOLD FORMATION IN AN OUTLYING DISTRICT

Bapong (population 5,000) is situated 35 kilometers from Brits. It is typical of the bantustan periphery where the inhabitants are dependent for their survival on migrant earnings and, more recently, on the earnings of commuter workers. Some residents work in the metropolitan areas of Johannesburg and Pretoria as migrants, while others commute to Brits. Buses run specially for the commuters arrive at 5:30 A.M. and deposit people back between 6:00 and 7:00 P.M.

The village and surrounding areas are occupied by Tswana-speaking people who have been settled there since the turn of the century. As is typical of bantustan villages, there is little infrastructure. Water is collected from various communal taps, although some of the residents have sunk boreholes. There is no electricity or sewage system. Most of the older houses are made of brick with corrugated iron roofs.

Although the community was always dependent on remittances from wage labor, in the past many people cultivated the soil for subsistence, and during the 1950s, many residents still owned cattle. Almost none of the residents are presently involved in agricultural activities, although a small number still keep cattle. The land is owned by the Bapo Tribe, and the village is governed by a chief under the Bophuthatswana government. The community is highly differentiated: Residents include small-business people who own local shops, taxi owners, farm laborers, commuter workers, migrant workers, hawkers, and the unemployed. It is especially difficult to assesses the magnitude and status of the unemployed given the absence of an elaborated state welfare assistance program.

THE HOUSEHOLDS

A sample of 32 households was studied. These households were chosen through a network sample, the sole criterion being that at least one woman was engaged in factory work. In-depth interviews were carried out with seven women. The majority of women interviewed had entered factory work between the ages of seventeen and twenty-eight. All of them had entered the work force in the early 1980s as Brits developed into an industrial zone. For most, this was their first experience of industrial work and their first job. A small minority had previously worked on the farms as laborers or in nearby towns as domestic workers. Moving to industrial employment was seen as attractive in contrast to lower-paying domestic and farm work due to the higher wages paid in this sector.

In the South African context, there is much debate over how to define households in circumstances of demographic instability caused by political and economic factors. In labor-supply economies and in circumstances of tight political controls, there is a continual movement of people in and out of households. This has recently become the concern of the anthropologists Andrew Speigle (1986) and Colin Murray (1981), who have questioned the relevance of the conceptual schema of a household "developmental cycle." In addition, feminist analysis has generally criticized the conventional anthropological literature for the conceptual deployment of households analyzed as static units within which resources are shared and where members constitute a community of interest. This definition omits conflicts of interest within households and omits analyzing the necessity of women's oppression in household reproduction. For the purposes of this discussion, households are defined here as residential sites where members who may be kin-related but are not necessarily so engage in conflictual relations of mutual obligation.

Among the households surveyed, there were a number of different forms. The most common household form was that of the three-generational family. The second most common was comprised of two-generational families with strong sibling links. The latter included households that had lost the first generation through death and therefore were in the same stage of the household cycle as three-generational

households. The most obvious characteristics of the majority of households was that conjugal ties only existed at the first generation: This
meant that most of the women workers were unmarried and still living
in their parents' households or with siblings and their children. Ten
percent of the women living in the three-generational households were
divorced and had returned to their parental homestead. In all the
households the women working in the factories played a central role
in the financial reproduction of the household and were, in most cases,
the dominant breadwinners.

Central to the organization of the households surveyed was the maintenance of a strong network of support, either from mothers of working
women or from unemployed siblings. As most of the women had children, this network of support was essential. The long hours commuting
and working also necessitated that women workers with children find
appropriate support systems. The women who were interviewed were
particularly conscious of choosing to avoid or delay marriage. A common feature of all the households was the women's avoidance of traditional patriarchal relations. Of the 32 households surveyed, 40
percent of the women had children, and only half of these maintained
links with the fathers of their offspring.

DOMESTIC SUPPORT NETWORKS

Tswana society is patrilineal and neolocal. Young women are expected to move out of their familial households into a newly established
household of their spouse. Working women who were interviewed for
this study indicated that they prolonged the period of time spent in
their natal households, and delayed marriage and subsequent neolo-
cality. This strategy, which was made possible only through access to
income through wage labor, also enables the women to escape the
patriarchy typical of Tswana domestic relations. The following examples are typical of the three-generation household.

Mary is thirty-four. She went to work in one of the factories in Brits
when she was twenty-six. She lives in her mother's house with her
brother and her two children. Mary is the only income earner and is
completely dependent on her mother for the daily domestic tasks. Her
male companion and the father of her two children lives in the Brits
location and visits weekly. They have been involved with one another
for six years. Mary admits that she does not want to get married. If
she did marry, she would have to move out of her mother's house in
Bapong and into a new home with her spouse or move into her mother-
in-law's house many miles from Bapong. Both options presented a
problem. If she moved into a house with her husband and kept her job,
she would have nobody to assist her with child care and other domestic

chores, which are presently carried out by her mother. She said that in this case she would probably have to give up work and, in addition, she would be forced to look after her husband. If she were to move to her mother-in-law's house, Mary would also have to give up work. In both situations, she would lose her economic autonomy and become reliant on the wages of her husband. Continuing to live with her mother and avoid marriage allows her to maintain her economic autonomy and escape patriarchal controls that would be imposed on her were she to get married.

Anna's three-generation household was recently formed by her return to her mother's household after her divorce. Anna had been working in the Brits industrial area for six years. She lived on her own during the week as her husband only returned on weekends from his job in Pretoria. Anna has two children who were cared for during the day by the local day care center. When she asked why she returned to her mother's house, she told the following story.

Living on my own was hard. I used to leave work and pick up the kids and then have to cook and clean. On weekends my husband came home and expected me to look after him. He would also drink. I got tired of this so I asked for a divorce. I prefer living with my mother—she helps me with the kids and the cooking.

Anna's mother was already looking after the two children of her second daughter. She now had four small children to care for but seemed accepting of her role. Furthermore, Anna's return to her natal household has placed considerable strain on other members of the household—the two grandchildren and a younger unemployed son. When interviewed, Anna's mother suggested that there was conflict emerging in the household over space and resources but that there was no other solution but to accept Anna and her children. Although Anna's mother maintained the authority as household head, Anna revealed in the discussion that she much preferred this to her husband's authority.

Edna's household is particularly interesting. It is comprised of her mother; her grandmother, who is in her eighties; an absent migrant father; two sisters; and one niece. All three sisters work in the factories. Their ages range from twenty-eight to thirty-three. Edna and her sisters contribute equally to the household expenses but keep their own money overall. All three sisters indicated a desire to be married in the future but only after they had accumulated enough money to enter into the marriage with some of their personal income. They were saving an average of R60 (US $23) per month. Although only one of them had a child, they were still dependent on their mother for household reproduction. They all indicated that they liked living together, as they felt "free" this way. Asked if they would feel as free if they were married, they answered that they would not unless they kept their jobs and had a lot of their own money.

A striking feature of all the three-generational families was the conscious distance maintained from male relationships. Where relationships existed, the male partner or, in some cases, the father of the women workers' children would make only weekend visits. The three sisters in Edna's household all had boyfriends but they lived in other parts of the region and, consequently, only visited irregularly.

Involvement of men was also absent in the women workers' parents' generation. Many of the older women were widowed or abandoned by their husbands, and others had husbands who still worked as migrant laborers. In most of these three-generational families, the mother of the factory worker played a major part in domestic reproduction.

Husbands of the first generation were, in most cases, absent from the day-to-day organization of the household, including child care, cleaning, and cooking. The mother was given a certain amount of income at the end of the month to cover household expenses. Despite almost total dependence on the daughter's income (only 3 percent received a small pension), the older women maintained the authority in the household with regard to the maintenance of traditional laws and customs and the delegation of the daily reproductive tasks. In all cases, women workers were exempt from fulfilling household chores during the week but were expected to do some work on weekends.

A substantial portion of the 34 households surveyed involved close and complicated relations with siblings of the working women. Forty percent were composed of two-generational households in which up to seven siblings and their families resided. Among all households, half were dependent on one income and half were dependent on two; in every instance, the female industrial worker was the highest income earner. The relatively superior earning power of the working women gave them increased power over their siblings. Younger siblings who were responsible for household tasks were often resentful, and the relations among siblings in these households were more conflictual. Arguments over money and resentment from younger siblings for having to carry out the major domestic tasks were often the sources of conflict.

In some cases, this mutual dependence has affected traditional gender roles. An account of Sina's household suggests the sources and resolution of new tensions arising from women's industrial employment in the Brits development zone. She is twenty-four and lives in her mother's house with two unemployed brothers, aged eighteen and twenty. She has two children whom she leaves daily in the care of her brothers. Her mother died three years ago and her father lives in Johannesburg. Sina's siblings have tried to find work but have only had limited success. The older brother worked temporarily in a mine but has never been able to find permanent work. The younger brother has finished school but has not yet found work. Sina is dependent on at least one of her brothers for child care, although she is aware that this arrangement may change if they find work. She currently supports both her brothers and her two children. The father of the children works about 30 kilometers away and visits irregularly. Sina has chosen not to marry as she would have to move to her husband's village and leave her job.

Another example of sibling conflict is in the Ramasea household. This household is comprised of three generations, and the nine children of the third generation are cared for by their grandmother. The second generation is comprised of three siblings—two females and one male. One female sibling works in the factories, while her brother is a policeman and her younger sister is still at school. Talita, the younger sister, hated living in the household, as she had to do all the chores for her working sister, her nephews and nieces, and her brother. She argued that she was the slave of the household because she had to work hard and help her mother when she came home from school. She argued that she has no life and is prevented from going out on weekends because there is so much to do. She expressed deep resentment toward her working sister.

The women who were interviewed were highly conscious of female subordination. The avoidance of marriage or the desire to delay marriage was captured in the following statements in response to the question of whether they wanted to marry sometime in the future. "I prefer not to marry, as I would have to serve my husband and my mother-in-law," said one interviewee. "I would like to marry if I could find somebody who would also help in the house," said another. Still another reported, "I need to work, and if I marry, I would not be able to support my children."

Some women argued that they would only marry after they had saved "enough" money. This statement was common among younger women who did not yet have children. Having access to a stable income and not having direct dependents gave these women the opportunity of saving money which would then enable them to enter a conjugal relationship with savings and, therefore, greater economic autonomy.

CONCLUSION

The entry of women into the work force has led to a number of important transformations at the level of the household. Despite ex-

ploitation on the factory floor, access to a higher income in industry
has given women workers some economic autonomy and enabled them
to make choices about their personal lives. The formation of three-
generational households headed by older women who became dependent on their daughters' income and households characterized by strong
sibling links has enabled women to receive the necessary support in
order to maintain their roles as mothers and working women. This
support would not have been the same had they entered marriage or
lived permanently with men. Women workers avoided or limited patriarchal control by constructing female-centered households and by
maintaining only limited involvement with men.

If this form of industrial development declines, it will likely affect
social relations and household organization. Women displaced from the
work force will become part of an unemployed rural proletariat or be
forced to look for work in urban areas and thus migrate. The recent
withdrawal of influx control has opened up the way for the development
of squatter settlements on the periphery of large urban areas. It is
most likely that women who are displaced from the decentralized work
force will have very little choice other than abandoning their rural
homesteads and moving, with or without their families, to informal
settlements on the urban periphery.

Part III

Worker Struggles and Survival in the New Industrial World

11

Labor-Managed Systems and Industrial Redevelopment: Lessons from the Fagor Cooperative Group of Mondragón

Davydd J. Greenwood

In this chapter, as in those that follow, the emphasis is on workers' efforts to improve their circumstances. Here Davydd Greenwood describes a usually neglected aspect of industrial cooperatives, how they function in competition with standard firms. He suggests that their success rests on their ability to pool capital and labor, a characteristic they share with household farms, which makes them highly flexible and adaptable systems.

The following chapter is a theoretical reflection on industrial redevelopment, and it centers on lessons of general importance learned from studying industrial cooperatives. Specifically, the chapter focuses on ways in which an examination of industrial cooperatives helps us understand the role of pooling capital and labor in successful adjustments to cyclical markets. As a theoretical discussion, it emphasizes argument over demonstration. My aim is to encourage comparative analyses of cases (including cooperatives) centered on the issues of labor and capital pooling and of economic cyclicity.

Because the industrial cooperatives of Mondragón (Guipúzcoa) in Spain are such successful examples of a labor-managed industrial system, clarity about which lessons to draw from studying them is important. Researchers and policymakers want to know what the key elements in Mondragón's success are, whether the structures invented and successfully deployed in these cooperatives can be transferred to other countries and different economic situations, and what the role of "culture" is in the cooperatives. All these issues are raised in the substantial literature on Mondragón.[1]

Unfortunately, the concern with their cooperative character obscures relationships between the economic success of such organizations and more generalized dimensions of industrial political economy. Mention of the cooperatives of Mondragón conjures either negative or romantic images of low technology and small scale, though this in no way characterizes their reality. Apparently, the high degree of participation and strong egalitarian ideology are assumed to require a noncompetitive economic and technological infrastructure.

This is a matter of ideological convenience, in my view. It liberates managers in noncooperative firms from explaining why the distribution of ownership, management responsibility, and economic rewards is so hierarchical. If the cooperatives are technologically backward and small in scale, then they can be viewed as an exotic plant, something that is nice to look at but would not grow in an ordinary garden. If, however, they are technologically sophisticated and large in scale, then the hierarchical character of most firms immediately becomes a political issue.

People concerned with cooperatives also tend to be quite inward-looking. The literature examines a host of issues of particular importance to cooperatives as firms and to potential cooperative leaders. Among the kinds of questions taken up are the following: Are non-Tayloristic production lines and other new forms of work organization an essential part of participation? How do cooperatives fit into the market and are they able to compete? Are self-consciously founded cooperatives essentially different from cooperatives that result from labor buyouts? What sort of internal statutory structure enhances the possibilities of commitment and growth?

Because mainstream scholars and those interested specifically in cooperatives both treat cooperatives as a special case, another set of potentially more significant questions has received less attention. These center on the comparative examination of labor–management cooperation and of cooperatives in the diversified international context of contemporary industrial economies. Where do cooperative organizations fit in? Are they the leading edge of a new growth sector, or will they forever constitute a tiny ideological fringe? Are they a sign of economic advance or decline? Do they have particular characteristics that enable them to successfully compete with ordinary firms under current conditions?

There is relatively little comparative analysis that contrasts industrial and/or agricultural cooperatives with other forms of self-managed organizations such as households, service organizations such as some colleges and universities, and some kinds of religious groups. There is even less direct comparison of the performance of firms that have been restructured as "participatory" workplaces with that of cooperatives.

As a result, many important issues have not been addressed in detail. How well do industrial cooperatives compete with standard firms? Can they survive such competition? Can cooperatives be linked to non-cooperatives as suppliers, in joint ventures, or as elements in multi-national corporations without destroying their internal structure? What are plausible paths to a future in which labor-managed systems play a significant role? Is a mixed cooperative–noncooperative economic system ideal, or even possible? What do other forms of labor-managed systems reveal to us about cooperatives?

Having formulated this set of questions, I do not actually intend to provide complete answers. This chapter simply aims to show how the study of cooperatives can be linked to the study of other forms of economic organization to gain some additional insight. In this case, I link the study of cooperatives to the examination of household farming production systems to show that both share some important characteristics that help explain their resiliency under certain conditions. If this approach seems useful, than I presume the case will be made for systematic pursuit of some of the other comparisons I have suggested.

THE BACKGROUND

The labor-managed industrial cooperatives of Mondragón (Guipúz-coa) in the Spanish Basque Country are one of the major examples of industrial democracy found anywhere in the world. Their particular importance stems from their improbable origin in the days of General Francisco Franco's fascism, their unique ability to operate effectively within unstable markets of market sectors, and their overwhelming economic success.

These cooperatives not only have outcompeted other Spanish industries and are exporting successfully, they have continued to do so through a severe worldwide recession, with minimal layoffs of members. They also recovered from the recession more quickly than other firms. How this was possible and its potential relevance to problems of industrial development and redevelopment are the subjects of this chapter. The answer can be found in their ability to pool resources and respond flexibly to changing market demand without impairing the social organization of production. I argue that there are useful analogies to be found in the way household farming systems pool resources to respond to cyclicity.

The Setting

The legally defined "Autonomous Community of the Basque Country" comprises 1.4 percent of the land surface of Spain and has a population of over 2 million, which is about 6 percent of Spain's total. Densely populated and highly industrialized from the late nineteenth century on, the Basque country has been one of the two major industrial centers of Spain, Catalonia being the other.

The region is well known to social scientists for a variety of reasons. The Basque language is unrelated to any other language currently spoken or historically known anywhere in the world. The Basque Country is known for its support of the Republic during the Spanish Civil War and, more recently, for recurrent waves of terrorism that it has experienced since 1968.

Since the 1970s, this area has undergone significant industrial decline. The smokestack industries on which it depended are either gone or in a state of collapse. In the early 1980s, Spain's unemployment rate hovered around 20 percent before falling back to about 15 percent, because the recession beginning in 1979 caused the 3 million–plus guest workers who were spread all over Europe to be sent back to Spain. In the Basque Country, the situation was even worse, with unemployment rising above 25 percent. At present, unemployment there has receded to somewhere between 10 and 12 percent.

By contrast, the region in which Mondragón is located, the Alto Deva, with a population of about 70,000, had an unemployment rate of only 12 percent at the worst point of the recession. Mondragón itself, a town of 27,000, had an unemployment figure of only 15 percent, despite many of the noncooperative firms in the community experiencing serious economic difficulties. The figure subsequently has fallen to below 10 percent. Although the labor-managed cooperatives only employ half the work force of the area, they are responsible for the much lower overall unemployment figures.

A Brief History of the Cooperatives

At present, the cooperatives of Mondragón are one of the largest and most successful complexes of labor-managed industrial cooperatives in the world. Founded as a single co-op in 1956 by 5 young men with 13 coworkers, the complex has grown to include about 100 producer cooperatives that employ around 20,000 worker-owners. They produce industrial robots, machine tools, semiconductors, computer circuit boards, refrigerators, dishwashers, stoves, microwave ovens, plumbing supplies, and a huge array of other products. In the midst of the worldwide recession, not only did the cooperatives remain solvent, they did not lay off their members. Thus, the system has not only continuously generated and maintained employment, it has also been able to move labor and capital around within its boundaries to create almost continual aggregate expansion. The annual growth rate has averaged 14 percent, and the cooperatives currently export over 24 percent of their products. This compares very favorably with the Spanish Basque Country's overall industrial export figure of 10 percent.

Membership and the Organizational Structure

The cooperatives are highly structured organizations with elaborate statutes and governing bodies. To enter, a worker must pay the equivalent of a year's wages. After a probationary period, the new worker becomes a full member.

Members do not receive salaries in the formal sense because member compensation is determined as a distribution of profits and shares in the cooperatives. Presented with the cooperative's business plan, including its capital requirements and anticipated revenues for the next year, the members vote and thus determine their own compensation. Over the years, the cooperatives have financed much of the production out of their collective resources, thereby avoiding dependence on outside capital.

The annual compensation arrived at by this process is distributed according to a functional classification of jobs in the cooperatives. Jobs are classified on a scale of approximately 1 to 3, with the lowest-paid worker receiving about one-third of the compensation given to the highest-paid manager. The low end of the scale is pegged to the entry level of unskilled labor in comparable firms in the area, though the benefits are better. This means that management generally is paid far less than in noncooperative industries. The logic of the compensation system is that cooperative members should neither exploit themselves and engage in unfair competition with private firms by underpaying themselves nor take excessive capital out of their cooperatives by overpaying themselves. The only way to get more income than workers in comparable private firms is to share in the profits of the cooperatives.

Management teams are elected by the membership for four years, and are subject to censure and recall at any time. The 100 producer cooperatives are backed up by important second-level cooperative organizations that provide social security, health care, financing, technical assistance, and education.

Many of the producer cooperatives are aggregated into larger groups: cooperative complexes with coordinating management boards. In my analysis, these groups play an especially significant role because they permit the pooling of resources and sharing of risks. Of the cooperative groups, the Fagor Cooperative Group is the largest, with 12 member cooperatives, including the first Mondragón cooperative, Ulgor, and a membership of around 7,000.

LESSONS FROM MONDRAGÓN

There are a wealth of lessons to learn from the study of these cooperatives. Our other writings examine conflicts between democracy in governance and democracy in production processes, the importance of debate and ideological conflict to the survival of cooperative systems, the continuous process of innovation that has kept them viable, and the character of PAR as a research method (Greenwood and González et al., 1990; Greenwood, in press; Whyte, Greenwood, and Lazes, 1989). Here I intend to highlight one specific dimension of the cooperatives that is relevant to larger issues of industrial development and redevelopment. I specifically have in mind the literature dealing with dualism and the craft economy.

In trying to find analyses that would permit me to fit the Fagor system into a larger view of industrial society, I was led to one particular corner of the literature on the structure of the contemporary industrial system. This material centers on the subject of dualism, postindustrial business organization, and shifting ideas about work life and leisure. The shelves are loaded with such materials,[2] all making contentions about the character of contemporary industrial society, the way people find meaning in work, and how different forms of socioeconomic organization in firms can have important consequences for the future of business.

As I read some of this material and examined what I had learned about Fagor, I found I had developed my own views on these issues. Some of the forces that enabled Fagor and the rest of the Mondragón cooperatives to succeed so dramatically have more to do with the ability to pool and move capital and labor around within the overall system than with formal features of democracy per se. This is not an argument against the importance of industrial democracy or self-management in general because I realize that democracy in Fagor has permitted the cooperatives to pool and transfer capital and labor more effectively than otherwise would have been possible. It is, instead, an argument for examining the pooling element in the cooperative system and comparing it with other systems' ability to pool capital and labor and to share risks.

Pooling of Capital, Labor, and Market Position

To present these views, I will begin with a brief overview of my sense of the history of the cooperatives from this perspective. The founding of the cooperatives, seemingly so modest in relation to their present significance, was accomplished by pooling the capital and labor of the first 5 members and their 13 coworkers, and by setting aside a portion of profits for investment in the enterprise. This process, including the payment of an entrance fee, has continued up to the present. In 1959, the cooperative bank was founded, Caja Laboral Popular, which took in the members' savings and attracted additional deposits from around the region. This bank then made (and still makes) loans to start new cooperatives on very favorable terms, permitting them a long period before the loans have to be repaid. Early in its history, the Caja developed an entrepreneurial division which supplies all kinds of consulting management services to those starting new cooperatives. Recently this entrepreneurial division has been made into a freestanding organization within the cooperative system. Thus, through the bank and the entrepreneurial group, the cooperatives have pooled capital from other cooperatives and from depositors within the region. The entrepreneurial division pools expertise to encourage further cooperative growth.

Rather than expanding indefinitely, the early cooperatives determined that internal areas of growth ought to spin off into new cooperatives. Thus, new cooperatives were founded to exploit particular market sectors. These cooperatives, in turn, were linked to each other by contracts of association and through the pooling operations of the bank.

Eventually, as the number and diversity of cooperatives increased, many of the cooperatives formed into groups in which they share central services and a joint management structure while retaining the internal independence of their operations. Fagor is the largest of these groups. Here again, the emphasis is on the pooling of resources, with the maintenance of coordination balanced by the maintenance of the useful diversity of the cooperatives themselves as they each face their particular markets.

This coordination permits the sharing of risks so that particular cooperatives that are in a downward cycle or that must reorganize substantially to meet competition can be subsidized for a time by the currently profitable cooperatives until they can return to profitable performance. The cooperatives are able to live up to their commitment to guarantee employment (though not specific jobs) by moving workers around within and between cooperatives from areas where the labor is not needed to areas where it is or where it can at least be profitably used.

None of these measures are accomplished easily. Adaptive features of a system do not guarantee that adaptation will be pleasant. The pooling of capital to help a cooperative in trouble can evoke considerable debate, controversy, and even ill will since it has a direct impact on the take-home pay of cooperative members. Those members who are uprooted from one cooperative and placed in another because of the shifting market conditions do not lose their jobs. They do, however, suffer dislocation and alienation in the process. Many experience this process as one of being singled out for ill treatment despite the fact that they are equal voting members of the cooperatives.

In effect, the conditions of cooperative membership are a complex mix of guarantees and liabilities. In downward cycles, the welfare of vulnerable members is maintained, but this occurs at the expense of every other member. There exists the potential for conflict over this. If members perceive that a cooperative is having trouble because of managerial incompetence or member laziness, they resent subsidizing them with the results of their own better performance. However, most members realize that the conditions may some day be reversed and that their current sacrifices are an insurance policy for themselves. In upward cycles these tensions are much less evident, since members are then voting on distributing gains rather than losses.

The democratic pay system also treats the upper ranks of cooperative management as servants of the system. That the highest-paid cooperative general manager does not earn more than three times the pay of the lowest-paid member means that the upper managers exploit themselves and their families for the benefit of the group. They are generally people with advanced technical or administrative skills that are in high demand, and could command much higher salaries outside the cooperatives.

These individuals rise within the cooperative system by demonstrating a combination of competence and willingness to work for the group rather than for personal economic benefit. In so doing, they become servants of the members, who can censure or dismiss them at any time. Their motives appear to me to be a complex mix of ethical beliefs and a strong sense of being respected for the work they do. Undeniably, these advantages cost them and their families a great deal of money.

From the initial moment of membership through the collective discussions in Social Councils, committee meetings, and General Assemblies, members are reminded of their "collective" interests and mutual responsibilities. Of course, ordinary firms, when under pressure, inform workers and unions of their need to "pull together" and make sacrifices. However, the constitutive elements of industrial democracy, from the self-determination of pay to the election of management, strongly reinforce the ability of the cooperative system to call on members to make these sacrifices. To object to pooling, whatever one's private feelings, is ideologically indefensible in the cooperatives.

This capability also enables the management of the cooperative groups to treat diversity of constituent units in the group as an advantage. By structuring cooperative groups like Fagor around a wide array of industrial processes and market sectors, Fagor is able to ride out market cycles affecting any one part of the business through subsidies from other parts of the system. Maintaining the diversity means supporting the activities of cooperatives that, at any one time, are not performing up to an international benchmark with resources from cooperatives that are. It also means, however, that as market cycles shift and the lead cooperatives fall on hard times, the others may be in a position to subsidize them.

LINKS TO A BROADER CONTEXT

This picture fascinates me for two reasons. It reminds me of lessons I had learned in my prior studies of the history of household farming systems in Europe (Greenwood 1974, 1976, 1978, 1980). It also links a variety of perspectives to be found in the literature on dualism and craft economy in contemporary industrial societies (Berger and Piore 1980; Piore and Sabel 1984; Schonberger 1982).

Pooling, Cyclicity, and the Political Economy of Agrarian States

Years ago I analyzed the sources of adaptability of household farming systems in a framework focusing on the political economy of states based on household agriculture (Greenwood 1974). My basic argument was that household farming is a highly flexible and adaptable system that gave household farm–based state systems an unusual degree of durability in the face of constant breakdowns of central governments. Further, I was able to demonstrate empirically that household farmers were able to outcompete large-scale capitalist agriculture in specific contemporary situations (Greenwood 1976).

Household farmers provide both their own subsistence and a surplus that is either extracted or sold. When the state is strong or the market active, household farmers either produce significant tax revenues or sell a substantial amount of products on the market. When the state weakens or collapses or when the market is disorganized, the household farm's subsistence activities ensure the survival of both its domestic groups and the continuity of the production system that can quickly be reintegrated by national political authority or reemergent market organization.

Thus, the highly diverse household farming systems of Europe both provided for the subsistence needs of the producers and provided a surplus to the state and market while demanding almost no services in return. The presence of this highly stable subsistence base, capable of providing valuable resources to the state in peaceful times and largely able to care for itself in periods of political disruption, deserves greater attention than it receives in the literature on European history. Understanding the workings of these systems is essential to an explanation of the way the nearly continuous political turmoil in European history occurred without more radically disorganizing agricultural production. By contrast, it appears that, once market-integrated agricultural systems came to predominate in Europe, political disorder and agrarian crises became more closely linked.

The household farming systems maximize stability rather than production, operate by pooling resources of the household or linked households, and occupy economic niches that simultaneously provide the minimum welfare of the family while underwriting the national government. At the farm level, these systems pool land, labor, and capital, providing a living for all household members and usually generating some surplus that is either sold or appropriated by outside authorities. Seen from the national level, the agrarian work force pays its own wages, maintains its own production systems, and produces food and taxes. These characteristics account for the highly cyclical political character and the extraordinary long-term stability of household farming–based states.

In a variety of contemporary situations, these same household farming systems have competed successfully with large-scale capitalist agriculture in some markets. Where the mixed subsistence–commercial producer does not have alternative use for land and labor resources, the opportunity costs of these factors of production approach zero and the cash cost of production is the only capital investment required. Under these conditions, so long as the profits made from selling products exceeds the capital costs, it makes sense to continue production. Further, in downward market cycles, household producers may discontinue production entirely for a period, relying on subsistence activities to carry them through. Then, as soon as the market improves, they may again begin to produce.

Large-scale capitalist producers face a different set of constraints. The costs of all the factors of production must be met, and sufficient profits must be generated above that to pay the costs of capital, inventory, and ongoing operations. A consistent negative return results in bankruptcy and the disappearance of the firm from the market. When the market again improves, it is unlikely that the now-defunct capitalist firm will reappear.

The "Second Industrial Divide"?

My research on household farming systems and my experience in Fagor were separate things until I read Suzanne Berger and Michael

Piore's *Dualism and Discontinuity in Industrial Societies* (1980), and, subsequently, Michael Piore and Charles Sabel's *The Second Industrial Divide* (1984). While I find Berger and Piore's use of the terms "dualism" and "traditional firms" misleading, their argument is provocative.[3] To simplify a great deal, Berger and Piore claim that it is only possible to understand the performance of industrial economies like Italy and France by recognizing that most industries contain two sectors, a quintessentially capitalistic sector, and a "traditional" sector. These sectors include:

a stable component which is met through a relatively extensive division of labor, utilizing highly specialized resources, and an unstable component, where production involves a less highly articulated division of labor, utilizing capital and labor which are less specialized and consequently susceptible to being shifted with fluctuations in demand to other activities. (Berger and Piore 1980: 7)

From their vantage point, the instability and flux in markets in industrial societies creates conditions that make this kind of dualism a persistent feature of society. The large capital-intensive, specialized firms cannot, and indeed do not wish to, occupy the total market for their products. For these, occupying the stable part of the market is the optimal strategy. They are happy to concede the fluctuating parts of the market to other producers that are organized in less specialized ways. Such large firms are also unwilling to enter some product areas at all for these reasons.

Mondragón, Agrarian States, and the "Craft" Economy

While I am not sure that "craft" firms can or should triumph over the large, capital-intensive firms, and gladly leave this for others to decide, the work by Berger, Piore, and Sabel intrigued me for two reasons. First, the logic of their arguments parallels what I used to analyze household farming systems. Given the volatile structure of markets and political systems, small-scale family producers have a niche that they exploit very successfully. This explains their remarkable degree of persistence in European history and the inability of large-scale capitalist agriculture to drive them out of certain sectors even now.

Second, the structure and performance of the Fagor Group and the Mondragón cooperatives generally can be seen as a solution to some of the structural problems of capitalism that Berger, Piore, and Sabel identified. The Fagor Group and the Mondragón cooperatives are large-scale, capital-intensive, highly specialized firms that often occupy a large sector of a market in direct competition with other large-scale, specialized firms. However, they simultaneously are cooperatives with a capacity and commitment to pooling resources in ways that permit them to shift labor and capital from one market to another, thereby addressing the cyclicity and uncertainty of their markets without disorganizing their overall socioeconomic structure.

While they cannot survive a universally depressed economy any more than other businesses can, they have unusual adaptive capabilities. Some units can produce at a loss for a period of time while stand-alone firms become bankrupt. They can reorganize using capital drawn from other member cooperatives. They can agree to decrease their own wages and shares and can maintain full employment through internal transfers to more productive sectors. As a consequence, they can return to full production rapidly. The success of the Mondragón cooperatives suggests that they have been able to do this better than the standard capitalist firms with which they compete.

Thus, it appears to me that the sources of the ability to deal with cyclicity and uncertainty that I saw in domestic farming systems and that Berger, Piore, and Sabel see in "traditional" and "craft" sectors is perhaps best embodied in the structure and operation of the Fagor Group and the Mondragón complex generally. Over and above the issues of industrial democracy and an idealized political future, perhaps the most important reason for understanding what is going on in Mondragón is that its members may have found a viable solution to key economic and social problems of industrial production under contemporary conditions, while using international state-of-the-art production technology.

IMPLICATIONS FOR RESEARCH

Since this chapter is a theoretical reflection, the main contentions have been already laid out. If these contentions are of interest to others, they directly imply a number of research tasks necessary for the further development of the argument. As is often the case, refocusing a theoretical question outstrips much of the available empirical data. Thus, an ambitious research agenda is involved.

Pooling and Cyclicity Strategies

To pursue these issues, we need comparable data about the different strategies for pooling and otherwise dealing with market cyclicity employed in multiunit firms of all types. It would be especially valuable to make comparisons of these strategies within particular product markets in order to examine the dynamics of the process closely.

Connections between Firms

Another major line of research implied by the theoretical perspective of this chapter focuses on the variety of types of connection between firms. Expanding and contracting activity, sharing risks, and so forth, are part of the response process in times of economic fluctuation. Different kinds of relations to subsidiaries, the wide variety of possible structures for joint ventures, and the diversity of kinds of original equipment manufacturer–supplier relations all have consequences for pooling and risk sharing. We even lack a basic typology of these relationships, and we certainly do not have a good understanding of their consequences in times of economic change.

Unions

The role of unions in this picture is clearly relevant in some industries and countries. Concessionary bargaining, the linkages between locals across an industry or a sector, different kinds of risk-sharing contracts, and so forth all have significant consequences for the ability of firms to meet economic demands. We know of examples in which union–management cooperation were essential in developing a successful response to highly stressful market conditions, but the study of these matters is in its infancy (Klingel and Martin 1988).

Diversification

The process of business diversification itself has been studied for a long time, and we know that companies have explicit, and often quite different, diversification strategies. We also know that many U.S. and European firms entered into a long phase of diversification only to find themselves incompetent and unsuccessful in many business areas. Thus, many firms failed to be able to use the market advantages of diversification because they found themselves unable to operate in such different markets and still maintain meaningful business connections. This resulted in the recent spate of sales of subsidiaries. Throughout this process, these diversification strategies were successfully pursued in Mondragón. What permits Mondragón to make diversity count economically should be a matter of some interest to those trying to design industrial redevelopment schemes for private firms and even entire industrial sectors.

Cross-National Comparisons

All the issues raised above need to be studied, not only within but also across national economies. For example, a comparison of Scandinavian and U.S. approaches to these issues would be valuable because the parameters and conditions in the countries are so different. By studying the processes of pooling and economic cyclicity in two such different situations, we are afforded the possibility of separating the idiosyncratic and local processes from those generic processes that apply to late-twentieth-century industrial organizations. We know that in Scandinavia, with full employment and a strong national commitment to industrial democracy, issues of diversification and pooling play out differently than in the United States, where there is significant unemployment, a negative balance of payments, major industries reeling from international competition, and labor unions in disarray; here, these issues raise a very different set of questions. To the extent that such comparisons reveal similarities and differences in the processes of pooling, they will be particularly valuable in the development of this theoretical perspective.

As is evident from this chapter, I firmly believe that the focus on diversity and pooling in relation to cyclicity in the economy is a key element in understanding the current dynamics of industrial systems. I am equally certain that understanding these processes is essential to the development of industrial strategies in the United States that will meet the test of international competition. Industrial redevelopment in the United States will only be possible if we abandon ideological recipes for the specificity of well-analyzed examples.

NOTES

I am grateful for important corrections and comments from William Foote Whyte and a variety of helpful suggestions from Michael Blim and Frances Rothstein.

1. The Mondragón sections of the chapter report on three years of participatory action research (PAR) by a team of 20 that I directed along with José Luis González. González was then director of personnel of the Fagor Group and president of the Fagor Electrotécnica Cooperative; he is now General Manager of the Orkide Cooperative Group. William Foote Whyte played a major role in getting this project started. For a full account of the study, see Greenwood and González et al., 1990.

There is an extensive literature on Mondragón. The best overview is Whyte and Whyte (1988), which contains ample bibliography on the subject.

2. Among them are Berger and Piore (1980), Piore and Sabel (1984), Schonberger (1982), Lawler (1986), and, in a popular vein, Ouchi (1982) and Peters and Waterman (1982).

3. It turns out that by "dualism," they do not mean two unitary and separate economic systems but two sectors, each differently organized. The "traditional" sector has a multiplicity of firms and strategies within it. I also object to the term "traditional" because no amount of redefinition can eradicate the semantic association between "traditional" and fixed or static. This association is in direct contradiction to the essence of their argument.

12

Tobacco, Textiles, and Toyota: Working for Multinational Corporations in Rural Kentucky

Ann E. Kingsolver

Ann Kingsolver begins with the premise that local decision making and traditions affect global processes and shows how workers in "Greenway County," Kentucky, resist control by multinational corporations by combining work in several economic sectors and/or industries. Their mixed livelihoods, which may include working for several multinationals, offer some rural Kentuckians a way of resisting a reduction of their choices.

Multinational corporations (MNCs) or, to refer back to Blim's introduction to this volume, managers of the "global factory," obviously cannot buy or build industrial manufacturing plants in an area without negotiating with *some* residents. Therefore, studies focusing on the control of capital on a world, or macro-socioeconomic, scale must be articulated with studies of local, or micro-socioeconomic, participation in the various decision-making processes through which work options in a region are determined. I would argue, further, that a vital aspect of such local involvement in global economic processes is indigenous participation in constructing *ideologies* of livelihood, that is, definitions of work, of who does what work, and of how resources and tasks are allocated, whether evenly or unevenly.

One of the disadvantages of macroanalyses is the blurring of regional processes into a single-voiced impression of a place. However, these reductions can be avoided by complementing such analyses of the global factory with long-term ethnographies of specific communities, through which we can learn much more about the complex contradictions and negotiations of identity and livelihood in which individuals are engaged daily, at *many* levels. Others, such as Taussig (1980), Ong (1987), and Kondo (1990) have documented the error of looking at *single* responses to MNCs in a locality. People construct livelihoods in complex, diverse, and changing ways.

This chapter is about how residents of a rural community in east central Kentucky mix work for three multinational industries producing tobacco, textiles, and automobiles.[1] It is based on ethnographic fieldwork conducted between 1986 and 1989 in "Cedar"—a community of under 2,000 residents—and "Greenway County." In this hilly area, far from major industrial processing and redistribution zones, mixing farm and factory work has long been a common practice. However, several recent changes affecting agricultural and manufacturing production in the region come up often in many Cedar conversations. One of these is the buyout of the locally owned textile and garment manufacturing mills by an MNC. Another is the coming of a Toyota assembly plant to Kentucky, for although the plant is not located in Greenway County, it is close enough for residents to commute to it. There is also the ongoing debate about whether the bottom is falling out of the tobacco industry or whether it is thriving; both versions appear to be promoted by tobacco MNCs at various moments, as each position at different times can aid in attempts to manipulate volume of production and control prices (Kingsolver 1991). A related event for this community is the shift in ownership and control of the two local banks from local shareholders and presidents to individual investors from outside Greenway County. Together, these changes have affected the availability of capital to small-scale farmers (who need it to complete the annual tobacco production cycle) as well as the way in which individuals go about getting factory jobs in the region.

It is my premise that by constructing livelihoods that combine work for two or three MNCs in different industries or economic sectors, Greenway Countians resist any one MNC's "intent" to centralize control of the labor force and, further, retain the livelihood flexibility afforded by ownership of a land base and multiple possibilities for off-farm employment in case any one of the plants relocates. My emphasis is not on the behavior of individuals according to a fixed identity such as small-scale farmer or merchant politician; indeed, in Cedar, an individual can have both these identities, and more, simultaneously.[2] Instead, I find more analytical richness, not to mention a more lifelike puzzle, in the ways that Greenway Countians manipulate constructions of identity and livelihood within the various networks in which they are embedded. These networks may be based on identification with certain constructions of gender, class, race, kinship, and ethnicity, or on regular contact with a group of people through workplaces, neighborhoods, informal socializing, or formal organizations. Through these "forms of life" (Finch 1977), Cedar residents, and others, negotiate the future of work in Greenway County.

I have made several fundamental assumptions in the project spawning this chapter: (1) Change does not emanate "from above," but is negotiated through a web of interactive, and sometimes contradictory, relationships and interpretations of identities and events. (2) All individuals, regardless of their residence in urban or rural areas, or whether they work as corporate executives or as nonwage farm hands, participate in forming assumptions about what work is desirable and appropriate in a region and in the allocation of authority to make decisions about work. Individuals may participate in multiple, and contradictory, constructions of desired livelihood in a region. Because individuals with mixed livelihood strategies have a wide variety of ways in which to identify themselves—for example, as *both* a farmer and a factory worker—I speak of how people "place" themselves and their views. This can clarify a microlevel study of the articulation of local and global socioeconomic processes, since the same individual might be speaking as an MNC manager and as a member of a kin-based farm-labor reciprocity network.[3] In doing this form of analysis, one needs to understand how these complex constructions of identity and interpretation are influenced by each role and how they play out in community decision making.

GREENWAY COUNTY

Cedar and a number of smaller communities are situated in Greenway County. The entire county has a total population of under 10,000. It is in a region of east central Kentucky between the Inner Bluegrass, known for thoroughbred horse farms and some high-technology manufacturing firms, and the Appalachian mountains (long mined for coal and ethnographies of poverty).

Most Greenway Countians are involved with burley tobacco production, either directly, themselves working in household, extended kin, or fictive kin groups that work together in the labor-intensive crop; indirectly, through relationships with people who do work in tobacco; or even more indirectly, through the complex system of lease and exchange agreements pertaining to the federally fixed tobacco allotments (by weight) that are attached to property deeds in the county. Hence, while the U.S. Census classified only one-sixth of the households in Greenway County as receiving any farm self-employment income in 1980, this reflected neither the total number of people working in tobacco (either as wage-earning or nonwage laborers) nor the percentage of Greenway County households in which members identify themselves, somehow, as farmers. Land ownership is not a necessary condition to identity as a farmer because of the social web of reciprocal obligation that can just as effectively link land with the landless laborer as with the owner.

At least one-third of the Greenway County labor force in 1980 was commuting to jobs in other countries, and 75 percent were listed as working in manufacturing, whether in or out of Greenway County (Kentucky, Cabinet for Economic Development 1988). The regional distribution of manufacturing jobs, and higher wages in those jobs, is weighted in the Inner Bluegrass, around Lexington, and thins out as one travels east. Greenway County exports twice as many daily commuters as it imports (*Commuting in Kentucky* 1984). Jobs available in Greenway County in 1980 were mostly in manufacturing (43 percent), with government being the second largest employer (18 percent),[4] followed by commerce (17 percent), services (12 percent), and finally, construction (3 percent) and other kinds of work.[5]

Average weekly wages *earned in the county* in 1986 ranged from $200 in construction and trade to $300 in manufacturing, banking, and real estate. The wages in manufacturing in Greenway County were two-thirds of average manufacturing wages in the state of Kentucky and were generally lower than those earned in counties toward the Inner Bluegrass and higher than wages in counties to the east. Men and women are fairly equally represented in the wage labor force.

Aspects of the labor force also important to note for the purposes of this chapter are the literacy rate (one in five adults in the county cannot read or write) and the uneven distribution of income in groups perceived as distinct not only by class but also by race. Twenty percent of Greenway Countians were reported in the 1980 U.S. Census data as living under the poverty level (one-third more than in the state as a whole), and 50 percent of African American households in the county were listed as earning less than poverty-level income in 1979 (United States Dept. of Commerce 1983: Table 57). Informal sector, or unreported, income is also significant to the construction of livelihoods in Cedar, as many households rely on barter of goods and services, exchanges of goods through yard sales, and subsistence activities like hunting, fishing, and gardening.

Making a living in Greenway County, then, engages household members in an ongoing negotiation of spatial factors (Who works where, and how do they get there?), social factors (Who owes whom work, wage or nonwage, and how is farmwork to be scheduled around, say, overtime demands at the factory?), and ideological factors (What activities are defined as work at all, and how does mixed employment affect perceptions of identity?). Mixed employment is a specialized way of life, with the skills of negotiating all these factors being as important as the skills required by the various forms of work comprising the livelihood. The next section describes how and why mixed-industry livelihoods work for those engaging in that way of life, and situates them in social science arguments about processes of labor-force proletarianization, or "modernization."

WORKING IN THE FACTORY, WORKING ON THE FARM

Hank Millerson, a Greenway Countian, was one of hundreds of applicants for his job at Toyota, but he got through all the preliminary screenings at a regional employment agency and was hired after a several-hour interview at the plant, about an hour's drive away. Not many Greenway Countians have been hired by Toyota. Hank said the main reasons they hired him were that they were looking for people who had not changed jobs a lot in the past, and they wanted people who could work very hard:

Somebody right off the street couldn't stand it, I tell you. It's like housing tobacco every day. But it's—you know—you're paid good, taken good care of, and you're interested in it. They'll do whatever it takes to see that everybody has got a good attitude toward work. . . . I guess it comes back to—you know, they pay you a good salary, good benefits, and have a bonus plan, retirement plan.

Hank considered his coworkers and the money he was making well worth the physical strain: he had lost weight since beginning work there, and recalled one stretch of working 19 days without a day off, as well as a lot of overtime. He laughed and said that with getting up at 4:00 A.M. and getting in after dark, he did not have much of a social life, but that he had always been a worker.

Hank Millerson also considered himself a farmer, having "always been associated with it." He said that his mother, who worked on the line at TexFlex (the local textile and garment manufacturing plant), as well as himself and other relatives, had always looked toward Christmas vacation as the time to get the tobacco stripped, instead of time to "sit back and watch football and stuff." Now, instead of mixing farming with schoolwork, he was farming at night after working on an automobile assembly line. The most difficult times of the year for him in combining farm and factory work were when the tobacco production cycle demanded a lot of time and when his beef cattle began calving. In the fall, "I'd work over there and then come home and work in [housing] tobacco about three and a half hours a night. That was killing me." He was hoping that his mandatory overtime would be cut down before calves started to come.

When asked whether he had thought about giving up the farm, Hank Millerson said that he had always been eager to do *more* on his family's farm, and he hoped to manage to get enough done at night to keep it going until he had more time for it. On the other hand, he said his factory job paid more money than he had ever seen in his life and he could not afford to quit. Maybe down the road, he postulated, the farm would help hold his taxes down and the salary would let him build up his herd. Hank laughed when he was asked whether he made any money on the farm, and said:

Probably not. There's not really a farm in this area that you could live on. And pay for your groceries and your liquid fuel and your taxes and your insurance. I mean just *live* there, and make a living and pay for the farm. And get whatever equipment you might need. There's not a farm in this area that will do that. Fifty years ago, when people used a team of horses or something, but not in this day and time. There's just not a farm that will do it.... You don't make much money on tobacco, but you can make more money out of tobacco than you can with peppers and tomatoes and they've had cucumbers and—it's just not a very good place in this area for alternative crops.... This is a general farming area.... It's just an area that it takes a combination of four or five different things to bring in a little bit of money to make it here.

While those who are combining several forms of work like Millerson usually have a work identity that they consider central to their person, each job has its own ethos for them. Why, then, would a farmer want to work in a factory and a factory workers want to farm? Tobacco production, with its highly specific and highly skilled labor process and extensive land and labor-exchange networks in the community, has developed a symbolic value beyond its monetary value.

Through their tobacco networks, Greenway Countians have often been ascribed other statuses—elected positions of authority, for example, or employment in manufacturing firms. TexFlex was begun by a local family of farm-based entrepreneurs, for example, and the labor force was built up through farm-related networks. Rather than detracting from the manufacturing labor pool or being incidental to it, the TexFlex management—even the new MNC spokespeople—consider farming households to be providing labor for them: specifically, women's labor for the sewing plant.

Tobacco production does not furnish enough profit for most households to live on through the year. In fact, payment for tobacco labor on small farms may be subsidized through other employment or through the sale of calves. What it *does* provide, in a more systemic view of household economics, is a sudden and fairly large infusion of capital in January. This is a time not only when holiday bills are due, but *many* debts in Greenway County are carried on a cycle coinciding with the arrival of the tobacco check.

Another facet of the farming side of mixed livelihood is a construction of identity: the independent, self-employed, American farmer. This image reflects cultural mythologies beyond the bounds of Greenway County. It is also largely an illusion, since all tobacco farmers are actually producing for MNCs and can be compared to homeworkers in other industries in that they cannot easily be organized, cannot negotiate their rates of payment, and end up performing several tasks in the vertical integration of the industry at high risk to themselves: processing, packaging, transportation, and the housing of surplus product. The costs of the latter (for example, space and insurance) are sometimes borne by the tobacco pool, but since this is a collective of the farmers, they are still, in a sense, paying.

On the other hand, farming households do have some flexibility in how they organize production and how they manage their investments and debts. Land ownership, even with liens, gives a certain buffer against a complete lack of autonomy in choosing work options, and formal and informal farming networks assure that a certain amount of labor is always available if unforeseen needs arise—reroofing after a storm, for example. Construction of identity as an independent worker also has its effects on where individuals "place" themselves in their perceptions of authority and decision making, and with what confidence opinions are expressed in public forums.

We have heard from Hank Millerson why a farmer might want to work in a factory. First, there is the outright financial need: both for total income and for *regular* income, which allows household disbursements to be planned rather than being dependent on conditions as random as the weather and wages, as do agricultural workers in other countries. Second, there are the benefits. Insurance is extremely important, since farming is a fairly hazardous occupation, especially when it is being done at night by tired people, and tobacco MNCs have no pension plan for retired farmers. Third, there are the social networks. It is not only through working in tobacco that other jobs are discussed; tobacco labor is sometimes planned while the same workers are on the shop floor.

Mixing farm work with work in other industries is not a new livelihood strategy in Cedar. There are records of tanneries and mills in the 1700s that were run by farming households, and trade—in goods or services—has nearly always been combined with agricultural interests in the county. What *is* new in this combination is the structure of ownership of the local banks and factories.

This recent integration of local sources of capital and manufacturing employment into the "global factory" affects mixed livelihoods in a number of ways, the most obvious being that relationships with management are less manipulable now within personal networks of reciprocal obligation and shifting loci of authority. What I mean by the last phrase is this: If a factory manager works at night in tobacco under the leadership of one of his or her shopfloor workers, they then in effect "swap hats," or trade places in perceived structures of authority. If the factory manager is not embedded in local networks of kin, fictive kin, and other complex relationships, then that manager wears the same "hat" in every interaction: one of authority. While Greenway Countians working at the new Toyota plant say that managers work *with* them as "teammates," they do not ever shift authority contexts (and thereby roles) with those managers—they have no "power over" them in, say, the tobacco barn, but only have the "power" to do their jobs at the plant well and keep them.[6]

Securing off-farm employment in the region is now a more "faceless" and uncontrollable task for Greenway Countians as well. The routing of all applications for factory jobs through the regional, federally funded employment service was done, one MNC representative said, to comply with affirmative action legislation and to receive the tax breaks and wage supplements afforded to plants hiring through federal programs.[7] While this would seem to make employment prospects more fair, it funnels all access to factory jobs through one office, concentrating its power and making its employees the subject of rumors of abuse of this power.

Conditions for mixing farm and factory work in Greenway County have shifted to, at least more *obviously* now, an international arena. The rules have changed with actually very little effect on the physical facade of work: Farmers still pull overtime shifts at TexFlex, but know they do so under MNC management. Problems of shifting from "face-to-face" to "face-to-faceless" interactions are by no means unique to Greenway County. They are probably experienced in any peripheral region with complex traditional forms of organizing livelihoods which is integrated rapidly—through the actions of both "outsiders" and "insiders"—into the global factory.

With blurred lines between rural and urban, and between small-scale and large-scale economic processes, individuals "placed" at every level of perceived hierarchies of job description and authority, and with various geographic identities, find some need to reconstruct their understandings of who does what, including decision making *about* livelihoods. For example, if the bank still looks like the same bank, how do employees and customers reinterpret their relative positions to an invisible owner who determines the policies governing their transactions?

The stresses of mixed livelihoods in Greenway County include this cognitive dissonance, or scramble to make sense of changes only partly discernible in the immediate environment, and also more tangible ones, especially physical exhaustion and illness from long, unpredictable workdays. Households are increasingly unable to organize extended-kin work parties, both because wages (which they cannot afford to pay) are now being demanded for formerly nonwage exchanges and because schedules are increasingly difficult to arrange. One TexFlex worker, who also farmed, told me that he had gone to work every day for the last year and a half without knowing when he would be allowed to go home—compulsory overtime could last hours beyond the end of the shift. For children, as well as women and men, increasing demands on household labor are stressful, since farmwork is often done at night after school and work.

Mixing farmwork with factory work is neither new to Greenway County, as I have stated, nor should it be viewed necessarily as a transition between full-time farming and full-time wage labor for MNCs. Where the land has always been conducive to part-time farming (because mechanized farming is impractical on steep, hilly, clay-soil land), it is especially possible to see mixed livelihoods as a way of life. Barlett (1986, 1989) has asserted, from her research in Georgia and surveys of the literature, that part-time farming is neither a sign of farm failure nor a temporary strategy in the process of proletarianization (labor being pulled off the land and into factory jobs): "In recent decades, it is clear that part-time farming is a permanent adaptation. Between a third and a half of family farms depend on their regular jobs for most of their income and carry out farming tasks in the evenings and on weekends" (Barlett 1989: 278). Barlett found, too, that many part-time farmers say they like farm life because it gives them satisfaction and makes them feel independent, and that off-farm employment gives them economic security to counterbalance unpredictable conditions in the agricultural market (Barlett 1989: 278–289).

Gladwin and Zabawa, who studied part-time and full-time farmers in yet another region of the United States—Florida—found that "the part-time family farmer is in a surprisingly stronger position than the full-time family farmer" in household economic terms, because the former could keep debts lower and could add off-farm wages to the farm budget (Gladwin and Zabawa 1987: 225). From international studies also—for example, Kada (1980), Bollman (1979), and others—it seems that part-time farming makes for flexible workers: One industry subsidizes another through the labor process. Therefore, in order to understand household economies or work in any one industry, in studies of the global factory where there are local options for mixed livelihoods

it is vital to focus on the interactive effects of mixed employment and
to research all the industrial sectors in which individuals in a community or household are working.[8]

Changes in regional demands for labor interact with changes in
indigenous definitions of the labor pool. In order to compensate for
nonwage labor no longer available through shrinking kin and fictive
kin reciprocity networks, there are changing constructions of appropriate work roles. In the late 1980s, more Greenway County women
were doing tasks in tobacco production that had been formerly labeled
as male tasks, especially "cutting" and "housing" tobacco.[9] Several
Cedar farmers in the same period came up with what they felt to be
an innovative solution to their labor shortage; hiring Mexican migrant
workers. Greenway County has not been on traditional migrant circuits, so some farmers drove to Texas to "import" laborers for the
summer, and others went to regional tobacco warehouses through
which Mexican workers were assigned farm work. Thus, new labor to
be exploited entered the regional system: lower wages than those being
demanded even by kinspeople were paid to the Mexican workers, who,
one farmer said, "don't seem to mind the hard work that local people
don't want to do any more."

THE CHANGING STRUCTURE OF MNCS IN
RURAL KENTUCKY

Kentucky is a state in which a majority of the population resides in
rural areas, and "its economic structure is predominantly industrial"—
manufacturing employs nearly a quarter of the labor force (Cromley
and Leinbach 1986: 333). Plants in rural Kentucky were found by
Cromley and Leinbach (1986: 341) to be mostly branch plants of corporations not headquartered in the burgeoning Sunbelt but linked to
and controlled from corporate "cores" in the Middle Atlantic and north-
east-central regions of the country. Rural Kentuckians are, then, as
members of a MNC proletariat, working for management sited mostly
in the rust belt and northeastern United States—where local job loss
shadows corporate gains. This pattern of shifting jobs contextualizes
to negotiations for new MNC plants; an endeavor in which many Kentucky state and local elected officials are very active.

Since the early 1980s, the Commonwealth of Kentucky has staffed
an office in Tokyo with the purpose of recruiting MNC-owned manufacturing plants to the state. This has been only one part of a strategy
to keep and recruit manufacturing firms, which was articulated by
three governors in turn. State government officials have encouraged
communities to organize local chambers of commerce and industrial
development authorities, both of which Greenway County did. Further,

contests and funds were established in the mid-1980s to encourage communities to assemble and distribute information about local attributes that might attract new manufacturing plants: primarily, low-wage, nonunionized labor forces and available sites (often, "industrial parks" which would be constructed at the community's expense).

It was through such a state campaign to attract new MNC plants that Toyota chose to site its $800 million assembly plant in central Kentucky. The plant, which drew 130,000 applications for work and gained both regional and national attention, was constructed on a site that the state actually purchased for it, and in all, the incentives package offered to Toyota by Kentucky officials totaled $125 million (Braden 1986).

While state officials felt that Toyota's choice to locate in Kentucky rather than one of the other 29 states competing for the plant was a result of the incentives offered by the state (Braden 1986: 32), it is probable that the MNC would have chosen the state or one of its immediate neighbors anyway. Mair, Florida, and Kenney (1989) explained that the "just-in-time" manufacturing system practiced by Toyota leads to a concentration of transplant assembly and supplier plants in one general region, in this case the Midwest, especially in rural areas where workers are not unionized and can be trained to be flexible on the line and in their hours to accommodate post-Fordist manufacturing techniques.[10] Kentucky workers were especially suited to work in a "just-in-time" system plant (more so, say, than Detroit workers) because they had never worked in the manufacturing sector of the automobile industry before and had no familiarity with (and therefore, no need to be retrained from) Fordist auto assembly techniques (Mair, Florida, and Kenney 1989: 370).

An additional argument for the lack of effect of the incentives offered by Kentucky on Toyota's final choice of a site is Harrison and Kanter's (1978) observation that an increase in the number of states offering incentives to MNCs to influence plant location, often in similar packages, leads to an actual decrease in the instrumentality of these incentives to the decision. The incentive package offered by the Commonwealth of Kentucky to Toyota may have had more ramifications in other groups than in the Toyota boardroom. The offer was challenged by several lawsuits: one from the Kentucky State Buildings and Trades Council and the AFL-CIO, one from a landowner whose property was condemned to become part of the site and one from within the administration to establish the constitutionality of the legal arrangements for channeling funds to Toyota (Green 1990); none of these resulted in blocking construction, and the plant is now in operation, and expanding, in central Kentucky.

Members of the Commerce Cabinet, specifically the Kentucky Department of Economic Development, sent letters in 1983 to 2,700 managers of manufacturing firms in the state, offering services and incentives to keep the "present industrial base."[11] These state services were invoked, with the governor herself mediating, when TexFlex was challenged in its effluent processing techniques by Kentucky's Environmental Protection Agency. Because of a dyeing process used at the TexFlex plant, high levels of sodium chloride were being released into the water source of several communities. Rather than the MNC paying for the change in processing, or shutting down the plant as it had threatened to do, a dilution (rather than recovery) project was funded by Greenway Countians—partly through a controversial payroll tax—and a matching grant from the state.

These examples of active recruitment of new MNCs to Kentucky and efforts to keep other MNC-owned plants in the state are intended to show the changing structure of MNC manufacturing employment. There are now manufacturers with post-Fordist (Graham 1990) techniques in Kentucky. Many Greenway Countians had hoped to attract a plant manufacturing supplies for the Toyota plant, but those suppliers were either already in place or were constructed on better road systems nearer to the assembly plant. Instead, Industrial Authority funds in the county have gone mostly to new and existing plants in the textile and apparel industries. State incentives are aimed at attracting new MNCs, and in Greenway County, money is being spent to keep local plants, whether they have been bought out by MNCs or not. I should point out here that MNCs that have long been present in Kentucky, the tobacco firms, are also supported by cooperative ties between state and federal legislators and land-grant university researchers, among others, and are also being subsidized by the state, in a sense, through policies favoring their activity in the region.

The overall structure of decision making about MNC-controlled manufacturing employment in rural Kentucky is changing in that political actors at all levels are very much involved in the process: MNCs are part of a public discourse of livelihood in the state. In Greenway County, visions of economic development are intertwined with constructions of identity (for example, as factory-working farmers) and appropriate work roles, and they are negotiated through numerous networks. Some, for example, are urging the construction of regionally owned agricultural-processing facilities; this form of manufacturing would complement the existing livelihood mix of combined farm and factory work. Others, through networks with more ascribed authority, are working with the state agenda to attract new MNCs to site manufacturing plants in the region. Those new plants that *have* been constructed in the region increasingly compete with the farm-related demands of mixed livelihood by, for example, requiring overtime and hiring managers unfamiliar with the mixed livelihood specialization's seasonal labor needs.

DISCUSSION

Although not everyone in Greenway County belongs to a household in which work for the tobacco industry is mixed with work for the textile and apparel or automobile industries, community life—in terms of economy *and* identity—is very much influenced by the mixed livelihood specialization. Business owners are accustomed to the tobacco debt cycle, for example, and have hours that accommodate factory workers. In festival parades, queens are crowned on tobacco wagons and TexFlex sponsors floats. One Cedar resident attends MNC board meetings held in other countries and farms tobacco and cattle in Greenway County with relatives. The global factory is not something for which residents of this peripheral region passively produce: They manipulate it as well.

Greenway Countians are involved with negotiations with MNCs to locate plants in the region and differ in their opinions on what kinds of jobs are desirable to attract. There are those who are landless and "placed" in networks with little authority or reciprocal potential who have little choice about where they work. However, many residents do have some relation to a land base and are "placed" in networks that give them access to more flexible household labor and to more choices about how to construct a livelihood.[12] Those who are working overtime in factory jobs and are also farming with little help outside the household say they "cannot keep it up much longer," and wait for something to happen to one of the industries. Sometimes what happens is surprising, like the recruitment of an additional supply of agricultural labor, Mexican migrants, along with the recruitment of additional manufacturing jobs for local workers.

This would tend to point toward a sectoral fragmentation of labor, but since there are so many small-scale farming households and small parcels of land, a shift to large-scale farms employing only migrant labor and a landless local proletariat is unlikely. Instead, I think it is more likely that the recruitment of migrant labor is, like the redefinition of gender-appropriate work roles, another manifestation of the effort in a mixed livelihood specialization to keep the labor supply flexible to meet fluctuating demands of combined farm and factory work, which does not seem itself to be a temporary or transitional strategy in the region.

The combination of many different types of subsistence activities, including work in several industries, appears to serve as a means of resistance to the reduction of work choices, thereby increasing workers' control. While MNCs choose the region primarily for its nonunionized labor, there are ways in which some skilled workers do protect themselves by preserving other work options—even when work for other industries can appear to cost rather than earn them money. This is one of the ways in which I believe tobacco is used as symbolic capital in the community and in which MNCs are manipulated against one another in a subaltern development discourse, or strategy of resistance, in the periphery.[13]

In order to avoid an overly protagonistic painting of the factory-working farmers, I must point out that within the specialization, as in other forms of work, there is unequal access to decision making and to higher wages and better working conditions. The redefinition of the least desirable farm tasks to make them appropriate for local women and Mexican migrant laborers reflects complex constructions of identity and authority as well as shifting demands for skilled labor. Greenway Countians are influenced by these constructions as represented in the presence of MNCs, and they also participate in producing and reproducing them—and their alternatives—locally.

Based on my observations of rural Kentuckians combining work for three different MNCs, I recommend that in macro-oriented studies of the global factory, we recognize the integration of individuals "placed" at multiple levels and in different, sometimes contradictory, roles and networks in the decision making that affects work patterns in a region. The texture of multiple cognitive and social domains in which individuals negotiate their livelihoods in the "periphery" is as important to understanding the global factory as the movements of international capital. The fine-grained analyses afforded by anthropologists' ethnographic techniques are what we can contribute to studies of the global factory. Through microlevel studies, complementing macrolevel work, we can answer such questions as who does what work and why, what people hope for in terms of work, and how contradictions of scale, authority, and identity—for example, gender and ethnicity—are played out locally. We all, ultimately, are working in a local context.

NOTES

I thank Julie Graham, Mark Whitaker, Sylvia Helen Forman, Michael Blim, and Frances Rothstein for their comments on drafts of this chapter, and the National Science Foundation for supporting me as a Graduate Research Fellow during much of my field research. As always, I am indebted to the residents of "Greenway County" for their words and thoughts offered in teaching me about making a living.

1. By "industries," in this chapter, I refer specifically to the overall segmentation of economic production by *product*. Emic usage of the term can

range from meaning manufacturing or *any* economic activity to a firm or plant. I have avoided that usage here in an attempt to minimize confusion.

2. Hopkins (1987: 155) stated this sentiment much more succinctly: "The focus is on what people do, not what they are."

3. This speech, when analyzed as heteroglossic discourse (see Bakhtin 1981), can read at times like code switching of ideologies.

4. Many part-time farmers have told me that the hours and benefits in government jobs are very compatible with farming. Health insurance is especially important. Nearly all elected officials in Greenway County are also active farmers, as are nearly all the postal workers.

5. These data are from the *1988 Kentucky Economic Statistics* (Kentucky, Cabinet for Economic Development 1988) and the Labor Force Characteristics of the 1980 U.S. Census (United States Department of Commerce 1983).

6. See Pred (1981) for a discussion of "power over" and "power to."

7. At least one motivation here was the transfer of any risk of affirmative action lawsuits from the plant and the MNC to the employment service; TexFlex changed its hiring policies after a 1988 monetary settlement of a discrimination lawsuit brought by a black applicant.

8. See Buck and Wenger (1988) on household labor and class processes in Kentucky burley tobacco production.

9. For a similar example of the redefinition of gender-appropriate work roles, see Anna Walsh's work on oil boom and bust cycles in Oklahoma—for example, Walsh (1988).

10. In the just-in-time system, in contrast to Fordist manufacturing, supply inventories are kept to a minimum through close ties with suppliers, and both machinery and workers are able to perform a variety of tasks to keep the production line flexible to make products already committed elsewhere for retail sale (Mair, Florida, and Kenney 1989: 354).

11. This information is from the local newspaper in Greenway County, which I do not cite specifically in order to maintain in confidence the name of the community.

12. While this chapter has not focused specifically on these differences, constructions of race and gender influence greatly an individual's access to networks with authority, especially electoral political authority. See Kingsolver (1990) for a discussion of gendered networks and authority in this same research context, and Buck (1989), Collins (1989), and Salamon (1989) for discussions of race and ethnicity in relation to employment and land tenure in U.S. agricultural communities.

13. See Bourdieu's (1977: 171–183) definition of symbolic capital, which I interpret as the value that an exchange comes to have beyond monetary value.

13

Women as Political Actors in Rural Puerto Rico: Continuity and Change

Ida Susser

In this, as in the following chapter by Kim, the focus is on overt political activity and we see the two arenas in which workers often struggle: their communities and their workplaces. In both case studies, women are important political actors, reflecting the increased attention of scholars to women and politics and the prominent role that women often play in politics, especially at the local level. In this chapter Ida Susser examines a community struggle over health issues and industrial waste and shows how women's role in politics changed from important but auxiliary efforts to leadership positions.

This chapter examines the impact on the lives of local residents of a U.S. industrial plant, Union Carbide Grafito, Inc., which was located in a semirural region of Puerto Rico from 1969 to 1989. The analysis focuses on the social movements among community residents and workers which developed in opposition to the plant's operation, and on the changing role of women in those movements.

Ethnographic research has documented that while women take political action and frequently play important political roles, they do not always act politically in the same manner or forum as do men, and their activities may rely on different strategies and emerge in different settings (Riegelhaupt 1967; Joseph 1973; Nelson 1974; McCourt 1977; Kaplan 1982, 1987; Susser 1982, 1986, 1987; Rapp 1987; Lamphere 1987; Sacks 1988; Martin 1990). Analysts have demonstrated that women frequently organize around community issues such as housing, health, food, and the environment (Kaplan 1977, 1982; Chaney 1979;

Susser 1982, 1987; Morgen 1987; Castells 1983; Martin 1990). Women's actions may also spur workers and unions led primarily by men to collective protest (Kaplan 1977; Castells 1983).

This chapter constitutes a case study of the changing roles of women in a conflict between industry, residents, and workers in a small rural proletariat community in Puerto Rico. Negotiations and confrontations between the corporation and the community progressed over time through several phases and, as we shall see, the roles played by women altered as the historical context changed. Responsible for the reproduction of households, women became politically active around issues that affected their environment and their children's health. Women's concern precipitated broad and long-lasting movements led initially by men and later by the women themselves. Not only were the situations of the company, the worker, and the community residents shifting over time, but so were the job opportunities for women and their ability to negotiate housework and reproductive decisions. This chapter documents the continuity in gender roles that led women to community concerns and examines the combination of changes that propelled women into leadership by the end of the 1980s.

It has been argued that industry leaves the mainland United States because workers elsewhere accept lower wages and are less well organized, and also because industry may pay lower taxes and be subject to less rigorous environmental regulation (Council on International and Public Affairs 1987). For the Union Carbide Grafito plant in the Yabucoa valley of Puerto Rico, most of these factors pertained (Susser 1985). However, the situation bred its own sources of conflict. It was the process of the battles between the company, the workers, the community surrounding the plant, and the governmental regulators that determined the changing environmental situation. Just as many analysts have come to see the structure of cities as the product of urban conflict, so it seems useful to view the issues of industrial pollution and occupational and environmental health hazards as changing in response to ongoing conflicts among workers, management, and the communities affected.

Over the 20 years in which Union Carbide operated in Yabucoa, the surrounding community, the workers, and the company changed in interaction with each other and with wider state and international forces. As a consequence of conflict and negotiation, the types and levels of pollution also changed, to the point where now, in 1991, the major issue is the hazardous waste left behind by a company that has accumulated its profits and transferred production elsewhere.

Over the same time period, women moved from auxiliary roles in local protest movements to leadership positions. Women emerged publicly as central to organizations to which they had always contributed in less visible ways. The following pages document the involvement of women at key junctures in the development of health concerns that became the basis for collective action. In a later section, the analysis traces the historical conditions that led women to assume more public responsibility in the struggle of local villagers against industrial pollution. It will become evident that as problems became more intractable and success less dramatic, men dropped from leadership positions while women kept the movement going.

THE EXPORTATION OF INDUSTRY TO PUERTO RICO

With the initiation of Operation Bootstrap—a joint effort of the U.S. and Puerto Rican governments to foster industrial development on the island of Puerto Rico—in the late 1940s, U.S. factories began to be established on the island (Baver 1979). Due to U.S. policy in combination with the Puerto Rican government, sugar cane plantations began to decline in importance. Whereas in 1950 the Puerto Rican economy depended almost completely on the production of sugar and, to a lesser extent, coffee, by 1990 these industries have come to represent only a small proportion of exports. In the 1950s the first companies to arrive represented low capital investment and low-wage industries, the majority of which were garment factories (Garcia 1978). Puerto Rican women hired to work for these factories became extremely proficient sewers. By the 1980s many of these factories had departed in the continuing search for cheaper labor. However, in the villages of Puerto Rico, needlework, either for neighbors or for U.S. companies, remains an important source of income for many women. In the early 1970s, large petrochemical and pharmaceutical plants were built by U.S. companies with the support of the government of Puerto Rico. While the decline in oil prices led to failures in the petrochemical industry, the number of pharmaceutical plants on the island continued to expand. Two petrochemical plants were established in the Yabucoa valley in 1969–1970. Each hired between 600 and 1,000 workers (fluctuating over time), most of whom were men. Women worked as secretaries, for which positions, bilingual skills were preferred.

In the decades following the establishment of the two petrochemical plants, health problems were documented among workers and residents, specifically in relation to the pollution caused by one plant, Union Carbide Grafito, Inc. The overall process through which community residents and workers endeavoured to make the company accountable are documented in an earlier publication (Susser 1985). Here, I shall focus on the significance of women's participation and their changing roles over time.[1]

GENDER AND SOCIAL ROLES

In Barrio Ingenio, women's social lives were distinctly different from men's. The differences in mobility of men compared to women was one of the greatest contrasts, which then defined also the locus of conversation and meeting places. If not working elsewhere for pay, women were nearly always in the house, and that was where they were expected to be. Men, whether working or not, were seldom home. The family car was the man's car, and he or a teenage son drove it. Men traveled from barrio to barrio, trading, visiting, picking up people and things, or simply stopping at various bars or beaches. Women mostly stayed home. They sent men or even children to do grocery shopping. If they wanted to visit a relative or a friend, they waited until they could arrange a ride. This was done despite our observation that most of the women who were confined to their houses knew how to drive. On one occasion, I traveled with four women to return goods they had sewn to the factory that was to pay them. The trip was about 20 miles and took a major organization of effort for one woman to have access to a car and for everyone to arrange to accompany her. On a second occasion, the same group of women asked me to drive them to the factory as no one had access that day to a car. Frequently, however, men ran most of the errands, and drove women and children to town, to the doctor's office, or to the welfare office.

The church was the one place to which women traveled independently. Many women attended church meetings two or more times a week. They often went alone or with other women, and sometimes went with husbands or children. Both Catholic and Pentecostal churches held numerous services in the area. The Catholic church services were led by male priests from the nearby town and were attended overwhelmingly by women. The two Pentecostal churches in the barrio were also headed by men, and they attracted both men and women to their nightly services. The church provided a justifiable reason for women to travel alone, attend meetings in the evening, and, in the process, develop strong community networks and support in addition to their kin-based groups. However, while the churches brought people together, none were supportive of the local political movements, and the Pentecostal churches tended to draw people away from participation in the protest against Union Carbide. If women mobilized for political action in Barrio Ingenio, it was despite rather than because of their attendance at religious services. It testified to the strength of the political movement that women provided support in the face of church opposition.

At the age of thirteen or fourteen, boys seemed to disappear from the home environment, only to appear for meals and to sleep. Teenage girls stayed closer to home, although on graduation from high school (and most of the girls we followed did graduate), they took jobs in nearby towns. Some girls pursued further degrees but remained tightly under the jurisdiction of their parents. For example, we shared a house with two unmarried young women and their unmarried unemployed brother, whose parents had moved to a house in the hills, about 18 miles away. After two months away, the parents ordered the nineteen-year-old daughter to come to live with them, which involved giving up her job in a nearby town. The unemployed son (age twenty-one and trained as an engineer), stayed on in the house without constraints. The older daughter, age twenty-three, who was a school teacher, was also allowed to remain in the old house as she was about to be married and, in fact, she did stay on in the same house with her new husband. Thus, young unmarried women left the house for work and training, and certainly were not in their kitchens as consistently as their mothers. However, even their freedom was curtailed in comparison to that of their brothers. Working teenage girls and young women were often picked up from work by relatives, whereas the young men would drive their own or their parents' cars to do the pickups. Teenage girls who wanted to visit a friend or congregate at a nearby store or park had to cajole their elders for a ride, while young boys simply left. Few boys had curfews for their return in the evening, whereas girls' departures and arrivals were planned and noted by their mothers. Frequently, girls were kept home because their help was needed with cooking and other household tasks. Such restrictions were not borne without resistance from teenage girls. Although I never observed a young girl or a woman who did not assist with household tasks, at least two teenage girls left to live with young men without their parents' permission. Of course, they then performed the same household tasks in a new domestic unit.

Division of tasks and socialization starts at an early age. At five years of age, little girls were given chairs to stand on so that they could wash the dishes after a meal. Most eight-year-old girls are already competent dishwashers, moppers, and sweepers. Our fourteen-year-old daughter was criticized for her lack of competence or interest in these areas of work (and I am sure the same was said of me, although not to my face). The boys learn none of these chores and are left to run free in the yard and wander the relatively safe streets of the barrio, where few cars pass and those that do go slowly to avoid the sludge and potholes. Thus, the pattern of women near the home and men wandering is initiated and reinforced from an early age. The tendencies for men to congregate away from home and women to stay near the kitchen determined political knowledge and manipulation. Men gathered around the local stores and bars, exchanging information and consolidating political factions.

They drove daily around the barrios, into neighboring towns, or as far as San Juan absorbing information, affirming long-standing political connections, and developing new contacts. However, while the women stayed home, they consolidated kin networks and mobilized neighbors to support a nascent political movement.

KIN CONNECTIONS AND POLITICAL ACTION

The significance of women in political action as consolidators of kin networks can be seen in the fact that the first leader of the social movement opposed to Union Carbide Grafito was linked by marriage to the second leader (his daughter-in law and the second leader's wife were sisters). In fact, three of the major actors in forming and maintaining the protest movement against the company were related through their wives, who were all sisters. Although the sisters' husbands were of different political persuasions (an *independista*, a socialist, and a more conventional democrat), all these men, who were related through the women, took leading roles in the development of the local protest movement.

In maintaining strong kinship alliances and reinforcing new local ties, the women also assumed the more expected tasks of providing large, filling, and acceptable meals for numerous people at short notice and for as little cost as possible. If the husband brought home a group of strangers or a member of a kin network, the visitors usually provided something toward a meal if they stayed. Guests might bring a live chicken, a rabbit, some salted cod fish, some plantains, or a breadfruit. To this offering the *ama de casa* (woman of the house) and most of the other women present would add whatever scraps were left in the refrigerator—beans, other vegetables, and pig's feet—and send children to the store for supplementary needs. Generally after two or three hours, a huge soup accompanied by large amounts of rice would appear. The men would arrive back from somewhere (the local bar or a visit to see a friend about a car) with beer and soda, and the dinner would proceed. Over the extensive preparations that such events required, the women exchanged information about other peoples' lives, children, and, to a certain extent, their own problems. They traded dress patterns, tried on clothes, watched the children, and passed on information about health and politics. Thus, while women usually stayed home unless taken somewhere by their husbands, they frequently spent long hours in other people's kitchens and front porches and had an intimate knowledge of community affairs.

Since social events such as that described above occurred every few weeks, and since visits to the beach on Sundays required similar collective and extensive preparations, women were well acquainted with the organization skills involved in mobilizing large groups of people. They could easily adapt these experiences to the task of working to achieve more ostensibly political goals, such as attending demonstrations in San Juan (a 40-mile drive from the barrio).

WOMEN'S CONCERN WITH HEALTH

As diagnosticians and healers, women play a central role within the community and within the home. Women keep track of the family's health history and accumulate knowledge, particularly about health problems of children. Women in charge of households kept a store of antibiotics and other prescription medicines which had been prescribed for the ailments of various children over a number of years. When asked, they could identify which bottle or pill had been used for which child when and could suggest what other purposes they might use it for.

Repeatedly we witnessed women performing a kind of "folk-differential diagnosis" with their own children, with ours, and with those of others. They displayed impressive skill in judging the severity of disorders and in their ability to compare and contrast the disorder in question with those they had experienced with other children in other contexts. The women's diagnoses frequently corresponded with the doctor's opinion when this was sought. For example, several small children in a neighbor's family had sores that refused to heal on their elbows and knees. The mother asked me if I thought it was impetigo. I was not in any way an expert on children's diseases, and said maybe it was just because the children kept reopening the scabs through falls. A few days later we took my one-year-old son to a pediatrician in a nearby town because my husband and I thought he had an ear infection. The pediatrician found no problem with the baby's ears but pointed out that our daughter, who had just accompanied us to the office, had impetigo. He prescribed antibiotics and careful washing of towels and clothes. On our return, I mentioned this diagnosis to our neighbors, and they asked what had been prescribed. The husband immediately drove to the local pharmacy to buy the same antibiotics (although U.S. laws officially apply in Puerto Rico, many prescription drugs can be bought directly over the counter), for his children. As the wife had suspected, the neighbor's children's scabs cleared up as soon as they were treated for impetigo. Although home treatments of this sort have been discouraged in the United States for fear of misdiagnosis and mistaken use of drugs, in Puerto Rico, home diagnosis is frequently practiced by women and on many occasions is probably accurate and useful. On other occasions, especially in the use of unclean needles for unneeded medical shots, such home practices may cause fatalities or at least more problems than they solve. In the particular households where we observed women providing medicines to their families, however, we never saw injections being given.

We interviewed people in 94 households about their health and other characteristics of household members. When we asked questions about children's health, the men gave general answers or suggested we ask the women for detailed histories. Mothers, grandmothers, and even the sisters of mothers provided us with chronologies of childhood asthma problems, ear infections, and skin infections. They remembered the dates when illnesses had occurred and, on occasion, brought the medicine to show us what had been prescribed by a doctor for treatment. Women were also well informed about preventive health care, well-balanced diets, and the health problems caused by unclean water and other sanitation inadequacies. Several women informed us that we should use less salt because of problems of high blood pressure. When we returned to Yabucoa in 1987, knowledge about HIV infection and its transmission was one of our concerns. Each adult woman I spoke to (several of whom had not finished high school and seldom left the barrio) knew the modes of transmission for HIV and knew that it could not be transmitted through casual contact. However, in this case, both men and women were aware of the issues, and one group did not appear more or less well-informed than the other, although women were more willing to state fears of AIDS and were possibly more judgmental than men. In general, women acted as and saw themselves as the guardians of health and repositories of knowledge about health in the barrio. While men might affect not to worry—for example, about salt in the diet—women would comment on these issues and try to alter the intake of husband and children. Men also expected women to keep track of the children's health and to cope with medical problems.

ENVIRONMENTAL AND OCCUPATIONAL HEALTH ISSUES

Concerns with occupational health and safety concentrate on conditions in the workplace and the hazards of production. In this instance, the workplace was largely manned by men: However, more than the workplace may be implicated in the hazards of production. Because of the proximity of Union Carbide Grafito to Barrio Ingenio, the population was exposed to some of the same hazards as were the men working in the plant. The gaseous, carbonaceous, and petrochemical by-products that afflicted workers were the same agents that appeared to be causing high rates of health disorders within the barrio. (For a discussion of health hazards in the plant and the community, see Susser 1985.)

The connections between plant and community problems was made apparent by the fact that protest was triggered not when the workers themselves became ill but when their wives and children living in the nearby barrio became affected. In the case of men who were highly active in organizing the community and leading the protest, their own accounts and those of their wives testify that it was the health problems of the family that alerted men to the prevailing conditions and prompted them to action. In one of these cases, the man concerned was an actual employee of the plant, and in the other, an independent craftsman. In both cases, however, it was the wives who pinpointed what they believed to be the cause of new health problems, and in both cases it was the fact that wives functioned as monitors of family health that prompted action.

Julio, the man who became the first recognized leader of the protest movement against industrial pollution, was one of the earliest plant employees. In fact, he was hired in the building of the Union Carbide plant. He lived in Barrio Ingenio with his wife and 13 children, and had previously led a successful movement to build a Catholic church in the barrio. Thus, he was well respected in the barrio as a builder and an organizer. With the advent of the new industrial plants, his wife, who had always had asthma, began to have attacks that were more frequent and severe. Eventually, on medical advice, they decided to move out of the barrio and into the mountains behind Yabucoa, where Julio began building a new house.

The independent craftsman, Juan, also lived with his wife and his six children in Barrio Ingenio, where he was renowned as a wrestler. His wife complained of the soot which accumulated on her floors in spite of mopping every morning. She attributed rashes that appeared on her babies' skin when they crawled on the floor to the dust which was precipitated by the new plant. Partly due to his wife's identification of the problem, and with her full support, Juan became the second leader of the protest movement after Julio made plans to leave the village. As mentioned earlier, Juan's wife was the sister of Julio's son's wife, which greatly facilitated communication and cooperation among the leading figures.

Thus, it was at the instigation of the women that community leaders originated complaints against the company. The community movement later provided a protective forum in which workers from the plant could voice their criticisms. The union, which became active around health issues, was formed after the community protests began and with the support and resources that the community leaders had already developed.

WOMEN AS PARTICIPANTS IN THE PROTEST MOVEMENT

In the organized protests, women have played, and continue to play, a significant part in organizing and demonstrating. At least half the demonstrators going to San Juan to protest before the Junta Calidad Ambiental (JCA, the Environmental Quality Board) were women. The first protest leaders were men, but women could be relied on to represent the barrio in picketing the plant and in helping to arrange for groups to travel to significant locations for protest. On one occasion, during an election year, when the governor of Puerto Rico visited the plant, a special women's delegation from the community met the governor at the plant gates in order to draw media and government attention to the pollution problems. This demonstration was spearheaded by Juan's wife, an extremely well-informed and articulate woman who left school at fourteen in order to marry and rear her children.

For the most part, in the first decade of protest (from 1975 to 1985), leadership and the political agenda was set by the men of the barrio, and women took less obvious supportive roles. Throughout these years, all members of the community's leadership committees were men. Important battles were fought. The JCA was forced to recognize the pollution problems, and in 1982 fined Union Carbide $550,000. In response to the rulings of the JCA, the plant began a new building program to reduce pollution from the incinerators. The union was organized and managed to enlist help from both the National Institute of Occupational Safety and Health (NIOSH) and the Occupational Safety and Health Administration (OSHA). Both NIOSH and OSHA produced reports citing the plant for pollution, some of which was found to be carcinogenic (NIOSH 1984). However, by the time the reports were printed, the union had been destroyed by the layoffs, for over six months, of more than 500 workers. During this same period, a law suit was brought by the residents of Barrio Ingenio against the Union Carbide Company, citing health complaints of community inhabitants resulting from plant pollution.

The law suit was long and drawn out, as cases tend to be when corporations work for delay. The delays, lack of success, and unreliability of the lawyers led villagers to mistrust and undermine their own leadership. As a result of the failures of legal recourse, Juan came under attack, and he and his committee abandoned their cause. It was after the hiatus caused by these setbacks that women emerged in leadership roles.

WOMEN AS COMMUNITY LEADERS

The first woman to take action, after Juan resigned from the committee under fire from his own community, was in her mid-thirties, about 20 years younger than Juan and a decade younger than his wife. Mercedes had four children; two were living with her in the barrio and the other two were with relatives in the United States. Mercedes herself had just returned from the United States and was fluently bilingual, in contrast to either of the previous leaders. Mercedes did not live with her husband and was explicit in our interview with her that she supported her household without his help. She was outspoken about her aims for the lawsuit. She had taken up the cause because she wanted to win the compensation and use the money to emigrate to the United States. In her statements there was no echo of criticism for irresponsible or exploitative U.S. investment such as the earlier protests had reflected. On discovering that the lawsuit had foundered through the neglect of the community's lawyers, Mercedes and her newly formed committee, which was made up of both men and women, sought out a new lawyer who was willing to fight their cause. Ironically, considering the lack of political critique among committee leaders, the lawyer they found was a well-known figure in the Puerto Rican Socialist party. After two years of energetic pursuit of the lawsuit, Mercedes went back to the United States, leaving the community once more without leaders to conduct their legal affairs.

In 1990, when I returned to Yabucoa once more, the lawsuit was still pending. The lawyer whom Mercedes and her committee had enlisted was still working on the case in an effort to reopen the issues. The new leadership that emerged at this time reflected the long history of the movement. The committee was now being led by Theresa, a bilingual mother of two young sons who had worked as a secretary at the plant and was the daughter of one of the original men who founded the first Ingenio committee. She was living with her husband, and both he and her parents supported her leadership role. She and her husband drove together with other Ingenio residents to San Juan to discuss the progress of the suit with their lawyer. In August 1990, the lawyer informed them that there was still some possibility that they might win the case, although they would have to wait for the decision of the Supreme Court judge. The decision would be made on the basis of written materials collected over 10 years by the company and the community, and required extensive work. However, the current leadership was not planning to move and was prepared to wait.

Thus, over a period of 15 years, the role of women in a local protest movement shifted from pressure behind the scenes to central leadership. This was partially due to changes in the success of the protest movement. As the union was destroyed and men from the factory were no longer coordinating strategy with the barrio residents, as the lawsuit became less hopeful, and as the original men who led the movement came under attack, women kept the lawsuit alive. Perhaps this also reflected changing expectations among a new generation of women who no longer saw themselves as dependent on the support of men in a household unit. However, the new women organizers framed their goals in very different language from the original leadership. Gone was the early idealism and emphasis on the collective good of the community. The idea of protest against U.S. investment or the exportation of hazardous industries was no longer voiced; in fact, not protest but legal recourse and compensation were the emerging emphasis.

Women were always central players in political organization and protest in the barrio. However, their locus of activity was in the household, and today remains largely in the kitchen. Both the new women leaders could be found most often in their own kitchens or on their own front porches. Men still drive from barrio to barrio and are more frequently absent than home. In spite of these continuities in the social organization of gender, women have emerged as accepted leaders in the last five years, whereas previously none had served on organizing committees. Women have not developed a feminist protest movement adversary to men. They have not taken up issues critical of men in the home or of their own subordination in certain areas. Instead, they have worked cooperatively with men to develop collective community responses. Nevertheless, in this context, women have managed to establish themselves as independent and respected actors in areas where they had not originally been accepted.

After early dramatic successes engineered by male leaders with women's support, the protest movement foundered on a long, tortuous, and possibly ill-conceived lawsuit. At this point, men gave up leadership positions (or were pushed out), and it was the previously less visible women who carried the suit forward. Theresa, the new leader, had worked for many years as a secretary for Union Carbide. As with the male leaders, Theresa was also related to previous leadership (as the daughter of a committee member). However, this time although her husband was active in the case, the woman herself was perceived by community members as the leader of the group.

In conclusion, Union Carbide Grafito, Inc., spent 20 years in the Yabucoa valley generating profits for the U.S. corporation. During this time, they consumed much of the water table and expelled pitch and polluting gases into the atmosphere. For example, it was possible to identify new leaves on plants around Barrio Ingenio in 1990 because they were not covered with the sticky black dust of leaves lower down the bushes, as by 1990, the corporation had removed most of its operation from the valley. However, the health problems of the population, the unused physical plant, and the waste precipitated by the chemical processes remained. Throughout the two decades, residents and workers struggled to cope with or prevent the deterioration of their

environment and health. Some major changes, such as improved in-
cineration at the plant, were won; and major defeats, such as the destruction of the union and the laying off of hundreds of workers with
plant seniority, occurred.

Women were central to all phases of the negotiations between plant
managers, workers, and community residents. However, as problems
became less dramatic and as failures loomed larger, it was the women
who continued to press for reparations and held tenaciously to the
original goals of the movement.

Over the same period, women have been struggling in the household
and the workplace to renegotiate their gender roles. I mentioned elope-
ments earlier; also, young women are having fewer children (two instead of six) and seeking birth control sooner, generally in the form of
sterilization or, less frequently, the pill. Men appear to be assisting
more in household tasks such as washing dishes, although such work
still remains occasional rather than customary. New chemical-
processing plants and fast food chains in nearby towns hire both young
men and unmarried girls, and some women have been appointed to
supervisory positions there. Some women drive themselves to visit
relatives and friends, and young teenage girls take as much freedom
as they can wrest from their households. Under these conditions, it is
not surprising that women have also emerged as visible public leaders
in community protest.

Fieldwork conducted over a decade has facilitated an analysis of the
changing power relations between U.S. corporate management, community residents, and workers in one plant in Puerto Rico. Intersecting
with these processes has been the emergence of women as visible political actors in the ongoing conflict. The environmental issue which
began as a major and active concern among community residents and
plant workers ground to partial defeat and abandonment by the mid-
1980s in the face of corporate firing of politically active workers combined with public relations and strategic improvements. By 1990, the
closed plant and the mound of chemical waste remaining represented
a festering sore and a chronic remainder of disappointment and bit-
terness. In this changing context, the role of women in the household,
the community, and the work force was constantly being modified,
although not transformed, by a struggle for independence and mobility.
The intersection of these changes is reflected in the various parts played
by women in the environmental movement. From providing the social
organization through which male leaders grouped and negotiated,
women, in the final stages, took over leadership and themselves conducted negotiations with community residents, lawyers, and corporate
representatives.

NOTE

1. The activities of women were studied using participant observation and ethnographic fieldwork methods. John Kreniske and I spent four months in Yabucoa in 1982; stayed for three months in 1983; and returned for shorter periods in 1985, 1987, 1988, and 1990. On these occasions, we interviewed and talked informally with barrio residents, Carbide workers, Carbide management, and state regulators and politicians. In 1982 and 1983 we conducted a systematic self-report survey of health in the barrio. We lived with two different families and sat for many hours in different kitchens and front patios observing interactions and talking with barrio residents. The interview survey (which, depending on the friendliness of the person, could take between one hour and an entire afternoon) allowed us to visit over 90 households and observe interactions among people in daily life. The data presented here are based on observations over a period of eight years in which we revisited the households of community leaders and other residents many times. The main locale of the study was Barrio Ingenio, a village of about 350 households in the municipality of Yabucoa, situated 500 yards from the Union Carbide Grafito plant.

14

Women Workers and the Labor Movement in South Korea

Seung-kyung Kim

In this chapter Seung-kyung Kim describes the process by which militant resistance to low wages and poor working conditions emerged among women workers in multinational corporations in the Masan Free Export Zone. Like the women of Barrio Ingenio described in the preceding chapter, women were involved in the struggle throughout, but their importance grew in the late 1970s and then again in the late 1980s when the repression of labor was greatest.

South Korea is now known for its spectacular economic growth, but as recently as the 1950s it was one of the poorest countries in the world. Since then, South Korea has made great progress in industrialization, although it remains heavily dependent on foreign capital, technology, and trade. A crucial factor for Korean economic development has been its well-disciplined, hard-working labor force. Korea's development strategy would not have succeeded without its workers' high level of productivity and their acceptance of low wages and long working hours.

Korea's export-oriented industrialization concentrated on light, labor-intensive industries, where cheap, unskilled labor was required (for example, textiles, rubber footwear, and electronics), and it absorbed massive numbers of women workers because young women were the least expensive labor force available. Newspapers and television often referred to these women as the backbone of Korean economic development. Despite the praise lavished on them, their hard work did not translate into higher wages or improved working conditions. During the 1980s, workers became more conscious of the gap between their own experiences and the "economic miracle," and became increasingly distrustful of such government slogans as "Development first, distribution later." In this chapter, I examine the women workers' labor movement, focusing on the Free Export Zone located in the southern port city of Masan.

The extent of women workers' involvement in the labor movement is illuminating because it contradicts the commonly held notion that women workers are docile and subservient (a major reason why multinational corporations hire women workers). I wish to delineate the process by which a working-class consciousness was developed among the workers of Masan and to examine the important roles taken by workers in organizing their own trade unions.

THE NEW INTERNATIONAL DIVISION OF LABOR

Beginning in the early 1960s, multinational corporations from developed countries (e.g., the United States, Japan, Western Europe) built factories in Third World countries to manufacture export goods for the world market. This export-oriented industrialization was promoted by the United Nations Industrial Development Organization, the World Bank, and the International Monetary Fund, and became a popular development strategy for Third World countries. The new international division of labor that was created by multinational corporations divided the production process among various plants of one firm that are located in different parts of the world (Frobel, Heinrichs and Kreye 1981).

The new international division of labor is a product of the collaboration of economic forces in both developed and developing countries. In the 1960s, the "deskilling process" was already going on due to the leap in manufacturing technology (see Braverman 1974). Technological advances made in communication and transportation made the flight of capital easy. Furthermore, many developing countries were experiencing failures in their attempts to modernize through import substitution. Due to the backwardness of the industries, wages were low and the domestic market could not absorb the goods that were produced (Safa 1981). Hence, many Third World countries tried to increase manufacturing as part of export-oriented development strategies, hoping specifically to (1) earn foreign exchange, (2) reduce high unemployment, and (3) transfer technology. Governments in developing countries regarded export processing as the answer to their problems of chronic high unemployment.

In the countries that chose a development strategy that relied on export processing, several problems eventually emerged. First, the only foreign exchange that the host country received from the multinational corporations was the wages paid, which were much lower than what the company would pay in a developed country; tax incentives practically eliminated any direct revenues for the host government; and multinational corporations operating in export processing zones (EPZs) were allowed to repatriate practically all the profits made from their operations, so the host government had no control over reinvestment. Second, the EPZ typically created a new, underpaid labor force of young single females instead of providing jobs at the wage levels needed to support families. Thus, even with EPZs, unemployment among males remained high. Third, the host government had to provide all the infrastructure needed for multinational corporations to operate in their countries, and since multinational corporations brought only the most labor-intensive part of the manufacturing process, the transfer of technology was minimal. With the new international division of labor, capital-intensive/high-technology manufacturing processes were kept in developed countries. The only reason for multinational corporations to move operations to Third World countries was because they provided cheap and abundant labor.

WOMEN'S POSITION IN THE LABOR MARKET

Export processing industries throughout the world depend on the labor of young, single females—sixteen to twenty-five years old (comprising 80 percent to 90 percent of their work force according to Fuentes and Ehrenreich 1983). "Women's nature" is often put forward as the main reason for the characteristics that make them initially the preferred labor force. However, "nimble fingers" and "docility" are not women's nature but rather characteristics that women acquire through socialization. In order to explain the preponderance of young female assembly-line workers, we need to inquire deeper than women's natural appropriateness.

Unrestricted by labor legislation or regulation, the multinational corporations have recreated industrial conditions similar to, or perhaps worse than, those found in the workshops of Europe and the United States more than a hundred years ago (Rosen 1987: 22). One researcher described labor conditions of the export processing industry as "wages on a par with what an 11-year-old boy could earn on a paper route, and living conditions resembling what Engels found in Manchester" (Ehrenreich 1982).

Women have traditionally been paid less than men, constituting a source of cheap labor for industrial capitalism (Saffioti 1978). This reflects the subordinate status of women both in society and in the family. The subordinate position of women paralleled the assumption that women's income is supplementary to that of a male provider (see Sacks 1974; Hartmann 1976). This pattern persists to the present day, even in areas of high male unemployment (e.g. Mexico, the Caribbean, and Malaysia) and even where a high percentage of women are heads of households (Safa 1981).

Although female workers are often perceived as compliant, submissive, and docile, researchers have discovered that management has to employ highly sophisticated techniques to manipulate women workers in order to gain control over their labor (Grossman 1979; Lim 1978; Mather 1983; Ong 1982, 1983, 1988). These researchers argued that in Southeast Asia, using the banner of "femininity" orientation (such as cosmetic classes and beauty contests), the management of the U.S.-owned company encourages "individualism" in a sense, manipulating "gender" into commodity, while the Japanese-owned company use "paternalistic" management to keep women workers subordinate to male supervisors. Thus, management uses both "traditional" and "modern" patriarchal ideology to manipulate workers in order to maximize profit and undermine worker organization.

Nevertheless, women working in the global assembly line have resorted to a variety of strategies to protest the conditions under which they work. Examples of these include Malaysian workers' resistance through mass hysteria (Ong 1987, 1988); Jamaican garment and textile workers' public demonstrations (Bolles 1983); Philippine textile workers' resistance to the Marcos regime (Enloe 1983); Caribbean countries' organized strikes ("Free Trade Zone Workers Fired" 1988). Korean textile workers are also well known for their militant resistance activities (Enloe 1983; Former Dong-il Textile Co. Labor Union 1985; Former Won-poong Textile Co. Labor Union 1988; Karl and Choi 1983).

THE MASAN FREE EXPORT AND SOUTH KOREAN ECONOMIC DEVELOPMENT

The South Korean development experience illustrates both the possibilities and limitations of capitalist development in the Third World. Korea has achieved remarkable economic development during the past 30 years while depending heavily on foreign capital, technology, and trade. Between 1962 and 1987, the South Korean economy grew at an average rate of 8.9 percent per year. Economic development has shifted "the composition of the Korean labor force from 79% engaged in the primary sector in 1961 to 70% engaged in the secondary and tertiary sectors in 1988" (Johnson 1989: 7). Korea's industrialization, however, was achieved at considerable political cost, as this same period saw the emergence and strengthening of authoritarian regimes.

The Masan Free Export Zones (MAFEZ) was established in 1970 as part of the export-oriented development plan. The South Korean government hoped to use direct foreign investment to introduce high technology and develop new foreign markets. To accommodate investors, the government promulgated the Foreign Capital Inducement Law (1969), which included tax incentives, simplified administrative procedures, waivers of the free trade union organization law, and other inducements for foreign investors. In other words, the government established the MAFEZ by providing land, labor, and other incentives in exchange for foreign technology, resources, and trademarks.

The South Korean government set the following goals for establishing the zone: first, export promotion—Korea would earn a sizable amount of foreign exchange by exporting everything manufactured in the zone; second, employment enlargement—since all the industries in the zone are labor-intensive, the zone would absorb underemployed labor from the countryside; third, technology advancement—there would be technology transfer since the zone would accommodate mostly electronics, precision equipment, and metal industries with highly advanced technologies; and fourth, community development—the zone would promote the migration of the farming population to an urban region, would establish Masan as an industrial area, and develop domestic industry to supply raw and subsidiary materials.

Initially, the Masan Free Export Zone was extremely attractive to foreign investors, and by 1975 there were 101 companies operating factories there. In the late 1970s, however, the number of companies began to decrease, and the drop continued until by 1987, there were only 76 companies operating in the zone (unpublished data provided by the South Korean Office of Administration, Masan Free Export Zone). Many of the companies that failed to survive were small- and medium-sized companies. In December 1978, just before an economic downturn that resulted in mass layoffs, 33 of the 95 operating companies employed fewer than 100 workers. When a recession hit the world economy, these small companies could not survive the competition and fled, leaving a large number of employees behind without paying overdue wages or severance pay (Korean Young Catholic Workers' Organization 1980).

The major investors in the Masan Free Export Zone are Japanese electronics companies. Of the 23 electronics factories operating in the zone, 21 are Japanese-owned. Most of the other industries are also dominated by Japanese or Japanese–Korean joint venture companies. The main industries represented in the zone are: electronics (23 companies), metal (18 companies), precision equipment (17 companies), and garment (12 companies, unpublished data provided by the South Korean Office of Administration, Masan Free Export Zone).

As of 1988, the companies in the zone employed a total of about

38,000 workers (male: 9,000, female: 29,000). The electronics industry employed the largest number of female workers (over 17,000—65 percent of the total female employees), followed by precision equipment and the garment and shoe industry (with about 3,000—12 percent each). The most prestigious jobs were in electronics companies, which did not accept job applications from women over twenty-two years old, arguing that older workers did not have the requisite manual dexterity. Women who leave jobs in the electronics industry for any reason are not able to return because of the age limit and must look for jobs in either garment companies or subcontracting factories outside the zone. The age limit was temporarily lifted in 1987 because of a labor shortage in the zone. At that time, the companies in the zone were willing to hire older women, including married women. The older workers, however, had to sign a temporary labor contract that specified that they could be laid off whenever the company wished. The labor shortage only lasted for the year of 1987, and in 1988, most married women were the first to be laid off.

WOMEN WORKERS IN THE MASAN FREE EXPORT ZONE

Local residents had little idea about the purpose of the zone when it first opened. One woman who worked in the zone during the early 1970s said, "When I first started to work there, I did not know what the Free Export Zone meant except that the place was for exports and mostly owned by Japanese." Many workers even today told me that they did not know what MAFEZ was before they started to work there.

At first most companies tried to hire only high-school graduates, but the competition for workers was such that many soon had to lower their requirements. Thirty-five-year-old Ms. Park remembers the day she went for an interview at Dongkwang Company, the second company to open in the zone:

They must have been hiring almost all the people who were applying. During the interview, I failed to answer a simple math question, so I thought I would fail. There were so many people who came to apply and so many high school graduates who did not have jobs at the time. I was surprised to receive a notice to come to work. When I first started to work, Dongkwang hired about 600 workers; now the company employs over 3,000 workers.

During the first phase of its establishment, most foreign companies brought their own technicians and managers, including some women workers, to teach Korean workers how to operate. Japanese workers were paid at a much higher rate than the local Koreans. As one worker recalled, "For the first year, there were Japanese women workers stationed to teach us basic skills. The wage difference between them and us was too much, even those women felt sorry for us; they received at least 6–7 times more than us."

Most women who worked in the zone during the 1970s remember working conditions as being very bad, especially long hours of mandatory overtime work. One worker recalled as many as 105 hours of overtime a month. There were over 50 labor disputes during this time period.[1]

In 1987, working conditions in the zone were still difficult. Garment and shoe factories had hot, dust-filled rooms with no fans during summer time. Electronics factories were usually clean and had air conditioners, but the reason for those air conditioners was not the workers but the delicate computer chips. Although work conditions in the electronics factories were considered better than those of the garment and shoe factories, the work was boring, repetitive, and confined the worker in one position for the whole day.

A twenty-six-year-old electronics factory worker complained:

"Compared to the textile company where I worked before coming to the zone, I thought that the work was a lot easier for the first month. However, after a year, I started to get migraines, I could not see well, and I was getting tired all the time. I realized that the assembly work in a conveyor line was not as easy as I first thought.

The labor process in the conveyor line was such that workers did not realize that the speed increased no matter how fast they worked. Furthermore, they could not even look the other way for a minute since the parts came down steadily. Managers adjusted the speed little by little so that workers could not really feel it right away. The techniques the management used to speed up the process in the garment factory were more direct:

They put an extra worker at the start of the 20-worker line. The number of parts increases and the rest of us have to finish whatever comes down to us. If we do not keep up with that, the manager yells at us. This way, the normal production quota of 200 pairs of pants per person goes up to 240, 280 and they even push us to produce up to 350 a day.

In Korea, Saturday is a full working day, so workers have only Sunday off, and factories often require overtime work on Sundays, too. Workers are paid once a month. The wages are divided into two parts: a basic wage and a set of allowances, which comprise nearly half the amount actually paid to workers. The process of getting paid these allowances is very complicated, and the whole system is used by management as a way of not paying full wage to workers, because these allowances are not paid in full unless workers have a perfect attendance record. Under this wage system, if workers are absent due to sickness or emergency, they lose that day's basic wage plus parts of each of the allowances, so the actual deduction is more than one day's wage. Workers are not given any sick leave, so they always try to come to work even when they are sick. Any bonuses are calculated from the basic wage rather than from the total paycheck. Since the wages are so low, workers usually welcome a few hours of overtime per day. Even with overtime, however, because of the high rent in Masan City, workers must live in crowded housing.

Despite their low wages, practically every worker saves some money every month by eating only rice and kim-chi (pickled cabbage) every day. Workers sometimes eat eggs, and they eat pork just once a month, right after payday. Many do not eat breakfast or dinner and rely only on the lunch provided by the company. By cutting back on necessities, factory workers save money for their dowry. The importance these workers attribute to the dowry reflects the high expectations that Korean women have for marriage. They are trying to improve their future status by creating a dowry that will enable them to marry a man from a better class background.

Young women workers are willing to tolerate low wages and poor working conditions because they anticipate spending only a short time in the factory before they get married and leave the labor force. They expect marriage to improve their status, and take it for granted that they will be supported by their husbands. This expectation inhibits their involvement in labor unions and other collective strategies to improve their working and living conditions.

Most women do marry and leave the labor force in their mid-twenties, so management does not have to worry about seniority-related pay increases. The turnover rate also diminishes labor militancy and makes workers more difficult to organize. Thus, multinational corporations benefit from the importance placed on marriage by the already existing patriarchal ideology of Korea. Indeed, workers older than twenty-six are pressured to quit and get married. One twenty-eight-year-old worker told me that she quit her job at an electronics company where she had worked for seven years because of the indirect pressure from coworkers and management. The pressure was not a direct demand; rather it took the form of teasing, such as "When are you getting married?" or "My God, you will be here until you get to be a grandmother."

Few women intend to work after they get married, and even then they prefer to have some other type of work besides factory work.[2] Most women give reasons related to their position in the patriarchal family to explain their desire not to work after marriage, for example, "I want to be a good wife and a mother." Some, however, give reasons directly related to their experience as factory workers, such as, "I am sick and tired of working in a factory."

After marriage, however, many women find that their husbands' salaries are inadequate to support their families, and they are forced to return to factory work under more arduous conditions. Working-class husbands cannot guarantee economic security for their wives, and these women become exploited both as workers and as spouses. Furthermore, they receive neither the protected status promised to women by patriarchal families[3] nor the freedom promised to women by their participation in the labor market.[4]

WOMEN WORKERS AND THE LABOR MOVEMENT

The 1970s saw a sharp increase in the number of female workers employed in the manufacturing sector (Kim 1986: 32). Between 1966 and 1978, female participation in the manufacturing labor force grew from 33.6 percent to 46.1 percent (Choi 1983: 82). Female workers' experience was even harsher than that of male workers since they had to work longer hours at lower wages. As in other parts of the world, female labor is treated as providing supplementary income and is con-centrated in unskilled, simple, repetitive jobs, which are the lowest paid. According to the statistics provided by the South Korean Labor Ministry for 1985, female workers work an average of 238.1 hours per month and 40.5 hours overtime while male workers in the manufac-turing sector work an average of 234.9 hours per month and 38 hours overtime.

During the 1970s the labor movement was not led by the formal national labor organization but was spontaneous and unorganized. Women workers sustained the Korean labor movement during the 1970s and became increasingly important after 1975. In-ryong Sin contended that from 1975 to 1980, only the women workers' movement was significant, and that during the repressive period immediately following the coup d'etat in 1980, women's labor movements were the only ones that existed (1985: 51).

Factors contributing to woman-initiated labor movements in the 1970s can be listed as follows (Sin 1985: 52–54):

1. Female workers historically had participated in the labor movement.
2. Women workers were working under worse conditions than male workers. They received less than half the male wage and were mistreated by both male managers and male production workers.
3. The labor struggle during the 1970s was severely repressed by the govern-

ment, so organizers had to risk being fired or imprisoned. Female workers risked less than men because their wages were so low to begin with.

4. Compared to male workers, female workers have marriage as an escape, and most of them have their families in the rural area to which they can return in an emergency. This might be a hinderance for the labor movement in the long run, but it made it possible for women organizers to be more militant in the short term.

5. Religious organizations (both Protestants and Catholics) influenced women workers. Since the end of the 1960s, these religious organizations have helped industrial laborers, especially female workers, to learn about their rights to organize and to raise their consciousness.

During the 1970s, the labor policy adopted by Japanese-owned companies in MAFEZ was one that coerced workers into loyalty to the company and was backed by threats of layoffs. Management enforced a demerit system according to which a worker would be laid off if she attained a certain number of demerits. The criteria for measurement in the demerit system were "sincerity, cooperation with the company, efficiency, attendance, and loyalty to the company" (Committee for Justice and Peace of South Korea 1976: 60). This led the workers to compete with each other. In addition to coercive labor practices, the Japanese supervisors exhibited an attitude of racial superiority over Korean workers. Workers confronted Japanese managers over three related issues: "general issues of workers' rights; discrimination against Koreans by Japanese; and sexual discrimination against women workers" (Committee for Justice and Peace of South Korea 1976: 61).

There were over 50 labor disputes reported during the first 10 years of MAFEZ (1970–1980). Most of these resulted in failure, and the workers involved in the disputes were fired. The number of disputes may not seem very high, but considering the government's restrictions, these were brave actions. Although the incidents were sporadic, resistance was always present. However, despite the courage and commitment of these women workers in Korea, they could not stand against "the combined power of the companies and the government" (Easter and Easter 1983: 22). After 1980, initiating disputes became almost impossible because the government began to enforce even harsher measures to prevent workers from organizing.

Despite laws prohibiting union activity in MAFEZ before 1987, several attempts were made to organize labor unions. The first was at Buknung (a food processing company) early in 1980 during the period of political uncertainty after the assassination of President Chung Hee Park. Soon after the labor union was established, however, the company closed down and left Masan. Workers in two other factories tried to organize unions but were prevented from doing so by management. In 1986, workers of the Sumida electronics company organized a union which management destroyed, dismissing the union leader. Thus, until 1987 there was only a "joint labor–management council" operating as a top-down organization in the MAFEZ.

Nevertheless, throughout the 1980s many women were becoming aware of unions and workers' rights, so when the nationwide labor uprising began in 1987, women in Masan area were active participants. The examples below show how, even before the 1987 uprising, the seemingly "passive and docile," workers were learning about their rights.

Women union leaders in Masan said that they became involved in the labor movement because of concern about poverty and inhumane working conditions. Most of them said that without help from the Catholic church organizations (especially *Jeunesse Ouvrière Chrétienne* or JOC, they would not have realized that their problems could be solved by organizing. Without help from JOC, their concerns would have remained only individual workers' personal complaints. Most of the union leaders of 1987 were either members of the JOC or became members while they were involved in the labor struggle.

The following examples illustrate the characteristics of women labor leaders in Masan and explain how they became involved in labor organizing. Eun-ja Kim started to work in Masan at a garment factory in January 1984. When I asked her how she became involved in the labor movement, she answered:

I am the oldest of four children [one boy and three girls]. My family was so poor working as tenant farmers that my parents decided to move to Masan, where they thought they would be able to get jobs. My father works as a day laborer and my mother works as a cleaning woman at a hospital. Even though four members of my family [father, mother, herself, and her younger sister] work hard, we are still poor. Not being able to get out of poverty made me think that something was wrong. Logically, if four of us are working, we should not be so poor, but we are. I did not know about how to fight for our rights until I started to go to JOC meetings. I learned that workers have the right to receive enough wages to support themselves, and that we should be united to organize a union to fight against the management. This is how I started to get involved in fighting against the management of the company where I am working.

At the garment factory, she met Jong-ja Lee, the president of JOC, who recruited her. Becoming a member of JOC transformed Eun-ja Kim from an angry but ignorant worker to a well-informed leader who is knowledgeable about labor law and other fields.

Eun-ja Kim became president of her factory union, which was organized in 1987. She had a hard time organizing a union since married women were afraid of losing their jobs during strikes. However, they continued a long fight under threat from the management to close down, and got a higher wage increase than management had first intended to give.

One of the strongest unions in the zone was at the Jungchon electronics factory which is owned by a Japanese firm. Their twenty-six-year-old union leader has worked in the zone for nine years, including five years at Jungchon. Before she became the union president, she was the representative of workers in the joint labor–management council; she had fought for better working conditions since 1986. One of the reasons why this union was so strong was that the leader had worked there for a long time; as a result, the workers trusted her and followed her direction. Moreover, she had close friends who were devoted to union activity, which helped a great deal. When I asked her how she came to work in the zone, she replied:

I have worked in the zone for nine years now [1978–1987]. I started at a shoe factory. I went to work for that company because they promised to send me to night school, but after 11 months, they told me that they decided not to send anyone that year. So I moved to another shoe factory. Since I had only a junior high school education, I could not apply to the electronics factory. Even at the second factory, I could not go to the industrial night school, so finally I paid for my own tuition to go to school. At the second factory, I worked for two and a half years and then moved to Jungchon electronics about 5 years ago. My plan was to learn as much as possible. I thought that education would solve my problems. . . . I tried four times to start a college correspondence course, but now I have given up since I realized that a college diploma did not mean much.

When she was working at the second shoe factory, she had to argue with the line leader every day in order to be allowed to go to school. She recalled how she decided to do something about the way workers were treated at the factory:

At Shinheung, about a third of the workers were students. The work at a shoe factory is hard, so the management used promises of education to lure young women to work in the factory. But they would not let students go to school whenever they needed overtime work. Students had to cry, fight, and run away to go to school. Seeing those incidents, I got angrier and angrier. From those experiences, I learned that we needed a union to protect our rights.

Organizing the union at the T. C. electronics factory transformed a worker from a weak, frightened woman to a strong-willed union leader. Mi-ja Park was only twenty-one years old in 1987, when the labor uprising erupted in the zone. She thought that the workers at T. C.

should go on strike too, and, since there was no one who wanted to be a leader, she was pushed to become one. At the time, she was ignorant about union activity. After she became a leader, however, JOC members contacted her and taught her how to organize her union. At first their efforts to organize a union failed because of management's intervention. When male workers threatened her, Mi-ja Park became afraid and did not know what to do. After management destroyed her union, she was transferred to another job in the factory, where she had to work by herself. Although she failed in 1987, she reorganized the union in 1988, and this time she succeeded. By then, she was quite determined and knowledgeable about unions. The case of T. C. will be discussed later in this chapter.

THE LABOR UPRISING IN JULY–AUGUST 1987

National Background

On June 29, 1987, in the midst of constant antigovernment demonstrations demanding "direct presidential elections," and "an end to the military dictatorship," the ruling party's presidential candidate, No Tae Woo, was pushed to announce the "June 29 Declaration." His declaration, however, made no mention of the rights of laborers, farmers, and urban poor. However, it provided an opening in the rigid facade of the military regime. Workers grabbed the opportunity to exercise their rights, and demanded "democratic labor unions," "wage increases," and "better working conditions."

The nationwide uprising began on July 5, in Ul-san at a subsidiary of the Hyun-dae company. The workers organized a democratic labor union, which sparked similar movements in other Hyun-dae subsidiaries. By August the struggle had spread around the country to workers in the other large conglomerates, and eventually workers in small- and medium-sized companies became involved. Between June and September there were over 3,000 labor disputes reported nationwide (*Kyounghyang Daily News*, 14 September 1987). According to Ministry of Labor statistics, disputes occurred at a rate averaging 44 cases a day. The events of 1987 are characterized as the first mass labor struggle to occur in Korean history.

The demands made during the uprising went beyond the demand for wage increases and better working conditions to include workers' rights to organize labor unions and democratize existing management-run unions. Unfair dismissals, interference with unionization, and other unfair labor practices were also issues.

The July-August labor uprising revealed growing national support for the movement. Most of the disputes were of a large size, and took place nationwide during a short period of time; the uprising was led by workers, not by a small number of activists. Moreover, it was backed by a strong nationalist movement, of which the student political movement was also a part.

The Labor Uprising in the Masan Area

Early in August the movement reached Chang-won, a heavy industrial estate that employs mostly male workers. Workers in Chang-won started strikes demanding democratic unions and wage increases. This uprising provided inspiration for female workers in nearby Masan, where unions were banned. By September, more than half the companies operating in the Masan Free Export Zone (41 out of 73) had experienced sit-in strikes. The four main demands of the workers were wage and bonus increases, better treatment, improved working conditions, and seniority allowances.

Most strikes in Masan were unorganized and were motivated by the need for higher wages. Management accepted the inevitability of increasing wages and bonuses, and went along with this and the other basic demands of the workers. However, allowing permanent labor unions to organize was another matter. After the initial disputes had been settled, management was able to persuade many workers to withdraw from the unions. Most workers were not aware of the importance of labor unions. For workers, paying union dues, even though they were very low, seemed like one more burden. Most of the unions were easily taken over by the management or disbanded. In the few cases where management encountered strong resistance, they organized male workers to threaten and physically abuse their female coworkers. In one exceptional case, management was able to turn female workers against the union organizers. These workers were told that they would be laid off because the union had frightened the parent company into canceling its orders. There were only six democratic unions still in existence at the end of the year. Even this small number, however, represented a significant gain, since no unions of any kind had been allowed before 1987.

The 1987 experience taught workers a valuable lesson about how to organize themselves to fight against management, and when they faced another labor struggle in March 1988, the women workers of Masan were able to organize more quickly and effectively. Union activities led to significantly higher factory wages in Masan, from US$4 a day in 1987 to US$7 a day in 1988. Workers' consciousness has also increased greatly in the past few years. Higher wages and increased union activities of women workers, however, have made the Masan Free Export Zone less attractive to its foreign investors.

The Continuation of the Struggle

The conflicting aims of multinational corporations and Korean workers is illustrated by the events leading up to the departure of the T. C. Electronics Company from the Zone. T. C., the largest U.S.-based company in Masan, was established in 1972, and was wholly owned by the Tandy Corporation. Its main products were stereo components, telephones, and computer components.

During 1988, workers seeking to unionize the company clashed with antiunion supervisors controlled by management at the T. C. Electronics factory. Several union women required hospitalization, but the labor union survived the confrontation. By mid-1988, about half the women workers had joined the union. The management of T. C. Electronics was disturbed by these developments and began to talk about closing down. The chairman of the Tandy Corporation in the United States threatened to move some production lines out of Korea because of the "general level of cultural change and political uncertainty" (quoted in the *New York Times*, 26 August 1988). However, he also stated that the company did not plan to pull out of Korea.

Management warned workers that orders from the parent company were decreasing. They instituted a hiring freeze in Masan and tried to move machines to subcontracting factories outside the zone. Union members threw themselves in front of the movers in an effort to stop the removal of the machines from the factory. In February 1989, management sued the union for its role in blocking the removal of equipment, and for obstructing daily procedures on the shop floor.

Both sides hardened their positions during these confrontations. Management accused the union members of slowing down productivity so that they could not rely on their workers to produce goods in time to meet shipping deadlines. The union accused management of hiring thugs to disrupt the operations of the factory so that T. C. Electronics could use "declining productivity" as an excuse to close. T. C. Electronics also described the confrontations at the factory as being between men and women workers, and thus as unrelated to management policies.

In April 1989, the workers' worst fear came to pass. Tandy Corporation declared that it was closing its factory in Masan and dismissed its entire staff. They paid the wages for April and the minimum legal severance payment (two months wages) to workers, following the legal requirements for closing the factory.

The core membership of the union refused to accept the plant closing and occupied the factory building, demanding that the company reopen the plant. When they were ignored by Tandy, about 20 workers went to T. C.'s research institute in Seoul. They found the company president in the institute and took him hostage, holding him for four days before he escaped. Their demand for direct negotiations with the parent company in the United States indicated that they still felt that the problems that had occurred in the Masan factory were due to local mismanagement rather than being intrinsic to the structural problems of export processing zones. They felt that perhaps if the head office understood their desperation, it would be sympathetic and reopen the factory. However, the union's kidnapping of the president of their Korean subsidiary did not convince Tandy to negotiate, but rather confirmed them in their decision to close their factory.

Eventually, the hopelessness of the union's position became clear, and the workers occupying the factory began to leave. There were only about 50 workers still in the factory when police came in and forced them out in December 1989. In 1990, the union president, Kim Chong-im, and 21 workers were jailed and their fight with Tandy was finished.

Tandy was the first major investor to pull out of Masan, but several other large companies have left or have threatened to leave the zone. Sumida Electronics left MAFEZ in 1989 without paying overdue wages and severance payments. If Tandy corporation closed its factory following all the "legal" procedure, Sumida did not even bother to follow that course. The owner of Sumida Electronics left Korea without any warning to workers and sent a fax announcing its bankruptcy ("Unions' Struggle across the Border": 59). After the plant closing, the union officers got together and organized a negotiation team to go to Japan. Only after demonstrations and public outcry in both Korean and Japanese newspapers were the union officers able to go to Japan, where they forced Sumida to send the workers their back wages. A year after the plant closing, workers' representatives are still continuing their struggle against Sumida with sit-ins and hunger strikes (*AMPO* 1990: 60).

CONCLUSION

The women workers in Masan have been a capitalist's ideal labor force, highly productive and characterized by low militancy and a willingness to work for low wages. The Korean tradition emphasizing female passivity led them to endure working long hours for low pay. Nevertheless, their recent political activism indicates that capitalists cannot expect female passivity to persist indefinitely.

In women's subordination as a gender, they often project a docile, subservient attitude toward men, especially those who occupy positions of authority over them. Women's apparent passivity is not a natural state, however, but rather, like the passivity of colonized peoples, it is produced through enormous efforts of self-repression; moreover, when action is eventually taken, it is intense and spontaneous (cf. Fanon 1968: 48). The political activism of the women workers in Masan was a response to their increasing frustration with the "Korean economic miracle."

Multinational companies set up assembly factories in Third World countries because of the availability of inexpensive, politically vulnerable labor. When workers at T. C. Electronics and Sumida Electronics organized militant unions, they forced the companies to improve wages. As a result, however, the operations in the zone were closed and the companies moved to cheaper, poorer countries. Even if workers in Masan were able to organize and temporarily achieve higher wages and better working conditions, are they better off if their employers leave Korea to find cheaper, unorganized labor?

Women workers in MAFEZ are not only part of the Korean labor movement, but as part of the new international division of labor, they are part of a global movement as well. From an international perspective, the closing of the T. C. Electronics factory may be a labor victory after all, since it radicalized workers and contributed to the development of a working-class leadership. The lives of many women were drastically changed by the 1987 labor uprising.

Workers in both developed and developing countries need to organize internationally to prevent multinational corporations from continually moving their operations to cheaper and more oppressed labor markets. "In order for those alliances to be effective, workers must extend their organizations to overseas branches to overcome the competitive downgrading of the wage scale worldwide" (Nash n.d.: 25). Unions from the developed and the developing countries must get together if they want to check the power of multinational corporations. Multinational unions are needed to deal with multinational corporations.

NOTES

This study is based on field research in Masan City from December 1986 to February 1988, which was funded by the National Science Foundation (BNS–440358) and the Andrew Silk Dissertation Fellowship, City University of New York Graduate Center. The names of factory workers are pseudonyms.

1. Besides the issues of wage increases and better working conditions which were in the center of the disputes in the first decade of MAFEZ, the problem of sexual relationships with foreign managers became an important political issue (see the Committee for Justice and Peace of South Korea 1976).

2. Out of the 675 women who responded to my questionnaire, only 10 percent intended to work after they got married.

3. The protected status that women are promised under "classic patriarchy" may offer real benefits to some women even though it is part of a system that

oppresses women in general. For a further discussion, see Johnson (1983), Kandiyoti (1988), and Wolf (1972).

4. Some married women workers are constrained by family obligations and forced to sell their labor through a system of homework.

15

Conclusion: New Waves and Old—Industrialization, Labor, and the Struggle for a New World Order

Frances Abrahamer Rothstein

Anthropology has had a long involvement with industrialization.[1] The chapters in this volume continue this involvement by building on the strengths of earlier approaches, including fieldwork, a concern with differences as well as similarities, processual accounts, and a holistic view that examines cultural, social, and political, as well as economic relations. However, the chapters in this collection build also on recent work in anthropology, as well as in other disciplines, in order to take into account the world as it exists today and its differences from even the recent past.

One of the most important commonalities in all the contributions is the recognition of a global capitalist system or international network of production, exchange, and consumption; that is, the global factory. Although each contribution focuses on the experiences of a specific community or region, the local context is seen as part of a dynamic global structure. Whether they are looking at Hong Kong investment in China, Japanese investment in Kentucky, or nonresident investment in India, and thus examining the movement of capital across national boundaries, or whether they are discussing the movement of people from country to city and back in Latin American or from *bantustan* to border industrial area in South Africa, all the authors set their research in a context of global capitalism. This recognition of a global model is a consequence both of the theoretical developments of the 1960s, 1970s, and 1980s discussed in Chapter 1 (dependency theory, Wallerstein's world-systems approach, and the more recent analysis of the new international division of labor) and of important changes in the world. It is impossible to avoid a global framework.

Not only are anthropologists, in this volume and in general, well past the era of treating communities as if they were isolated (the model suggested by George Foster in the 1950s), but as anthropologists and as citizens, we are constantly reminded of the interconnections in the contemporary world. Johanna Lessinger met the son of a family she knew when she was in a student training program in rural Ecuador 20 years ago, now selling textiles in front of the New York City Public Library. A rural Mexican woman I know flew to New York with US $1,500 that had been collected by a group of factory workers to buy South African ostrich feathers (at half the price they were selling for in Mexico City) for the Carnival celebration in San Cosme. Wherever we are in the "developed" world, we are increasingly likely to encounter people from the countries that anthropologists have traditionally studied. Moreover, when we are in the field in the "developing" world, there are constant reminders of the First World. The overlap in people, things, behavior, and ideas between the First and Third, core and periphery, or developing and developed, worlds and the variations within these categories are so great that the categories are useful only if we see them as points on a continuum, approximations, or parts in a system, and *not* as discrete entities. The concept of a global factory, as Michael Blim emphasized in Chapter 1, incorporates the fluidity and flexibility that characterizes contemporary processes and units. It is important to stress also that the concept of the global factory goes beyond the idea that global capitalism influences and is influenced by local actors and events (see Smith 1984c, Rothstein 1988). The global factory *is* comprised of local actors and events, but the stage on which they play is the world.

Another important common denominator of the approach used in the articles here is that the authors all take their cues from the particular situation or situations in which they have lived and studied. Traditional anthropological ethnography is used along with quantitative analysis, historical analysis, and a global theoretical framework, but a heavy emphasis is placed on ethnography and the view of the participants. This is most explicit in the chapter by Ann Kingsolver, Ida Susser's discussion of Puerto Rican women's everyday healing behavior, and Alan and Josephine Smart's analysis of gift exchange in China. Even where the authors do not explicitly focus on the emic view, the problems they stress are derived from an inside view rather than an outsider's etic perspective; Frances Rothstein's emphasis on return migration, for example, comes not from the literature on migration (that is, outsider views, which, she suggests, have treated migration as a unidirectional flow) but from the repeated comings and goings that give a particular rhythm to life in San Cosme. It is probably because of their heavy reliance on ethnography also that although some of the papers focus on transnational corporations and the global assembly line (Kingsolver, Kim, and Susser), and all the others acknowledge the presence and influence of transnational corporations, small-scale production with diverse linkages to the international market figures prominently in most of the analyses. In stressing small-scale production, these chapters remind us that "the TNCs are neither all-powerful nor fully equipped to shape a new world economy themselves. They require workers and they require consumers" (Gordon 1988: 64). Via the ethnographic approach, the chapters make clear also that participants in the global factory are not simply workers and consumers. We are women or men, young or old, and we are also family members and members of racial-ethnic groups, with religious, regional, and national identities.

CONNECTIONS

Although the chapters in this book focus on the concrete lives of people in relatively small communities, because the authors also see those communities and their residents as participants in a global network of production, distribution, and consumption, the chapters reveal connections and similarities as well as diversity and contrast.

Not surprisingly, more interconnections among the world's players means also that new interconnections and relations are emerging. We are accustomed to think of capital and manufactured products flowing from the "advanced" capitalist world to the developing countries, and primary products flowing from the developing countries to the developed countries. Today, however, there are a number of different flows. The flow of manufactured products from the developing countries has grown significantly since the 1960s. While the flow of capital from the developed countries continues and has grown, especially in the form of direct foreign investment, the flow of capital from the developing countries to the developed countries, sometimes through "capital flight," has also grown. The chapters by Smart and Smart and by Eugene Cooper and Xiong Pan describe how capital from such newly industrialized countries as Hong Kong is now playing a significant role in China.

In one way or another, all the chapters focus on new patterns of connection—in the flows of capital, people, and/or products—and their consequences. One of the most important characteristics of contemporary industrialization, as noted in Chapter 1, is the increasing stress on export production.[2] Given the pressure being exerted by transnational corporations, the International Monetary Fund, and the World Bank, especially in countries such as Mexico or Egypt which have large debts, to replace import substitution industrialization with export production, it is likely that export production will be even more common in the near future. Many of the articles explicitly or implicitly analyze correlates of this new flow of industrial production from formerly "underdeveloped" countries. Seung-kyung Kim describes how in order to promote export production, the South Korean government increased state involvement, first in the creation of export processing zones and then in labor control. Johanna Lessinger describes a different state strategy to increase export production in which the Indian government is attempting to encourage foreign investment not by transnationals but by NonResident Indians (NRIs).

The new integration of the Common Market in 1992 is a strategy of 12 European nation-states to facilitate export production. In their examination of Spanish public- and private-sector preparations for the new integration, Hans and Judith-Maria Buechler show how individual, family, community, regional, and national economic planning interact, combine, and sometimes conflict. Conflict figures also in Cooper and Pan's analysis of the Changping District of China where, they suggest, successful entrepreneurs in the rapidly growing export processing rural industries may represent a threat to local Communist party control. Similarly, Lessinger notes that the NRI phenomenon in India has generated a great deal of opposition from the Indian business class as well as progressives, and politicians.

Not only capital and products but people also are increasingly on the move in new directions in the global factory. The movement of people within and between nations is not new, but today's movement differ even from the earlier migrations associated with capitalism. Until recently, massive labor relocations flowed from less dynamic areas to regions where economic growth was centered.[3] Today, however, there are large migrations from areas such as Asia and the Caribbean which, because of the growth of export production, are themselves among the most dynamic (Sassen 1988). The chapters by Douglas Caulkins and by Rothstein are concerned with an analogous form of migration in which workers from urban industrial centers (that is, the growth centers), are leaving the cities and moving back to the countryside of Latin America and the United Kingdom. Although not the focus of their chapters, return migrants and their remittances are important also in the Buechlers' discussion of rural Spain and Koptiuch's discussion of Egypt. The Indian migrants discussed by Lessinger similarly sometimes move back from the United States or Great Britain. Lessinger's analysis makes explicit a point that is implicit in many of the articles. Although there is a common pattern in the flow of people going home, important class differences affect who goes home, how they go, and where in the economic and political hierarchy they reenter.

GLOBALIZATION AND DIVERSITY

At first glance, the new movements of people, products and capital; the overall general growth of global industrialization; and the growth of capitalism and export production in socialist as well as capitalist economies, along with increasing privatization in countries such as Mexico and Egypt, suggest that the global factory is a homogenizing agent and part of a homogenized world. However, as the chapters all indicate, despite an important grid of similarities, old differences are being maintained and/or reworked, and new differences are being created. The Nonresident Indian investors discussed by Lessinger, for example, are neither completely Indian nor completely non-Indian. As she indicates, their "transnational" interests bring them into conflict with other Indians at home and with other overseas immigrants abroad. They almost seem more similar to the returning native sons described by Caulkins than to Indians or other immigrants; like the returning native sons, they combine investment in high-tech export-oriented production with "traditional" regional identities.

HOMEWORK, PETTY COMMODITY PRODUCTION, AND GLOBALIZATION

Ironically, even as production becomes more similar in terms of being oriented for the same international market, on the surface, at least, more diverse production relations are developing and coexisting. This is particularly evident in the chapter by the Buechlers, in which they show that small-scale, large-scale, agricultural, and industrial production are all increasing. Often members of the same household or the same individual at different points in the life cycle will be involved in different kinds of production relations. As Kingsolver indicates, Toyota workers in Kentucky combine farm and factory work. In San Cosme, where farm and factory work has also been combined for many years, now different forms of industrial production are also combined. For example, one woman runs a small workshop with three machines in which low-paid workers make girls' dresses. Her husband is a relatively well-paid worker at a large transnational chemical manufacturing plant. His annual bonus provided the capital to start the workshop. For now, at least, the couple sells their products themselves at regional markets. In this as well as other examples in the collection, "modern" production facilitates or is facilitated by traditional or small-scale production.

Until recently, the common view of industrialization held that large-scale factory organization would replace household-based petty commodity production. Several of the chapters in this volume add to a growing body of evidence indicating that small-scale production is still very much a part of "modern" production. In fact, the case studies by Buechler and Buechler, Cooper, Smart and Smart, and Kristin Koptiuch suggest that in many areas globalization has increased household-based production. Sometimes homework is directly connected to large-scale transnational export production; some small-scale production is for the regional or local market but, as Koptiuch suggests, the importance of many "informal" enterprises depends on their role in maintaining low reproductive costs for workers in highly capitalized enterprises.

Not only is there a mix of petty commodity production (of both autonomous and nonautonomous varieties), homework, and large-scale monopoly capitalist enterprises in today's global production but, as the articles by Cooper and Pan and by Smart and Smart indicate, within socialist economies there are similar mixes of large- and small-scale capitalist units *and* government-run cooperatives. As these authors make clear, actual relations of production cannot be read off simply from whether the national economy is socialist or capitalist.

Research on small-scale production over time in both capitalist and socialist economies is necessary to determine how autonomous small producers are and whether they can stay that way for any length of time. For the moment, small size and independence from each other enables the small firms described by Smart and Smart to deal more effectively with the Chinese bureaucracy. Blim's re-studies of Italian shoe factories and artisan firms competing on the international market suggest that the success of small-scale producers was short-lived because of their limited capital. Even the supposedly flexible small firms that relied on a great deal of "informal" labor were unable to withstand global market fluctuations and competition.

Davydd Greenwood's analysis suggests that large-scale industrial cooperatives in Spain were able to avoid some of the adverse effects of changed market conditions because their structure enabled them to pool resources, rearrange labor, and shift profits from more to less profitable branches. The case described by the Buechlers suggests that at the household level, as well as at the level of the firm, flexibility is crucial. Reliance on homework, for example, seems possible only when the homeworker can allocate many hours and when supplementary sources of income and labor are available. It should be noted, however, that if alternatives (rather than supplements) are present, as in one of the cases cited by the Buechlers, individuals may resist homework. Some homeworkers and small-scale production units may persist therefore, despite losses, only because there are few alternatives. A similar dependence and resistance to such dependence is mentioned by Caulkins in his analysis of enterprises run by "local heroes." These owners of the smallest firms, ranging in size from 1 to 10 employees, frequently rely on subcontracts from larger national and multinational corporations, but Caulkins notes at least one case of a firm which did not accept a contract with a large transnational corporation because they preferred to maintain a diverse customer base.

GLOBALIZATION AND KINSHIP

Contrary to the old modernization thesis, which predicted the decline of kin ties with the spread of industrialization, in all the cases discussed here, family and kinship ties continue to be important. Often they are an important source of the flexibility that underlies contemporary industrialization. Georgina Jaffee stresses the support of mothers and siblings in enabling South African women to be employed. Wives are an important source of labor in several of the small enterprises discussed by Caulkins. Smart and Smart stress the role of kin ties for Hong Kong capitalists trying to establish industrial enterprises in China. Although kin ties help some individuals and units, such as families, households, or firms, survive and even succeed, the benefits of success are often distributed unequally within the family, household, or family firm. Sometimes the relations between kin may be exploitative as in the case of nonresident Indians using kin ties overseas to get cheap labor. Within household enterprises, internal power dynamics and distribution patterns may also be unequal. There has been a tendency to treat households as representing a unity of interests. As noted in Chapter 1, recent research on household-based production has suggested that hierarchical gender and age relations are often reenforced in household enterprises (Boris 1985; Benería and Roldán 1987; Truelove 1990; Babb 1990). Whether they are entering the market as wage laborers (as in the cases discussed by Jaffee and Kim) or providing unpaid labor in a household enterprise (as in many of the cases described by Buechler and Buechler) women rarely have many alternatives, and their access to capital and wages is almost always less than men's. In contexts where household-based production or wage labor increases their alternatives and access to capital or wages, women's autonomy may be increased. In the case described by Jaffee, women's use of kin ties to get access to the unpaid labor of other women enables at least the wage-working women to increase their access to wages and to reduce patriarchal control. More often, women are excluded from all but the very lowest-paying jobs, and they have little choice but to become dependent on and subordinate to husbands. Despite their economic dependence, however, as Susser shows, women may be important links in kinship networks which can be utilized and mobilized for a variety of purposes, including, as in the case of the women of Yabucoa, sustained political action.

NEW WAVES AND OLD

If there is a single theme that emerges from the studies in this collection it is that contemporary industrialization with its heavy reliance on small-scale production and kinship in a global context, differs sharply from the industrial transformation of the West. In that first industrial experience, factories grew larger and larger and social relations became more impersonal. Some of that impersonality and factory growth has been exaggerated by social science models which focused on those aspects of industrialization and ignored the persistence of kin relations and other "traditional" behaviors. However, although recent historical research has documented the continued presence of family and ethnic ties, petty commodity production, and homework not unlike that described in the case studies here, there was a clear and significant decline in such patterns.

It may be that the prominence of small-scale production and kinship in the industrialization of the late twentieth-century simply represents an early stage and, like the industrial transformation of the West, these features in today's global factory will gradually disappear. Not only is small-scale production still important in the developing world, however, but the resurgence of household-based production and sweatshops in the United States suggests that history is not simply repeating itself. It may be that the new forms of technology, especially new forms of communication and information processing and relatively cheaper transportation, which link people and places despite great physical distances, have allowed a new system to emerge.[4] In the first industrial revolution, "the dispersed organization of labor gave way to the development of a new form of productive enterprise, the factory" (Wolf 1982: 274). Concentration "under one roof" of workers and phases of work was the hallmark of that factory. In contemporary industrialization, modern technology allows dispersal. Capitalists can now invest on a global scale. This had led some observers to suggest that capital's new "lever of exploitation"—capital mobility—has placed labor in a weakened position and given capitalism a new freedom and power (Ross and Trachte 1990). There is no doubt that labor in the United States and other Western countries such as Great Britain is weaker now than it has been. However, the global factory means that labor is not just

Western labor. The cases in this volume document the numerous and diverse efforts that working people throughout the world have made to improve their lives. As the studies here by Kim and Susser show, periodically these efforts take the form of conscious political struggle. The obstacles to successful struggle are no doubt great. Ultimately, Union Carbide moved; the Tandy Corporation closed its factory in the Masan Free Export Zone in South Korea. However, workers also move, either temporarily or permanently. Perhaps the mobility of labor and the social connections that go with it, along with the same modern technology which allows production to occur on a global scale, will also allow workers to unite on a global scale.

NOTES

1. For useful summaries of anthropology and industrialization in general, see Burawoy (1979a) and Holzberg and Giovannini (1981). For a discussion of applied anthropology and industry, see Baba (1986).

2. All countries have been heavily involved in export production for a long time, but until recently, the developing countries exported only primary products. Since the 1960s, however, there has been a significant growth in their export of manufactured products (World Bank 1987; Gordon 1988; Ross and Trachte 1990).

3. See Wolf (1982: 361–379) for an excellent summary and analysis of the first three major waves of migration in the development of capitalism.

4. I am not suggesting that technology occurs in a vacuum or that technology is causal. Both transportation and information technology have been spurred on by capital's constant search for profit and the crisis that monopoly capitalism faced in the 1970s and 1980s.

Bibliography

Abdel-Fadil, Mahmoud. "Informal Sector Employment in Egypt." *Cairo Papers in Social Science*, 6, no. 2 (1983), 55–89.

Aglietta, Michael. *A Theory of Capitalist Regulation: The U.S. Experience.* London: New Left Books, 1979.

Ahluwalia, Isher Judge. "Industrial Policy and Industrial Performance in India." In *The Indian Economy, Recent Development and Future Prospects*, ed. Robert Lucas and Gustav Papanek, pp. 151–162. Boulder, Colo.: Westview Press, 1988.

Alavi, Hamra. "The Structure of Peripheral Capitalism." In *Introduction to the Sociology of "Developing Societies,"* ed. Hamra Alavi and Teodor Shanin, pp. 172–191. New York: Monthly Review Press, 1982.

Alderson-Smith, Gavin. "Confederations of Households: Extended Domestic Entrprises in City and Country." In *Miners, Peasants and Entrepreneurs: Regional Development in the Central Highlands of Peru*, ed. Norman Long and Bryan Roberts, pp. 217–234. Cambridge: Cambridge University Press, 1984.

Alonso, Jose Antonio. "The Domestic Clothing Workers in the Mexican Metropolis and Their Relation to Dependent Capitalism." In *Women, Men, and the International Division of Labor*, ed. June Nash and Patricia Fernandez-Kelly, pp. 161–172. Albany, N.Y.: State University of New York Press, 1983.

Altamirano, T. "Regional Commitment among Central Highland Migrants in Lima." In *Miners, Peasants and Entrepreneurs: Regional Development in the Central Highlands of Peru*, ed. Norman Long and Bryan Roberts, pp. 198–217. Cambridge: Cambridge University Press, 1984.

Almanac Editorial Board. *1986 Almanac of China's Foreign Economic Relations*. Beijing, 1986.
American Anthropological Association. The Anthropology of the European Community, Symposium at the 87th Annual Meeting of the American Anthropological Association, Phoenix, Ariz., November 1988.
Amin, Ash, and John Goddard. "The Internalization of Production, Technological Change, Small Firms and Regional Development." In *Technological Change, Industrial Restructuring and Regional Development*, ed. Ash Amin and John Goddard, pp. 1–22. London: Allen and Unwin, 1986.
Amin, Ash, and Ian Smith. "The Internationalization of Production and its Implications for the U.K." In *Technological Change, Industrial Restructuring and Regional Development*, ed. Ash Amin and John Goddard, pp. 41–76. London: Allen and Unwin, 1986.
Amin, Samir. *Unequal Development: An Essay on the Social Formations of Peripheral Capitalism*. New York: Monthly Review Press, 1976.
Amsden, Alice. "The State and Taiwan's Development." In *Bringing the State Back In*, ed. Peter Evans, Dietrich Rueschmeyer, and Theda Skocpol, pp. 78–106. Cambridge: Cambridge University Press, 1985.
———. "Third World Industrialization: 'Global Fordism' or a New Model?" *New Left Review*, 182 (July–August 1990), 1–32.
Andors, P. "Women and Work in Shenzhen." *Bulletin of Concerned Asian Scholars*, 20, no. 3 (1988), 22–41.
Anselmi, Sergio. "Presupposti storici del recente sviluppo regionale." In *L'industria a domicilio: Aspetti dell'economia marchigiana negli ultimi decenni*, ed. Sergio Anselmi, Ugo Ascoli, and Riccardo Mazzoni, pp. 13–36. Ancona, Italy: Cooperative Giulio Pastore, 1983.
Arizpe, Lourdes. "Relay Migration and the Survival of the Peasant Household." In *The Political Economy of Urbanization in Third World Countries*, ed. H. Safa, pp. 19–46. Delhi: Oxford University Press, 1982.
Arrighi, Giovanni. "International Corporations, Labor Aristocracies, and Economic Development in Tropical Africa." In *Imperialism and Underdevelopment*, ed. Robert Rhodes, pp. 220–267. New York: Monthly Review Press, 1970.
———. "Fascism to Democratic Socialism: Logic and Limits of a Transition." In *Semiperipheral Development*, ed. Giovanni Arrighi, pp. 243–279. Beverly Hills, Calif.: Sage, 1985a.
———, ed. *Semiperipheral Development: The Politics of Southern Europe in the Twentieth Century*. Beverly Hills, Calif.: Sage, 1985b.
Ascoli, Ugo. "Le tendenze del mercato del lavoro in una regione ad economia periferica: Le Marche negli anni '80." University of Ancona, Italy. Mimeograph, n.d.
Baba, Marietta. "Business and Industrial Anthropology: An Overview." *NAPA Bulletin* (Washington, D.C.: American Anthropological Association), 2 (1986), 1–45.
Babb, Florence. "Women and Work in Latin America." *Latin American Research Review*, 25 (1990), 236–247.
Bagchi, Amiya Kumar. "Foreign Capital and Economic Development: A Schematic View." In *Imperialism and Revolution in South Asia*, ed. Kathleen

Gough and Hari Sharma, pp. 43–76. New York: Monthly Review Press, 1973.

Bagnasco, Arnaldo. *Tre Italie: La problematica territoriale dello sviluppo italiano*. Bologna: Il Mulino, 1977.

———. *La costruzione sociale del mercato*. Bologna: Il Mulino, 1988.

Bagnasco, Arnaldo, Rosella Pini, and Carlo Trigilia. "Sviluppo economic e trasformazioni sociopolitiche nei sistemi territoriali a economia diffusa." *Quaderni di Fondazione Giagiacomo Feltrinelli*, no. 14 (1981), 1–25, and no. 15 (1981), 1–21.

Bakhtin, M. M. "Discourse in the Novel." In *The Dialogic Imagination: Four Essays by M. M. Bakhtin*, ed. Michael Holmquist, trans. Caryl Emerson and Michael Holmquist, pp. 259–422, Austin, Texas: University of Texas Press, 1981.

Balassa, Bela. *New Directions in the World Economy*. New York: New York University Press, 1989.

———. "Korea's Development Strategy." Ed. Jene Kwon, pp. 3–18. New York: Greenwood Press, 1990.

Balasubramanyam, V. N. *The Economy of India*. London: Weidenfeld and Nicolson, 1984.

Balloni, Valeriano, and Roberto Vicarelli. "Il sistema industriale marchigiana negli anni settanta." *Economia Marche*, 5 (1979), 43–73.

Banco de España. *Informe annual 1988*. Madrid: Banco de España, 1989.

Baran, P. "Are Toy Makers Moving Base to China?" *Hong Kong Business*, September 1985, 12–13.

Barker, Jonathan, and Gavin Smith, eds. "Rethinking Petty Commodity Production." *Labour, Capital and Society* (Special Issue), 19, no. 1 (April 1986).

Bartlett, Peggy F. "Part-time Farming: Saving the Farm or Saving the Lifestyle?" *Rural Sociology*, 51, no. 3 (1986), 290–314.

———. "Industrial Agriculture." In *Economic Anthropology*, ed. Stuart Plattner, pp. 253–291. Stanford, Calif.: Stanford University Press, 1989.

Barrett, Richard, and Soomi Chin. "Export-Oriented Industrializing States in the Capitalist World System: Similarities and Differences." In *The Political Economy of the New East Asian Industrialism*, ed. Frederic Deyo, pp. 23–43. Ithaca, N.Y.: Cornell University Press, 1987.

Bartra, Roger. *Estructura Agraria y Clases Sociales en Mexico*. Mexico City: Serie Popular Era (Instituto de Investigaciones Sociales/UNAM), 1974.

Basch, Linda, Nina Glick-Schiller, and Christina Szanton. *The Transnationalization of Immigration: New Perspectives on Ethnicity, Race, Class and Nationalism*. New York: Gordon Breech, in press.

Basok, Tanya. "How Useful Is the 'Petty Commodity Production' Approach? Explaining the Survival and Success of Small Salvadorean Urban Enterprise in Costa Rica." *Labour, Capital, and Society*, 22, no. 1 (April 1989), 41–64.

Baver, S. "Policy Making for Industrialization in Puerto Rico, 1947–76." Ph.D. diss., Columbia University, 1979.

Beedham, B. "East of Eden: A Survey of Eastern Europe." *The Economist*, 12 August 1989, S3–S18.

Beinin, Joel, and Zachary Lockman. *Workers on the Nile: Nationalism, Communism, Islam, and the Egyptian Working Class, 1882–1954.* Princeton, N.J.: Princeton University Press, 1987.

Bell, Peter F. "Marxist Theory, Class Struggle, and the Crisis of Capitalism." In *The Subtle Anatomy of Capitalism*, ed. Jesse Schwartz, pp. 170–194. Santa Monica, Calif.: Goodyear Publishing Co., 1977.

Bell, Peter F., and Harry Cleaver. "Marx's Crisis Theory as a Theory of Class Relations." *Research in Political Economy*, Vol. 5, ed. Paul Zarembka. Greenwich, Conn.: JAI Press, 1982.

Bendix, Reinhard. *Work and Authority in Industry: Ideologies of Management in the Course of Industrialization.* Berkeley: University of California Press, 1956.

Bener í a, Lourdes. "Subcontracting and Employment Dynamics in Mexico City." In *The Informal Economy*, ed. A. Portes, H. Castells, and L. Benton, pp. 173–188. Baltimore, Md.: Johns Hopkins University Press, 1989.

Bener í a, Lourdes, and Marta Rold á n. *The Crossroads of Class and Gender: Industrial Homework, Subcontracting, and Household Dynamics in Mexico City.* Chicago: University of Chicago Press, 1987.

Bener í a, Lourdes, and Gita Sen. "Accumulation, Reproduction, and Women's Role in Economic Development: Boserup Revisited." In *Women's Work*, ed. Eleanor Leacock and Helen Sofa, pp. 141–157. South Hadley, MA: Bergin and Garvey, 1986.

Bener í a, Lourdes, and Catharine Stimpson, eds. *Women, Households, and the Economy.* New Brunswick, N.J.: Rutgers University Press, 1987.

Benton, Lauren. "Uso politico e sopravivenza dei ceti in declino." In *Il caso italiano*, ed. Fabio Cavazza and Stephen Graubard, pp. 291–313. Milan: Garzanti, 1974.

———. *Invisible Factories: The Informal Economy and Industrial Development in Spain.* Albany, N.Y.: State University of New York Press, 1990.

Berger, Suzanne. "Problems and Prospects of Egyptian Small-Scale Industry." Draft Report. Cairo: USAID, 1978.

Berger, Suzanne, and Michael Piore. *Dualism and Discontinuity in Industrial Societies.* Cambridge: Cambridge University Press, 1980.

Berik, Gunseli. *Women Carpet Weavers in Rural Turkey: Patterns of Employment, Earnings and Status.* Geneva: International Labor Office, 1987.

Berry, Mike. "Industrialization, Deindustrialization, and Uneven Development: The Case of the Pacific Rim." In *Capitalist Development and Crisis Theory: Accumulation, Regulation, and Spatial Restructuring*, ed. M. Gottdiener and Nicos Komninos, pp. 174–216. London: Macmillan, 1989.

Birch, David. *Job Creation in America.* New York: Free Press, 1987.

Blim, Michael. "Searching for the Small and Beautiful: Labor Process and Class Formation in the Industrialization of a Central Italian Shoe Town." Ph.D. diss., Temple University, 1987.

———. "Economic Development and Decline in the Emerging Global Factory: Some Italian Lessons." *Politics and Society*, 18 (1990a), 143–163.

———. *Made in Italy: Small-Scale Industrialization and Its Consequences.* New York: Praeger Publishers, 1990b.

Bluestone, Barry, and Bennett Harrison. *The Deindustrialization of America:*

Plant Closings, Community Abandonment, and the Dismantling of Basic Industry. New York: Basic Books, 1982.

Block, Fred. *The Origins of International Economic Disorder.* Berkeley: University of California Press, 1977.

Boissevain, Jeremy. "Small Entrepreneurs in Contemporary Europe." In *Ethnic Communities in Business: Strategies for Economic Survival,* ed. Robin Ward and Richard Jenkins, pp. 20–38. Cambridge: Cambridge University Press, 1984.

Bolles, Lynn. "Kitchens Hit by Priorities: Employed Working-Class Jamaican Women Confront the IMF," In *Women, Men and the International Division of Labor,* ed. J. Nash and M. P. Fernandez-Kelly, pp. 138–160. Albany: State University of New York Press, 1983.

Bollman, Ray D. *Off Farm Work by Farmers.* Ottawa: Statistics Canada, 1979.

Boris, Eileen. "Regulating Industrial Homework: The Triumph of 'Sacred Motherhood.'" *Journal of American History,* 71, no. 3 (1985), 745–763.

Bourdieu, Pierre. *Outline of a Theory of Practice.* Trans. Richard Nice. Cambridge: Cambridge University Press, 1977.

Brada, J. C., E. A. Hewett, and T. A. Wolf. "Economic Stabilization, Structural Adjustment, and Economic Reform." In *Economic Adjustment and Reform in Eastern Europe and the Soviet Union,* ed. J. C. Brada et al., pp. 3–36. Durham, N.C.: Duke University Press, 1988.

Bradby, Barbara. "The Destruction of Natural Economy." In *The Articulation of Modes of Production,* ed. Harold Wolpe, pp. 93–127. London: Routledge and Kegan Paul, 1980.

Braden, Maria. "Kentucky's Far East Connection." *Rural Kentuckian,* 40, no. 7 (1986), pp. 6–22.

Braverman, Harry. *Labor and Monopoly Capital: The Degradation of Work in the Twentieth Century.* New York: Monthly Review Press, 1974.

Breheny, Michael J., Paul Cheshire, and Robert Langridge. "The Anatomy of Job Creation? Industrial Change in Britain's M4 Corridor." In *Silicon Landscapes,* ed. Peter Hall and Ann Markusen, pp. 118–133. Boston: Allen and Unwin, 1985.

Breheny, Michael J., and Ronald McQuaid. "H.T.U.K.: The Developments of the United Kingdom's Major Centre of High Technology Industry." In *The Development of High Technology Industries,* ed. Michael Breheny and Ronald McQuaid, pp. 296–354. London: Croom Helm, 1987.

Brenner, Robert. "The Origins of Capitalist Development: A Critique of Neo-Smithian Marxism." *New Left Review,* 104 (July–August 1977), pp. 25–92.

Brewer, Anthony. *Marxist Theories of Imperialism: A Critical Survey.* London: Routledge and Kegan Paul, 1980.

Bromley, Ray, ed. "The Urban Informal Sector: Critical Perspectives. *World Development* (Special Issue), 6, nos. 9–10 (1978).

Bromley, Ray, and Chris Gerry, eds. *Casual Work and Poverty in Third World Cities.* New York: John Wiley and Sons, 1979.

Brusco, Sebastiano. "The Emilian Model: Productive Decentralization and Social Integration." *Cambridge Journal of Economics,* 6 (1986), 167–184.

Brush, S. "Peru's Invisible Migrants: A Case Study of Inter-Andean Migration." In *Land and Power in Latin America*, ed. B. Orlove and G. Castred, pp. 211–228. New York: Holmes and Meier, 1980.

Buck, Pem Davidson. "Racial Representations and Power in Southern Dependent Development." Paper presented at the 88th Annual Meeting of the American Anthropological Association, Washington, D.C., November 1989.

Buck, Pem Davidson, and Morton Wenger. "The Domestic Dynamics of Development: Articulation, Rearticulation, and the Rural Family." Paper presented at the 86th Annual Meeting of the American Anthropological Association, Phoenix, Ariz., November 1988.

Buechler, Hans. "Cooperatives and Inequality in Spanish Galicia." In *Research in Inequality and Social Conflict*, ed. I. Wallimann and M. Dobkowski, Vol. 1, pp. 131–164. Greenwich, Conn.: JAI Press, 1989.

Buechler, Hans., and Judith-Maria Buechler. *Carmen: The Autobiography of a Spanish Galician Woman*. Cambridge: Schenkman, 1981.

Buechler, Judith-Maria. "Women in Petty Commodity Production in La Paz, Bolivia." In *Women and Change in Latin America*, ed. June Nash and Helen Safa, pp. 165–188. South Hadley, Mass.: Bergin and Garvey Publishers, 1986.

Buechler, S. "The Autonomous Communities in Spain: Historical, Political and Legal Elements of an Ever-Evolving System." Ms., independent project in political science, Syracuse University. 1986.

Bulmer, M. "Employment and Unemployment in Mining." In *Mining and Social Change*, ed. M. Bulmer, pp. 150–165. London: Croom Helm, 1978.

Burawoy, Michael. "The Anthropology of Industrial Work." *Annual Review of Anthropology*, 8 (1979a), 231–266.

———. *Manufacturing Consent*. Chicago: University of Chicago Press, 1979b.

———. "Between the Labor Process and the State: The Changing Face of Factory Regimes under Advanced Capitalism." *American Sociological Review*, 48 (1983), 587–605.

———. "Marxism as Science: Historical Challenges and Theoretical Growth." *American Sociological Review*, 55, no. 6 (December 1990), 775–793.

Butterworth, D., and N. Chance. *Latin American Urbanization*. Cambridge: Cambridge University Press, 1981.

Capecchi, Vittorio. "The Informal Economy and the Development of Flexible Specialization in Emilia-Romagna." In *The Informal Economy: Studies in Advanced and Less Developed Countries*, ed. Alejandro Portes, M. Castells, and L. Benton, pp. 189–215. Baltimore, Md.: Johns Hopkins University Press, 1989.

Cardoso, Benjamin, and Enzo Faletto. *Dependency and Development in Latin America*. Berkeley: University of California Press, 1979 [1971].

Castells, Manuel. *The City and the Grass Roots*. Berkeley: University of California Press, 1983.

———. *The Economic Crisis and American Society*. Princeton, N.J.: Princeton University Press, 1980.

Castells, Manuel, and Laura D'Andrea Tyson. "High Technology and the Changing International Division of Production: Implications for the U.S. Economy." In *The Newly Industrializing Countries in the World Econ-*

omy, ed. Randall Purcell, pp. 13–50. Boulder, Colo.: Lynne Rienner Publishers, 1989.

Castro Cotón, M. "La financiación de las empresas gallegas ante la perspectiva de adhesión a las Comunidades Europeas." In *Galicia ante el Mercado Común*, ed. L. Caramés Viéitez, pp. 99–115. La Coruña, Spain: Velograf, 1985.

Caulkins, Douglas. "Is Small Still Beautiful? Images of Success among Scotland's High Technology Entrepreneurs." Paper presented at the meeting of the Central States Anthropological Society, St. Louis, Missouri, 25 March 1988a.

————. *Networks and Narratives: An Anthropological Perspective for Small Business Research*. Scottish Enterprise Foundation Occasional Paper Series, no. 01/88. University of Stirling, 1988b.

Cavazza, Fabio, and Stephen Graubard, eds. *Il caso italiano*. Milan, Italy: Garzanti, 1974.

Censis. *Dal sommerso al post-industriale: evoluzione delle piccole e medie imprese industriali negli anni '70*. Milano: Franco Angeli, 1984.

Chai, J. "Industrial Cooperation Between China and Hong Kong." In *China and Hong Kong: The Economic Nexus*, ed. A. Youngson, pp. 104–155. Hong Kong: Oxford University Press, 1983.

Chaney, E. *Supermadre*. Austin: University of Texas Press, 1979.

Chase-Dunn, Christopher. *Global Formation: Structures of the World-Economy*. Oxford: Basil Blackwell, 1989.

Chen, J.Y.S. *Hong Kong in the 1980's*. Hong Kong: Summerson, 1982.

Choi, Jang-jip. "Interest Conflict and Political Control of South Korea: A Study of the Labor Unions in Manufacturing Industries, 1961–1980." Ph.D. diss., University of Chicago, 1983.

Chossudovsky, M. *Towards Capitalist Restoration? Chinese Socialism After Mao*. Houndmills, England: Macmillan, 1986.

Christiansen, Robert, et al. "Issues of Political Economy in Formulating Donor Policy toward Sub-Saharan Africa." In *Africa's Development Challenges and the World Bank*, ed. Stephen Commins, pp. 91–114. Boulder, Colo.: Lynne Rienner Publications, 1988.

Clammer, John, ed. *The New Economic Anthropology*. New York: St. Martin's Press, 1978.

Clammer, John. *Anthropology and Political Economy: Theoretical and Asian Perspectives*. New York: St. Martin's Press, 1985.

————. "Peripheral Capitalism and Urban Order: 'Informal Sector' Theories in Light of Singapore's Experience." In *Beyond the New Economic Anthropology*, ed. John Clammer, pp. 188–201. New York: St. Martin's Press.

Cobbett, William, et al., "South Africa's Regional Economy: A Critical Analysis of Reform Strategy in the 1980's." *South African Review* (Johannesburg), 3 (1986), 3–23.

Cockcroft, James, Andre Gunder Frank, and Dale Johnson. *Dependence and Underdevelopment: Latin America's Political Economy*. Garden City, N.Y.: Anchor Books, 1972.

Cohen, Stephen, and John Zysman. *Manufacturing Matters: The Myth of the Post-Industrial Economy*. New York: Basic Books, 1987.

Collins, Jane. "The Household and Relations of Production in Southern Peru." *Comparative Studies in Society and History*, 28 (1986), 651–671.

Collins, Thomas W. "Rural Economic Development in Two Tennessee Counties: A Racial Dimension." Paper presented at the 88th Annual Meeting of the American Anthropological Association, Washington, D.C., November 1989.

Colombo, Umberto. "Computer-Aided Design and Manufacturing in the Rejuvenation of Traditional Sectors in Italy." *Italian Journal*, 4 (1987), 29–31.

Committee for Justice and Peace of South Korea. "A Fact-Finding Survey on the Masan Export Processing Zone." *AMPO: Japan-Asia Quarterly Review*, 8, nos. 1, 2 (1976), 58–64, 58–69.

Commons, Stephen, ed. *Africa's Development Challenges and the World Bank*. Boulder, Colo.: Lynne Rienner Publishers, 1988.

Commuting in Kentucky. Frankfort, Kentucky: Kentucky Department of Economic Development, 1984.

Conference Board. *Global Economic Trends: What Lies Ahead for the '90's*. New York: Conference Board, 1989.

Connell, J., et al. *Migration from Rural Areas. The Evidence from Village Studies*. Delhi: Oxford University Press, 1976.

Cook, Scott. "The 'Managerial' versus the 'Labor' Function, Capital Accumulation and the Dynamics of Simple Commodity Production in Rural Oaxaca, Mexico." In *Entrepreneurship and Social Change*, ed. Sidney Greenfield and Arnold Strickon, pp. 54–95. Lanham, Md.: University Press of America, 1986.

Cooper, Eugene. *The Wood-Carvers of Hong Kong: Craft Production in the World Capitalist Periphery*. Cambridge: Cambridge University Press, 1980.

Council on International and Public Affairs (CIPA), *Industrial Hazards in a Transnational World*. New York: Friedrich Neumann Foundation, 1987.

Cowling, Keith. "The Internationalization of Production and De-Industrialization." In *Technological Change, Industrial Restructuring and Regional Development*, ed. A. Amin and J. B. Goddard, pp. 23–40. London: Allen and Unwin, 1986.

Craig, Ann, and Wayne Cornelius. *Politics in Mexico: An Introduction and Overview*. San Diego: University of California, Center for U.S.-Mexican Studies, 1984.

Cromley, Robert G., and Thomas R. Leinbach. "External Control of Nonmetropolitan Industry in Kentucky." *Professional Geographer*, 38, no. 4 (1986), 332–342.

Dahl, Robert. *A Preface to Economic Democracy*. Berkeley: University of California Press, 1985.

Davis, Eric. *Challenging Colonialism: Bank Misr and Egyptian Industrialization, 1920–1941*. Princeton, N.J.: Princeton University Press, 1983.

de la Pena, Guillermo. *A Legacy of Promises: Agriculture, Politics, and Ritual in the Morelos Highlands*. Austin: University of Texas Press, 1981.

Delbecq, Andre L., and Joseph Weiss. "The Business Culture of Silicon Valley: Is It a Model for the Future?" in *Futures of Organizations*, ed. Jerald Hage, pp. 123–141. Lexington, Mass.: Lexington, 1988.

Dertouzos, Michael, et al. *Made in America: Regaining the Productive Edge*. Cambridge, Mass.: MIT Press, 1989.

Desai, Ashok. "Technology Acquisition: Interpretations of the Indian Experience." In *The Indian Economy*, ed. R. Lucas and G. Papanek, 163–184. Boulder, Colo.: Westview Press, 1988.

Development Board for Rural Wales. *1984: A Year of Mid Wales Development*. Annual Report 1983/84. Newtwon, Powys: Development Board, 1984.

Deyo, Frederic, ed. *The Political Economy of the New East Asian Industrialism*. Ithaca, N.Y.: Cornell University Press, 1987.

Dinerman, Ina. "Patterns of Adaptation among Households of U.S.-Bound Migrants from Michoacan, Mexico." *International Migration Review*, 12, no. 4 (1978), 485–501.

Dirlik, A. "Postsocialism? Reflections on 'Socialism with Chinese Characteristics.' " *Bulletin of Concerned Asian Scholars*, 21, no. 1 (1989), 33–44.

Dongguan County Government (People's Republic of China). *Dongguan xian canguandian jianjie* (An Introduction to Places of Interest in Dongguan County). Dongguan, PRC: People's Government, 1984.

Dore, Ronald. "Goodwill and the Spirit of Market Capitalism." *British Journal of Sociology*, 34, no. 4 (1983), 459–482.

Douglas, Mary. *Cultural Bias*. London: Royal Anthropological Institute, 1978.

Douglas, Mary, ed. *The Sociology of Perception*. London: Routledge and Kegan Paul, 1982.

Dutt, Ela. "Boom Eases, Immigrant Mix Changes." *India Abroad*, 21 July 1989, p. 17.

Easter, D., and M. Easter. "Women Fight Back: South Korea Case." *Multinational Monitor*, 4, no. 8 (1983), 12.

Economic Research Department. "Industrial Processing in China." *Hang Seng Economic Monthly*, April 1987, pp. 1–3.

Economist Intelligence Unit. *County Report: Hong Kong, Macao*. London: Economist Publications, 1987.

Edelman, Marc. "Agricultural Modernization in Smallholding Areas of Mexico: A Case Study in the Sierra Norte de Puebla." *Latin American Perspectives*, 7 (1980), 29–49.

Edwards, Richard. *Contested Terrain: The Transformation of the Workplace in the Twentieth Century*. New York: Basic Books, 1979.

"Egypt in Crisis." *MERIP Reports*. no. 56 (April 1977).

Ehrenreich, Barbara. "The Nouveau Poor." *Ms.*, 10, no. 1 (1982), 215–224.

Eisenstadt, S. N. *Modernization: Protest and Change*. Englewood Cliffs, N.J.: Prentice-Hall, 1966.

Ejnavarzala, Haribabu. "Political Economy of International Migration: A Study of Potential Professional Emigrants from India." Paper presented at the 11th World Congress of Sociology, New Delhi, August 1986.

England, J., and J. Rear. *Chinese Labour under British Rule*. Hong Kong: Oxford University Press, 1975.

Enloe, Cynthia H. "Women Textile Workers in the Militarization of Southeast

Asia." In *Women, Men, and the International Division of Labor*, ed. J. Nash and M. P. Fernandez-Kelly, pp. 407–425. Albany: State University of New York, 1983.

Epstein, A. L. *Ethos and Identity: Three Studies in Ethnicity*. London: Travistock Publications, 1978.

European Community Commission. *Bulletin of the European Community Commission*, 21, no. 718 (1988).

Evans, Peter. *Dependent Development: The Alliance of Multinational, State, and Local Capital in Brazil*. Princeton, N.J.: Princeton University Press, 1979.

————. "Class, State, and Dependence in East Asia: Lessons for Latin Americanists." In *The Political Economy of the New East Asia Industrialism*, ed. Frederic Deyo, pp. 203–227. Ithaca, N.Y.: Cornell University Press, 1987.

Evans, Peter, Dietrich Rueschemeyer, and E. H. Stephens. "Introduction." In *States versus Markets in the World-System*, ed. Peter Evans, Dietrich Rueschemeyer, and E. H. Stephens. Beverly Hills: Sage, 1985, pp. 11–30.

Evans, Peter, Dietrich Rueschemeyer, and Theda Skocpol, eds. *Bringing the State Back In*. Cambridge: Cambridge University Press, 1985.

Fabian, Johannes. *Time and the Other: How Anthropology Makes its Object*. New York: Columbia University Press, 1983.

Fainstein, Susan, and Norman Fainstein. "Technology, the New International Division of Labor, and Location: Continuities and Disjunctures." In *Economic Restructuring and Political Response*, ed. Robert Beauregard, pp. 17–41. Newbury Park, Calif.: Sage, 1989.

Fanon, Franz. *The Wretched of the Earth*, trans. Constance Farrington. New York: Grove Press, 1968.

Feindt, W., and H. Browning. "Return Migration: Its Significance in an Industrial Metropolis and an Agricultural Town in Mexico." *International Migration Review*, 6 (1972), 158–166.

Ferleger, Lou, and Jay Mandle. "Capitalism and Third World Development." *Socialist Review*, 89, no. 4, 1989, 139–144.

Fernandez-Kelly, Maria Patricia. *For We are Sold, I and My People: Women and Industry in Mexico's Frontier*. Albany: State University of New York Press, 1983.

Fernando, Laksiri. "The Challenge of the Open Economy: Trade Unionism in Sri Lanka." In *Trade Unions and the New Industrialisation of the Third World*, ed. Roger Southall, pp. 164–181. Pittsburgh, Pa.: University of Pittsburgh Press, 1988.

Figueroa, A. *Capitalist Development and the Peasant Economy in Peru*. Cambridge: Cambridge University Press, 1984.

Finch, Henry Le Roy. *Wittgenstein—The Later Philosophy: An Exposition of 'The Philosophical Investigations.'* Atlantic Highlands, N.J.: Humanities Press, 1977.

Former Dong-il Textile Co. Labor Union. *The History of Dong-il Textile Company Labor Union Movement* (Dongil Bangjik Nodong Johap Undong-Sa). Seoul: Dolbegae, 1985.

Former Won-poong Textile Co. Labor Union. *Ten Years of Democratic Labor Union* (Won-poong Mobang Nodong Johap Hwaldong Gwa Tujaeng). Seoul: Pulbit, 1988.

Foster-Carter, Aidan. "Can We Articulate 'Articulation'?" In *The New Economic Anthropology*, ed. John Clammer, pp. 210–249. New York: St. Martin's Press, 1978a.

———. "The Modes of Production Controversy." *New Left Review*, 107 (January-February 1978b), 47–77.

Frank, Andre Gunder. *Capitalism and Underdevelopment in Latin America*. New York: Monthly Review Press, 1967.

———. "The Development of Underdevelopment." In *Imperialism and Underdevelopment*, ed. Robert Rhodes, pp. 4–17. New York: Monthly Review Press, 1970.

"Free Trade Zone Workers Fired." *Caribbean Association for Feminist Research and Action Newsletter*, 2, no. 2 (June 1988).

Frischtak, Claudio. "Structural Change and Trade in Brazil and the Newly Industrializing Latin American Economies." In *The Newly Industrializing Countries in the World Economy*, ed. Randall Purcell, pp. 159–186. Boulder, Colo.: Lynne Reinner Publishers, 1989.

Frobel, F., J. Heinrichs, and O. Kreye. *The New International Division of Labor: Structural Unemployment in Industrialised Countries and Industrialisation in Developing Countries*. Cambridge: Cambridge University Press, 1981.

Fua, Giorgio, and Carlo Zacchia (a cura di). *Industrializzazione senza fratture*. Bologna, Italy: Il Mulino, 1983.

Fuentes, Annette, and Barbara Ehrenreich. *Women in the Global Factory*. Boston: South End Press, 1983.

Gallin, Rita. "Women and the Export Industry in Taiwan: The Muting of Class Consciousness." In *Women Workers and Global Restructurings*, ed. Kathryn Ward, pp. 179–192. Ithaca, N.Y.: ILR Press, 1990.

Garcia, N. "Puerto Rico Siglo XX: Lo Historico y lo natural en la ideologia colonialista." *Pensamiento Critico*, 8 (September 1978), 1–28.

Garonna, Paolo, and Elena Pisani. "Italian Unions in Transition: The Crisis of Political Unionism." In *Unions in Crisis and Beyond: Perspectives from Six Countries*, ed. Richard Edwards et al., pp. 114–172. Dover, Mass.: Auburn House, 1986.

Geertz, Clifford. *Peddlers and Princes: Social Development and Economic Change in Two Indonesian Towns*. Chicago: University of Chicago Press, 1963.

Gill, Stephen, and David Law. *The Global Political Economy: Perspectives, Problems and Policies*. Baltimore: Johns Hopkins University Press, 1988.

Giner, Salvador. "Political Economy, Legitimation, and the State in Southern Europe." In *Uneven Development in Southern Europe: Studies of Accumulation, Class, Migration, and the State*, ed. Ray Hudson and Jim Lewis, pp. 309–350. New York: Methuen, 1985.

Gladwin, Christina H., and Robert Zabawa. "Transformation of Full-Time Family Farms inthe U.S.: Can They Survive?" In *Household Economies and Their Transformation*, ed. Morgan D. Maclachlan, pp. 212–227. New York: University Press of America, 1987.

Gledhill, John. "Agrarian Social Movements and Forms of Consciousness." *Bulletin of Latin American Research*, 7, no. 2 (1988), 257–276.

Glick-Schiller, Nina, and Georges Fouron. " 'Everywhere We Go, We Are in Danger': Ti Manno and the Emergence of Haitian Transnational Identity." *American Ethnologist* 17, no. 2 (1990), 329–347.

Gluckman, Max. "Anthropological Problems Arising from the African Industrial Revolution." In *Social Change in Modern Africa*, ed. Aidan Southall, pp. 67–82. London: Oxford University Press, 1961.

Gmelch, George. "Return Migration." *Annual Review of Anthropology*, 9 (1980), 35–155.

Goddard, J., A. Thwaites, and D. Gibbs. "The Regional Dimension to Technological Change in Great Britain." In *Technological Change, Industrial Restructuring and Regional Development*, ed. A. Amin and J. B. Goddard, pp. 140–156. London: Allen and Unwin, 1986.

Godelier, Maurice. *Perspectives in Marxist Anthropology*. Cambridge: Cambridge University Press, 1977.

———. "The Appropriation of Nature." *Critique of Anthropology*, 13–14 (1979), 1–26.

Goodman, Edward, and Julia Bamford, with Peter Saynor, eds. *Small Firms and Industrial Districts in Italy*. London: Routledge, 1989.

Gordon, David. "The Global Economy: New Edifice or Crumbling Foundations?" *New Left Review*, 172 (1988), 14–64.

Gordon, David, Richard Edwards, and Michael Reich. *Segmented Work, Divided Workers: The Historical Transformation of Labor in the United States*. Cambridge: Cambridge University Press, 1982.

Graham, Julie. "Fordism/Post-Fordism, Marxism/Post-Marxism: The Second Cultural Divide?" Unpublished manuscript, Department of Geology and Geography, University of Massachusetts at Amherst, 1990.

Gramsci, Antonio. *Selections from the Prison Notebooks*. Ed. and trans. Quintin Hoare and Geoffrey Nowell Smith. New York: International Publishers, 1971.

Granovetter, Mark. "Small is Bountiful: Labor Markets and Establishment Size." *American Sociological Review*, 49 (June 1984), 323–334.

Green, James. *The World of the Worker*. New York: Hill and Wang, 1980.

Green, P., and Alan Hirsch. "Manufacturing Industry in the Ciskei." In *Homeland Tragedy: Function or Farce*, Sars Information Publication, no. 6. Braamfontein South Africa: The Service, 1982.

Green, William. "State Constitutions, Industrial Recruitment Incentives, and Japanese Automobile Investment in Mid-America." *The Urban Lawyer*, 22, no. 2 (1990), 245–283.

Greenhalgh, Susan. "Families and Networks in Taiwan's Economic Development." In *Contending Approaches to the Political Economy of Taiwan*, ed. Edwin Winckler and Susan Greenhalgh, pp. 224–245. Armonk, N.Y.: M. E. Sharpe, 1988.

Greenwood, Davydd J. "Political Economy and Adaptive Processes: A Framework for the Study of Peasant-States." *Peasant Studies* 3, no. 3 (1974), 1–10.

——. *Unrewarding Wealth: Commercialization and the Collapse of Agriculture in a Spanish Basque Town.* Cambridge: Cambridge University Press, 1976.

——. "Community-Region-Government: Toward an Integration of Anthropology and History." In *Homenaje a Julio Caro Baroja*, ed. A. Carriera, J. A. Cid, and M. Gutiérrez Esteve y R. Rubio, pp. 511–531. Madrid: Centro de Investigaciones Sociológicas, 1978.

——. *Community-Level Research, Local-Regional-Governmental Interaction and Development Planning: A Strategy for Baseline Studies.* Rural Development Occasional Paper, no. 10, Center for International Studies, Cornell University, 1980.

——. "Collective Reflective Practice Through Participatory Action Research: A Case Study from the Fagor Cooperatives of Mondragón." In *The Reflective Turn*, ed. Donald A. Schön. New York: Teachers' College Press, in press.

Greenwood, Davydd J., and José Luis González, et al. *Culturas de Fagor: Estudio antropológico de las cooperativas de Mondragón.* San Sebastian: Editorial Txertoa, 1990.

Gressel, D. "People's Republic of China: The Problems of Structural Change." *Asian Monetary Monitor* 11 (1987), 39–63.

Grindle, Merilee S. *Searching for Rural Development: Labor Migration and Employment in Mexico.* Ithaca, N.Y.: Cornell University Press, 1988.

——. "The Response to Austerity: Political and Economic Strategies of Mexico's Rural Poor." In *Lost Promises: Debt, Austerity, and Development in Latin America*, ed. W. Canak, pp. 190–215. Boulder, Colo.: Westview, 1989.

Gröger, B. *The Transformation of Peasants into Consumers of Machines: Big Tractors on Small Fields in a French Community.* Ph.D. diss., Columbia University. Ann Arbor: University Microfilms, 1979.

Grossman, Rachel. "Women's Place in the Integrated Circuit." *Southeast Asia Chronicle*, no. 66 (1979), 2–17.

Grunwald, Joseph, and Kenneth Flamm. *The Global Factory: Foreign Assembly in International Trade.* Washington, D.C.: Brookings Institution, 1985.

Guangdong Provincial Government (People's Republic of China). *Guangdong sheng xiangzhenqiye yijiubasi nien gongzuo zongjie he yijiubawu nien gongzuo yijian* (Guangdong rural enterprise: Summary of work in 1984 and suggestions for 1985). Guangzhou: Provincial Rural Industrial Bureau, 1985.

Hadjicostandi, Joanna. "Facon: Women's Formal and Informal Work in the Garment Industry in Kavala, Greece." In *Women Workers and Global Restructuring*, ed. Kathryn Ward, pp. 64–84. Ithaca, N.Y.: ILR Press, 1990.

Haggard, Stephen, and Tun-jen Cheng. "State and Foreign Capital in the East Asian NICs." In *The Political Economy of the New East Asian Industrialism*, ed. Frederic Deyo, pp. 84–135. Ithaca, N.Y.: Cornell University Press, 1987.

Hall, Peter. "Technology, Space, and Society in Contemporary Britain." In *High Technology, Space and Society*, ed. Manuel Castells, pp. 41–52. Urban Affairs Annual Reviews, 28. Beverly Hills, Calif.: Sage, 1985.

Hall, Peter, and Ann Markusen, eds. *Silicon Landscapes*. Boston: Allen and Unwin, 1985.

Hall, Stuart. "Notes on Deconstructing 'the Popular.' " In *People's History and Socialist Theory*, ed. Raphael Samuel, pp. 227–239. Routledge and Kegan Paul, 1981.

Hammam, Mona. "Capitalist Development, Family Division of Labor, and Migration in the Middle East." In *Women's Work: Development and the Division of Labor by Gender*, ed. Eleanor Leacock & Helen Safa, pp. 158–173. South Hadley, Mass.: Bergin and Garvey, 1986.

Hansen, Bent, and Samir Radwan. *Employment Opportunities and Equity in a Changing Economy: Egypt in the 1980s. A Labor Market Approach.* Geneva: ILO, 1982.

Harding, S. *Remaking Ibieca: Rural Life in Aragon under Franco*. Chapel Hill: University of North Carolina Press, 1984.

Harrison, Bennett, and Sandra Kanter. "The Political Economy of State Job-Creation Business Incentives." *Journal of the American Institute of Planners*, 44 (October 1978): pp. 424–435.

Hartmann, Heidi. "Capitalism, Patriarchy, and Job Segregation by Sex." In *Women and Workplace*, ed. M. Blaxall and B. Reagan, pp. 137–169. Chicago: University of Chicago Press, 1976.

Harvey, David. *The Condition of Postmodernity*. Cambridge, Mass.: Basil Blackwell, 1989.

Hendry, John. *Innovating for Failure: Government Policy and the Early British Computer Industry*. Cambridge, Mass.: MIT Press, 1990.

Hindess, Barry, and Paul Hurst. *Pre-Capitalist Modes of Production*. London: Routledge and Kegan Paul, 1975.

Hindson, Doug. *Pass Controls and the Urban African Proletariat*. Johannesburg: Ravan Press, 1987.

Hobsbawm, Eric. "The Crisis of the 17th Century." In *Crisis in Europe, 1560–1660*, ed. Trevor Aston, pp. 5–62. New York: Anchor Books, 1966.

Holzberg, Carol S., and Maureen J. Giovannini. "Anthropology and Industry: Reappraisal and New Directions." *Annual Review of Anthropology*, 10 (1981), 317–360.

Hong Kong. *Hong Kong 1987*. Hong Kong: Government Printing Department.

Hong Kong. Census and Statistics Department. *Hong Kong Review of Overseas Trade in 1988*. Hong Kong: Government Printer, 1989.

Hong Kong. Trade Development Council. *Survey on Hong Kong Re-Exports*. Hong Kong: Trade Development Council, 1988.

Hopkins, K., ed. *Hong Kong: The Industrial Colony*. Hong Kong: Oxford University Press, 1971.

Hopkins, Nicholas S. "The Agrarian Tradition and the Household in Rural Egypt." In *Household Economies and Their Transformation*, ed. Morgan D. Maclachlan, pp. 155–172. New York: University Press of America, 1987.

Hu, Tai-li. "The Emergence of Small-Scale Industry in a Taiwanese Rural

Community." In *Women, Men, and the International Division of Labor*, ed. June Nash and Patricia Fernandez-Kelly, pp. 387–406. Albany: State University of New York Press, 1983.

Hua, Guocang. "China's Opening to The World." *Problems of Communism*, 35 (November/December 1986), 59–77.

Hudson, Ray. "Producing an Industrial Wasteland: Capital, Labour and the State in North-East England." In *The Geography of De-Industrialisation*, ed. Ron Martin and Bob Rowthorn, pp. 169–213. London: Macmillan, 1986.

————. "Labour-Market Changes and New Forms of Work in Old Industrial Regions: Maybe Flexibility for Some but Not Flexible Accumulation." *Society and Space*, 7 (1989), 5–30.

Hugon, Philippe, ed. "Secteur informel et petite production marchande dans les villes du tiers monde." *Tiers Monde* (Special issue), 21, no. 82 (1980).

Humphrys, Graham. "Industrial Wales." In *Wales: A New Study*, ed. David Thomas, pp. 154, 189. Newton Abbott: David and Charles, 1977.

Indian Investment Centre. *Myths and Realities of Foreign Investment in India*. New Delhi: Indian Investment Centre, n.d.

International Medical Science City, Advertisement in *India Abroad*, 26 January 1990, 21.

International Monetary Fund. *World Economic Outlook, May 1990*. Washington, D.C.; IMF, 1990.

Isbell, Billie Jean. *To Defend Ourselves: Ecology and Ritual in an Andean Village*. Austin: University of Texas Press, 1978.

Islam, Iyanatul, and Colin Kirkpatrick. "Export-Led Development, Labor-Market Conditions, and the Distribution of Income: The Case of Singapore." *Cambridge Journal of Economics*, 10 (1986), 113–126.

Ismael, Jacqueline. "The Conditions of Egyptian Labor in the Gulf: A Profile on Kuwait." *Arab Studies Quarterly*, 8, no. 4 (1986), pp. 390–403.

Instituto Centrale di Statistica (ISTAT). *Le Regioni in Cifre*. Roma: ISTAT, 1986.

Jacobs, P. "Hong Kong's Role in China's Economic Development." *Business PRC* (May/June 1986), 113–117.

Jaffee, Georgina. "The Incorporation of African Women into the Industrial Workforce: Its Implications for the Women's Question in South Africa." In *After Apartheid: Renewal of the South African Economy*, ed. J. Suckling and L. White, pp. 90–108. London: James Curry, 1988.

Jain, R. K. *Guide on Foreign Collaboration, Policies and Procedures 1987–88*. Delhi: S. S. Books Associates for India Investment Publications, 1987.

Jaycox, Edward. "What Can Be Done in Africa? The World Bank's Response." In *Africa's Development Challenges and the World Bank*, ed. Stephen Commins, pp. 19–52. Boulder, Colo.: Lynne Rienner Publishers, 1988.

Johnson, Chalmers. "South Korean Democratization: The Role of Economic Development." *The Pacific Review*, 2, no. 1 (1989), 1–10.

Johnson, Kay A. *Women, the Family and Peasant Revolution in China*. Chicago: University of Chicago Press, 1983.

Joseph, S. "Working-Class Women's Networks in a Sectarian State: A Political Paradox." *American Ethnologist*, 10, no. 1 (1983), 1–22.

Kada, Ryohei. *Part-Time Family Farming: Off-Farm Employment and Farm Adjustments in the United States and Japan*. Tokyo: Center for Academic Publications, 1980.

Kamel, Rachel. *The Global Factory: Analysis and Action for a New Economic Era*. Philadelphia: American Friends Service Committee, 1990.

Kandiyoti, Deniz. "Bargaining with Patriarchy." *Gender and Society*, 2 (1988), 274–290.

Kaplan, Temma. "Female Consciousness and Collective Action: The Case of Barcelona in 1910–1918." *Signs*, 7, no. 3 (1982), 545–566.

———. "Women and Communal Strikes in the Crisis of 1917 to 1922." In *Becoming Visible*, ed. Renate Bridenthal, Claudia Koonz and Susan Stuard, pp. 38–68, Boston: Houghton Mifflin, 1987.

Karl, Marilee, and Wan-cheung Choi. "Resistance, Strikes and Strategies." In *Of Common Cloth: Women in the Global Textile Industry*, ed. W. Chapkis and C. Enloe, pp. 91–97. Washington, D.C.: Transnational Institute, 1983.

Katznelson, Ira. "Working-Class Formation: Constructing Cases and Comparisons." In *Working-Class Formation: Nineteenth-Century Patterns in Western Europe and the United States*, ed. Ira Katznelson and Aristide Zolberg, pp. 3–44. Princeton, N.J.: Princeton University Press, 1986.

Kearney, Michael. "From the Invisible Hand to Visible Feet: Anthropological Studies of Migration and Development." *Annual Review of Anthropology*, 15 (1986), 331–361.

Keating, M., and B. Jones. *Regions in the European Community*. Oxford: Clarendon Press, 1985.

Keeble, David, and Egbert Wever. *New Firms and Regional Development in Europe*. London: Croom Helm, 1986.

Kentucky Cabinet for Economic Development. *1988 Kentucky Economic Statistics*. Frankfort, Ky.: Department of Business Development, 1988.

Keren, Donna. "A World after Its Own Image: Capitalism and Crisis in Mexico." Paper presented at the 87th Annual Meeting of the American Anthropological Association, Phoenix, Arizona, November 1988.

Kim, Illsoo. *The New Urban Immigrants: The Korean Community in New York*. Princeton, N.J.: Princeton University Press, 1981.

Kim, J. "China's Modernizations, Reforms and Mobile Population." *International Journal of Urban and Regional Research*, 12, no. 4 (1988), 595–626.

Kim, Kum-su. *Hanguk Nodong Munje ui Sanghwang gwa Insik* (The circumstances and interpretation of the Korean labor problem). Seoul: Pulbit, 1986.

Kingsolver, Ann E. " 'Not If She Had Wings': Expressions of Resistance to Women in Politics, from Rural Kentucky." Paper presented at the Conference on Women, Politics and Change in Twentieth-Century America, New School for Social Research, New York, 1990.

———. "Tobacco, Toyota, and Subaltern Development Discourses: Constructing Livelihood and Community in Rural Kentucky." Ph.D., diss., University of Massachusetts at Amherst, 1991.

Klingel, Sally, and Ann Martin, eds. *A Fighting Chance: New Strategies for Saving Jobs and Reducing Costs.* Ithaca, N.Y.: ILR Press, 1988.

Kondo, Dorinne K. *Creating Self: Power, Gender and Discourses of Identity in a Japanese Workplace.* Chicago: University of Chicago Press, 1990.

Koo, Hagen. "The Interplay of State, Social Class, and World System in East Asian Development: The Cases of South Korea and Taiwan." In *The Political Economy of the New East Indian Industrialism,* ed. Frederic Deyo, pp. 165–181. Ithaca, N.Y.: Cornell University Press, 1987.

——. "From Farm to Factory: Proletarianization in Korea." *American Sociological Review,* 55, no. 5 (October 1990), 669–681.

Koptiuch, Kristin. "Egypt's Informal Sector: Continuity or Simulacrum?" Paper presented at the Social Science Research Council Workshop on the Informal Sector in the Middle East, July 1986. Tutzing, West Germany.

"Korea Is Urgently Seeking Cheaper Credit: Seoul Starts to Overhaul Its Outmoded Financial Markets." *Wall Street Journal,* 27 January 1989.

Korean Association of Women Workers. *Hanguk Yosong Nodong ui Hyonjang* (The scene of Korean women workers). Seoul: Baeksan Sodang, 1987.

Korean Young Catholic Workers' Organization (JOC). *Masan Export Processing Zone Report on Company Suspension and Closure.* Seoul: JOC, 1980.

Krugman, Paul, et al. "Developing Countries in the World Economy." *Daedalus,* 118, no. 1 (Winter 1989), 183–203.

Kung, J., and T. Chan. "Export-Led Rural Industrialization: The Case of Dongguan in the Pearl River Delta in China." Paper presented at the Conference on Chinese Cities in Asian Context, University of Hong Kong, 17–19 June 1987.

Kwon, Jene, ed. *Korean Economic Development.* New York: Greenwood Press, 1990a.

——. "The Uncommon Characteristics of Korea's Economic Development." In *Korean Economic Development,* ed. Jene Kwon, pp. 33–50. New York: Greenwood Press, 1990b.

Laclau, Ernesto. "Feudalism and Capitalism in Latin America." *New Left Review,* 67 (May-June 1971), 19–38.

Laite, Julian. *Industrial Development and Migrant Labor.* Austin: University of Texas Press, 1981.

Lamphere, Louise. *From Working Daughters to Working Mothers: Immigrant Women in a New England Industrial Community.* Ithaca, N.Y.: Cornell University Press, 1987.

Lange, Peter. "Semiperiphery and Core in the European Context: Reflections on the Postwar Italian Experience." In *Semiperipheral Development,* ed. Giovanni Arrighi, pp. 179–214. Beverly Hills, Calif.: Sage, 1985.

Langley, Winston. "What Happened to the New International Economic Order?" *Socialist Review,* 90, no. 3 (1990), 47–62.

Lash, Scott, and Urry, John. *The End of Organized Capitalism.* Madison: University of Wisconsin Press, 1987.

Lawler, Edward, III. *High-involvement Management.* San Francisco: Jossey-Bass, 1986.

Lawson, Fred. "Social Origins of Inflation in Contemporary Egypt." *Arab Studies Quarterly,* 7, no. 1 (1985), 36–57.

Lazerson, Mark. "Organizational Growth of Small Firms: An Outcome of Markets and Hierarchies." *American Sociological Review*, 53 (1988), 330–342.

Leacock, Eleanor, and Helen Safa, eds. *Women's Work: Development and the Division of Labor by Gender*. South Hadley, Mass.: Bergin and Garvey, 1986.

Leeds, Anthony. "Forms of Urban Integration: 'Social Urbanization' in Comparative Perspective." *Urban Anthropology* 8, nos. 3/4 (1979), 227–247.

———. "Work, Labor, and Their Recompenses: Portuguese Life Strategies Involving 'Migration'." In *Migrants in Europe*, ed. Hans Buechler and Judith-Maria Buechler, pp. 9–60. Westport, Conn.: Greenwood Press, 1987.

Lenin, Vladimir. *Imperialism, The Highest Stage of Capitalism*. Peking: Foreign Language Press, 1970.

Lessinger, Johanna. *Research Report on Indian Immigrant Entrepreneurs in New York City*. New York: Rockefeller Foundation, 1986.

———. "The Tyranny of the American Dream: New York's Indian Immigrants as Workers and Investors." Paper delivered at the 88th Annual Meeting of the American Anthropological Association, Washington, D.C., November 1989.

Leung, W. Y. *Smashing the Iron Rice Pot: Workers and Unions in China's Market Socialism*. Hong Kong: Asia Monitor Resource Center, 1988.

Levy, Marion. *Modernization and the Structure of Society*. Princeton, N.J.: Princeton University Press, 1960.

Lim, Linda. *Women Workers in Multinational Corporations: The Case of the Electronics Industry in Malaysia and Singapore*. Ann Arbor, Mich.: University of Michigan Occasional Papers in Women's Studies, 1978.

———. "Capitalism, Imperialism, and Patriarchy: The Dilemma of Third-World Women Workers in Multinational Factories." In *Women, Men, and the International Division of Labor*, ed. June Nash and Maria Patricia Fernandez-Kelly, pp. 70–92. Albany, N.Y.: SUNY Press, 1983.

———. "The Impact of Changes in the World Economy on Developing Countries." In *Cooperation for International Development: The United States and the Third World in the 1990s*, ed. Robert Berg and David Gordon, pp. 21–47. Boulder, Colo.: Lynne Rienner Publishers, 1989.

Lipietz, Alain. "New Tendencies in the International Division of Labor: Regimes of Accumulation and Modes of Regulation." In *Production, Work, Territory*, ed. Allen Scott and Michael Storper, pp. 16–40. Boston: Allen and Unwin, 1986.

Litvak, Isaiah, and Christopher Maule. "Comparative Technical Entrepreneurship: Some Perspectives." *Journal of International Business Studies*, 71 (1976), 31–38.

Long, Norman, and Paul Richardson. "Informal Sector, Petty Commodity Production, and the Social Relations of the Small-Scale Enterprise." In *The New Economic Anthropology*, ed. John Clammer, pp. 176–210. New York: St. Martin's Press, 1978.

Long, Norman, and Bryan Roberts, eds. *Miners, Peasants and Entrepreneurs:*

Regional Development in the Central Highlands of Peru. Cambridge: Cambridge University Press, 1984.

Lucas, Robert. "India's Industrial Policy." In *The Indian Economy*, ed. R. Lucas and G. Papanek, pp. 185–202. Boulder, Colo.: Westview Press, 1988.

Lynd, Robert, and Helen Lynd. *Middletown.* New York: Harcourt, Brace and World, 1929.

———. *Middletown in Transition.* New York: Harcourt, Brace and World, 1937.

McCourt, K. *Working Class Women and Grass Roots Politics.* Bloomington, Ind.: Indiana University Press, 1977.

McMichael, Philip. "Social Structure of the New International Division of Labor." In *Ascent and Decline in the World System*, ed. Edward Friedman, pp. 115–146. Beverly Hills, Calif.: Sage, 1982.

Mager, Anne. "Moving the Fence: Gender in the Ciskei and Border Textile Industry, 1945–1986." *Social Dynamics*, 28 (1989), 1.

Mair, Andrew, Richard Florida, and Martin Kenney. "The New Geography of Automobile Production: Japanese Transplants in North America." *Economic Geography*, 64, no. 4 (1989), 352–373.

Mandel, Ernest. *Late Capitalism.* London: NLB, 1975.

Mangin, William. "The Role of Regional Associations in the Adaptation of Rural Migrants to Cities in Peru." In *Contemporary Cultures and Societies in Latin America*, ed. Dwight Heath and Richard N. Adams, pp. 311–323. New York: Random House, 1965.

Martin, Emily. *The Woman in the Body.* Boston: Beacon, 1987.

Martin, J. "Motherhood and Power: The Production of a Woman's Culture of Politics in a Mexican Community." *American Ethnologist*, 17, no. 3 (1990), 470–490.

Martin, Ron. "Thatcherism and Britain's Industrial Landscape." In *The Geography of De-Industrialisation*, ed. Ron Martin and Bob Rowthorn, pp. 238–290. London: Macmillan, 1986.

Martin, V., and Chris Rogerson. "Women and Industrial Change: The South African Experience." *South African Geographical Journal*, 66 (1984), 1.

Marx, Karl. *Capital, Vol. I*, trans. Ben Fawkes. New York: Vintage Books, 1977.

———. *Capital, Vol. II.* New York: International Publishers, 1967.

———. *Capital, Vol. III*, trans. David Fernbach. New York: Vintage Books, 1981.

———. *The Eighteenth Brumaire of Louis Bonaparte.* New York: International Publishers, 1963.

Mason, Edward, et al. *The Economic and Social Modernization of the Republic of Korea.* Cambridge, Mass.: Harvard University Press, 1980.

Mather, Celia. "Industrialization in the Tangerang Regency of West Java: Women Workers and the Islamic Patriarchy. *Bulletin of Concerned Asian Scholars*, 15, no. 2 (1983), 2–17.

Mauss, M. *The Gift.* London: Cohen and West, 1954.

Mazzoni, Riccardo. "Ridistribuzione delle attivta producttiva." In *L'industria a domicilio: aspetti dell'economia marchigiana negli ultimi decenni*, ed. Sergio Anselmi, Hugo Ascoli, and Riccardo Mazzoni, pp. 37–60. Ancona, Italy: Cooperative Giulio Pastore, 1983.

Mehta, Fredie. "Growth, Controls and the Private Sector." In *The Indian Economy*, ed. R. Lucas and G. Papanek, pp. 185–202. Boulder, Colo.: Westview Press, 1988.

Meillassoux, Claude. "From Reproduction to Production: A Marxist Approach to Economic Anthropology." *Economy and Society*, 1, no. 1 (1972), 93–105.

———. *Maidens, Meal and Money, Capitalism and the Domestic Community*. Cambridge University Press, 1981. (original French publication 1975.)

Meixide, Vecino, A. "El problema del empleo en Galicia ante la integración en la CEE: Algunas consideraciones." *In Galicia ante el Mercado Común*, ed. L. Caramés Viéitez. La Coruña, Spain: Velograf, 1985.

Merli, Rosanna. "Dinamiche strutturali e caratteristiche dell'economia marchigiana negli anni '70." In *Una economia in mezzo al guado*, ed. Domenica Baglione et al., pp. 115–152. Ancona, Italy: Ediesse, 1984.

Mies, Maria. *Patriarchy and Accumulation on a World Scale: Women in the International Division of Labour*. London: Zed Books, 1986.

Mintz, Sidney. "The Plantation as a Sociocultural Type." In *Plantation Systems in the New World*, ed. Angel Palerm and Vera Rubin, pp. 42–50. Social Science Monograph, no. 7. Washington, D.C.: Pan American Union, 1959.

———. *Sweetness and Power: The Place of Sugar in Modern History*. New York: Penguin, 1985.

Mitchell, J. Clyde. "Distance, Transporation, and Urban Involvement in Zambia." In *Urban Anthropology: Cross-Cultural Studies of Urbanization*, ed. Aidan Southall, pp. 287–314. New York: Oxford University Press, 1973.

Moench, Richard U. "Oil, Ideology and State Autonomy in Egypt." *Arab Studies Quarterly*, 10, no. 2 (1988), 176–192.

Monck, Charles, ed. *Science Parks—Their Contribution to Economic Growth*. Proceedings of the U.K. Science Park Association's Annual Conference, 6 December 1985, in association with Peat Marwick.

Moore, Barrington. *Social Origins of Dictatorship and Democracy*. Boston, Mass.: Beacon Press, 1966.

Morgan, Kevin. "Re-Industrialisation in Peripheral Britain: State Policy, the Space Economy and Industrial Innovation." In *The Geography of De-Industrialisation*, ed. Ron Martin and Bob Rowthorn, pp. 322–359. London: Macmillan, 1986.

Morgen, Sandra. " 'It's the Whole Power of the City against Us!': The Development of Political Consciousness in a Women's Health Care Coalition." In *Women and the Politics of Empowerment*, ed. Ann Bookman and Sandra Morgen, pp. 97–115. Philadelphia: Temple University Press, 1988.

Morris, M. L. "The Development of Capitalism in South African Agriculture: Class Struggle in the Countryside." In *The Articulation of Modes of Production*, ed. Harold Wolpe, pp. 202–253. London: Routledge and Kegan Paul, 1980.

Morsey, Soheir A. "U.S. Aid to Egypt: An Illustration and Account of U.S.

Foreign Assistance Policy." *Arab Studies Quarterly*, 8, no. 4 (1986), 358–389.

Moser, Caroline O. N. "Informal Sector or Petty Commodity Production: Dualism or Dependence in Urban Development?" *World Development*, 6, nos. 9/10 (1978), 1041–1064.

Munck, Ronaldo. "Capital Restructuring and Labour Recomposition under a Military Regime: Argentina (1976–83)." In *Trade Unions and the New Industrialisation of the Third World*, ed. Roger Southall, pp. 121–143. Pittsburgh, Pa.: University of Pittsburgh Press, 1988.

——, ed. *The New International Labour Studies: An Introduction*. London: Zed Books, 1988b.

Murray, Colin. *Families Divided: The Impact of Migrant Labor in Lesotho*. Cambridge: Cambridge University Press, 1981.

Myers, J. "Modernization and 'Unhealthy Tendencies.' " *Comparative Politics*, 21, no. 2 (1989), 193–213.

Nash, June. "Segmentation of the Work Process in the International Division of Labor." Manuscript, n.d.

——. *We Eat the Mines and the Mines Eat Us: Dependency and Exploitation in Bolivian Tin Mines*. New York: Columbia University Press, 1979.

——. "Ethnographic Aspects of the World Capitalist System." *Annual Review of Anthropology*, 10 (1981), 393–423.

——. "Cultural Parameters of Sexism and Racism in the International Division of Labor." In *Racism, Sexism, and the World-System*, ed. Joan Smith et al., pp. 11–38. Westport, Conn.: Greenwood Press, 1988.

——. *From Tank Town to High Tech: The Clash of Community and Industrial Cycles*. Albany, N.Y.: State University of New York Press, 1989.

Nash, June, and Patricia Fernandez-Kelly, eds. *Women, Men, and the International Division of Labor*. Albany, N.Y.: State University of New York Press, 1983.

Nash, Manning. *Machine Age Maya: The Industrialization of a Guatemalan Community*. Chicago: University of Chicago Press, 1958.

Negri, Antonio. *Marx Beyond Marx. Lessons on the Grundrisse*. Trans. Harry Cleaver, Michael Ryan, and Maurizio Viano, ed. James Fleming. South Hadley, Mass.: Bergin and Garvey Publishers, 1984.

Nelson, C. "Public and Private Politics: Women in the Middle Eastern World." *American Ethnologist*, 14 (1974), 551–1323.

Nelson, Joan. "Sojourners versus New Urbanites: Causes and Consequences of Temporary versus Permanent Migration in Developing Countries." *Economic Development and Cultural Change*, 24, no. 4 (1976), 721–757.

Ninan, T. N. "Business and Economy: Reaching Out and Upward." In *India Briefing 1989*, ed. Marshall Bouton and Philip Oldenburg, pp. 35–59. Boulder, Colo.: Westview Press, 1989.

"NRI Entrepreneurs, a Mixed Homecoming." *India Today*, July 31, 1989, 90–93.

"NRI Investment on the Rise." *The Hindu*, July 13, 1989, 9.

Nutini, H., and B. Isaac. *Los Pueblos de Habla Nahuatl de la Region do Tlaxcala y Puebla*. Serie de Antropologia Social, no. 27. Mexico City: Instituto Indigenista, 1974.

Oakey, Ray. "High-Technology Industries and Agglomeration Economies." In *Silicon Landscapes*, ed. Peter Hall and Ann Markusen, pp. 94–117. London: Allen and Unwin, 1985.

Oakey, Ray, and Roy Rothwell. "High Technology Small Firms and Regional Industrial Growth." In *Technological Change, Industrial Restructuring and Regional Development*, ed. Ash Amin and John Goddard, pp. 258–283. London: Allen and Unwin, 1986.

O'Connor, James. "The Meaning of Crisis." *International Journal of Urban and Regional Research*, 5, no. 3 (1981), 301–329.

———. *The Meaning of Crisis: A Theoretical Introduction*. New York: Basil Blackwell, 1987.

Ong, Aihwa. "Women and Industry: Malay Peasants in Coastal Selangor, 1975–1980." Ph.D. Dissertation, Columbia University, 1982.

———. Global Industries and Malay Peasants in Peninsular Malaysia. In *Women, Men, and the International Division of Labor*, ed. J. Nash and M. P. Fernandez-Kelly, pp. 426–439. Albany, N.Y.: State University of New York Press, 1983.

———. *Spirits of Resistance and Capitalist Discipline: Factory Women in Malaysia*. Albany, N.Y.: State University of New York Press, 1987.

———. "The Production of Possession: Spirits and the Multinational Corporation in Malaysia." *American Ethnologist*, 15, no. 1 (1988), 28–42.

Orellana, Carlos. "Mixtec Migrants in Mexico City: A Case Study of Urbanization." *Human Organization*, 32, no. 3 (1973), 273–283.

Ouchi, William G. *Theory Z: How American Business Can Meet the Japanese Challenge*. New York: Avon, 1982.

Owen, Roger. *The Middle East and the World Economy, 1800–1914*. London: Methuen, 1981.

———. "The Study of Middle Eastern Industrial History: Notes on the Relationship between Factories and Small-Scale Manufacturing with Special References to Lebanese Silk and Egyptian Sugar, 1900–1930." *International Journal of Middle East Studies*, 16, no. 4 (1984), 475–487.

Paci, Massimo. *Mercato del lavoro e classi socialis in Italia*. Bologna, Italy: Il Mulino, 1973.

———. "Ristrutturazione industriale, piccola impresa, e lavoro a domicilio." *Inchiesta*, 5 (1975), 20.

———. *Famiglia e mercato del lavoro in un'economia periferica*. Milano: Franco Angeli, 1980.

———. *La struttura sociale italiana*. Bologna, Italy: Il Mulino, 1982.

Palerm, Angel, and Vera Rubin, eds. *Plantation Systems in the New World*. Social Science Monograph, no. 7. Washington, D.C.: Pan American Union, 1959.

Parsons, Talcott. *The Evolution of Societies*. Englewood Cliffs, N.J.: Prentice-Hall, 1977.

Patwardhan, M. S. *Oil and Other Multinationals*. Bombay: Popular Prakashan, 1986.

People's Republic of China, Rural Industrial Bureau. *Xiang Zhen Qi Ye* (Rural enterprise). Beijing, 1984.

———. *Xiang Zhen Qi Ye* (Rural enterprise). Beijing, 1985.

People's Republic of China. State Statistical Bureau. *China Statistical Yearbook 1988*. Beijing: China Statistical Information, 1988.

Pérez Touriño, E. "La PAC y la evolución de las agriculturas de la CEE. Análisis de las estructuras productivas de la agricultura de Galicia dada la perspectiva de la integración." In *Galicia ante el Mercado Común*, ed. L. Caramés Viéitez. La Coruña, Spain: Velograf, 1985.

Peters, Thomas, and Robert Waterman. *In Search of Excellence*. New York: Warner Books, 1982.

Petras, J. "Contradictions of Market Socialism in China." *Journal of Contemporary Asia*, 18, no. 1 (1988), 3–23.

Petras, James, and Dennis Engbarth. "Third World Industrialization and the Capital-Labour Relations in the Third World." In *Trade Unions and the New Industrialisation of the Third World*, ed. Roger Southall, pp. 81–112. Pittsburgh, Pa.: University of Pittsburgh Press, 1988.

Piore, Michael, and Charles Sabel. *The Second Industrial Divide: Possibilities for Prosperity*. New York: Basic Books, 1984.

Pizzorno, Alessandro. "I ceti medi nei meccanismi del consenso." In *Il caso italiano*, ed. Fabio Cavazza and Stephen Graubard, pp. 314–337. Milan, Italy: Garzanti, 1974.

Polanyi, K. *The Great Transformation*. New York: Rinehart and Co., 1944.

Portes, Alejandro. "The Informal Sector: Definition, Controversy, and Relation to National Development." *Review*, 7, no. 1 (1983), 151–174.

Portes, Alejandro, and Lauren Benton. "Industrial Development and Labor Absorption: A Reinterpretation." *Population and Development Review*, 10 (1984), 589–611.

Portes, Alejandro, Manuel Castells, and Lauren Benton, eds. *The Informal Economy: Studies in Advanced and Less Developed Societies*. Baltimore, Md.: Johns Hopkins University Press, 1989.

Portes, Alejandro, and John Walton. *Labor, Class and the International System*. New York: Academic Press, 1981.

Powdermaker, Hortense. *Copper Town: Changing Africa*. New York: Harper and Row, 1962.

Pred, Allan. "Power, Everyday Practice and the Discipline of Human Geography." *Lund Studies in Geography* (Sweden: University of Lund), 48 (1981), 30–56.

Purcell, Randall, ed. *The Newly Industrializing Countries in the World Economy: Challenges for U.S. Policy*. Boulder, Colo.: Lynne Rienner Publishers, 1989.

Raatgever, Reini. "Analytic Tools, Intellectual Weapons: The Discussion among French Marxist Anthropologists about the Identification of Modes of Production in Africa." In *Old Modes of Production and Capitalist Encroachment: Anthropological Explorations in Africa*, ed. Wim van Binsbergen and Peter Geschiere, pp. 290–330. London: KPI, 1985.

Radwan, Samir. *Capital Formation in Egyptian Industry and Agriculture 1882–1967*. London: Ithaca Press, 1974.

Rapp, Rayna. "Review of Claude Meillassoux, *Femmes, Greniers et Capitaux*." *Dialectical Anthropology*, 2, no. 4 (1977), 317–323.

———. "Urban Kinship in Contemporary America: Families, Classes and Ideology." In *Cities of the United States*, ed. L. Mullings, pp. 219–243. New York: Columbia University Press, 1987.

Raskin, Marcus, and Stephen Muller. *Global Reach: The Power of the Multinational Corporations*. New York: Touchstone, 1974.

Ray, Shantanu. "Professionals Seeking Visas." *India Abroad*, 17 July 1989, p. 15.

Regione Marche (Italy). "L'industria delle calzature nelle Marche." *Quaderni della Programmazione 2*. Ancona, Italy: 1982.

Reich, Robert. *The Next American Frontier*. New York: Penguin, 1983.

Reich, Robert, and Ira Magaziner. *Minding America's Business: The Decline and Rise of the American Economy*. New York: Vintage, 1982.

Rempel, Henry, and Richard Lobdell. "The Role of Urban-to-Rural Remittances in Rural Development." *Journal of Development Studies*, 14 (1978), 324–341.

Reserve Bank of India. *Foreign Collaboration in Indian Industry, Fourth Survey Report 1985*. Bombay: Reserve Bank of India, 1985.

———. *Annual Report 1988–89*. Bombay: Reserve Bank of India, 1989.

Rey, Pierre-Phillippe. *Les Aliances de Classes*. Paris: François Maspero, 1973.

———. "The Lineage Mode of Production." *Critique of Anthropology*, 3 (Spring 1975), 27–79.

Reynolds, Clark, and Robert McCleery. "The U.S.-Mexican Trade Relationship: Past, Present, and Future." In *The Newly Industrializing Countries in the World Economy*, ed. Randall Purcell, pp. 115–158. Boulder, Colo.: Lynne Rienner Publishers, 1989.

Rhodes, Robert, ed. *Imperialism and Underdevelopment: A Reader*. New York: Monthly Review Press, 1970.

Richards, Alan. *Egypt's Agricultural Development, 1800–1980: Technical and Social Change*. Boulder, Colo.: Westview Press, 1982.

Richards, Alan, P. Martin, and R. Nagaar. "Labour Shortages in Egyptian Agriculture." In *Migration, Mechanization and Agricultural Labor Markets in Egypt*, ed. Richards and P. Martin, pp. 21–41. Boulder, Colo.: Westview Press, 1983.

Riegelhaupt, J. "Saloio Women: An Analysis of Informal and Formal Political and Economic Roles of Portuguese Peasant Women." *Anthropological Quarterly*, 40, no. 3 (1967), 109–126.

Ritchie, John. "Enterprise Cultures: A Frame Analysis." In *Deciphering the Enterprise Culture: Entrepreneurship, Petty Capitalism and the Restructuring of Britain*, ed. Roger Burrows, pp. 17–34. London: Routledge, 1991.

Rohatyn, Felix. "A New Reconstruction Finance Corporation?" *New York Review of Books*, 5 February 1981.

Roseberry, William. "Political Economy." *Annual Review of Anthropology*, 17 (1988), 161–185.

———. *Anthropologies and Histories: Essays in Culture, History, and Political Economy*. New Brunswick, N.J.: Rutgers University Press, 1989.

Rosen, Ellen Israel. *Bitter Choices: Blue-Collar Women In and Out of Work*. Chicago: University of Chicago Press, 1987.

Ross, Robert, and Kent Trachte. *Global Capitalism: The New Leviathan.* Albany, N.Y.: State University of New York Press, 1990.

Rostow, W. W. *The Stages of Economic Growth: A Non-Communist Manifesto.* Cambridge: Cambridge University Press, 1971.

Rothstein, Frances. *Three Different Worlds: Women, Men and Children in an Industrializing Community.* Westport, Conn.: Greenwood Press, 1982.

———. "The New Proletarians: Third World Reality and First World Categories." *Comparative Studies in Society and History,* 28, no. 2 (1986), 217–238.

———. "Anthropologizing Western Feminism." Unpublished paper presented at the 88th Annual Meeting of the American Anthropological Association, Washington, D.C., November 1989.

———. "Global Views and Human Action in a Rural Community in Mexico." *Urban Anthropology,* 17, no. 4 (1988), 363–378.

Rothwell, Roy, and W. Zegveld. *Innovation and Small and Medium Sized Firms.* London: Frances Pinter, 1982.

Rubinstein, Hymie. "Remittances and Rural Underdevelopment in the English-Speaking Caribbean." *Human Organization,* 42, no. 4 (1983), 295–306.

Rudolf, Gloria. "Panamanian Insights into a Common Third World Trio: Capitalism, Labor Migration and Class Conflict." In *Panama in Transition: Local Reactions to Development Policies,* ed. J. Bort and Mary Helms, pp. 129–160. Columbia: University of Missouri, 1983.

Rueschemeyer, Dietrich, and Peter Evans. "The State and Economic Transformation: Toward an Analysis of the Conditions Underlying Effective Intervention." In *Bringing the State Back In,* ed. Peter Evans, Dietrich Rueschmeyer and Theda Skocpal, pp. 44–77. Cambridge: Cambridge University Press, 1985.

Russell, Raymond. "Using Ownership to Control: Making Workers Owners in the Contemporary United States." *Politics and Society,* 13, no. 3 (1984), 253–294.

Sabel, C., and J. Zeitlin. "Historical Alternatives to Mass Production: Politics, Markets, and Technology in Nineteenth Century Industrialization." *Past and Present,* 108 (August 1985), 133–176.

Sabel, Charles. *Work and Politics.* Cambridge: Cambridge University Press, 1982.

Sacks, Karen. "Engels Revisited: Women, the Organization of Production and Private Property." In *Woman, Culture, and Society,* ed. M. Rosaldo and L. Lamphere, pp. 207–222. Stanford, Calif.: Stanford University Press, 1974.

———. *Caring by the Hour.* Urbana: University of Illinois Press, 1988.

———. "Toward A Unified Theory of Class, Race, and Gender." *American Ethnologist,* 16, no. 3 (August 1989), 534–550.

Safa, Helen I. *The Urban Poor of Puerto Rico: A Study in Development and Inequality.* New York: Holt, Rinehart, and Winston, 1974.

———. "Runaway Shops and Female Employment: The Search for Cheap Labor." *Signs,* 7, no. 2 (1981), 418–433.

Saffioti, Heleieth. *Women in Class Society*. New York: Monthly Review Press, 1978.

Salamon, Sonya. "Land Tenure Implications of Ethnic Beliefs in Illinois Agriculture. Paper presented at the 88th Annual Meeting of the American Anthropological Association, Washington, D.C., November 1989.

Sassen, Saskia. *The Mobility of Labor and Capital: A Study of International Investment and Labor Flow*. Cambridge: Cambridge University Press, 1988.

Sayer, Andrew. "Industrial Location on a World Scale: The Case of the Semiconductor Industry." In *Production, Work, Territory*, ed. Allen Scott and Michael Storper, pp. 107–125. Boston: Allen and Unwin, 1986.

Sayer, Andrew, and Kevin Morgan. "The Electronics Industry and Regional Development in Britain." In *Technological Change, Industrial Restructuring and Regional Development*, ed. Ash Amin and John B. Goddard, pp. 157–186. London: Allen and Unwin, 1986.

———. "High Technology Industry and International Division of Labour: The Case of Electronics." In *The Development of High Technology Industries*, ed. Michael Breheny and Ronald McQuaid, pp. 10–36. London: Croom Helm, 1987.

"SBI Helps NRIs Raise Capital." *India Abroad*, 10 November 1989, 19.

Scase, Richard, and Robert Goffee. *The Real World of the Small Business Owner*. London: Croom Helm, 1980.

Schonberger, Richard. *Japanese Manufacturing Techniques*. New York: Free Press, 1982.

Schryer, Franz. "Class Conflict and the Corporate Peasant Community: Disputes over Land in Nahuatl Villages." *Journal of Anthropological Research*, 43, no. 2 (1987), 99–120.

Scobell, A. "Hong Kong's Influence on China: The Tail that Wags the Dog?" *Asian Survey*, 28, no. 6 (1988), 599–612.

Scott, Allen, and Michael Storper, eds. *Production, Work, Territory: The Geographical Anatomy of Industrial Capitalism*. Boston: Allen and Unwin, 1986.

Scott, Michael. "Graduates into Enterprise." *The Times Higher Education Supplement* 30, no. 1 (1987), 14.

Seddon, David. "Economic Anthropology or Political Economy? (I): The Barotse Social Formation, a Case Study." In *The New Economic Anthropology*, ed. John Clammer, pp. 31–60. New York: St. Martin's Press, 1978.

Shunde People's Government (People's Republic of China). *Shunde xian qu xiang qiye gaikuang jianjie* (An introduction to the general situation of district and sub-district enterprises of Shunde county). Shunde, PRC: Government Press, 1983.

———. *Kaichuang qu xiang qiye fazhan xin jumian* (Breakthrough in the development of district and subdistrict enterprises). Shunde, PRC: Government Press, 1985.

Shutes, M. "Cows, Co-Ops and the Common Market: Changes in a Rural Irish Parish Resulting from EEC Membership." Paper presented at the symposium on the Anthropology of the European Community, 87th Annual

Meeting of the American Anthropological Association, Phoenix, 16–20 November 1988.

"SICOM—An Entrepreneur-Friendly Organization." *News India*. 5 October 1990, 33, 39.

Sikri, Aprajita. "Big Market for Plastic Lenses." *India Abroad*, 3 February 1989, p. 21.

Simmons, Alan, and Ramiro Cardona. "Rural-Urban Migration: Who Comes, Who Stays, Who Returns? The Case of Bogota, Colombia, 1929–1968." *International Migration Review*, 6 (1972), 166–180.

Sin, In-ryong. *Women, Labor, and Law* (Yosong, Nodong, Beob). Seoul: Pulbit, 1985.

Singh, Ajit. "Third World Competition and De-Industrialization in Advanced Countries." *Cambridge Journal of Economics*, 13 (1989), 103–120.

Sirianni, Carmen. "Worker Participation in the Late Twentieth Century: Some Critical Issues." In *Worker Participation and the Politics of Reform*, ed. Carmen Sirianni, pp. 1–29. Philadelphia: Temple University Press, 1987.

Sit, V.F.S. "Industries in 'Shenzhen: An Attempt at Open-door Industrialization." In *China's Special Economic Zones*, ed. Y.C. Jao and C.K. Leung, pp. 226–246. Hong Kong: Oxford University Press, 1985.

Sit, V.F.S., S. L. Wong, and T. S. Kiang. *Small-Scale Industry in a Laissez-Faire Economy*. Hong Kong: University of Hong Kong, Centre of Asian Studies, 1979.

Sivanandan. "Imperialism and Disorganic Development in the Silicon Age." *Race and Class*, 21, no. 2 (1979), 111–126.

Skocpol, Theda. "Wallerstein's World Capitalist System: A Theoretical and Historical Critique." *American Journal of Sociology*, 82, no. 5 (March 1977), 1075–1090.

——. *States and Social Revolutions: A Comparative Analysis of France, Russia, and China*. Cambridge: Cambridge University Press, 1979.

Smart, Alan. "Invisible Real Estate: Investigations into the Squatter Property Market." *International Journal of Urban and Regional Research*, 10, no. 1 (1986), 29–45.

——. "Forgotten Obstacles, Neglected Forces: Origins of Hong Kong's Public Housing." *Environment and Planning D: Society and Space*, 7, no. 1 (1989).

Smart, Josephine. *The Political Economy of Street Hawking in Hong Kong*. Hong Kong: Centre of Asian Studies, 1989.

Smart, Josephine, and Alan Smart. "Personal Relations and Divergent Economies: A Case Study of Hong Kong Investment in South China." *International Journal of Urban and Regional Research* (1989).

Smelser, Neil. "Mechanisms of Change and Adjustment to Change." In *Industrialization and Society*, ed. B. F. Hoselitz and W. E. Moore. The Hague: Unesco-Mouton, 1963.

Smith, Carol A. "Forms of Production in Practice: Fresh Approaches to Simple Commodity Production." *Journal of Peasant Studies*, 11, no. 4 (1984a), 201–221.

——. "Labor and International Capital in the Making of a Peripheral Social

Formation." In *Labor in the Capitalist World-Economy*, ed. C. Bergquist. Beverly Hills, Calif.: Sage Publications, 1984b.

———. "Local History in Global Context: Social and Economic Transitions in Western Guatemala." *Comparative Studies in Society and History*, 26 (1984c), 193–228.

Smith, David. *North and South: Britain's Economic, Social, and Political Divide*. London: Penguin, 1989.

Solé Tura, J. *Nacionalidades y nacionalismos en España: Autonomías, Federalismo, Autodeterminación*. Madrid: Alianza Editorial, 1985.

Southall, Roger, ed. *Trade Unions and the New Industrialisation of the Third World*. Pittsburgh, Pa.: University of Pittsburgh Press, 1988.

South China Morning Post (SCMP), [Hong Kong daily newspaper], various issues.

Speigle, Andrew. "Rural Differentiation and the Diffusion of Migrant Labour Remittances in Lesotho." In *Black Villages and Industrial Society*, ed. P. Mayer, pp. 109–168. Oxford: Oxford University Press, 1980.

———. "The Fluidity of Household Composition in Matatiele, Transkei." *African Studies*, 45 (1986), 17–36.

Spivak, Gayatri Chakravorty. "The Rani of Sirmur." In *Europe and Its Others*, Vol. 1, ed. Francis Barker et al., pp. 128–151. Proceedings of the Essex Conference on the Sociology of Literature, July 1984, Colchester: University of Essex Press, 1985.

Stephen, Lynn. *Zapotec Women*. Austin: University of Texas Press, 1991.

Stephen, Lynn, and Kathleen Logan. "Women in Mexican Popular Movements: A Critical Discussion of New Social Movements Theory." Paper presented at the 89th Annual Meeting of the American Anthropological Association, New Orleans, Louisiana, November 1990.

Stern, Steve. "Feudalism, Capitalism, and the World-System in the Perspective of Latin America and the Caribbean." *American Historical Review*, 93, no. 4 (1988), 829–872.

Steward, Julian. *The People of Puerto Rico: A Study in Social Anthropology*. Urbana: University of Illinois Press, 1956.

Stinchcombe, Arthur. "Flexible Specialization." *Sociological Forum*, 1, no. 2 (1987), 185–190.

Storey, David. *Entrepreneurship and the New Firm*. London: Croom Helm, 1982.

———. "The Economics of Smaller Businesses: Some Implications for Regional Economic Development." In *Technological Change, Industrial Restructuring and Regional Development*, ed. Ash Amin and John Goddard, pp. 215–232. London: Allen and Unwin, 1986.

Sullivan, K. "The Impact of Migration: Social Change among Returned Emigrants in a Spanish Town." Ph.D. Dissertation, University of California at Santa Barbara. Ann Arbor, Mich.: University Microfilms, 1979.

"Survey of the Italian Economy," *The Economist*, 27 February 1988.

Susser, I. *Norman Street: Poverty and Politics in an Urban Neighborhood*. New York: Oxford, 1982.

———. "Union Carbide and the Community Surrounding It: The Case of a

Community in Puerto Rico." *International Journal of Health Services*, 15, no. 4 (1985), 561–583.

———. "Political Activity among Working Class Women in a U.S. City." *American Ethnologist*, 12, no. 1 (1986), 108–117.

———. "The Welfare Trap: A Public Policy for Deprivation." In *Cities of the United States: Studies in Urban Anthropology*, ed. J. Kreniske and L. Mullings, pp. 51–71. New York: Columbia University Press, 1987.

———. "Working-Class Women, Social Protest and Changing Ideologies." In *Women and the Politics of Empowerment*, ed. S. Morgen and A. Bookman, pp. 257–271. Philadelphia: Temple University Press, 1988.

Tarrow, Sidney. "The Crisis of the Late 1960's in Italy and France: The Transition to Mature Capitalism." In *Semiperipheral Development*, ed. Giovanni Arrighi, pp. 215–241. Beverly Hills, Calif.: Sage, 1985.

Taussig, Michael T. *The Devil and Commodity Fetishism in South America*. Chapel Hill: University of North Carolina Press, 1980.

Taylor-Awny, Elizabeth. "Labour Shortage in Egyptian Agriculture: A Crisis for Whom?" In *Peasants and Peasant Societies: Selected Readings*, 2nd ed., ed. Teodor Shanin, pp. 166–173. Oxford: Basil Blackwell, 1987.

Terray, Emmanuel. *Marxism and "Primitive" Societies*. New York: Monthly Review Press, 1972.

Thompson, E. P. *The Making of the English Working Class*. New York: Vintage Books, 1966 [Originally published 1963].

Tong, Z. G. "Trade Between China and Hong Kong." *Hong Kong Manager*, October 1984.

Toth, James. "Labor Surplus to Labor Shortage in Rural Egypt." Draft paper, 1984.

Trimberger, Ellen Kay. "World Systems Analysis: The Problem of Unequal Development." *Theory and Society*, 8, no. 1 (1979), 127–137.

Trotsky, Leon. *The Age of Permanent Revolution: A Trotsky Anthology*, ed. Isaac Deutscher. New York: Dell, 1964. (Original ed. Ann Arbor, Mich.: University of Michigan Press, 1932.)

Truelove, Cynthia. "Disguised Industrial Proletarians in Rural Latin America." In *Women Workers and Global Restructuring*, ed. K. Ward, pp. 48–63. Ithaca, N.Y.: ILR Press, 1990.

"Turning on the Northern Lights." *Economist*, June 3, 1989, pp. 33–42.

Unione Regionale delle Camere di Commercio delle Marche. *Sintesi congiunturale dell'industria manifatturiera delle marche nel 1986*." Ancona, Italy: Unione Regionale della Camere di Commercio delle Marche, 1987.

———. *Giuria della congiuntura: Sintesi dell'industria manifatturiera delle marche nel 1987*. Ancona, Italy: Unione Regionale delle Camere di Commercio delle Marche, 1988a.

———. *Ruolo e prospettive della calzatura nella realta marchigiana*. Ancona, Italy: Unione Regionale delle Camere di Commercio delle Marche, 1988b.

———. *Giuria della congiuntura: Indagine dell'industria manifatturiera delle marche, sintesi 1988*. Ancone, Italy: Unione Regionale delle Camere di Commercio delle Marche, 1989.

———. *Giuria della congiuntura: Indagine dell'industria manifatturiera delle marche, sintesi 1989.* Ancona, Italy: Unione Regionale delle Camere di Commercio delle Marche, 1990.

"Unions' Struggle across the Border: Mass Dismissals at Korea Sumida," *AMPO: Japan-Asia Quarterly Review*, 21, no. 4 (1990), 59–63.

United States Office of Technology Assessment. *Computerized Manufacturing Automation: Employment, Education and Workplace.* Washington, D.C.: U.S. Government Printing Office, April 1984.

———. *Technology, Innovation, and Regional Economic Development.* Washington, D.C.: OTA-STI-238, July 1984.

United States Department of Commerce. Bureau of the Census. *1980 Census of the Population: General and Social Characteristics, Kentucky.* Washington, D.C.: U.S. Government Printing Office, July 1983.

Van Hear, Nicholas. "Recession, Retrenchment and Military Rule: Nigerian Labour in the 1980s." In *Trade Unions and the New Industrialisation of the Third World*, ed. Roger Southall, pp. 144–163. Pittsburgh, Pa.: University of Pittsburgh Press, 1988.

Vence Deza, X. *Capitalismo e Desemprego en Galicia.* Vigo, Spain: Edicións Xerais de Galicia, 1986.

Wallerstein, Inmanual. *The Modern World System I: Capitalist Agriculture and the Origins of the European World-Economy in the Sixteenth Century.* New York: Academic Press, 1974.

———. *The Modern World System II: Mercantilism and the Consolidation of the European World-Economy 1600–1750.* New York: Academic Press, 1979.

———. *The Politics of the World-Economy.* Cambridge: Cambridge University Press, 1984.

———. "The Relevance of the Concept of Semiperiphery to Southern Europe." In *Semiperipheral Development*, ed. Giovanni Arrighi, pp. 31–39. Beverly Hills, Calif.: Sage, 1985.

Walsh, Anna G. "The Relationship between Women's Gender Roles and the Economy." Paper presented at the 87th Annual Meeting of the American Anthropological Association, Phoenix, Arizona, November 1988.

Walton, John. "The Third 'New' International Division of Labor." In *Capital and Labor in the Urbanized World*, ed. John Walton, pp. 3–16. London: Sage, 1985.

———. "Theory and Research on Industrialization." *Annual Review of Sociology*, 13 (1987), 89–108.

Walton, John, and Charles Ragin. "The Debt Crisis and Political Protest in the Third World." *American Sociological Review*, 55, no. 6 (December 1990), 876–890.

Wang, G. G. *China's New Investment Laws: New Directions.* Singapore: Butterworths, 1988.

Wang, N. T. *China's Modernization and Transnational Corporations.* Lexington, Ky.: Lexington Books, 1984.

Wangel, Arne. "The ILO and Protection of Trade Union Rights: The Electronics Industry in Malaysia." In *Trade Unions and the New Industrialisation of the Third World*, ed. Roger Southall, pp. 287–305. Pittsburgh, Pa.: University of Pittsburgh Press, 1988.

Ward, Kathryn, ed. *Women Workers and Global Restructuring*. Ithaca, N.Y.: ILR Press, 1990.

Warner, W. Lloyd, et al. *The Social System of the Modern Factory, Yankee City Series*. New Haven, Conn.: Yale University Press, 1947.

Warr, Peter. "Export Promotion via Industrial Enclaves: the Philippines' Bataan Export Processing Zone." *Journal of Development Studies*, 23, no. 2 (January 1987), 220–241.

Waterbury, John. *The Egypt of Nasser and Sadat: The Political Economy of Two Regimes*. Princeton, N.J.: Princeton University Press, 1983.

Waterman, Peter. "Understanding Relations amongst Laboring People in Peripheral Capitalist Societies." *Labour, Capital, and Society*, 14, no. 1 (April 1981), 88–108.

Whyte, William Foote, Davydd J. Greenwood, and Peter Lazes. "Participatory Action Research: Through Practice to Science in Social Research." In *American Behavioral Scientist*, 32, no. 5 (1989), 513–552.

Whyte, William Foote, and Kathleen King Whyte. *Making Mondragón: The Growth and Dynamics of the Worker Cooperative Complex*. Ithaca, N.Y.: ILR Press, 1988.

Wiemann, Jurgen. *India in Transition*. New Delhi: Allied Publishers, 1986.

Wiest, Raymond. "Anthropological Perspectives on Return Migration: A Critical Commentary." *Papers in Anthropology* (University of Oklahoma), 20, no. 1 (1979), 167–187.

Wilkens, Paul H. *Entrepreneurship: A Comparative and Historical Study*. Norwood, N.J.: Ablex, 1979.

Williams, Karel, et al. "The End of Mass Production." *Economy and Society*, 16, no. 3 (1987), 405–439.

Williams, Shirley. *A Job to Live: The Impact of Tomorrow's Technology on Work and Society*. Harmondsworth, U.K.: Penguin, 1985.

Wolf, Eric. "Specific Aspects of Plantations Systems in the New World." In *Plantation Systems in the New World*, ed. Angel Palerm and Vera Rubin, pp. 136–146. Social Science Monograph, no. 7. Washington, D.C.: Pan American Union, 1959.

——. *Europe and the People without History*. Berkeley: University of California Press, 1982.

Wolf, Margery. *Women and the Family in Rural Taiwan*. Stanford, Calif.: Stanford University Press, 1972.

Wolfe, Alvin. "The Supranational Organization of Production: An Evolutionary Perspective." *Current Anthropology*, 18, no. 4 (December 1977), pp. 615–620.

Wolpe, Harold, ed. *The Articulation of Modes of Production*. London: Routledge and Kegan Paul, 1980a.

——. "Capitalism and Cheap Labour-Power in South Africa: From Segregation to Apartheid." In *The Articulation of Modes of Production*, ed. Harold Wolpe, pp. 289—319. London: Routledge and Kegan Paul, 1980b.

Wong, E. L. "Recent Developments in China's Special Economic Zones." *The Developing Economies*, 25 (1987), 73–86.

World Bank. *Employment and Development of Small Enterprises*. A Sector Policy Paper. Washington, D.C.: World Bank, 1977.

————. *Arab Republic of Egypt: Survey of Small Scale Industry.* Washington, D.C.: World Bank, 1978.

————. *World Development Report, 1987.* New York: Oxford University Press, 1987.

Xu, X. Q., and W. X. Zhang. "A Preliminary Study of the Driving Force behind Rural Urbanization in Areas Open to the Outside World." *Chinese Sociology and Anthropology*, 21, no. 2 (1989), 35–51.

Yang, Mayfair Mei-Hui. "The Gift Economy and State Power in China." *Comparative Studies in Society and History*, 31, no. 1 (1989), 25–54.

Yin, Ying. "Environmental Regulations and the Relocation of Capital." Unpublished paper, Department of Sociology and Anthropology, Northeastern University, 1991, 20 pp.

Young, Kate. "The Creation of a Relative Surplus Population: A Case Study from Mexico." In *Women and Development: The Sexual Division of Labor in Rural Societies*, ed. L. Benería, pp. 149–177. New York: Praeger, 1982.

Young, Lord, of Graffham. "Science Parks—Their Contribution to the National Economy." In *Science Parks—Their Contribution to Economic Growth*, ed. Charles Monck. Proceedings of the U.K. Science Park Association's Annual Conference, in association with Peat Marwick, 6 December 1985.

Zeitlin, Jonathan, ed. "Local Industrial Strategies." *Economy and Society*, 18 (1989), 4.

Index

Berger, Suzanne, 186–188

capitalism: in Africa, 9–12; agriculture and, 37–40, 106–9; in Asia, 9–12, 47–82; in China, 47–61; dependency theory and, 34–36; development and, 152, 220, 220–37; in Egypt, 149–60; in England, 119–21, 132–34; entrepreneurs and, 53–60; export processing zones and, 4, 17–19, 139, 221–22; gift exchange and, 53–60; in India, 62–82; industrialization and, 12–14; international division of labor and, 221–22, 236; in Italy, 85–99; in Latin America, 9–12, 34–37; Marxist theories of, 2–5; in Mexico, 34–41; migration and, 44–46; new international division of labor and, 4–5, 49–50; petty commodity production and, 86–90, 149–60, 242–43; socialist societies and, 9,
47–61, 136–38; in South Korea, 220–37; in Spain, 109–115; in United States, 191–206; world economic growth and, 9–14

class structures: in Asia, 21, 25; in China, 136–37, 144, 146–47; communities and, 23–26; development and, 20–26; in Egypt, 149–50, 151–52, 157–58, 159; entrepreneurs and, 21–22, 86, global factory and, 20–26; households and, 23–24; in India, 73–80; industrialization and, 20–26, 86; international division of labor and, 4–5, 157–59; in Italy, 23–25, 92–93, 98–99; in Latin America, 20–21; workers and, 22–24

deindustrialization. See industrialization
development: in Africa, 9–12; in Asia, 9–12, 47–61, 65–68; in

China, 47–61, 136–48; combined and uneven, 6–8; in England, 119–23; entrepreneurs and, 53–60, 124–30; export-processing zones and, 4, 221–22; gender and, 16–17, 23; global factory and, 8–19; in India, 65–68; industrialization and, 12–14; in Italy, 85–99; Marxist theories of, 3–5; migration and, 33–36, 44–46; in South Korea, 220–21, 223–25; in Spain, 102–6, 115–18; states and, 19–20; theories of, 33–35, 88–89; world economy and, 9–12

entrepreneurs: in Asia, 53–60, 73–79; characteristics of, 53–60, 124–30; in China, 53–60, 146, 241; cooperatives and, 98–99; descriptions of, 124–30; in Egypt, 154; in England, 124–30, 244; global factory and, 14–16; in India, 73–79; investments and, 126–30; in Italy, 86–98; in Spain, 109–15; theories of, 124–30; transnational corporations and, 16–17, 97–98
Evans, Peter, 20

Frank, Andre Gunder, 3–4
Frobel, Folker, 4

gender relations: global factory and, 166–68; industrialization and, 112–15, 160 n.11, 161–74; labor and, 203; politics and, 206–19; in Puerto Rico, 206–19; in South Africa, 161–74; in Spain, 113–15
global factory: anthropology and, 26–28; described, 5–8; dimensions of, 8–26; ethnography and, 191–92, 204, 239–40; flexible specialization and, 16–19, 85, 88–89
Gordon, David, 17
Gramsci, Antonio, 157, 159

Hobsbawm, Eric, 16
homework: gender and, 242–43; global factory and, 16–17; and in-

dustrialization 242–43; in Italy, 86–87; in Spain, 110–12
households: capitalism and, 38–39; class structure and, 23; defined, 169; development and, 86–87; informal sector and, 40–41; migration and, 38–40; mixed livelihoods of, 196–97, 199, 203; relationships in, 170–74

industrial cooperatives, 177–90
industrialization: in Africa, 14; anthropology and, 238; in Asia, 13–14, 47–82; in China, 47–61, 136–48; and deindustrialization, 119–23; in England, 119–23; environment and, 148, 206–19; gender and, 160 n.11, 161–74; global factory and, 12–19; in India, 62–68; in Italy, 85–88; kinship and, 244–45; in Latin America, 13–14; in Mexico, 18–19; petty commodity production and, 14–17; in Puerto Rico, 206–19; regional development and, 88–89, 102–4, 115–21, 161–74; socialist societies and, 47–61; in Spain, 109–15; transnational corporations and, 17–19; trends in 12–14
informal economy. See global factory
informal sector, 40–41; in Egypt, 149–60
international division of labor. See capitalism; development
investment: in Asia, 49–53, 62–82; China, 49–53, 137, 140; in England, 121–30; forms of, 49–53, 60–65; in India, 62–82; in Italy, 95–96; nonresident, 62–82; in Spain, 107–15; transnational, 17–18

kin: accumulation and, 86–87, 97; in Asia, 55–60, 77–78; in China, 55–60, 140; entrepreneurs and, 55–60; industrialization and, 77–78; investment and, 55–60; 126–30, 140; in Italy, 86–87, 93; labor and, 86–87, 89; in South Africa, 169–74

labor markets: in Asia, 53; capitalism and, 22–23, 155–57; in China,
   53; composition by age, occupation, and sex, 86–87, 163–65; development and; in Egypt, 155,
   157, 158; export processing zones
   and, 222–23; gender and, 203;
   global factory and, 22–23, 86–87;
   in Italy, 86–87; in Kentucky, 200,
   203
labor processes: global factory and,
   22–23; industrial cooperatives
   and, 177–90; industrialization
   and, 22–26; in Italy, 86–87, 92–93;
   in South Korea, 226–27; in Spain,
   110–14, 177–90; undocumented labor and, 87, 110
Leeds, Anthony, 45
Lenin, Vladimir, 7, 23

Mandel, Ernest, 7–8
Marx, Karl, 6–7, 13, 19
migration: in Asia, 53, 68–73; capitalism and, 33–36, 44–46; in
   China, 53; class structure and,
   242; development and, 33–36, 44–
   46; in Egypt, 150, 155; entrepreneurial, 128–30; gender and, 34–
   35; global factory and, 241; households and, 38–44; India and, 68–
   73; in Kentucky, 203; in Mexico
   and elsewhere in Latin America,
   33–46; politics and, 42–44; remittances and, 39, 144, 155–56, 168,
   241; return, 37–44; in South Africa, 163, 168; in South Korea,
   163, 168

Piore, Michael, 187, 188
politics: in Asia, 72–82; class formation and, 24–25, 93; in India, 73–
   79; industrialization and, 72–82;
   in Italy, 93; in Mexico, 44–46; in
   Puerto Rico, 206–19; in Spain,
   103–6; Women and, 206–19, 220–
   37
production processes: in Asia, 77–78;
   cooperative forms, 98–99, 177–90;

in England, 130–32; households
   and, 86–87; in India, 77–78; in Italy, 86–87, 90–97; in Spain, 109–
   13; technology and, 130–32

Roseberry, William, 6
Rothstein, Frances, 19

Sabel, Charles, 187, 188
Sacks, Karen, 23, 26
Sassen-Koob, Saskia, 4
Sayer, Andrew, 19
Skocpol, Theda, 19
socialsim, 243; Chinese, 140; in
   Egypt, 154–55
state policies: in Asia, 51–53, 62–82;
   capitalism and, 19–20, 87; in
   China, 51–53, 136–48; development and, 18–20, 149–60; 200–
   203; in Egypt, 156; in England,
   119–20, 132–34; global factory
   and, 18–20, 241; in India, 73–82;
   industrialization and, 73–82, 136–
   48; investment and, 18–20, 62–82;
   in Italy, 87, 98–99; in Kentucky,
   200–203; labor and, 17, 19–20; in
   Latin America, 20; 161–63; in
   South Africa, 161–63; in South
   Korea, 222–23, 242; in Spain,
   103–8, 241; unions and, 20; in
   United States, 208; world market
   and, 17–20

technology: agriculture and, 107–8;
   entrepreneurs and, 124–32; global
   factory and, 13–14, 245; transfers
   of, 90–97, 130–32
Thompson, Edward, 23
Trotsky, Leon, 7–8

unions, 189; in Italy, 24–25; politics
   and, 93; in South Africa, 163–64,
   166; in South Korea, 220–37;
   women and, 228–37

Wallerstein, Immanuel, 2
Waterman, John, 16
Wolf, Eric, 6

women: development and, 87, 110–
  15; global factory and, 16–17;
  health and, 212–13, 214; homework and, 86–87, 110–115; households and, 169–74; in Italy, 98–99;
  kin networks and, 211–12; migration and, 34; politics and, 206–19;
  in Puerto Rico, 206–19; in South
  Africa, 161–74; in South Korea,
  220–37; in Spain, 113–15; unions
  and, 24, 228–37
working class: in Asia, 25–26; composition of, 22–26; in Egypt, 149–
  60; formation, 23–26; global factory and, 245–46; in Italy, 24–25,
  92–93; in Kentucky, 191–206; organization of, 23; politics and, 25–
  26, 206–19, 220–37; in Puerto
  Rico, 206–19; in South Korea, 25–
  26, 220–37; unions and, 228–37
world market: descriptions of, 2–26;
  development and, 2–26, 94–99;
  global factory and, 5–12; industrialization and, 12–14; labor and,
  14–26; regional development and,
  88–89, 102–4, 115–21; theories of,
  2–5; world-system and, 2

Yang, Mayfair, 56–59

About the Contributors

MICHAEL L. BLIM, Assistant Professor of Sociology and Anthropology at Northeastern University, is the author of *Made in Italy: Small-Scale Industrialization and Its Consequences* (Praeger Publishers, 1990) and of several articles on economic development and redevelopment in English and Italian publications.

HANS C. BUECHLER is Professor of Anthropology at Syracuse University. His most recent publications include *The Masked Media: Aymara Fiestas and Social Interaction in the Bolivian Highlands*; *Carmen: The Autobiography of a Spanish Galician Woman*, co-authored with Judith-Maria Buechler; and *Migrants in Europe: The Role of Family, Labor, and Politics*, co-edited with Judith-Maria Buechler (Greenwood Press, 1987). He has also co-produced, with Hans-Ulrich Schlumpf, Judith-Maria Buechler, and Rainer Trinkler, a film, *Die Welt der Sofia Valazquez: La Paz, Bolivien*, whose English version is titled *The World of Sofia Valazquez.*

JUDITH-MARIA BUECHLER is Professor of Anthropology at Hobart and William Smith Colleges. Her publications include *The Bolivian Aymara*, and *Carmen: The Autobiography of a Spanish Galician Women*, both co-authored with Hans Buechler; and *Migrants in Europe: The Role of Family, Labor, and Politics*, co-edited with Hans Buechler (Greenwood Press, 1987). With Hans-Ulrich Schlumpf, Hans Buechler, and Rainer Trinkler, she has also co-produced the film *Die Welt der Sofia Valazquez: La Paz, Bolivien.*

DOUGLAS CAULKINS, Professor of Anthropology at Grinnell College, has held visiting postdoctoral fellowships at the Universities of Kansas, Trondheim (Norway), and Durham (England). He is a contributor to *Technology, Innovation, and Regional Economic Development.*

EUGENE COOPER is Associate Professor of Anthropology at the University of Southern California. His publications include *The Woodcarvers of Hong Kong: Craft Production in the World of Capitalist Periphery* and numerous articles on Chinese folk habit, custom and culture.

DAVYDD J. GREENWOOD is Professor of Anthropology and John S. Knight Professor and Director of the Center for International Studies at Cornell University. His publications include *Unrewarding Wealth: The Commercialization and Collapse of Agriculture in a Spanish Basque Town* (1976); *Nature, Culture, and Human History: A Bio-Cultural Introduction to Anthropology,* co-authored with William A. Stini; *The Taming of Evolution: The Persistence of Non-Evolutionary Views in the Study of Humans,* and *Culturas de Fagor: Un Estudio Anthropologico de las Cooperativas de Mondragón,* co-authored with José Luis Gonzalez.

GEORGINA JAFFEE is currently working in a small development agency in South Africa that provides assistance to groups wanting to form cooperatives. She formerly taught at the University of the Witwatersrand.

SEUNG-KYUNG KIM is Assistant Professor of Women's Studies at the University of Maryland, College Park.

ANN E. KINGSOLVER is Assistant Professor of Anthropology at Lawrence University.

KRISTIN KOPTIUCH recently received her Ph.D. in anthropology from the University of Texas at Austin. She has contributed articles to *Social Text* and *Critique of Anthropology.*

JOHANNA LESSINGER is the co-editor, with David Hakken, of *Perspectives in U.S. Marxist Anthropology* and, with Amy Swerdlow, of *Class, Race, and Sex: The Dynamics of Control.* She has published articles in *Feminist Studies* and *Manushi.*

XIONG PAN has taught at Zhongshan University in Guangzhou and at the University of Southern California. He is the author of *Xifang Renleixue de Lishi* (The History of Western Anthropology).

FRANCES ABRAHAMER ROTHSTEIN is Professor of Anthropology at Towson State University. Her publications include *New Directions in Political Economy: An Approach from Anthropology*, edited with M. Barbara Leons (Greenwood Press, 1979), *Three Different Worlds: Women, Men and Children in an Industrializing Community* (Greenwood Press, 1982), and numerous articles in such journals as *Comparative Studies in Society and History* and *Latin American Perspectives*.

ALAN SMART is Assistant Professor of Anthropology at the University of Calgary. He is the author of *Making Room: Squatter Clearance in Hong Kong* and articles in *City and Society, International Journal of Urban and Regional Research, International Journal of the Sociology of Law*, and *Critique of Anthropology*.

JOSEPHINE SMART, Assistant Professor of Anthropology at the University of Calgary, is the author of *The Political Economy of Street Hawkers in Hong Kong* as well as articles in *The Asian Journal of Public Administration* and *The Canadian Journal of Development Studies* and in various collections.

IDA SUSSER is Associate Professor of Community Health at Hunter College, and Associate Professor of Anthropology, at the Graduate Center of the City University of New York. She is the author of *Norman Street: Poverty and Politics in an Urban Neighborhood* and of articles in *Medical Anthropology Quarterly, International Journal of Health Sciences*, and *American Ethnologist*.